i

CONTENTS

Cricut for Beginners

Cricut Maker Mastery

Cricut Project Ideas

Cricut Explore Air 2 Mastery

Cricut Design Space for Beginners

Cricut Joy Mastery

1.

CRICUT FOR BEGINNERS

The Unofficial Step-By-Step Guide to Cricut Explore Air 2 Machine, Accessories and Tools + Tips & Tricks + Easy DIY Projects and Smart Business Ideas for Everyone. 2021 Edition

Philippa Smalley

CRICUT FOR BEGINNERS

Introduction

You may have received a Cricut machine on Christmas or for your birthday that you put away and is still lying in its case. Maybe you are just someone who wants to design an item, or you've seen some amazing project images and wondered: "how do they cut those complicated designs?" You may have also asked yourself: "What is the Cricut machine? What could I do with it?" If you've thought of these questions, you are in the right place! This book will teach you everything you need to know about the Cricut Explore Air machine and inform you of all the fun stuff you can do with it.

Most Cricut machines operate with Bluetooth or Wi-Fi, and you can use them through your iPad or iPhone, or laptop.

Cricut machines are relatively simple to use, completely adjustable, and the only limit is your imagination.

What Does the Cricut Machine Come With?

1. Warranty
2. Power and USB cord
3. Fine-point blade
4. A "getting started" package
5. Rotary blade and instructional manual
6. Fine-point pen
7. Fabric and a piece of cardstock
8. 12 x 12-inch fabric and light grip mat
9. 50 free project ideas as well as 25 sewing projects

This chapter provides a general overview of the Cricut machine and further sheds light on various types of Cricut machines that are available. It also discusses several advantages of the Cricut Explore Air 2 machine, which is the model that is discussed in this book.

1. What Is the Cricut Machine?

A Cricut is a cutting machine that can cut various materials, such as paper, vinyl, and cardstock for your art projects. You can also cut thin wood, cloth, silk, and more with certain Cricut machines. You can wirelessly link your machine to your device, build or import designs to your computer, and upload them to be cut by your Cricut. Cricut has applications called Design Room (which are available for Windows, MAC, and smartphones) that help you build and import machine-cut designs. A tiny blade (or rotary cutter, pen, and scoring instrument) is installed within the Cricut. You should attach your preferred material to a 12-inch wide cutting mat until you have a design that is ready to be cut in Design Space. Then, send your design to your Cricut wirelessly from your phone, and wait for the material to load into your system. In this way, you can begin cutting your project with the click of a button. Since professional cutting equipment is used by Cricut machines, there is no detail that is too specific. You can create the most complicated and intricate designs, write out a "handwritten" note in ink, or expertly rate a pop-up card. Each piece will always turn out exactly how you wanted due to Cricut's precision.

Do you want to have a perfect finish? Putting smaller pieces together is what makes Cricut Basics a delight. You can easily create a fantastic project much larger at any step of the way. In other words, the options are infinite with your Cricut machine.

All you need is a Cricut machine, anything to cut, Design Space, and an imagination.

What can you do with a Cricut machine?

There are many things you can design with a Cricut machine. We can't really mention all of the options that are available, but there are a few popular projects that we have listed below so that you can see what the machine is capable of doing:

1. Design a T-shirt or a onesie
2. Create a bracelet from leather
3. Create buntings and other party decorations
4. Make your own art stencils
5. Create a vinyl patch for your car's windshield
6. Mark things in your kitchen or in your kid's playroom

7. Create pillows with monograms
8. Design ornaments for Christmas
9. Label a packet
10. Decorate a cup, tumbler, or mug
11. Glass etching at home
12. Create your own decals for walls
13. Create a wooden, decorated sign
14. Create your own window clings
15. Cut quilt squares or appliques

What can you do with a Cricut?

Using the latest Cricut Maker, you can cut fabrics and even tougher material. You may also cut intricate designs with precision, including lace stationery patterns, perfect snowflakes, and spider webs for seasonal decor.

Write

Create "handwritten" cards and projects using Cricut pens. You may select the design you prefer from over 370 fonts or choose your computer's favorite font for free.

Score

The Cricut Explore machine makes great folding cards or lines, envelopes, frames, 3-D paper creations, acetate crescents, and so much more using the scoring stylus.

2. Different Types of Cricut machines, Their Features, and Advantages

Original Cricut

Though it might be considered outdated, the machine that began it all was the Cricut Personal. This device utilizes Cricut cartridges and does not require a computer for it to work. It is quite a tiny machine with a very small cutting area. It was not able to make exceedingly complicated cuts nor to complete projects longer than 5.5 x 11 inches. The diameter of the cutting mat was just 6 inches high, meaning that it was just a simple handicraft cutting unit.

Cricut Maker

The very next machine set out by Cricut (widely recognized as Provo Craft) was the Cricut Create. This machine is the exact size of the initial Cricut machine, although some improvements were made to this version. Compared to the first machine, it has a completely different shape and uses more colors. The display screen is also of a higher quality due to technological and hardware enhancements, which were also expanded. In addition, an 8-way tactical blade also came with it.

Cricut Expression

The next type is the Cricut Expression, which is a substantively improved version.

Most importantly, with a 12 x 24-inch cutting capacity, it is considered to be the first Cricut machine while also making more intricate cuts, thereby making it easier to use. This machine can also cut a larger variety of items, including thicker material, such as poster boards and vellum.

This program could still be used without a computer; however, the program for computer use was undoubtedly improving in terms of quality. Cricut Craft Room was the predecessor to Cricut Design Space, and in this version, this software began being used.

Cricut Expression 2

A very famous computer in its day was Cricut Expression 2. This machine's design had been changing, but we can all accept that it's considered a little ugly. In addition, it had a faster, larger full-color screen that made it much simpler to use.
It also had wonderful features and enhancements were made to this device, such as:

- Offering over 200 designs that are preloaded (images, fonts, sayings, etc.)
- Better deception designs, such as mirroring, resizing, flipping, and rotation

Cricut was progressively becoming well-known and more famous among crafters by the time that Expression 2 was released.

Cricut Imagine

The most common question asked by Cricut beginners is: "can you get print using the Cricut machine?" Cricut Imagine is special as it's the only version that can print as well as cut. Cricut partnered with HP so that it could offer black and tri-color ink cartridges to be used by this version.

Regrettably, at the time, the machine was not the most popular, and it was consequently discontinued quite quickly. As such, the manufacturers of Cricut tried to design machines that were better aligned with the original.

Cricut Mini

The Cricut Mini cutting machine, which is not to be mistaken with the Cricut Easy Press Mini, was just another little personal cutter.

It was the initial unit that required a computer to be used with a narrower cutting range of 8.5 inches. While it was not as successful as the Expression series, this machine was marketed as a smaller and more portable version.

Cricut Cake Machine

The Cricut Cake machine was included in the Cricut Martha Stewart range. Basically, this machine was used to decorate cookies, cupcakes, and cakes. The machine can cut frosting sheets, fondant, gum paste, and other types of baking material.

Cricut Explore One

The Cricut Explore One is the very first machine that looks pretty much the same as the other machines. It takes after the styles of the modern and current Cricut machines.

You can use your favorite free fonts and scalable vector graphics (SVGs) with Explore One or make a selection from the Cricut image library's tens of thousands of graphic files. This machine was much simpler to use and worked well with computers as it contains compartments where you can store pens, extra blades, and other equipment. Moreover, with a Bluetooth adaptor, it can be used wirelessly.

Cricut Explore Air

The Explore Air was an immensely famous model, and it was the first Cricut machine to contain a dual tool holder. The variety of items that can be cut with the Cricut Explore Air machine also increased, and over 60 other suggestions are offered to users. This machine contains a built-in Bluetooth, and in relation to general settings, it contains the smartest dial.

While there is always a place to add a Cricut cartridge, the configuration files are connected to your account. As such, you can practically get away with the cartridge.

Cricut Explore Air 2

The Cricut Explore Air 2 is a hugely famous machine and considerably cheaper than the Cricut Maker. The former also offers more colors than any other machine. The Cricut image library and craft room became the Cricut Design Space, which significantly improved the machine in that it is not browser-based.

Cricut Maker

Cricut Maker is one of the best models invented as it has the greatest capabilities and highest specs. It's a huge improvement from Explore Air 2 and is the best option that you should consider if you can afford it.

The Cricut Joy

The Cricut Joy is the smallest and most recent Cricut machine invented. Its size is approximately one-fourth that of the Maker and Air 2 models, with a cutting width of 4 inches. The major difference is that with this machine, you can cut up to 20 feet worth of material, which is more than any other machine.

3. Advantages and Features of Different Types of Cricut Machines

In terms of crafting and plotting, and precision cutting, this machine can make any kind of project relatively simple. Cricut machines allow you to make all types of projects, from vinyl decals to papercrafts. All you have to do is link a Cricut to your smartphone, PC, or tablet, which is already a great first step to starting your project.

There are a range of Cricut models from which you can choose for your projects; if you intend to buy a Cricut for business or individual use, you must consider the differences between the different models in greater depth.

The next section explores the advantage and features of using each type of Cricut model.

Cricut Maker

With the help of the Cricut Maker, you can create everything. This is the flagship model of Cricut machines and can work with any material, ranging from paper to balsa wood. The Cricut Maker contains an expandable range of instruments, such as a pen, scoring tool, and blade. When using the rotary blade, which is also included in the Cricut Creator, any type of fabric can be easily cut with precision.

Using the device's knife blade, one can create particularly deep cuts using thicker and heavier materials, such as balsa wood and a mat board. You can also choose from among the thousands of electronic designs offered by the Cricut database, all of which can be easily cut and marked by the machine. As such, all you need to do is finish your project. Quilting and sewing work gets pretty simple with the Cricut Maker as you even have the choice of opting for your own layout and designs, which makes it one of the most well-liked models.

Features

- Includes expandable devices, such as knife blades, a rotary blade, and pens
- The rotary blade can cut accurately and quickly through material
- The knife blade can cut through thin and thick material
- 12 by 12-inch cutting mats along with a fine-point pen
- Contains several digital sewing patterns
- Using an easy design app, it is possible to load many projects onto a mobile device or computer
- Your own templates can be used
- Includes a kit docking slot
- Has wireless Bluetooth technology and a USB port so that your device can be charged while you are using it

Advantages

- Allows you to cut a range of materials
- Comes with adjustable instruments

- Includes a number of distinct designs
- Enables use of mobile devices or computers with the Cricut
- Permits greater interaction with the machine with the help of a device dock

Cricut Explore Air 2

A lot of things can be done with your personalized Cricut Explore Air 2 machine, like the creation of home décor and personalized vinyl stickers. With this machine, you can upload the designs you made or even use those from the vast collection in the library.

You can create your designs on your computer, personal mobile phone, or tablet and then easily import it to the Cricut Design Space, which works with both iOS and Android devices.

Cricut Explore Air 2 has a function called smart set dial, which allows users to use over 100 materials. This machine can be connected to your device or PC through Bluetooth in order to cut different materials. People who have Android generally don't experience issues with using this machine, although it may be difficult for a few individuals who use iOS to operate Design Space. That is why it is recommended that you choose a Cricut model that fits your computer if you're using an iPad or items with the iOS framework.

Features

- Cuts and shapes detailed material with great accuracy
- Makes handwritten cards and various projects with the help of Cricut pens
- Offers over 370 fonts to choose from
- Includes a scoring stylus which helps fold boxes, cards, acetate, and 3D paper crafts
- Comes with a two-times-faster cutting mode
- Cuts through over 100 types of materials
- Design Space can be used to import files from any kind of device
- Compatible with iOS and Android devices
- Comes with Cricut picture library
- Enables linking to the Cricut machine through Bluetooth

Advantages

- Cuts with absolute accuracy
- Writes using over 370 fonts
- Scoring stylus bends lines for various projects
- Writes and cuts up to two-times faster
- You can work with over 100 materials
- Uses Design Space
- Connects to devices via Bluetooth

Cricut Explore Air

You can wirelessly work on projects using the Cricut Explore Air. This cutting device has wireless Bluetooth functions that allow you to work via iPad, smartphone, or tablet. It has dual cartridges, which enable you to write, score, or cut in one move. You can also upload your own pictures for free to Cricut Design Space, as nearly all design files are supported by this app. Even if you are working on various projects, you can quickly and reliably cut over 60 types of materials, so you won't waste costly materials, such as leather. With a smart set dial, you can also create simple settings, which is quite easy even if you haven't used it before. You may use your own designs or others from its vast library collection. In addition, you can also utilize Cricut cartridges. In sum, using the Cricut Explore Air is a breeze, but it may be costly to use for the long term if you don't plan to create your own designs, as the prices of fonts and pictures start at $0.90. However, creating original designs is easy.

Features

- Finish your work wirelessly with the help of Bluetooth
- Contains a dual cartridge, which helps in writing, scoring, or cutting simultaneously.
- Compatible with .dxf, .bmp, .svg, .png, .jpg, .gif files
- Cuts over 60 distinct materials
- Operates with all sorts of Cricut cartridges
- Comes with integrated components for storage

Advantages

- A person can operate the machine wirelessly
- You can cut and score or cut and write simultaneously
- You can use pictures you created or those from the image library
- You can use storage knives, pens, and other items included in the storage compartments
- This machine is compatible with other Cricut cartridges

Cricut Explore One

Cricut Explore One allows you to make projects and cut various types of materials. This cutting tool has a wireless Bluetooth connection, enabling work on any type of Bluetooth device to make projects come out perfectly. You can also upload your own pictures and designs for free and even cut these with ease.

You can cut a wide range of material from vinyl and paper to leather and cotton both smoothly and effortlessly with the Cricut Explore One machine. You can also select images to use from the Cricut image library, which provides a selection of over 50,000 images. Old cartridges are also compatible with this Cricut device.

The use of Cricut Explore One is convenient due to the fact that you can experience wireless plotting and cutting. However, this machine doesn't have built-in wireless features. If you want to use this feature, you must buy the wireless Bluetooth device separately, which increases the cost of the Cricut machine. Apart from this, you'll also have to pay an additional price to use images and fonts from the picture library.

Features

- You can upload your own designs for free or select an image you like from the Cricut image library.
- You can use the Cricut Design Space from your iPhone, Mac, PC, or iPad
- If you add a wireless Bluetooth device, you can connect to the Cricut machine wirelessly
- This machine works with various materials
- You can use all the fonts which are installed on your PC
- It is compatible with .dxf, .gif, .jpg, .svg, .png and .bmp files
- You can use the cartridges designed for Cricut machines
- Comes with convenient accessories and a tool holder
- You don't have to build your own customized settings or have a setup with the smart set dial
- Projects can be created in minutes

Advantages

- With the help of a Bluetooth adapter, you can work wirelessly
- It includes over 50,000 fonts and images in the image library of Cricut
- You can upload your own designs for free
- You can create designs using your own device or PC through Design Space
- You don't have to do anything to your settings for the smart set dial
- This machine allows you to cut and print quickly

Cricut Expression 2

You can use your device, computer, or the convenient Cricut Expression 2 LCD touchscreen. This is a brand-new model that is quite compact; you can carry it everywhere if you wish to create projects, cut images, and fonts, and create your own customized designs. This machine also works with the Cricut cartridges, meaning that you have the option of using existing cartridges used for former Cricut models. Through the LCD touchscreen, you can more easily operate the machine and work with all types of materials.

The Cricut Expression 2 allows you to control the projects you have through the screen, whereby you can adjust the speed and pressure settings or even customize your settings for some specific types of material. This includes thick materials, such as chipboard, cardstock, or vinyl, as well as thin materials such as foil, fabric, or paper. It contains three Cricut cartridges with a limited number of phrases, images, and fonts. To get access to more fonts, you must buy additional Cricut cartridges.

Features

- It has a full-color LCD touchscreen
- Compatible with different Cricut cartridges
- The content of the Cricut cartridge is already loaded inside the machine
- The machine links with the Cricut Design Space for free
- It contains many features for editing images, including horizontal and vertical flipping, image sizing, or image rotation

- It offers three types of fonts, 110 layered images and 40 phrases that are already loaded
- It comes with a Cricut alphabet cartridge and the essentials cartridge
- It fits materials that are a variety of sizes and kinds
- Uses a cutting mat of 12 x 24 inches, which is sold separately
- It comes with extra features, such as fit to page, quantity, and auto-fill
- You must have a computer if you wish to cut and design through the Cricut craft room
- You can use pictures from Cricut's image library

Advantages

- You don't have to link to the computer, and you can get your work done through the LCD touchscreen
- You can see pictures from the LCD screen
- There is a control that can be used in relation to the Cricut craft room
- You can adjust the speed and pressure of cutting through the LCD screen
- It contains preloaded Cricut cartridges
- It can be used with all types of materials
- You can make more use out of items with the fit to page function

Cricut Expression 1

You can create several customizations for various projects with the help of the Cricut Expression 1 machine. This cutting machine operates through a craft room where one can improve output and edit designs.

You can create multiple projects using four functions and six modes. Users may also take advantage of the fast plotting and cutting options, meaning that projects can be made more quickly. This machine is suitable for business purposes and is quite versatile as it can be carried anywhere, including to one's home, office, or school. Although it contains an LCD screen, it is not considered a touchscreen. You don't have to buy a cutting mat as this machine has a 12 x 12-inch cutting mat available.

Cricut Expression 1 is compact and works effectively as you can create several kinds of designs. However, you must purchase your own cartridges as this machine doesn't have any.

Features

- The machine connects with the Cricut craft room
- It contains four distinct functions and six modes that enhance customization
- The machine is capable of cutting 23.5-inch designs to 0.25-inch images.
- It has a standard LCD screen
- The device is portable
- It includes a 12 x 12-inch cutting mat.
- It can cut efficiently and quickly

Advantages

- It has four functions and six modes
- It is completely customizable for the purpose of creating effective designs
- The machine has portable designs
- It includes a 12 x 12-inch cutting mat
- The machine is compatible with the Cricut craft room

Cricut Mini

You will love the Cricut Mini because, despite its small size, the machine is capable of cutting 8.5 x 12-inch materials as well as fonts and shapes that are even smaller extremely precisely. As the name suggests, this machine is very light and portable, meaning that you can carry it with you wherever you wish to go. To get a connection to the device, you must have a computer or laptop that is connected to the internet. If you wish to save space or if you ever need a portable machine, then this machine could be the best option for you.

Features

- It can cut materials larger than 8.5 x 12 inches
- This machine allows you to cut fonts and shapes that are extremely small as well as much larger cuts
- To operate the device, your machine must be linked to a computer or a laptop
- You don't have to pay for the Cricut craft room online software
- One can get access to various pictures from the Cricut library
- You can edit your designs through the slant, flip, rotate, or size features
- It can be used to cut all types of materials regardless of thickness
- Portable and small
- Easy to use
- Lightweight
- It includes four free cardstock sheets that are 8.5 x 11 inches.

Advantages

- It includes Craft Room, which is an online app
- You can edit projects by flipping, slanting, resizing, and rotating
- It can cut a significant number of materials, including foil, vinyl, and chipboard
- Easy and simple to use
- Contains an 8.5 x 12-inch cutting mat

4. Comparison of All Cricut Machines

Explore Air 2 vs. Cricut Maker

The biggest difference between the Cricut Maker and Explore Air 2 is that the former contains a knife blade, which helps you to cut thicker and tougher materials, such as leather, chipboard, and balsa wood. The Maker is also heavier since the knife blade can apply more pressure when handling a material. However, while Explore Air 2 may cut thick items, the Maker can cut more precisely and quickly with the help of a knife blade.

With the new enhanced sensor, Cricut Maker has the advantage of cutting colored and patterned paper, although Cricut Explore Air 2 can only cut white papers. Cricut Explore Air 2 also has a smart dial that allows you to select the materials you want to use. However, it appears that it operates with only a few materials in comparison to the Cricut Maker, which has the advantage of cutting through both thick and thin materials easily and quickly.

The Cricut Maker, with certain metal components, also has a stylish look. It even has several compartments, including a device holder, to store accessories, such as scissors, pens, markers, and blades. This is unlike Cricut Explore Air 2, which only has one compartment for tools and accessories.

The Cricut Maker is particularly useful because of its multiple functions. If you're looking for a Cricut machine that can cut through mediums quickly and efficiently regardless of thickness and includes ample storage space, then you must opt for the Cricut Maker. Among all the Cricut machines, the Cricut Maker is the most expensive. However, if you intend to work on simple projects and want a portable device, then you should purchase the Cricut Explore Air 2 machine.

Explore Air vs. Explore Air 2

Both Cricut Explore Air 2 and Cricut Explore Air are the most famous Cricut models released in the explore line. However, there are clear differences between the two, which should be noted before selecting one to purchase. Both machines contain the smart set dial, which allows you to operate the machine with the materials which you wish to cut. You can work wirelessly through Bluetooth on both machines, and each can also use various Cricut cartridges. A person can also use fonts and images from the image library through both machines, and neither has a rotary blade, knife blade, or tool to cut fabrics.

The primary difference between both is that the Explore Air 2 can cut and write material twice as quickly as the Explore Air. In addition, Explore Air comes in colors such as wild orchid, teal, blue, and gold, whereas Explore Air comes in rose, lilac, blue, and mint. If you want a faster and more powerful Cricut machine, then Explore Air 2 is the better option. On the other hand, if the slower speed is not an issue for you and you want to pay less for your Cricut model, then you can choose Cricut Explore Air.

Explore One vs. Explore Air

The Cricut Explore One and Cricut Explore Air are both Cricut models that are light and portable. These can be taken wherever you want, such as the workplace, home, or school. With the help of a smart set dial, the two machines are designed to allow you to easily set the machine and work on different kinds of materials. A selection of fabrics ranging from heavy leather and vinyl to thin paper can be cut using both Cricut Explore machines. However, Cricut Explore One doesn't have a built-in Bluetooth option that would enable wireless cutting. To have this, you must buy a Bluetooth connector from Cricut to enable the machine to operate wirelessly. While both machines can be attached to a Mac, iOS devices, or PC, Cricut

Explore One uses an accessory device that must be bought separately. This adapter would allow the one pen connector to be attached so that you can use the Cricut Explore One machine. As such, Explore Air may be preferable if you wish to have a Cricut machine that is already wireless. It also contains a dual cutting and writing tool holder, which means that you don't have to buy an adapter for the tool. When looking at the additional gadgets and tools you would need to upgrade Explore One; it can be seen that you can save time and money by using Explore Air.

Explore Air Gold vs. Explore Air

When comparing and contrasting Explore Air Gold and the Explore Air models, it is important to determine which machine is better and more suitable for individual users. In general, it should be noted that there is simply no distinction between the specs of the models. In addition, both devices contain a smart set dial to set the sort of material you are going to work on, use Bluetooth to enable wireless cutting and writing, and contain a double holder for speedy cutting and writing.

Both Cricut machines allow you to cut a wide range of materials and use the Design Space software to create your own photos for free. In both models, Cricut cartridges can be used, and you can also connect the iOS device, Mac devices, or PC to Explore Air and Explore Air Gold as well. The main difference is the design of the machines, as Explore Air Gold has a gold band running across the lower section of the machine's body, which makes it look more stylish and consequently is more expensive than the standard Explore Air.

The Cricut Explore Air Gold machine looks fantastic for office purposes and is a great cutting tool. If you consider yourself among the many people who find Explore Air Gold to be more visually appealing, then you might not mind paying more for it. However, Cricut Explore Air seems to be a better option if you are more interested in the value than the design.

Expression 2 vs. Explore One

There are a few main differences between the two models of Explore One and Expression 2. The latter has a small touch screen where the machine's primary control panel is mounted. Through the LCD touchscreen, you can adjust your design and increase the speed and pressure applied to the material you are cutting. However, the Cricut Explore One machine doesn't have an LCD screen; however, if it has a Bluetooth connector in place, the machine can be operated by a PC or mobile. Both machines cut materials of various kinds and can use Cricut cartridges.

Cricut Expression 2 is largely different from Expression 1 as the former has an LCD touch screen, superior design and specs, and the wireless networking option. Although it's heavy, unlike Explore One, its fantastic features and design still make it the better model.

Cricut Mini vs. Expression 1

If you wish to use and buy a Cricut but you can't because it is too expensive, then the best option for you could be the Cricut Mini. With its power to cut and write on 8.5 x 12-inch paper and make tiny to larger cuts, this cutting model is a smaller version of standard Cricut models. It can cut a range of materials and is light and portable. The price of this machine is a fraction of the usual Cricut versions. As such, you may ask yourself, especially if you wish to design larger and more complicated projects, whether this affordable Cricut alternative is a better option.

Let's take a look at some increasingly common Cricut designs:

When comparing Expression 1 with the Mini, the latter can print, cut, and write on most items. Moreover, the machine must be linked to a laptop or PC, which is further linked to the internet. While Cricut Mini is definitely light, you must bring your laptop so that you can use it anywhere.

Expression 1 comes with an LCD screen and buttons, which will help you when editing your template. This further means that you don't need a laptop or computer. Through the LCD screen, you can adjust the pressure and pace. In order to conveniently select the best environment for your cutting or plotting needs, you can even utilize six cutting modes and four functions.

Expression 1 is obviously heavier in comparison to Cricut Mini. However, if you wish to have a small, lightweight cutting machine that can be taken anywhere, then you should think about purchasing the Cricut Mini. On the other hand, if you like to have a more efficient cutting tool, regardless of its weight, the better choice for you would be Expression 1.

Cricut Joy vs. Cricut Maker and Cricut Joy vs. Cricut Explore

Cricut joy has a few limitations when it is compared to the other Cricut machines. However, it also has capabilities that other machines don't have. Firstly, Cricut Joy is easy to use as it does not have any buttons; when it is plugged in, it is turned on. The machine has a cut width of 4.5 inches, whereas Cricut Explore and Cricut Maker can cut material that is up to 11.5 inches wide. There is only one blade with a point. Due to the "smart" sticky vinyl and iron on items, which have a thick supporting material that acts as a mat, you do not need a real cutting mat. The sticky smart vinyl comes in many lengths, including a mega long 20-inch roll in a few colors. Individual cuts might be approximately 4-inches long, and you can cut all 20 inches of vinyl in one go if you're creating smaller shapes shorter than that (such as wall decals). Hence, despite being a small machine, the matless cutting feature enables the cutting of many images in one go, and you won't need to purchase new mats.

5. What Can Be Made with the Cricut Joy Machine?

The Cricut Joy is perfect as a lightweight cutter when it comes to making labels, minor heat transfer, and making cards and vinyl decals. It is also convenient to transport and is a nice addition to any craft room. Cricut Joy is known as a portable cutting machine that is less than half the size of Cricut Maker and Cricut Explore. This makes it ideal for people who don't have a designated crafting area. It also comes with a pen holder and a single blade. As such, you shouldn't be deceived by the size as this machine has certain amazing features.

The Cricut Joy machine is built as a supplementary device to be paired with the already-owned Cricut. You can use it without destroying your Cricut Maker or Cricut Explore or making it run at the exact time as the other devices when you're creating several projects rather quickly.

You can make various easy projects using Cricut Joy as you can select one application, color, and cut per project. Hence, it's great for basic ideas and brand-new users of Cricut. In mere minutes, you can have some fun by making things like:

- Wall borders and decals
- Vinyl stickers for basic baby bodysuits and shirts
- Banners, party decorations, and cardstock cards

Can you use any of Cricut Explore or Cricut Maker's mats, blades, and materials for Cricut Joy?

Blades: No, Cricut Joy's blade and design are distinct as they match the smaller size of the unit.

Mats: You must use the Cricut Joy mats. However, since the smart vinyl and iron-on items do not require the use of a cutting mat, you may end up purchasing fewer mats in general.

Materials: Of course, you can use many materials. With the help of a standard iron-on, you can cut out a shape you desire and apply it with the Cricut Joy mat. This also applies to adhesive vinyl, cardstock, and other materials that may be cut with a pointed blade.

1. Unboxing Your Cricut Explore Air 2

You must first check to ensure that you aren't missing any items.

If you find that certain things are not included, you must return the machine to the market where you bought it or get a replacement.

If there's something special included that typically isn't, then that's really a good bonus.

At the very least, your kit should include the following:

- Instructional manual
- Cricut mat for cutting
- Pre-installed cutting blade
- Cricut Explore Air 2
- USB cords and power plug
- Pre-installed accessory adapter and silver pen
- Vinyl samples and cardstock

2. Cricut Explore Air 2 accessories and tools

Initially, you are not actually required to get each, and everything included as Cricut has a few important items that are needed. The following list specifies what the Cricut Explore box contains:

Supplies and accessories present in the Cricut Explore box:

- Premium point blade and sheath
- Light grip 12 x 12-inch mat
- Point Cricut pen (not part of the Cricut Explore One)
- Accessory connector (not part of Cricut Explore One)
- Sample of content (for the initial project)
- USB cord and power adapter
- Supplies and accessories present in the Cricut Maker box
- Premium point blade and housing
- Rotary blade and sheath
- Light grip 12 x 12-inch cutting sheet
- Fabric grip 12 x 12-inch cutting sheet
- Fine-point Cricut pen
- Sample cardstock and cloth (for initial projects)

- Adapter for accessories
- USB cord and power adapter

Now, what are the must-have Cricut accessories?

Important accessories: Cricut tools

Necessities: Some simple equipment, especially a weeding instrument and a scraper, which are very helpful.

Why you must have them: You are almost definitely going to have a weeding device if you shred vinyl, as you will need to extract all the vinyl scraps you don't need. When chopping paper, a scraper is handy since it requires a bit of effort to remove all the little pieces of paper from your cutting mat.

Necessary accessories: Cricut cut blade or Cricut knife

Necessities: You can cut thicker material with the deep cutting blade (for the Cricut Explore and Maker models) and a knife blade (used for the Cricut Maker). If you bought a special package, none of these items would arrive with the Cricut.

Why you must have them: If you wish to cut materials that are thicker, you will require one or perhaps both blades, as this will give you a lot of slashing options.

Necessary accessories: Cricut stylus or scoring tool

Necessities: Among the great accessories, we suggest that a person buying a Cricut machine for the first time must purchase a stylus (that is for Cricut Explore) or a scoring tool (for the owners of Cricut Maker). The owner of a Cricut Maker can even utilize the stylus for scoring if desired, although a deeper score can be obtained with the help of the scoring tool.

Why you must have it: You can create different types of paper crafts with a scoring gadget. Remember that you do not require this accessory if you are not going to complete a project that involves paper crafting.

Accessories you must have: a ball of aluminum foil

What you need to have: A layer of standard aluminum foil that is scrunched up.

Why you must have it: A ball of aluminum foil will allow you to keep the blades clean and sharp and will hopefully ensure that you will not need to purchase new blades for a long time.

Supplies you must have for Cricut

Cardstock
You will require cardstock if you'd like to start making paper-related projects with the Cricut.

Vinyl
You'll require vinyl if you want to begin creating projects with vinyl using the Cricut. For a number of vinyl designs, we suggest you use both self-vinyl and iron-on (often referred to as HTV).

Transfer tape
Vinyl projects will require one transfer tape roll to enable you to transfer the vinyl to the surface of a project. Make sure to use the standard Cricut grip tape, not the strong grip transfer tape.

Useful accessories

Cricut mats

To get your machine to work effectively, certain designs may really require you to use a new mat, which is quite sticky. You can choose to clean your old mats, but this is very time-consuming. As such, purchasing fresh mats is simpler. If you want to create any bigger designs, you must get each of these Cricut mats or any 12 x 24-inch mats.

Cricut Easy Press

The Easy Press is the perfect accessory if you are trying to prepare designs made from iron vinyl, which makes the creation of iron-on stuff easier.

Cricut pens

Grab a few Cricut pens if you think you're going to want to do some letter labeling or writing as they work with the accessories clamp and on card designs as well as label writing.

Cloth and cloth marking pen

If you have a Cricut Maker, you will notice that it very beautifully cuts through cloth. As such, it may be useful to use with a limited stock of felt and other materials. You will want to get a cloth marking pen as well.

Items you may purchase later:

You don't really need perfect blades for replacement purposes or every color and kind of vinyl or cardstock. You should purchase your materials based on the projects you want to make.

3. What Is a Cricut Mat?

If you're feeling overwhelmed due to the wide variety of Cricut mats that exist and the kind of items that should be used with each Cricut mat as well as how to care for and clean them, then this is surely the best place for you. In essence, a Cricut mat consists of an area upon which to cut each project. At present, there are around four distinct kinds of mats, such as a pink one made of fabric, a standard grip green mat, a purple, strong grip mat, and a light grip blue one.

Based on the resources you are using, you may need a different mat. If you do not use the right mat for a particular project, this can pose a problem later on when you are trying to separate your materials from the Cricut mat.

Everything you need to know about Cricut mats

To complete any project, you must use a Cricut mat because each item that you cut must be placed on a surface. Otherwise, it will move around, which can be problematic.

Cricut mats have the quality of being sticky, with the degree of stickiness differing based on the material being gripped. Tighter grips are better for tougher materials (such as think cardstock or chipboard), unlike light material, which does not need to be gripped as firmly, such as vinyl or regular paper.

Mats are elastic, which is very useful because they can bend, which helps detach certain projects.

Protective cover: Transparent covers have been placed on the latest Cricut mats to better protect them.

Outer mat: There is no grip (or stickiness) on this section of the cutting mat and you can also see the title of the cutting mat that you are working on along with the dimensions, both in inches and centimeters.

Inner mat: The inner section of the mat is separated by squares of 1x1 inches, which is very useful so that you can clearly see where the material is at all times when you are about to cut anything.

What is the difference between all the Cricut mats?

You must get a different kind of mat every time you work on a specific kind of project, and this further depends on the resources you are using to make your project. You must learn or at least notice what mats are best suited for particular purposes as the Design Space won't recommend to you which mats should be used for various kinds of projects.

For this reason, it's better to purchase all the mats and then just select the one you need for the project you are making.

Blue light grip mat

This is specially made to cut light materials.

The type of mat comes in sizes of 12 x 24 inches and 12 x 12 inches.

It would be extremely difficult for you to extract a particular substance from your Cricut mat if you put a thin material or layer on a thicker grip mat.

Using a light grip Cricut mat, the most popular materials that can be cut are:

- Thin cardstock
- Normal paper
- Construction paper
- Vinyl

Green standard grip mat

The most popular and inexpensive mat is the standard grip kind, which was designed to work for materials of average weight. It typically comes with any Cricut machine you buy (however, be sure to read the label on your device) and is green.

Using this kind of mat, the most popular materials you may cut are:

- Removable or permanent vinyl
- Cardstock
- HTV

Purple standard grip mat

This cutting mat was built to keep heavy items in place.

The grip of this mat is not sufficient when using hard material, such as balsa basswood. In such instances, it may be better to use painter's tape to bind the material to the cutting mat.

The most popular materials which can be cut are:

- Glitter and thick cardstock
- Basswood and balsa wood
- Chipboard
- Leather
- Posterboard

Pink fabric grip mat

The latest mat is the pink mat, which comes with the Cricut Maker model.

This fabric grip cutting mat is built to cut material made of fabric. It is often paired with a Cricut model or with the rotating blade and Cricut Maker.

This mat requires the most upkeep and gets dusty easily.

The most popular materials that can cut by the strong grip cutting mat are:

- Bonded fabric
- Any kind of rotary blade cloth (as used by the Cricut Maker)

4. Dos and Don'ts When Cleaning Cricut Explore Air 2

Cricut Explore machines can get messy because of all the scraps that form when cutting glitter paper, vinyl, or cardstock. As such, there are some things you can do to keep your Cricut Explore in good condition.

Dos:

- Switch your computer off when cleaning your machine
- Clean the machine with a clean cloth or a non-alcoholic baby wipe
- Wipe the handles to remove any leftover residue
- To clear any residue, clean the blade to keep the area tidy
- Move the casing carefully to one end to clear the case

Don'ts:

- Never explicitly spray the cleaner on the machine
- Don't ever clean the shelf that has the casing as the grease is important
- Never try to hold the chain of the gear that is placed toward the back of the machine
- Don't vacuum when your screen is switched on

5. Differences between Explore Air and Explore Air 2

A frequent question that people ask pertains to the difference between Explore Air and Explore Air 2 because they look the same and have similar characteristics. In response to this, the key distinctions relate to speed and color. The Explore Air 2 has a mode that allows one to cut material twice as fast, which works with iron-on, cardstock, and vinyl. It consists of three main colors: pastel pink, sky blue, and mint green. Let us take a peek inside now.

6. Inside Cricut Explore Air 2

The main characteristics of Explore Air 2 are illustrated below.

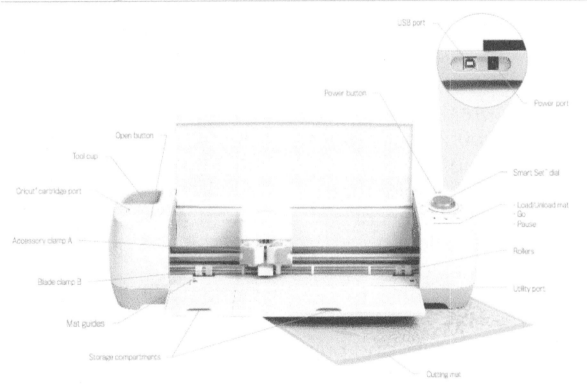

Cricut Explore®: Overview

Cricut Explore Air 2

PROS

- Cuts, writes, & scores
- Double accessories clamp
- Built-in bluetooth
- Cut dozens of materials
- Fast Mode
- Free access to Design Space
- Cut SVGs and print then cut images
- Upload your own images
- Cartridge slot
- Less expensive than the Maker

CONS

- Requires bonded fabrics
- Not compatible with Rotary Blade, Knife Blade, Scoring Wheels
- Not the best long term value
- Cannot cut delicate materials like crepe paper
- Thicker materials like wood may not cut as clean

- **Tool cup:** contains scissors, pens, etc.
- **Clamp A:** The accessory connector is pre-installed, where one can add a pen for illustration purposes. It's also good for carrying blades for scoring.
- Blade clamp B: It includes a pre-installed blade. If you want to remove or replace the vinyl, then you must take a look at it.
- **Storage spaces for accessories:** Besides the tool cup, there are two holding compartments available in relation to the Explore Air 2. On the left side, the smaller compartments carry blades, an extension adapter, and the blade sheath. To hold the replacement blades securely in place, a magnetic strip has been attached. The larger storage space is suitable for longer pens and tools.
- **Smart set dial:** To pick the item you will be cutting, turn the dial. The 2x quick mode enables you to switch and demonstrates which items can be cut.
- **Cutting mat:** This will be how much of the content will be loaded into your Cricut machine. To keep our material tightly in place, it's one side sticky.

A quick note on the blade and accessory clamps: If there's a need to detach the accessory clamp and blade, just pull the lever and the metal casing. The blade has been placed inside, and toward the top, you can see a small plunger. To see the magnetic blade, you will need to push it down. If you want to swap the blade, just take out the previous one and insert the new one.

- If you wish to use a pen, open accessory clamp A, lower it, and then close the clamp.
- Connect your machine and install the needed drivers.
- Link the MAC/PC/iPad to the computer
- While this Cricut Explore Air 2 can be used wirelessly, you can set it up with a USB cable. You can start by putting it behind on a platform with 10 inches of space left as the mat that is used to cut moves back and forth within the machine.
- Plug the device in and then attach the USB cable and power adapter.
- Switch on your computer along with Explore Air 2 machine.

The cutting mat

Perhaps the essential accessory you're going to use is the cutting mat, which will assist in loading most of the items into the machine. On the one hand, it's sticky, which helps the material be kept in place when it's being inked, scored, or cut.

There are three basic types of cutting mats. Each is used with a particular collection of materials, so you can use all three of them based on what you usually deal with.

Light blue grip mat

- Light cardstock
- Construction paper
- Cardstock light
- Scrapbook and printer paper
- Vellum

Green standard grip mat

- Embossed as well as regular cardstock
- Standard vinyl and heat transfer
- Window clings
- Backed fabric
- Vinyl

Purple strong grip mat

- Chipboard
- Perforated cardboard
- Suede and leather
- Foam
- Magnetic substance
- Posterboard
- Wood (including balsa)
- Cricut tool simple set collection

More tools you can buy

Scissors

Tweezers

They are reverse grip, meaning that the handle is pressed to open and released to shut. It is extremely effective for keeping projects as soon as they dry as well as for many other small functions.

Scraper

Important for vinyl work and cleaning the cutting mat.

Spatula

Used for the thorough removal of material from the cutting pad.

Weeder

It helps in extracting vinyl from the lining or removing tiny cuts.

7. Use of the Cricut Explore Air 2: Your First Design

Now we are going to walk you through a sample project using only the materials that came along with the machine you purchased.

You have to be selective as your sample consists of cardstock, a cutting mat, a silver pen, and paper. You must remove the protector from the cutting mat to work, and you can add it again later after finishing your project. It must be preserved when it is not being used.

- Place the cardstock over the cutting mat. Hold it sideways on the cutting mat with the layered side facing up. It must be positioned just below the Cricut logo in the upper-left corner.

- Mount the mat through the rig. In accordance with the instructions, insert the mat. Here is a photo that illustrates what it must look like at this stage. When clicking the unload/load button located over the top right, hold the mat down, pushing tightly with the rollers. This item looks like a double-arrow package.

- Insert the silver pen. Then, open connection clamp A. Remove the cap of the pen and place the tip in the casing until you can no longer see the arrow of the pen. Then, proceed to close the clamp.

Tip: Attach the cap to the bottom of the pen so that you don't lose it.

- Check the pattern on the preview screen of the mat. Then, press the go button.
- Now, get your device set up on the dial that is suitable for cutting cardstock
- Then, to begin, press the flashing "C" button.
- Let the mat unload. Click the unload/load button until the project is completed and detach the pen. You can store yours in the component compartment. However, if you want to have easy access to it, there is also a convenient bin on the left side of the unit where you can store it.
- Put the mat face down on a smooth surface and curl the side up that is facing you. The material can then be separated from the mat, so just continue curling the cutting mat to make it a little easier to remove.

Fold over the card and press down, squeezing it in two. Do the exact same step with the blue paper and put the grey card inside. If you wish, you can stick this in place.

Presto, your finished object should look like this:

Cricut Access

Cricut Access is a high price service that is provided by Cricut to individuals with a subscription that gives you access to designs, fonts, or 10% percent cash back on all transactions based on the proposal you have chosen.

If you find yourself purchasing a number of items through the Cricut Design Space app, Cricut Access might be worth it for you.

However, if not, then it would likely be better to buy designs as they are needed and to acquire them in this way.

Utilization of Bluetooth

The Explore Air 2 has Bluetooth in the box so that it can work wirelessly with your desktop, iPad, or iPhone. Cricut contains a page covering Windows, Android, iOS, and Mac devices, which can help you combine it with your desktop.

Tricks and tips

You can use Design Space with nearly any picture you find. Just make sure to check and follow the step-by-step directions from Cricut.

Always make sure to test your project on a tiny portion of the material. It might take extra time, but it can save you some money if you have set up all the settings correctly and have an oily blade.
The Explore Air 2 machine can be used without an internet connection if you just attach it with Android or any iOS (iPad/iPhone) device.

8. Projects you can make with Cricut Explore Air 2

1. Iron on pajamas

With Cricut Explore Air 2 and iron-on, you can design all kinds of clothing. You can use a single sticker or picture on a tee or even create "patterned" clothes, such as pajamas for Valentine's Day.

Material:

- Cricut Explore machine along with a sharp point blade
- Blue light grip or standard grip mat
- Weeding tool
- Cricut iron-on in a selection of colors
- Cricut iron-on glitter in a number of colors
- Washed pajamas
- Cricut Mini Easy Press or a regular easy press

- Scissors
- Rotary cutter and acrylic ruler (optional)

Directions:
- Arrange your file in the Design Space
- Shorten your project
- Place your iron firstly onto the shiny side of your mat. Make sure that the setting of the material is suitable to the form of iron that is in use
- Afterward, insert the mat into the Cricut. To begin cutting the mat, tap the blinking C button
- Now, you must weed the project
- After you are done cutting the project, you need to remove everything you don't want using the weeding hook
- Stick the iron to the vinyl material
- Make sure to pre-wash your pajamas to ensure that the velvet can be ironed. You can even use the Cricut Easy Press (the tiny one is perfect in terms of its size)
- Grab your source of heat

XOXO Pajama

- We can begin by placing the key decal on the front of the XOXO pajama. Heat up the heating device you have or the Easy Press. Then, place the pajamas on the mat of the Easy Press or any other surface to apply pressure to it after having placed the sticker in the center of the tee.
- The next step is to use a heating device, be it the Easy Press or any other device. If you wish to use it with the Cricut Mini, shift it back and forth on the iron. It just needs around thirty seconds, depending on your decal's size. Then, peel off the plastic liner carefully. If you notice that the material has not become fully stuck, then you have to put the liner back and iron it until it has completely adhered. Then, switch your shirt and heat it for almost 15 seconds. Allow it to cool properly before handling.
- Complete the remainder of the tiny lips and mustaches, randomly putting them across the pants and tops of the pajamas. Then, repeat the previous step in terms of your handling of the key decal.

2. DIY symbol - sticker on wood

Making interior design signs with Cricut Explore Air 2 is a fun activity as there are many ways in which one can do this. In the case of raw wood, we suggest that you continue to iron but that you use adhesive vinyl for painted wood. For example, you should do so when dealing with the "create, hustle, replay" sign since a heating element will damage the paint.

Materials
- Cricut Explore machine
- Wild rose kit, which contains nearly everything you need to complete this project
- Black adhesive vinyl
- Pink adhesive vinyl
- Transfer tape
- Scraper

- Weeding tool

You will also need:
- A wooden sign
- Paintbrush
- White paint
- Clearcoat (not necessary)

Directions
- The first step is to paint the sign you have chosen
- If the sign which you have selected is made of raw wood, then you will likely want to get it painted. If the surface is rough, then make sure it is smooth because cleaner wood will strengthen the likelihood that the vinyl will hold better. As such, we suggest that you select smooth wooden pieces, to begin with.
- Now, you can begin painting. Keep in mind that you must use at least two coats of paint. You may use white acrylic paint for the sign. Then, allow your sign to dry, which may take over 24 hours.
- Proceed to open a file in the design file
- Resize the project
- Trim the vinyl

When the project is correctly sized, you can proceed to split two vinyl colors using Design Space. It's NOT vinyl iron, so don't mirror your picture. Instead, place the colored side of the vinyl on the mat. Then, put it into the Cricut and press the flickering "C" button.

- Weed the vinyl. Use the weed tool to scrape the unwanted vinyl off the project until your design is cut. If you are struggling to match the sign, then take out the remaining parts.
- Attach transfer tape to the image. Use the scraper to burnish the vinyl on the transfer tape. If it is important to your project, then you can cut the words so that they are apart from one another. After that, you must take care to ensure that the vinyl sticks to the transfer tape when peeling the carrier sheet.
- Align vinyl on the sign. Place your vinyl and transfer tape on your project. Until you have burnished it, you should ensure that it is correctly aligned.
- Burnish your sign. Use the scraper to clean the words on your wooden tag.
- Peel your transfer tape. Burnish again if you think it's not sticking, as this can be challenging with certain types of wood that have been painted.
- Include a clear coat. Apply a transparent coat to your project if you like. We recommend MOD Podge as it is a product that dries as a hard and clear coat.

3. Huge paper flowers by cardstock

Cardstock is one of the simplest materials to cut with Cricut Explore Air 2. However, it's also a very malleable material that can be used in an infinite number of ways. Cardstock is great for creating 3D projects such as frames, wreaths, interior design, and multilayer cards. For example, you can create large beautiful paper flowers if you purchase certain materials and follow the instructions stated below.

Materials

- Cricut Explore machine
- Teal flower
- Pink flower

Directions

- Download the prototype for a large paper flower
- Assemble the huge paper flowers
- Once you are done cutting each and every piece, you will notice that every flower petal contains a slit that begins at the petal base
- Now, apply some craft glue and cover the base to create certain dimensions using every petal. It does not matter how much overlap there is, as you should just make sure to be consistent when using the flower petals.
- When dry, all the flower petals should be glued together to make them "bloom." You can start from the bottom with the largest petals, which you can glue in a circle on the highest point of the piece of the ring design. Once you've finished the initial layer, do the next layers you've completed the entire flower.

4. Tote bag with infusible ink

Cricut is still creating various new materials, many of which can be cut with the Cricut Explore Air 2. There are various projects that can be made with infusible ink, such as T-shirts, coasters, tote bags, and baby onesies.

Materials

- Cricut Explore machine
- Standard grip cutting mat
- Sheet for the transfer of infusible ink
- Blank tote bag with infusible ink
- Easy Press 2 or a heat press
- Easy Press 2 cutting mat
- Tweezers
- White cardstock
- Butcher paper, which is included in the transfer sheet
- Lint roller
- Heat-resistant tape

Directions

- Sketch your idea in the Design Space
- Cut your template using Cricut Explore
- Put the infusible ink sheet liner on the side of the cutting mat. Then, insert that into the machine and cut.
- Remove the infusible ink liner

- Get the tote bag
- Pack the tote bag before actually completing your move. You can begin by placing the easy press cutting mat and part of your cardstock into the tote bag. The white cardstock helps keep the Cricut Easy Press cutting mat free of ink, especially if it hasn't leaked. You might need the white cardstock for the next project that involves infusible ink.
- Use a lint brush to remove any dust and dirt from the tote bag
- To transfer your infusible ink, you should use the Cricut Easy Press
- The first thing you need to do is cover the tote bag with butcher paper, which is already included. You have to wait until the transfer sheet is applied, as this will help in flattening the surface and drying the moisture over the bag. Push the button for about 15 seconds and make it completely cool down. Notice the temperature as you reach the cutting mat and cooler bag.
- As soon as the bag has completely cooled down completely, you may include the transfer sheet. Put the baking paper above the transfer sheet and then gently apply the Easy Press to the project using consistent and light pressure. You must ensure that the whole material being transferred must be covered by the Easy Press. You must not switch the easy press as this can make the transferred material change and blur its edges. Thus, make sure to hold it carefully in place for forty seconds
- Make sure you cool the transfer and select it carefully

5. Cleaning labels

Using the Cricut Explore Air 2 machines, you may print and cut material as this will enhance the creativity of the output made. You are not confined to vinyl colors and designs only as you can print anything using your printer, and your Cricut machine can also cut across edges. A basic example of this is cleaning labels; however, other things can also be made, such as stickers, cards, and gift tags.

Materials
- Cricut Explore machine
- Printable vinyl
- A blue light grip or standard grip green cutting mat
- Numerous plastic, metal, or glass containers and bottles

Directions
- Sketch the file in Cricut's Design Space
- Cut out the cleaning labels that were placed over Cricut
- On the screen, the Cricut Design Space recommends that the user should print out a picture on vinyl. Make sure to have an inkjet as a printer. To do this kind of project, make sure to get a bleed check.
- As soon as the labels get printed through the printer, place them over a green or blue cutting mat.
- Through the Cricut Explore, select your material through the custom option and then click "printable vinyl." If you are using the Cricut maker, then just click "printable vinyl" directly.
- Then, insert your cutting mat into the device and cut circles through the labels with the Cricut machine.
- Troubleshooting: When your computer cannot interpret the marks, focus your attention on the machine. You should also make sure that the registration points can be seen and that your device is

not in a shadowy corner of the craft room.

• Now, pick the labels you want, such as stickers, and put them over the jars and containers.

6. Cup of joy mug with adhesive vinyl

A mug is one of the best projects you can design with the Cricut Explore Air 2. Using the vinyl, cut the point razor and add a piece of transfer tape to your cup. You can also pack the cup with peppermint chocolate supplies, a wonderful holiday gift concept.

Materials

• Cricut Explore machine
• Cutting mat in green and blue (a blue cutting mat is already included with the Cricut Explore machine)
• Three enduring vinyl shades
• Weeding tool
• Transfer tape
• White mug
• Hot chocolate material
• Paper Filler Crinkle
• Ribbon for adornment (in-store)

Directions

• Attach it to the Design Space with the insert tool situated in the panel over the left-hand side of the canvas.
• Split it on the Cricut. Notice that it is not possible to mirror standard adhesive vinyl like iron-on-vinyl. You should remove each bit from your pictures and eliminate any excess content.
• Split a bit that is smaller than the words on a sheet of transfer tape. Peel the paper off the tape and get it over the words, scraping the tape to sharpen the vinyl.
• Once you remove the tape, the letters should be stuck. You can then align the mug and put your sticker on the mug, beginning in the center. Remove the tape, and it can stick to the mug with the vinyl. It can stay like that if it doesn't rub a bit harder against the material.
• Fill up your mug with paper on the lower side and all the ingredients needed to prepare hot chocolate, such as mini marshmallows, candy cane, and hot chocolate mix. Use a bow, and then your gift is ready to be given.

7. Painted sign with stencil blank

Did you know that the Cricut Explore Air 2 can trim stencils as well? You can operate the Cricut machine in various ways to create a stencil. This Christmas sign was made with the help of a stencil blank (which is made of a tougher plastic canvas material). However, if you want, you may also use Cricut vinyl, standard vinyl, or even freezer paper.

Materials

• Cricut Explore machine

- Green standard grip or purple strong grip cutting mat
- Wood design frame
- Stencil blank
- Masking tape roll
- Craft paint with numerous colors, including white
- Brushes with a sponge stippler
- Tiny, stiff brush with paint
- Paint tray
- Bright and merry SVG

Directions

- Prepare the canvas in the Cricut Design Space
- Choose the latest project you want
- Cut out the stencil. The "press" button makes it, which is located to the right of the canvas. Once you are on the ready screen, there's nothing else to do, so you should press "Proceed". Then, select the custom dial that is desired and place the stencil on the mat. Position the mat underneath the guides and put the cutting mat into the system by selecting the flashing arrow. Then, press the flashing "C" button, and the stencil film will be cut out by your Cricut. Once you extract the cutting mat from your device after cutting, check it to ensure that it actually cut it. If not, press the "C" button again and wait for it to cut. This is because if the cutting mat is removed from the machine before you have checked, you cannot do this. Thus, make sure to check whether it's been cut along with the cutting mat inside the Cricut.
- Stenciling the interior design label. The next step involves stenciling the sign. You should begin by taping the inside of the frame with the stencil because you want to keep it in place. Scrap away the tape until the paint has set, and then gently lift your stencil (doing this will help keep the paint from pulling up and sticking). If a small amount of paint is being used along with a standing motion, then it must not be exceeded. You may utilize a tiny stiff and white paintbrush to touch up areas that require repainting. Once it is dried, you can apply a polymer coating if you intend to use it indoors. However, if not, then you can skip this step.

This method can be applied to every kind of sign that is stenciled. This bright and merry sign will be quite attractive if painted green and red. You can also choose to use white chalk on the chalkboard.

9. What Are the Best Projects for Mats in Different Sizes?

Cricut mats come in two separate sizes, which are 12 x 12 inches and 12 x 24 inches, are typically available. If you plan to cut an exact pattern a few times or create anything which is larger than the 12 x 12-inch mat, then make sure to get the 24 x 24-inch mat size.

Let's just say that if you have a Cricut Maker, you will need wood and fabric as materials. You may cut larger wood sizes to create designs for your home with 12 x 24-inch mats. The same applies to fabric, as large cloths can be cut, and a fluffy pillow cover can later be sewn. There is no limit other than your imagination!

10. How Do You Clean and Care for Your Cricut Mat?

It's necessary to take care of the mat and ensure that its cuts are nice and smooth. By giving your mats some "extra love," their longevity will get extended, and you can save some money in the future.
Here are some of the best ways that you can achieve this:

- Cover your mat as soon as you are done
- Never throw away the protective cover, as this will ensure that your mat does not gather debris and dust. This will also help keep the mat less sticky.
- As soon as you finish your project, make sure to cover it.
- Use the right items for your Cricut Mats

Each mat is built for use with various kinds of materials. However, if it gets messed up or its functionality decreases, you might have a hard time removing any scraps.
If a light item is placed on a purple mat, it can be very difficult to remove that material. Moreover, this process can increase the wear and tear of the mat. The way in which you extract materials placed on the cutting mat is also important as you must be very careful and try to remove any elements with patience and care.

Over time, the cutting mat will start to lose its grip as material builds up on it, which can make it difficult to remove the mat and replace it with another.
Until you have a new mat, make sure to clean your mat periodically. There are a few distinct methods to clean your mat.

Strong, light, and standard grip mats

- Scraper: After you are done with a project, make sure to remove any paper scraps with your scraper.
- Lint roller: To remove small material and scraps left on the Cricut mat, use a lint roller. This is of particularly great use in removing unwanted fabric.
- Baby wipes (non-alcohol): For instant cleaning, you can use baby wipes as this can work effectively if the mat contains only a small amount of dirt or leftover material.
- Soapy water: To deep clean your mat, you can use a clean washcloth and soapy water.

If water is required to clean your wat met, you must dry it first. This is an important step as a wet mat will not just damage your machine but can even destroy your materials.

Fabric mat:

The pink mat is really special and requires special handling, unlike the other cutting mats. Below are a few of the easiest washing and maintenance techniques for your fabric mat.

- You should not make use of the scraper as this mat was designed to grip fabrics. It's also very light, so the scraper will not be able to be applied to the mat's surface.

- You may use a lint roller to remove any fabric which might be leftover from the Cricut mat.
- It is possible to make use of transfer tape
- You shouldn't use water or soap on this mat
- While moving the mat to get the fabric on it, make sure that your fingers are off the handle
- Cover your mat after you are done

Can adhesive spray be used if the Cricut mat loses its stickiness?

Cricut has four types of mats, with four unique grips.

We realize that everyone wants to save money but purchasing and applying adhesive spray to the mat does not return it to its original state. You might be applying additional stickiness, but this does not work for every material and mat.

Now, what's the next step?

There are various possibilities; you can get the right mat for your project, but if you use the wrong one, you may ruin the mat or your materials. As such, there is a risk factor involved. You may use it until you have had your machine for a year, as this can void the warranty of the machine. Cricut mats are undoubtedly expensive, but you can prolong their life by covering them once you finish your projects, washing them, and handling them with great care.

You can make clean cuts with your Cricut machine by following the troubleshooting tips. Cricut machines are great for cutting material as they can help you create various lovely things. However, you may not always obtain the clean cut that you want, and it's not always clear what can be done to get it fixed. There are five things you should pay attention to while cutting something using your Cricut Maker or Cricut Explore machine. You can solve almost every problem related to Cricut cutting and even make clean, beautiful cuts.

1. Clean Cutting Solutions

The five aspects that you need to pay attention to are the blade, setting, mat, pattern, and material.

Cricut cutting solution 1: sticky mats must be used

You must use a sticky Cricut mat to make clean cuts. This means that if the cuts are jagged, you must first replace your mat. Your problem can be solved instantly with a new Cricut mat. However, if you do not want to or cannot purchase a brand-new mat, you can just wash yours with dish soap and let it dry so that it can become sticky. A mat that's sticky can make a big difference in how your cut turns out.

Cricut cutting solution 2: use a sharp, clean blade

Make sure that the blade you are using is sharp and clean. You can sharpen or clean it by using an aluminum foil sheet. Remove the blade from its casing, compress the plunger, and gently push it in and against the aluminum ball around 50 times. This process will help remove any residue on the blade, such as vinyl or paper. This method works well for long or fine-point blades, ultimately helping you when you want to cut something which requires great care or handling.

If you are concerned because your blade is actually cutting the material too much, then you must not be using the right blade. Go through the package as you must be using a fine-point premium blade with the Cricut Maker and Explore machines. You can learn about which blades are appropriate for use as those with a fine point that have red or white caps. You must not use caps with gray blades as these are specifically made for the older Cricut machines and are not designed to be used by the Cricut Maker and Explore models.

Cricut cutting solution 3: use high-quality items

The material you have can make a huge difference in terms of how it's being cut. For instance, not every paper should be cut down in the same way. If the material is shorter or more delicate, then you have to tear more. If you notice that your paper is not being cut nicely even after you use a clean blade and sticky mat, then the problem will likely be with the paper you are using. As such, we recommend that you use Cricut paper because it is of high quality.

Cricut cutting solution 4: check the settings

You must select the correct settings based on the material you are cutting, as this is an essential step. To change the settings of the material, using the Cricut Design Space is better than the Cricut dial. To change the settings on your Cricut Explore, customize the dial, and then pick the material you want to cut. If this still doesn't help, consider increasing the Cricut pressure.

Cricut cutting solution 5: check the pattern

Notice that every pattern can be cut rather neatly. The more detailed, intricate, and smaller it is, the more difficult it can be to cut certain patterns. At times, you may notice that such patterns are quite small. In this case, you can increase the size if you have this option. If a cardstock needs to be cut down and everything you have done so far hasn't worked, then the material can be cut intricately. You can also tape it if you are working with vinyl. While these options might not actually provide you with any sort of guarantee, you can still try them at least once to see if they will work. Lastly, you may notice that a few patterns are too small or too detailed to cut. However, don't worry. This does not mean that your work is in vain, as you can still cut it and clean it with a knife or scissors later.

2. 15 Cricut hacks

We understand that it can be very intimidating to start using Cricut as a beginner because you might not know what things need to be purchased, what you must learn, and at what point you should start. You also might have a limited budget. As such, these hacks are excellent techniques that are used by experienced crafters that can save you money and energy.

- Buy contact paper instead of transfer paper. When faced with different options, select cheaper products. This is a good hack as transfer paper can be expensive. As such, you can get your work done by using contact paper, which is also useful for transferring images.
- Remove tiny scraps from inside the Cricut by using a sticky lint roller. Lint rollers might even be helpful in clearing glitter or debris that is left over on the cutting mat. As such, it helps the mat stay sticky.
- To get sharpies to fit into Cricut Explore's pen holder, you should use a pencil.
- Clean the Cricut mat with the cheapest method by using warm water and soap. Moreover, if you just want to clean your mat, use (non-alcoholic) baby wipes.
- How to get your mat to be sticky (after it loses its adhesive quality). When you originally purchased a Cricut mat, you will find that it is very sticky. At some point, the mat will become less sticky. As such, in order to get your mat to last longer so that you don't need to get it replaced as often, cut the mat edges with the tape of the printer. Then, spray the stuff gently over the mat so that it can become sticky again.
- You can stick vinyl over textured walls with a tennis ball.
- When using the burnishing tool, you should use a gift or credit card, which can be used to transfer a

design after you are done weeding.

- To make a stencil, trim freezer paper using the Cricut machine.
- Use the sheet that covers your mat when you first bought it and put it back in its place after you are done using it, so that pet hair or dust doesn't decrease the mat's stickiness.
- Place the vinyl rolls on the holder.
- Tie masking or painter's tape to your hand to remove scraps easily when weeding. This will definitely speed up the weeding process, which can be rather tedious.
- To make sure that it is correctly loaded, label the upper side of the cutting mat. This is essential for newcomers to prevent them from making costly mistakes, which can damage the cutting mat or machine if it is incorrectly loaded.
- To sharpen the Cricut blade, push it in and out of an aluminum foil ball. This hack is probably the most useful one.
- Spice up your templates using new fonts.
- Get Inkscape to make the SVGs without any cost

3. Cricut Machine Routine Maintenance

To prolong the life of any object, you must make sure to take extra care of it.

Cleaning your Cricut machine

- Carefully wipe the external panels with a wet cloth.
- Dry any excess moisture instantly with a soft cloth or chamois.
- Don't use alcohol or chemical cleaners on the machine. Cleaning tools and scratchy cleaners must be avoided. You should also refrain from dipping any component of the machine in water.
- Remember not to drink and eat when operating the machine.
- Keep it in a dust-free, dry spot.
- Don't leave the device in any vehicles where high temperatures can melt or destroy plastic parts. This will also help you avoid any excessive heating and cooling.
- Don't expose the machine to direct sunlight for a prolonged period

Caring for your cutting mat

- You must anticipate that you can use your Cricut mats for cutting anywhere between 25 to 40 times before they must be replaced.
- The lifespan of a cutting mat will vary based on the configurations used and the paper that is being cut.
- It's necessary to change the mat when papers no longer stick to it.
- We recommend that you only use Cricut substitutes.

4. Techniques and Tips for Maintaining Your Cricut Machine

Peel the mat away from the material

It could seem instinctual to strip the material (i.e., vinyl or cardstock) from the mat. However, it's usually easier to gently curl and peel your mat away against the material. This helps avoid damaging the finished product.

Use a plastic IKEA bag to store vinyl

IKEA storage bags are particularly useful as you can store vinyl rolls in them.

Sharpen your blade with tin foil

You can potentially increase the lifespan of your point blade by sharpening it with the help of tin foil. You can even lengthen the blade by using tin foil. To sharpen the blade, remove it from the clamp and push the sharp point of the blade against some aluminum foil around 10 to 12 times.

Hold the blades in the Cricut machine

Your machine can store your small tools and blades in a dust-free container.

A lint roller can be used to remove cutting scraps from the mat

You can catch any particularly tiny scraps using the lint roller, which can help you save time, especially if a complicated pattern is carved out on vinyl or on paper.

Use pen adapters so that more Cricut pens can be used

The writing feature of the Cricut machine is amazing because it does all the writing by itself. You may definitely wish that other pens could be used other than the Cricut brand ones. The good news is that if you have Cricut Explore 2 or any other new Cricut machine, then you can buy a pen adapter, which will let you use pens from every brand.

Use your nail polish container for vinyl

This hack is definitely pretty great as you can collect little pieces of vinyl when weeding by purchasing an inexpensive nail-paint holder.

Learn how to make your SVG file in Inkscape for free

Seeking freebies and buying Cricut Access may seem like it's the best option to use SVG files in the Design Space. However, have you ever thought of making your own?

Inkscape is an option that can be downloaded to create your own SVG files and convert pictures to structured SVG files.

A single click can transform a picture into an SVG file

If you are still unable to figure out how to create SVG files of your own, then you must consider converting pictures to SVG with a single click.

You can place all your Cricut supplies on a pegboard

Pegboards are very important in keeping all your supplies sorted as your empty wall space can also get utilized.

Clean your mat with non-alcoholic baby wipes.

You can remove all the debris on your mat by using baby wipes. By spraying easy tack over the surface of your mat, your mat can then become sticky.

Use slap armbands to hold vinyl rolls

Inexpensive slap armbands can be used to tie vinyl rolls.

Sort your vinyl

It is essential to keep track of the kinds of vinyl you have (be it textured, iron-on, or adhesive). You can use a small storage container that is labeled in order to identify the material.

Vinyl must be trimmed with a straight edge to remove uneven edges

Vinyl is an item that is easy to lose control over if you are not cautious. Your edges can be straightened, and waste can be reduced by trimming the vinyl in advance.

For thicker items, make sure to use painter's tape

If your goods move on the mat, your best friend will be painter's tape. It is extremely useful to use with chipboard materials and wood projects.

Make slits in the transfer tape on curved surfaces

How can you have a smooth vinyl on a surface that is curved? One technique that you can use, apart from practice, is cutting slits on the sides around the transfer tape.

1. Decorating a Notebook with Iron-on Foil

1. Go to the project canvas in the Design Space.

2. To cut the pattern out of foil vinyl, follow the onscreen directions. Try to mirror the image because you will need to iron it on your notebook in reverse.

3. Follow the suggested vinyl configuration to iron the pattern onto the notebook.

2. DIY Mini Gift Box and Bow with SVG Cut File for Christmas

Materials

1. Cricut Explore machine
2. Cricut Space Architecture
3. Cardstock in different colors
4. Adhesive (i.e., hot glue)

Directions

1. Upload the SVG cut file gift box to the Cricut Design Room

2. Adjust the measurements based on the desired size.

3. Apply glue to the body flaps.

4. Fill it with something you'd like.

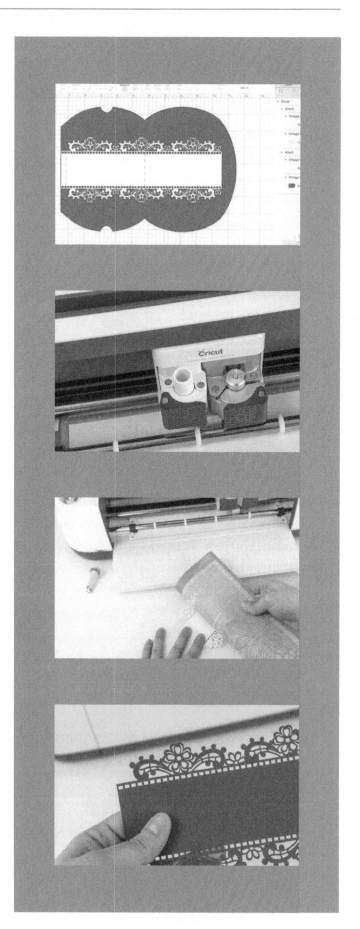

5. Try to fold the top sections. You may also glue them together.

6. Attach a bow and ribbon. Then, glue together the ends of each bow.

7. To create layered loops for the bow, glue the centers together. Then, add a second layer of loops to it, glue the bow back, and lastly, wrap it in place with the tiny centerpiece and glue.

3. Fancy Christmas Tree Card

You can beautify this Christmas tree card by simply changing the colors of the papers you use. If you'd like to simplify this project a little, cut out one tree and apply it to the card.

Mat erials
- Glue
- Cardstock and foil
- Cricut Explore machine
- Tree cut design
- Mat
- White cardstock
- Cricut Design Space
- Cardstock and foil

Directions
1. Place the coil above the cardstock.
2. Follow the instructions.
3. Use the scoring plane, and do not use a pen.
4. Brush the mod lodge and bind the tree cut together with the base.
5. Bind the metal and emboss the card stick together.
6. Now stick the card and tree together firmly.

4. DIY Hand-Drawn Ornament

Without drawing them yourself, you can design stunning ornament gift tags. Using your Scrapbook Explore cutting machine, you may create a collection of DIY gift tags. In order to do so, you can customize the doodle decorations, ornament colors and add additional embellishments, which serves as the perfect finish to all your gifts. On your favorite decorative papers, apply glitter and watercolors, or you can also just opt to print them out. The job is up to the Cricut, but the look is up to you.

Materials

- Cricut Explore machine
- Cricut Design Space apps
- Printer
- Project for ornament gift tags designed by Jen Goode
- Standard Grip 12 x 12-inch Cricut mat
- White and gold cardstock
- Glue
- Coloring accessories, embellishments, or paint (optional)

Directions

- Cut the designs based on the computer's instructions.
- Cut out different layers together. To make thicker gift tags or design and cut an entire gift layout, such as a single cutout piece, further change the center.
- Further decorate your extra accessories with paint, mini crystals, or glitter.
- Hang tape or tie decorations with a ribbon onto your presents.

5. Make a Wreath for an Ugly Sweater

To decorate your wreath and make the best hideous sweater decor ever, use recycled fabrics, children's art supplies, or your favorite bucket of glitter! This project was originally planned as a Cricut project, but you can also print and cut it out with a pair of scissors.

Materials

- Cricut Explore machine
- Created by Jen Goode, Christmas accessories cut-out file.
- Card stock in a variety of colors and patterns
- Ribbon
- A wreath to adorn
- Scissors and glue

Directions

1. You can begin to make a handmade wreath by covering it with a large red ribbon and then adding a decorative ribbon that is orange or gold.
2. Proceed to cut out and personalize your ugly paper sweaters. You can then print out your favorite patterned papers by cutting out hideous sweaters or using a specific template. You can also combine the Thanksgiving accessories with the sweater cut to produce a few sweater designs.
3. You can also cut out some of Christmas accessories and stick them onto individual paper sweaters (i.e., reindeers, trees, and joyous ornaments). Do something that appeals to your sense of style and taste. You can also set out the sweaters at your gathering and have each guest decorate theirs, and then add the finished parts to your wreath.
4. Glue the hideous paper sweaters to your wreath.
5. Attach a bow and enjoy!

6. Cute and Simple Cricut DIY Pumpkins

Decorating Halloween pumpkins is one thing that all kids want to do. This cute and simple Cricut DIY Pumpkins project is great if you want to have some family fun, set up class Halloween parties, or organize community activities. It's perfect for people of all ages and is practically mess-free. This is also great for all kinds of decorating projects as an easy-to-make Halloween craft, and it's also easy to help the kids make the vinyl stickers.

To make thousands of variations, mix up the pumpkin face pieces that were cut with your Cricut unit. To help them make and design their own pumpkins, you can pre-cut all the facial features and allow the children to choose their favorites.

Materials

- Cricut Machine
- Black vinyl
- Pumpkins
- Ribbon or cloth scraps (optional)

Directions

1. With a damp cloth, clean your pumpkin and wipe it dry.
2. Download an SVG file and upload it to the Cricut Space. Ungroup and change the size of each pumpkin face to any size you like.
3. To cut out the pumpkin faces, follow the on-screen directions.
4. Apply each face to the individual pumpkin.
5. Finish your pumpkin with strips of ribbon or fabric that can be wrapped and tied around each pumpkin's stem.

Tip: use adhesive vinyl outdoors or glue to ensure that it sticks well to the pumpkin.

7. DIY Spider Web Garland for Halloween

Materials

- Cricut machine
- File cut by spider web
- Black paper
- Glue
- Parchment paper (optional)

Note: Look for a spider web template that you can cut out rather than cutting a stencil fragment, especially if you don't have a Cricut Explore machine or the ability to cut out your own files. Follow the instructions based on the desired template file.

Directions

1. Upload and cut several sizes of the spider web SVG format.
2. Spread out several pieces of parchment paper in order to cover your workspace. The parchment paper will allow the glue to dry without making the garland stick to the table.
3. To get the look you want, spread the spider webs out. The longer the working surface, the more space you will need to design the garland without needing to stick it to a surface.
4. Use glue on overlapping edges to tie the webs together until you're pleased with the layout. This can be tricky because there aren't that many edges.
5. When it's thoroughly dry, pick up the garland carefully and verify if you have enough points attached to one another. Do it now if you need to add glue to other parts of the webs.
6. Wait for it to finish drying.
7. Decorate the webs as you please.

8. Sugar Skulls Cupcake Decorations

Materials

- Cricut Explore machine
- Cricut Design Space apps
- Sugar Skull print-outs
- 12 x 12-inch regular Cricut mat grip
- Printer
- White paper or cardstock
- Toothpicks
- Glue

Directions

- Print out and then cut two sugar skull models per cupcake. Follow the on-screen instructions.
- Glue two sugar skull designs together, putting a toothpick between each two skulls so that they are back-to-back.
- Glue or attach a toothpick to the rear of one of the items (optional).

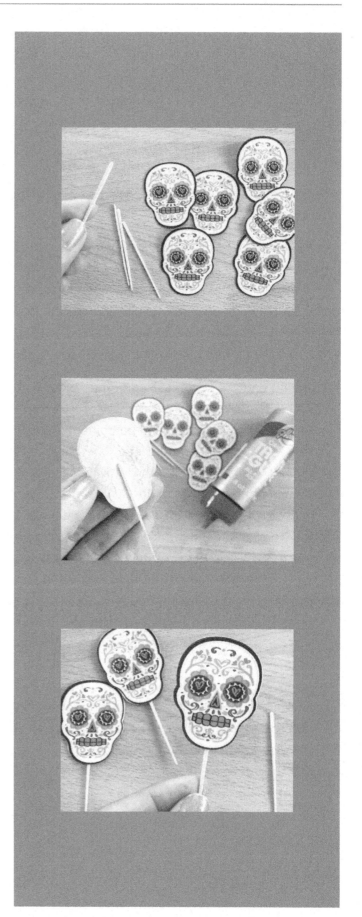

9. DIY Lit Spider Web Decoration

Using only a few Cricut cut spider web templates, you can make your own stylish lit spider web decoration. You can make a nice Halloween decor design in about 30 minutes, which looks fantastic, especially at night.

In just a few easy steps, you can create a spooky spider web fluorescent bulb for Halloween. Go and get ready to get crafty with a small container and some black cardstock.

Materials
- Computer
- Cricut Explore machine
- Cricut Design Space apps
- Split template spider web
- 12 x 12-ich regular grip mat
- Back cardstock
- Painter's tape or another tape that isn't too sticky
- Glue
- Quart size mason jar
- Battery-powered votive candle

Directions
1. To cut two sets of spider webs, follow the on-screen instructions.
2. Wrap a strip of tape around the middle of the Mason jar's center, leaving the sticky side facing outside.
3. To create the look that you want, tree trunk pieces to the tape.

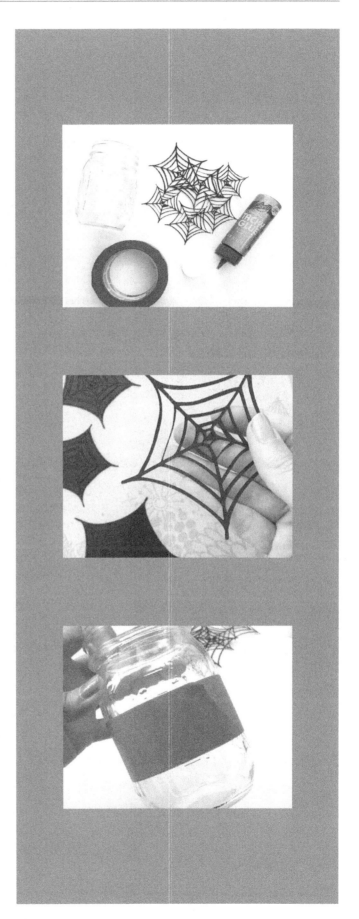

4. Use glue to stick the parts of the web together. Wait for it to dry.

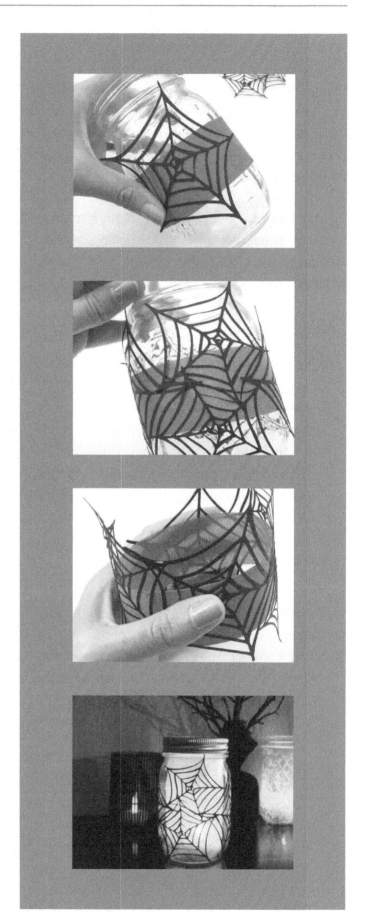

5. Slip the piece away from the container, including the tape.

6. Remove the tape from either side of the jar very carefully. Place the spider web on the jar again. Alternatively, you can glue it in place.

7. Place the candle inside the pot and light it.

10. Girl and Doll Matching Art Shirts

If you have a Cricut machine, you will know that it's perfect for crafting paper. How about using it to make some gifts for your kids too?

Materials

- Computer
- Cricut Explore machine
- Free online design tools by Cricut Design Space
- 12 x 12-inch standard grip cutting pad
- Gold iron-on glitter
- White T-shirt for a doll
- Black T-shirt for a girl
- Iron
- Jen Goode's "Love Art" picture, which is available via Cricut Design Space

Directions

1. In the Cricut Design Room, click the Girl and Doll matching shirt project link.
2. To cut out the templates, follow the on-screen directions.
3. Remove the excess vinyl glitter so that only the art design appears.
4. Iron each pattern onto the required shirt.
5. Wrap it and put a gift tag on it.
6. To design both shirts, you only need one piece of shimmer iron-on vinyl and one pattern. You will be able to resize the cut design as you please by using the Design Space software. It is SO EASY!
7. To create a different look, you can change the colors or the type of shirt that you are using. Use pink vinyl for a spring look on a teal shirt, or use white vinyl on a black shirt to have some great contrast. Even by only changing the colors, you can make the shirt far more appealing. Regardless of whatever you are thinking, this gift will definitely be loved by your child!

11. DIY Necklace Puzzle Piece

I think it is a lot of fun to be able to design your own jewelry. You may have asked yourself: Is it possible to design jewelry using your Cricut machine? Yes, it's possible! You can make this beautiful little DIY puzzle piece necklace in about 30 minutes with your Cricut machine. To pick the colors and style that suits you, you may customize this fun Cricut project. You can further use some polish or fabric glitter. Either way, it's completely up to you.

If you want to make a personalized for a special someone in your life, this will surely be the perfect project for you. This puzzle piece can be used to create jewelry through one necklace. Get imaginative and have fun designing themed jewelry.

Materials

- Cricut Explore machine
- Cricut Design Space apps
- The project's puzzle piece necklace
- Standard 12 x 12-inch grip mat
- White cardstock
- Glue
- Glitter
- Chain necklace

Directions

1. Printed and cut puzzle pieces based on the directions on the tablet.
2. Depending on how thick you want the bracelet pendant to be, repeat the cut to produce 4 to 7 puzzle pieces.
3. Remove the middle heart from the center of the puzzle pieces.
4. Spread glue across the different layers of the puzzle. To create a strong seal between the layers, press down firmly. Wait for it to dry.
5. Add glue to half of the puzzle piece and sprinkle some glitter on it.
6. Finish the pendant.
7. Link it to a chain necklace.

12. DIY Valentine's Day wreath

To make your holiday decorations, repurpose the paper crafts and other Valentine's Day ornaments! This will not take much time, and it's quite easy. You can use print-then-cut art, but you can also make use of your favorite colored paper.

Materials

- Cricut Explore machine
- Workspace
- Wreath
- Ribbons, cords, and pieces of yarn or cloth
- Glue

Directions

1. Wrap the wreath with a combination of ribbon pieces, twine, and other cloth. A piece of fleece piece was used for this example, which was cut into strips and then wrapped around the wreath. You can also decorate your foundation using paint and glitter.
2. To create the design that you want, upload the heart SVG to the Cricut Design Space and lay out the pieces. You can make a few hearts to create a beautiful piece of decor in different sizes and colors.
3. Glue the hearts in place before adding some extra ribbons and a gift tag to top it all off.

Tip: plan it out the way you want and make sure everything looks the way you imagined before you start gluing it in place. Instead of using a lot of glue, move stuff around as this is much simpler.

13. DIY Pillow Box Hugs and Kisses

Do you want to make a cute package for your sweetheart? If you follow the instructions below, you can make a box to fil with all sorts of different treats. This is a Cricut project that you can make with your favorite colored papers, or you may alternatively use a Design Space printable pattern. Then, use your Cricut machine to cut out the box template. You can add some pretty designs or even create a paper bow with glitter or a ribbon.

Materials

- Cricut Explore machine
- Cricut Design Space apps
- Jen Goode's "Pillow Collection and XO Cut" designs
- 12 x 12-inch regular grip Cricut mat
- White card stocks
- Printer
- Candy
- Glue or double-sided tape

Directions:

1. In order to create a cushioned box, select the desired confetti and candy tags. Then, follow the on-screen instructions.
2. Fold the box carefully along all its edges. To seal the box's ends, the curved parts should be moved so that they fold inward.
3. Put some glue on the box's side flap and close one of its ends. You can the end in place if you'd like but that is not needed.
4. Apply the XO chocolate tags to the candy bottoms.
5. Load and close the box with chocolate and confetti.

Tip: Change the package size to create mini treat packages for parties and friends for Valentine's Day.

14. Pretty Flower-Designed Cupcake Wrappers

These floral lace cupcake wrapper templates, which are accessible through the Cricut Design Room, are a Cricut project that you can create. The cut-out file comes with several bits that you can use with your cupcakes to make pretty party pieces. To add a bit of extra sparkle, choose your favorite paper colors and use glitter or adhesive foil.

To give all your spring celebrations an elegant floral dimension, you can make a few pretty cupcake wrappers. With various paper colors, you can split a single festive paper into pieces or create layered designs.

Material:
- Cricut Explore machine
- Cricut Design Space apps
- Jen Goode's "Garden Birthday Party Cupcake Wrap" cut designs
- 12 x 12-inch regular grip Cricut mat
- Cardstock in different shades

Directions
1. Use the basic cupcake wrapper cut to make a sample to ensure that your size is right for the cupcakes you are using.
2. To cut out the cupcake wrappers, follow the on-screen directions.
3. Wrap the cupcake wrapper and keep it together with tape or glue.

15. DIY Flower Art for a Simple Napkin Ring

With this simple DIY flower art napkin ring that you can make with your Cricut machine, you can beautify your table for any occasion. To start this project, set up your table and select the paper colors and pen colors you want.

Materials

- Cricut Explore machine
- Cricut Design Space apps
- "Garden Birthday Party" by Jen Goode Cut and Draw Designs
- 12 x 12-inch regular grip Cricut mat
- Cardstock
- Cricut pens
- Glue

Directions

1. To draw and cut out the napkin ring elements, follow the on-screen instructions.
2. Layer each part of the napkin ring and put it in place.
3. Wrap the ring and keep it in place with glue.

16. DIY Season Gift Tag

You can make a few unique gift tags with a pleasant spring style. These are perfect for gatherings in the spring as you can use guest tags to beautify any gift bags.

Materials

- Computer
- Cricut Explore machine
- Cricut Design Space apps
- Jen Goode's "Flower Baby Day Activity and Mini Label" Cut Designs
- 12 x 12-inch regular grip Cricut mat
- Cardstock
- Cricut pens
- Glue
- Ribbon

Directions

1. Follow the instructions in order to display and clip the different tag components together.
2. Layer different components of the tag and put them into place.
3. Attach a ribbon to your name and then tie it to the gift tag.

17. Create a Cricut Flower Coloring Card

Choose your favorite cardstock colors and get ready to create your card. You may opt to keep the card white if you want to design one that is simpler and more sentimental. Otherwise, you can also use some markers or watercolor pencils.

Materials

- Cricut Explore Machine
- Cricut Design Space apps
- Flower cutouts and heart accessories
- Standard 12 x 12-inch grip Cricut mat
- White cardstock and paper
- Black Cricut pen (.03 midnight, fine-point size)
- Optional colored pencils and markers

Directions

1. In the Cricut Design Room, follow the instructions on how to draw and cut flower coloring card designs.
2. Color the shapes in the card using the colors you like.
3. At the back of the envelope, fold the final scores and glue the side flaps together.
4. Put confetti inside the envelope, seal, and then send it.

A Cricut machine provides you with many innovative business ideas that you can choose to implement.

1. Craft Supply Shop

You can open a craft supplies retail store to sell and advertise items after making your own crafts with the Cricut. This type of retail sector would require considerable investment from start-ups; however, this can be well worth the effort based on the profit that can be earned as a result.

This type of business enterprise should usually be situated inside a city in a highly visible and readily accessible venue. Also, make sure to offer a full range of art materials. Building a loyal customer base is the secret to good retail, and the only way you can do this is to keep the shop fully stocked with goods and supplies that cater to different clients.

2. Making T-Shirts

Making T-shirts is a big industry that you can try to tap into and one of the ways you can create your own T-shirt Company is by using your Cricut machine. If you intend to produce multi-colored T-shirts, it is better to also buy a printer and use this together with your Cricut.

You'll also need a heat press as well as a vinyl cutter and machine. Use the Cricut to make a design and then cut the model with a vinyl printer. You can then use a stick blender to permanently stick the design to the front of any T-shirts, coats, or jerseys.

3. Christmas Decorations

Billions of dollars are spent on holiday decorations worldwide each year, which makes it a pretty lucrative market. This kind of venture is easy to initiate and can be launched by anybody because it does not require any particular knowledge or expertise in the industry.

You can create, manufacture, and sell one-of-a-kind personalized Christmas decorations made with your Cricut. If you check out what is desirable in the market and create some unique collector's items, you can earn a tidy sum with each sale you make. In any famous Christmas theme, decorations can be made using almost every kind of raw material.

4. Crafts Company

If you are skilled in a specific art, you can please others and yourself by making use of your skills by using your Cricut. It's just important to learn how to sell your creations for enough cash in order for you to make a profit that is in accordance with the time you spent and the money you paid for your materials. You can also think more about where you will be selling your merchandise.

It's fun to go to art fairs and craft shows, but individuals who visit these spaces prefer to shop only if the crafts are cheap. As such, selling products to wholesalers or sales agents who will transform and market them to customers is a good way to fix this issue.

5. Split Coast Stampers

Coasters have a practical appeal, but they are much more enticing when they are creative or visually appealing, regardless of whether you sell them or want to use them for yourself. As such, think this through as it can stimulate your sales as well as make a good impression on customers who are considering buying your products.

6. Designer Pillows

You can make a lot of money with a cutter, needle, and thread by making custom-made pillows. The pillows can be finished individually, or you can make several and sell them as a set on an online platform or in an actual store. Since interior designers might be your biggest customers for customized pillows, make sure that you network with such professionals to make the most out of your business. It is also possible to make some extra money by making customized pillows and pillow covers with intricate designs.

7. Vinyl Lettering

By offering a range of fonts and sizes, you can attract consumers by producing separate words that can be used by a client or placed on custom-made posters. As such, you can use your Cricut machine to make such designs. However, you'll need to buy self-adhesive vinyl for your creations.

8. Toy Boxes Theme

It can be quite profitable to establish a home-based business enterprise that produces themed toy boxes or packaging. In fact, with less than $1,000 spent on overhead costs, you can launch a fantastic business. Remember that the trick to effectively manufacture and market the toy boxes is to ensure that the prototypes are original. The toys that are placed in these kinds of packaging should be exclusive. The final product should be colorful and have a theme that is appealing to children, such as ponies, cowboys, or dragons.

Toy boxes can be sold to stores on a wholesale basis, online or through trade shows, a shopping sales kiosk, via mail order, or directly to customers. You can consider producing wicker baskets and placing a wooden toy in each toy box as a unique bonus gift, as an extra income source, or as a publicity tactic.

9. Smartphone Art Gallery

Art is a big business and launching a mobile art gallery can set you on the path to wealth. You can build one-of-a-kind items, create an art gallery, and show your products or those of others to the world!

Although it's not that easy, you can make a decent income from this kind of business. You would probably want to collaborate with a thousand or more artists in this enterprise as such an operation necessitates working with others and having enough artwork to display. If you have chosen the artists, proceed to create areas where their works of art can be displayed.

10. Paper Art Designs

It is also possible to work on certain materials using a Cricut machine, which involves using paper as well as plastic forms. Therefore, this method is a blessing for those who like making paper crafts since it will offer them opportunities for growth.

11. Detailed Designs

Although many organizations have pushed as far as they can to build models in the digital world, they also have to create functioning models at some stage. To create these templates for different companies, a Cricut may be used.

A 3D printing firm would like to partner with any industry that wants extremely accurate templates to be designed in a short time. As such, you can look at libraries, architectural companies, interior design services, or inventors to get some inspiration before setting up your own business for cutting and printing 3D objects.

12. Service Embroidery

Some of the latest advances in technology have been made in the billion-dollar embroidery industry, which makes launching an embroidery service very easy, even for beginners. Cricut machines and other embroidery devices can help create multiple items at a time.

These new devices rely on computers to draw designs before finishing up any patterns using an embroidery machine to finish stitching any patterns. From a home-based venue, a company can be comfortably run.

13. Children's Clothing Manufacturer

There are many options you have to advertise your products. For example, you can visit any nearby children's boutiques to see if they would be interested in buying your clothes. Through your website, you can also try to sell your clothes online. A decent market for your products can also be any local craft and art fairs. You can even host monthly fashion shows in your kitchen!

14. Marketing Items

Remember that North American corporations invest billions of dollars annually in advertising products to consumers, including T-shirts, markers, caps, and calendars. While you can essentially secure only a small fraction of this very lucrative market, it can still make you wealthy. If you are in the business of advertising branded merchandise, the secret to profitability is not to create and also market your own goods.

15. Decorative Handset and Notebook Covers

Vinyl decal pieces have become highly common and pretty popular accessories. Normally, these decorative

items are sold with an adhesive sticker so that they can stick quite easily to a certain object. They are very popular for personal decorative functions as well as company branding. They can also be offered as souvenirs for marketing purposes.

16. Automated Printing Service

Through the establishment of new media, the publishing industry has been revolutionized. Company owners and clients are no longer at the mercy of print shops in order to manufacture their short-run publicity brochures, event programs, and invitations. Instead, many of these types of printed products can now be printed in full-color digital format without charging additional money for pricey print plates.

A digital printing service can be run conveniently from one's home. As such, a decent laptop, design software, and a good-quality printer are all that you need to get this company up and running.

17. Indigenous Art

Some of the most wonderful kinds of music available have been produced by indigenous peoples in the US and Canada, with these paintings being in short supply, especially in overseas markets. Remember that if you have an established clientele in foreign countries, the market for indigenous art can serve as a great marketing opportunity for you.

Bear in mind that this kind of work also makes it easy to earn money as a well-paying broker by supporting local indigenous artists and arranging any overseas sales. However, another option is that you can arrange distribution networks representing musicians from international nations while you reside in the US.

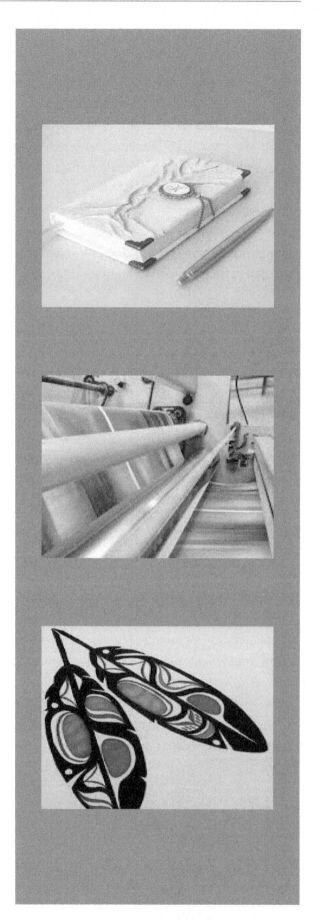

18. Christmas Ornaments

With a Cricut machine, you can start a company that produces Christmas decorations, which will serve as a supplementary income. For example, coasters and garlands are very easy to create while also being affordable to produce. They can also be sold in bulk or directly to customers at a retail kiosk in a mall or art shows, including to retailers. You can run your small business from home, and the overhead cost is practically nonexistent.

19. Manufacturing Mirror Art

Mirror art essentially represents small mirrors that have been pieced together to create an image, landscape, and an abstract design in different colors and shapes. A trip to the local glass store can offer you insight into a selection of mirrors that are available and can be purchased relatively cheaply. Most mirror shops have mirror cut-off pieces, which are too tiny to market. However, you can capitalize on this and negotiate with the store owner to give them to you for free or for a small sum, as these are perfect for making mirror art.

20. Banners

For special events, you can make large curtains using embroidery and vinyl materials. These can be sold and marketed for use at different events, such as for marriages, celebrations, or family reunions.

Commercial consumers that wish to promote their products or property, make an art show more cheerful or adorn a billboard can be targeted. If you plan to join the vinyl banner manufacturing market, creating a website for your company is a smart idea so that consumers can order the signs they want online.

21. Vinyl Signs

Signs cover our planet, ranging from invitations, warnings of imminent danger, or shining fluorescent beacons of warmth. There are several ways to draw people's attention, and you can start a company that creates signs and points out directions for corporations or people. The demands are quite vast as every company wants to have signs to give directions to people or guide customers.

22. Kit Creation Services

Most producers understand that packaging can be almost as important as the product itself in terms of revenue and overall performance. This is why many suppliers, when it comes to producing or updating the packaging of their products, usually employ the services of an expert. For enterprising companies, this is a perfect opportunity to capitalize on this by launching your own packaging development services.

23. Doll-Making Business

On a part-time basis, you can launch a doll-making company from home and sell your dolls via retail, booths, home delivery, craft exhibits, as well as the internet. Relatively little money needs to be spent in order to start, and the average monthly overhead is consequently rather minimal.

24. Web Exhibits of Craft

You may also opt to create a website for e-crafts or that serves as a virtual craft exhibition. The website can be indexed into different crafts types, and users can pick the segment they want to see. Craftspeople can get a listing that would provide information about their unique products and also display photos of their products with a link to a website.

To enter payment and delivery records, customers wishing to buy a product can select their price range and will be connected to the central e-crafts shop. Remember that by selling your own crafts or getting commission by listing and selling the products of others on your website, you can earn some income, which will also help maintain the website and e-craft shop.

25. Niche Greeting Cards

If you want to make some money and are capable of making attractive and desirable designs from paper, then you should attempt to design and sell specialty greeting cards. By sending personalized cards to others for big occasions, such as weddings or events, you can help organizations build and sustain a bond with their client base.

You can even send cards advertising special occasions for customers and sensationalize cards with your customers' signature and logos. The perks of starting such a company are that it can be started part-time and can be very fun and creative as a personal endeavor.

26. Murals from Curtains

Most building and company owners want to design or decorate their offices so that it is appealing to customers. This is something you can capitalize on by running a small, custom mural-painting business.

27. Home-Based Tailor

Note that men's formal and corporate clothing stores will likely not have an in-house manufacturer, and modification work is normally outsourced to outside tailors. However, this reality provides people with sewing skills and a Cricut machine with opportunities to capitalize on this by starting a crafting service from home.

The easiest way to set this up is to sell your services to men's clothing stores on a contractual basis and then schedule the same time of the week to pick up clothes to be tailored and return them the next day.

28. Creation of Handbags

Beginning with a Cricut machine, designing and making handbags is a great business idea to pursue. There will also be very little overhead and costs with the exception of the material you buy.

Remember that it can be to your benefit to use innovative prototypes and unconventional fabrics to manufacture handbags. Then, any finished goods can be sold to fashion outlets or put in nearby discount stores for shipment. You can also show off your fashion sense in art shows or market your products in person or online, such as by selling your purses on eBay or Amazon.

29. Ad Brochures

Promotional pamphlets serve as much more than just a few words on a website followed by a shiny image, much like company presentations. In fact, the value of effective advertising brochures should not be underestimated when establishing a new company as it can significantly boost your marketing and sales.

30. Instructional Material for Arts and Crafts

Knitting, drawing, carving, and staining are techniques used in different arts and crafts. Arts and crafts can be practiced from a home-based workshop during the day, evening, or over the weekend. Renting out commercial property together with a crafts manufacturer is also a good idea to set up a small workspace in an isolated or

unused space in order to really develop your business. This could be a good option if it takes off, and your income begins to grow from this endeavor.

You can also promote courses for arts and crafts retailers by designing newspaper ads, networking for businesses and social events, putting updates on group bulletin boards, and exhibiting products at art and crafts shows.

31. Modification Service

With a Cricut, you can provide clothing and fabric modification services from your home workroom and use your sewing skills to make a bunch of money in the process. Potential clients of your service would be dry cleaners, apparel retailers, dress manufacturers, wedding dress boutiques, textured fabric studios, and resale clothes stores.

You will notice that prospective buyers for this kind of company are all firms that sell retail or rent apparel of some sort. As such, put on a nice pair of shoes and go contact these firms in person to offer your tailoring services. You can also offer free collection and delivery, short processing times, outstanding service, and high quality at a reasonable price, which could help you compete with other tailors.

1. Do I need a Cricut machine?

For many crafters out there, a Cricut machine is a dream come true because it can be used to design and create several items, including cards and home décor material. If you are enjoying crafts and often find yourself making several crafts by hand, then you will surely benefit from getting a Cricut machine. However, if you're not into arts and crafts, you will likely not end up using a Cricut machine even if you bought one.

2. Are there other computers that are capable of doing the same thing?

Yes, you will find that several other types of machines can do what the Cricut machine does to some degree. There are also two other big brands on the market that cut a wide range of materials.

3. Can you profit from getting a Cricut machine and earn back the money you would have spent elsewhere on items that you could've designed using the machine?

Yes, purchasing a Cricut machine can be well worth the effort as you can use it for different purposes.

4. What's the best Cricut machine that I could get?

The best Cricut machine that you can get for its price is the Cricut Explore Air 2, hands down.

5. What is the best Cricut machine for me?

You should purchase a Cricut machine based on three factors. First, it depends on what you can afford, the model that can cut the materials that you want to use, and the one that will leave you with enough money to buy any additional materials you need.

6. May I get my Cricut model upgraded later?

If you already have a Cricut machine, then let us tell you that you ROCK! Are you considering making an upgrade, or would you prefer to purchase the latest version? Or is it the case that you want to update your model because you have a new computer? If your answer to the second question is yes and you have the budget for it, then you can purchase the Cricut Builder model.

7. What materials am I going to cut with a Cricut machine?

There are literally thousands of materials that you can cut with this incredible machine, some of which are:
1. Any kind of cardstock
2. Metallic paper
3. Vinyl (including iron-on, glitter, permanent, removable types)
4. Tissue and textiles

5. Faux leather
6. Corrugated papers
7. Thin forests (only with Cricut Maker)
8. Paper sticker
9. Parchment paper

8. Are Cricut's goods expensive?

Cricut products can be fairly costly, depending on the designs you choose to cut. This is why devices that also will give customers items that they can already cut should be purchased.

If you don't have enough extra money to invest in for you to cut some other resources, it can be useless to obtain the Cricut Builder. Little costs can add up, and materials such as basswood can also be very costly.

9. May I use off-brand materials for my Cricut?

Yes, you don't need to be confined to the materials made by Cricut. There are hundreds, if not thousands, of awesome items that you can get online or at your local craft shop.

10. What's the mystery box offered by Cricut, and how does it work?

A mystery box is released every month by Cricut. This box is packed with cool materials that are not known to buyers until they get the package. The wonderful thing about this box is that you're going to get more than you paid for. What we mean by this is that the price would have been so much higher if you were going to buy all the goods that come in the box individually. They get sold out quickly though, so make sure to get yours at the beginning of each month if this intrigues you.

11. What is the framework for the Cricut adaptive instrument?

An extraordinary and efficient feature that only the Cricut Creator has is the Cricut Adaptive Device, which controls the path and blade. This tool is particularly useful as it can change the blade pressure to match the products that you work with. This technology enables the Cricut Creator to cut ten times faster than any other device in the Cricut Explore Family.

12. Does Cricut print it out?

There is no Cricut computer printing. However, all the current machines they sell except the Cuttlebug have the option of drawing and outlining items such as letters and shapes.

13. Do you need ink for a Cricut?

To use your Cricut, you don't need ink if it's not writing. If you're going to use the illustration option, however, in order for it to be able to draw, you need pens. There is a wide selection of choices for you to choose from.

14. Does the Cricut emboss material?

The Cricut Cuttlebug is the only Cricut Machine that was and is capable of embossing. However, some of the other machines use workarounds, produce stencils, and emboss almost everything that your heart desires.

15. Does the Cricut sew material?

No, the Cricut doesn't sew materials, although it's understandable why you might have assumed that it was able to do that.

16. Does Cricut cut cloth for you?

Yes, Cricut machines can cut cloth. The Cricut is your best and most trusted cutting assistant if you work with garments and need to cut large quantities of cloth into various shapes and sizes. The Cricut machine helps you cut fabric without any secured product. Hence, if your profession involves sewing or weaving, then you can greatly benefit from getting a Cricut machine. With a few Cricut Explore Family devices, you can cut cloth. However, it is important to tie the cloth together.

17. What is backing material, and how does it apply to fabric cutting?

The Cricut Explore Family and Cricut Builder machines are capable of cutting cloth. However, there is a major caveat, which is that you need backup content to be able to cut cloth with the Explore Family devices.

In the world of Cricut and die-cutting machines, backup, which is also referred to as "heat and bond," is a type of material that helps you secure fabrics onto a cutting pad. In other words, when you use Cricut Explore Devices, if you do not apply this material to your fabrics, the fabrics may not be cut correctly and could instead be destroyed and spread out.

18. Does Cricut cut wood?

Yes and no. Of all the cutting machines that were designed by the Cricut firm, Cricut Builder is the only one that can cut timber, balsa, and basswood. You will need to bear in mind that the Cricut Maker itself does NOT cut wood with the usual blade that comes with it. You would need the knife blade for these types of ventures, which is a type of blade that is specially designed to cut through thick materials.

19. What are some of the projects I can make with a Cricut machine?

There are several projects that you can make with a Cricut machine! This is just a short list of some of the stuff that you can create.

Home decoration:
This includes window decals, walls, personalization of items like baskets, cooking spice containers, etc.

Stickers:
These can be used for journaling, organizing, and other purposes.

Greeting cards:
You can design high-end greeting cards like those sold in the supermarket!

Clothing items:

It is possible to cut and iron material onto your T-Shirts in stunning and customized styles.

3D projects:

This pertains to gift boxes and even paper toys!

You can cut wood with the Cricut Creator and build 3D and durable designs. You can also use this for your clothes in order to cut fabric and make fashion pieces. The sky is the limit!

20. What is Cricut Infusible Ink?

Cricut Infusible Ink is a form of technology that enables you to build and apply a base material to your designs. What makes this technology so special is that the Infusible Ink transfer allows you to fuse together your base material with the project you are making.

21. What are Cricut mats, and which one do I need?

The surface you use in general upon which you will cut particular materials is called a Cricut pad or mat. They are available in 2 different sizes: 12 x 12 inches and 12 x 24 inches. Cricut mats are sticky, and you're better off using ones with varying degrees of stickiness based on the substance you're going to cut. There are also a few so-called handles too.

There are four styles of Cricut Explore and Builder mats:

1. Light grip(blue)
2. Strong grip (purple)
3. Normal grip (green)
4. Cloth grip (pink)

There are three distinct mats used by Cricut Joy:

1. Light grip (blue)
2. Normal grip (green)
3. Card mat (blue), which is designed for cut-out cards

When you're just starting out, the best mat to have is the regular grip kind. The harder the grip, the more durable substances you can use. For example, if you are cutting regular thin paper, you can use a light grip mat. However, with a hard grip mat, it is better to cut heavy material, such as thick cardstock. A basic grip mat comes with just about any unit. Before you purchase your device, make sure you read the label to see what is included in the box.

22. What are Cricut blades, and which one would I need?

A knife cuts the materials. However, before you start and if you intend to cut tougher materials, there is something really important for you to remember. There are seven types of blades and several other crafting tools that can be used by larger machines (Explore and Maker).
• Fine-point blade:

This is suitable for materials such as paper, vinyl, and cardstock, which are light and medium. It comes in gold.

• **Deep-point blade:**

This is useful for dense materials such as plasterboard, thick cardboard, foam mats, etc.

• **Bonded-cloth blade:**

This can be used on a wide range of fabrics! It is important to bind the fabric together.

• **Rotary blade (Cricut Creator only):**

It cuts almost any form of cloth, and the fabric can be laid directly on the mat.

• **Knife blade:**

(Cricut Creator only) It can be applied to very dense materials, such as basswood, which can be sliced by this amazing little blade.

• **Fast-switch perforation blade:**

This unique blade will allow you to build tear-finished projects, with a new universe of possibilities opening up with this method. It is only offered by the manufacturer of Cricut.

• **Quick swap wavy blade:**

This blade can cut material in waves instead of cutting clean lines like the rotary or fine-point blade.

• **Quick swap debussing guide:**

This tip forces the material in and can create beautiful and comprehensive designs. Through the specifics you will apply to your creations, the debossing may elevate your projects to a whole new level. It is only offered by the Cricut firm.

• **Engraving tip for fast Swap:**

The engraving tip is exactly what many artisans have been waiting for! You'll be able to embroider a wide range of materials with this kit as it is only offered by the manufacturer of Cricut.

• **Tips for fast swap scoring wheel:**

Counting tire is a tool that helps your materials be folded in elegant, edgy, or fluffy designs. It only works with Cricut models.

• **Foil Switch Kit:**

The foil transfer kit helps produce stunning and crisp foil results and designs. It works with the Cricut Builder and some of the other models in the Explore line. This kit can be considered to be three devices in one as Cricut has fine, average, and bold tips to better suit different projects.
• The Cricut Joy model uses a fine-point blade, so it works only for that unique unit.

23. Which blades does each Cricut machine come with?

They normally come with a blade when you only buy a computer (no bundle).

• **Cricut Explore Air 2:**

a fine-point blade

• **Cricut Maker:**

Rotary blade and fine-point blade

• Cricut Joy:

a fine-point blade

24. How long will do a Cricut blade last?

This depends on the material you cut, and the number of times you use them as there is no designated expiry date. Once you notice that the fabrics are not being cut as well as they used to be, it's time to substitute them.

25. What is the Cricut Simple Press?

A Cricut Simple Press is a cool gadget that enables you to move T-shirts, sweaters, quilts, and more on to your Iron-On vinyl. It comes in three different sizes, and the one that suits your needs can be purchased.

These are the sizes:

- 9 inches: This scale is ideal for converting patterns to T-shirts for adults.
- 6 to 7 inches: This is suitable for ironing small clothing pieces, such as onesies and other items for infants.
- 10 to 12 inches: This is ideal for ironing material on wide surfaces, such as quilts and blankets.

Transfer tape: this can be used to press HTV onto small items, such as bags and caps. You can read a review of the Easy Press Mini to learn more about it.

26. Is the Cricut Quick Press worth it?

You may be wondering if you need to be tech-savvy in order to use Cricut machines. In general, you don't need to be. However, you need to know the basics of how computers operate, and you should also have some rudimentary knowledge of how machines work, such as if you have a mobile and you want the computer to work with an app. If you are a bit worried about whether you can pick this up, you really shouldn't be. It only takes a little bit of practice to adjust to using the Cricut machine and the accompanying apps or tools.

27. What systems do I need to operate my Cricut machine?

You must use a computer to operate Cricut in most cases. In addition, only Mac and Windows operating systems are compatible with Cricut. In other words, when you're using Cricut Machines, you will need to have Windows installed.

28. May I attach my Cricut to my phone or device through Bluetooth?

It depends on the computer you have. If you want to use your laptop or tablet, the Explore Air 2, Creator, and Joy include built-in Bluetooth technology.

29. Do I need the internet to use Cricut?

No, you do not require an internet connection to work on your projects. However, to get your computer up and running, you need to be connected to the internet so that you can also access the Cricut Design Space.

30. Is there any alternate program through which I can use Cricut?

There used to be a way to do this with third-party software, but it is not compatible with newer computers.

31. How does Cricut work?

Cricut machines use a variety of instruments and equipment, including mats, knives, and fabrics. However, how does this operate in relation to a Cricut machine itself? You must use it together with the Cricut Design Room for the Cricut Machine to carve as you must first determine the design you want before allowing the device to cut the desired pattern.

32. Is Cricut Architecture free?

Yes, it's free if you have a phone. Your templates can be submitted to be cut out. To make basic cuts for free, you can also use your system's fonts and some other shapes. However, what is restricted is Access Cricut.

33. What is Access by Cricut?

Cricut Connectivity is a massive repository that enables you to pick and build pre-prepared designs. If you are just beginning to use Cricut, this can be very helpful. If you have Scrapbook Access, then you can pick specific fonts, textures, 3D designs and attempt to implement them. They have created projects for nearly every purpose and with so many different types of resources, which is pretty impressive.

34. What's Friday's Free Cut Cricut?

Cricut publishes several cut files for FREE on Friday. Each week, you can access only certain files, which is pretty awesome because it allows you to continue using your computer to test out new apps. You can look for it in the Code Composer Room.

2.

CRICUT MAKER MASTERY

The Unofficial Step-By-Step Guide to Cricut Maker Machine, Accessories and Tools + Design Space + Tips and Tricks + DIY Projects for Beginners and Advanced Users. 2021 Edition

Philippa Smalley

CRICUT MAKER MASTERY

Designed to meet all your crafting needs, Cricut Maker is one of the most useful Cricut models that has been released by Cricut, Inc. This machine can cut hundreds of items, ranging from thin materials, such as cloth and paper, to thicker types, including mats, boards, and leather. It can also cut iron as well as your favorite kinds of plastic!

Cricut Maker uses excellent equipment and hardware and many of Cricut, Inc.'s most common blades, markers, and instruments. For example, this includes a rotary cutter, knife blade, scoring wheel, and washable cloth pen, some of the company's latest additions!

You can also connect to an online library with hundreds of design templates from labels such as Simplicity® and Riley Blake®. As such, once you choose a project and gather all the needed components, you can proceed to cut material using your device. Just sit back and relax while allowing your machine to do all the work, which also helps you save your energy for the more enjoyable task of piecing your object together!

Not only can the Cricut Maker cut all the parts by itself, but you can also choose to label your template components and other fabrics with your washable cloth marker so that you can keep track of how to use your fabrics during a project. This is an amazing feature, although it is optional and entirely up to the user!

This device can be used everywhere, including colleges, workplaces, and design stores. You can also use your machine for class assignments, paper stock ventures, and iron-on projects. You may also opt to cut and re-design your curtains.

The Cricut blade, which comes separately, acts effectively as an X-ACTO blade to hack into thicker materials, such as 2.5-millimeter-thick balsa wood and matt surfaces. You definitely won't be able to wait to get your hands on this! Some of the beautiful items that the blade can produce, like these kinds of prototypes, can be bought at certain stores.

Yes, the machine can cut hundreds of diverse materials. Every day, users can cut different types of materials, which is a truly exciting endeavor.

The Cricut Maker provides users with the ability to use the Cricut Design Space, where you can build or upload and design your templates. As such, there are unlimited opportunities to create new objects and designs!

It also includes a wireless charging port and a smartphone or desktop charger, meaning that users don't have to worry about charging their devices when completing late-night tasks! Users can also operate the Cricut Design Space directly from their phone, which is pretty great and simple to use!

If you have not noticed the latest buzz surrounding Cricut Maker, get ready to have your mind blown! What is particularly awesome about this device is that Cricut, Inc. frequently releases new tools for users to enjoy, which means that you can look forward to occasionally purchasing new tools. This can also enable you to cut your material in different ways.

The rotary blade, which was crafted especially for the Cricut Maker device, is a real game-changer! The blade slices through nearly every cloth material quite quickly and reliably with its gliding, rotating movements.

The Cricut machine is flexible and can be used to attach various materials to make creative objects. This book is for beginners as well as more advanced Cricut users and includes some practical projects that can be made. In fact, through this book, users can learn everything that they need to know about what Cricut machines are and how you can make the most out of them. If you read this manual and begin practicing, you will surely become an expert in no time!

Although people really like working with felt, they often don't choose the best machine or tools that are needed to cut this particular material. The Cricut Explore model cuts through the material much more efficiently, leaving behind smooth edges, which is generally desirable. When working with the Cricut Maker and rotary knife, one of the first cloth materials you can experiment with is thick wool felt.

A Cricut can perform the following functions:

Cutting
It is used to cut materials with great precision, especially those with intricate designs, including raindrops, elegant jewelry patterns, and silk webs. The current Cricut Maker can even cut through natural fibers as well as less conventional materials.

Scoring
The Cricut Explore device can easily make ideal folding cards or outlines, frames, boxes, candy canes, 3D scoring stylus.

Writing
You can use a Cricut device to make "handwritten" creations with your Cricut pens. You can choose one of the hundreds of fonts that exist and wait for your Cricut machine to do the work for you – it's really quite simple!

You can also make use of this gadget to create stylish accessories and jewelry. The Cricut Maker helps anyone make use of fake leather to design extraordinary items. In addition, very young children and their teachers can also utilize this device to print pictures or photos from a computer, such as printable posters, stamps, gift cards, coloring books, and so on!

The contents of this book are truly inspirational! If you have ever wanted to make beautiful crafts but have lacked the means to do so, this is your opportunity to purchase a Cricut and begin putting your creativity to the test. Read on to learn more about Cricut, the wonderful designs you can make, and how such machines can be used!

If you are not familiar with Cricut devices and how they work, keep reading this book to learn more. Cricut devices are particularly great tools capable of slicing, cutting, debossing, engraving, writing, etc.

As kids, many of us used to create things out of anything that could be found around the house (i.e., boxes, cardboard scraps, construction paper, glue, markers/pens, and pipe cleaners). In the present, the designing world has evolved, and there are many choices out there that can enable you to put a creative twist to just about everything!

1. What You Need to Know about Cricut Machines?

A Cricut is a cutting device that can cut various materials such as fabric, vinyl, and cardboard. It is also possible to cut thinner timber, leather, textiles, and other material with Cricut Maker. In general, Cricut Maker is a computer-controlled cutting machine that cuts designs or patterns that users can sketch through Cricut Design Space (which is very similar to Adobe Illustrator). Ranging from paper and clothing to wooden materials, there are many types of resources that can be used in your projects. There are also many Cricut cutting devices currently being sold, including Cricut Explore 2 and Cricut Maker.

2. How Do Cricut Devices Work?

You can wirelessly link a Cricut to any smart device, create or download patterns to your computer, and then upload them to be cut by the Cricut. Cricut has an application named Design Space (which is compatible with Windows, MAC, and mobile phones) that can be used to create and upload templates. A small blade (and rotating cutter, pen, or scoring instrument) is installed within the Cricut. You can then attach your preferred instrument to a broad 12-inch cutting mat. Once you have a template that you are prepared to cut in Design Space, transfer the design to the Cricut wirelessly from your phone and, afterward, load the material into your Cricut. It will begin cutting the project with the click of a button.

3. Why Would You Need to Buy a Cricut?

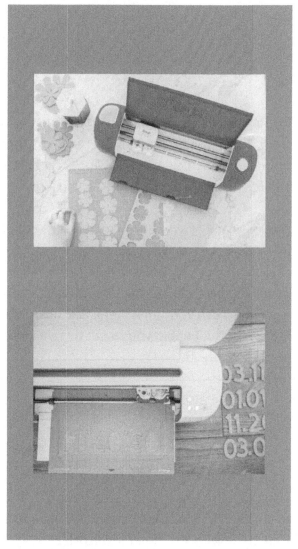

When the first Cricut model was released into the market, many people were unsure of what it had to offer, especially since other tools can be used to cut out shapes and designs, such as scissors. However, upon testing it out, many artists became avid users due to its usefulness. This device is extremely efficient as it cuts material very precisely, leading to final products that would amaze everyone. No matter how complex the layout is, the cuts appear to be smooth.

Students created "test projects" included in the package when they first received their Cricut. The prototype project familiarizes users with the device and what it can do, with the first task being the creation of a greeting card using materials that are already included with the Cricut Maker, including three supplies and a black pen. It is an easy project that gives individuals an understanding of what can be achieved. Those who tested out the machine discovered that this task could be just one of multiple projects that could be created in the future, including seasonal greeting cards, gifts, and other items.

Another explanation for why scissors are limited in their function is that when users are working with vinyl and glue, there are only a certain number of activities they can do. Scissors are not as adaptable as razors, which can cut material quickly because Cricut mats can keep them in place. Both Cricut devices are efficient and can be kept in a spot where any intricate cutting can be carried out.

For example, you can cut out and store sticky cursive initials in a jar. This would have ended up being a total nightmare if it had been attempted with scissors. Those who were able to cut the symbols and move them to the container quickly with transfer tape after having utilized the Cricut cutting device will not have experienced any difficulties. In general, however, you should concentrate on the layout of a project when operating this device and should refrain from thinking about how everyone else might cut such objects. The cutting stage, in truth, is the most uncomplicated phase!

4. What is Cricut Design Space?

Cricut has a program that can be used to create designs, namely Cricut Design Space, which can be connected to via one's personal computer (with the support of both Mac and Windows) or mobile (both Apple iOS and Android phones are supported). Other tools like Adobe Illustrator can also be used, and the files can be submitted to Cricut Design Space for cutting. This particular program is quite simple to use. Even if it takes you longer to adjust to using Cricut Design Space, you will eventually get the hang of it. There are several reputable training resources and teaching materials that are available that can enable you to learn the basics. Cricut also provides users with an impressive information base where answers to all kinds of concerns can be found.

5. Is it Possible for Cricut Maker to Cut Textiles, Leather, and Wood?

Yes, Cricut Maker can cut material such as cloth, leather, wood, paper, vinyl, and cardboard! Read on to learn which devices can cut materials that are stronger or more delicate.

6. Which Cricut Should You Purchase?

Three models of Cricut are presently available in the industry: Cricut Joy, Cricut Explore Air 2, and Cricut Maker (which just came out recently). Deciding which device to purchase depends on what sort of task users want to perform. All devices come with a number of free Design Space tools.

7. Cricut Explore Air 2

This is the device that most users consider buying. It's the most common Cricut model and can cut most materials anyone needs for a broad range of creative projects, such as vinyl, paper, cardboard, and wood. With this device, one can cut about a hundred materials.

8. Cricut Maker

In addition to cutting thick or thin items like leather, thinner woods, and garments, this device does everything that Cricut Explore Air 2 can do. In fact, Cricut Maker can cut around 300 materials, with users able to utilize around twelve types of tools for cutting, typing, and scoring. This is the perfect machine if you want to be able to make more complex projects and work with a wider range of materials.

9. Cricut Joy

The newer Cricut device, Cricut Joy, is more easily transportable than the other two models discussed. It can cut material up to 5.5 inches long, meaning that users can buy material that is up to 20 feet long. It can slice through more than 50 materials and can make use of two cutting and typing tools. If anyone wants to pay less and make easy projects with vinyl tags, cards, and tiny iron-on patterns, this is the ideal gadget.

10. Where Can You Buy a Cricut Machine?

Users can purchase Cricut from the main Cricut website, Amazon, or from big craft stores, such as Michaels and JOANN. It's also possible to order additional accessories or gadgets online for your Cricut if you are looking for more specific material.

11. Are Cricut Machines Challenging to Operate?

An extensive online tutorial comes with all Cricut devices; you can use it to learn about how to operate these machines. In addition, there are several other online Cricut tools that can explain to you all the basics, which will enable you to adjust to such tools rather quickly. Both Cricut Design and Cricut machines are user-friendly, meaning that users do not require a lot of knowledge of graphic design to make use of them. However, if you are someone who is familiar with graphic design programs, this can help you design more complex programs soon after purchasing such a machine. You can also make your own designs as well. Otherwise, you may make use of the library of photos and templates that already exist, which you can further alter when making your own new project. If you want to access some exclusive designs, you can also purchase a few with a discount.

12. Are Cricut Devices Worth Purchasing?

If you love crafting, a Cricut device is a useful investment, especially if you want to make items out of paper and vinyl. It will make your cutting projects have smoother edges while also making designs appear to have been professionally made. With your Cricut, you can also have the opportunity to earn money by designing and selling personalized T-shirts, lovely mugs, and decals online. You can even accept orders from people and make other unique items that can be sold at local art fairs. There are so many things that you can make with your Cricut machine, which would enable you to earn back the money you spent on it easily. As such, the device is utterly worth it if you plan to use it every now and then or even more regularly for your projects.

13. What Resources Do You Need for Projects?

Thus far, you have read a lot about the different materials that can be cut by Cricut machines, as well as some of the advantages that come along with having one. However, it may still be unclear to you exactly what tools and resources you will need to operate your device, including additional accessories that can help you attain the desired shape or object that you want. The following list includes some necessary tools that every Cricut owner should possess.

Necessary tools

Cricut Simple Tool Kit: This kit includes a few necessities, including tweezers, a weeder, and a scraper. XL Scraper: Although the Simple Tool Kit has a tiny scraper that is perfect for minor tasks, it can be more useful to purchase an XL scraper to strip material from the mats.

Device Mat Variation Pack: These four packs of mats have varying levels of traction that users require while cutting to hold certain materials. The pads are sticky, which enables certain substances to be "gripped" by the mat. They hold the substance when the template is being cut or drawn by the Cricut device. At least one mat will be included with your Cricut device (based on the model that users get). As such, be sure to buy a few others that are compatible with other varieties of materials. If you have some money to spare, you can also buy one or two spare mats in different colors, which can be used when your original mats lose their stickiness.

Other tools

The Cricut EasyPress

The Cricut Easy Press is an excellent tool to have if you want to carry out projects utilizing iron-on items or infusible dye. You can change the temperature based on the particular project form that you are working on and the time that is needed to transfer one item to a project. Although you can also achieve this by using a household iron, it is more difficult to control the temperature and is consequently less flexible. Therefore, this is a useful tool to purchase if you plan to work with iron-on items and are, for example, interested in making customized shirts.

Cricut EasyPress mats

These are crucial to have since they come in different sizes. When users intend to transfer heated material to other projects, the mats provide a level of insulation that prevents other surfaces from being damaged. These mats can also prevent the material that is being ironed-on from being damaged or wrinkled due to the mats' special design.

Cricut pens

As indicated earlier, Cricut devices can also be used to sketch and draw designs. In fact, users can create fashionable envelopes or bedazzled invitations with the multiple types of Cricut pens that exist. You can use your chosen fonts, create an outline, and let the Cricut device draw the shape for you. The different

Cricut pens often appear in several shades and distinct ink forms. To sketch or write material, users can choose from a number of Cricut markers.

Cricut blades (exclusively for the Cricut Maker model)

Strong knife blade

Although this item is good to have, depending on what you choose to cut, it will become a necessity if you intend to cut heavier or denser materials, including timber or chipboard. You don't have to already know how to use the blade when you have purchased your Cricut Maker, as it will take you a bit of time to adjust anyway.

Debossing tip

This is one of four blades released by Cricut in August 2019. This blade makes it easy for anyone to deboss designs. Debossing is a way to puncture or create an indentation in paper or other material. It is possible to deboss items in order to create things like monograms, which will help them appear somewhat multi-dimensional. While it may be more challenging to use this tool, it yields nice results.

Wavy blade

The wavy blade, the second of the four blades launched by Cricut in August 2019, helps one to cut patterns with a wavy tip. It is great to use when making invitations, decorative items for birthdays, or other enjoyable crafts!

Engraving tip

The engraving tip, the third of the four blades, enables one to engrave designs on items such as metals, leather, or acrylic! This particular tool helps inscribe more detailed and lasting designs on a range of products. Users can design embossed jewelry or name tags in this way.
Perforation blade
The perforation blade, the fourth of the four blades, is perfect for projects that encourage one to strip away a segment of a paper. You can also find that depending on the package that you have purchased; you may also be given instructions on how to complete a prototype project, which is really exciting!

Scoring wheel

The Cricut Maker's scoring wheel serves as an alternative to the scoring stylus. If users make anything, such as a card or gift, this wheel will create creases to enable you to make a simplified fold. It creates indentations in the material you are handling in order to show users where folds can be made without actually cutting through it completely.

Double scoring wheel tip

The double scoring wheel tip helps users by making two parallel creases that can enable them to make flawless folds when working with specific types of thick material.

14. What Materials Can a Cricut Cut?

There are many types of material that can be cut by your Cricut device as the range of choices is rather long (and even more extensive if you have a Cricut Maker). Some of the most common materials that you can initially purchase are listed below.

Cardstock

This is the most common material that can be cut by Cricut devices. There are many different types of cardstock that are sold by Cricut, Inc.; however, users can also purchase cardstock from the nearest craft shop. If they are searching for a particular weight or size, there are many excellent online websites that you can find cardstock on, including LCI Paper, the Paper Mill Shop, and Scrapbook.com.

Vinyl

Vinyl is excellent to deal with, and it can be applied to many different surfaces, including water bottles, mugs, tags, decorations, notepads, and fancy journals. There are several different styles, shades, and vinyl finishes that can be selected, so make sure to check out the options that are available and buy something you find appealing.

Transfer tape

If you want to make vinyl designs, you will need some transfer tape because it makes it so much simpler to transfer vinyl to your finished product! You can also add transparent transfer tape to a weeded template or lettering when it's on the mat. When the tape has been applied, smooth it out and carefully raise it. Next, press the tape to the main surface. Carefully cut the tape while ensuring that the vinyl is stuck to the surface. You can also view a tutorial on how to use transfer tape alongside vinyl when preparing certain projects.

Iron-on vinyl

If you want to make personalized T-shirts or other things like tote bags, then you'll adore Cricut iron-on vinyl products. There are many iron-on fabrics that you can choose from, including mesh, foil, mosaic, shimmer, holographic, patterned, and SportFlex materials. The kind you use depends on the design you want to have. You can look into the different effects that these designs will have before selecting which one would be best suited for the project you have in mind.

Infusible ink

Infusible Ink is the latest addition to the Cricut content line-up. It allows you to add ink to and permanently dye your T-shirts, backpacks, coasters, or other projects. Although there are different ways of adding certain materials or tools to products, such as by using iron-on, infusible ink is rather unique because it is washer-proof and does not cause your material to peel or crack.

15. Other Materials

Chipboard

Chipboard is a great material to use when making items such as posters or DIY notebooks because of its durability. You can utilize the knife blade on the Cricut Maker to cut this material rather quickly. While Cricut, Inc. sells specific types of chipboard, you can also find other varieties that are sold online, such as through Amazon, for a range of high and low prices.

Thin types of wood

Thin types of wood are suitable when making three-dimensional decorations or more concrete items, such as airplanes. In Design Space, you can carve or create complicated designs with the knife blade, thereby enabling you to cut and design your wooden material effectively!

Leather

You can use the Cricut Maker to create a leather journal or notebook covers. To make your own unique creations, you can emboss patterns onto leather. There are a lot of different leather options to select from, so make sure to check out the different varieties that exist and the products you can make with this material.

Stencils

You can utilize Cricut Maker to create your own stencils, which you can later use for other crafts. In fact, you can cut your own words or create models to make personalized labels for spray paint designs. Of all the Cricut models that exist, only Cricut Maker provides you with this particular option.

16 Is a Cricut Maker a Worthwhile Investment?

In the field of crafts, having a Cricut machine is incredibly beneficial. It is especially helpful to get one if you want to build stuff and engage in new and exciting projects. Although Cricut Maker can be considered to be a bit expensive, it is ultimately worth it if you intend to make good use of it and try out different arts and crafts.

You should read the newcomers tutorial for Cricut in order to learn more about how to operate the machine. Cricut Maker specifically offers a more comprehensive list of functions that can be carried out. As such, make sure to begin educating yourself about this process by reading books and guides, such as this one, which will enable you to get to know the ins and outs of your machine in no time.

When it comes to the individual components that can be used with Cricut devices, there's a wide variety of options to pick from. In fact, you might feel overwhelmed with the choices that you have, especially if you come across an entire aisle that is filled with all kinds of Cricut products and gadgets. While you will eventually learn which products will be better suited for certain projects, you can begin by making sure you have a certain number of simple tools. This will enable you to begin some projects and start getting acquainted with your Cricut machine.

1. Collecting Simple Tools

It is important to collect a number of tools to begin operating your Cricut Maker. For example, you will surely need a scraper kit and weeding equipment, so make sure to get those.

2. Mats

StandardGrip mats

These kinds of mats are really great tools to have in your arsenal. When you begin using them, make sure to take advantage of the plastic lining that comes along with the mats.

LightGrip mats

These types of mats are great for cutting lightweight material, including light cardstock, printer paper, vellum, and more!

When they're not in use, make sure to add the plastic cover on top of the mat to ensure that the mat remains sticky and does not accumulate dust or other unwanted material.

3. Vinyl

Iron-on vinyl

There are many types of iron-on vinyl that you can pick from! In fact, you can use vinyl to further beautify tops, caps, bags, pillows, and sheets. People often use other types, including Cricut Everyday Iron-On Nylon, Cricut Iron-On Lite, Cricut Iron-On Foil, and SportFlex Iron-On. It is also important to note that iron-on vinyl is also known as heat transfer vinyl (HTV) online as well as by Cricut, Inc., which can help you recognize it when you see either term.

With a standard iron fabric, you can utilize iron-on vinyl while further placing a dishtowel between the fabric and iron. If you intend to use a lot of iron-on material in your projects, it can certainly be helpful to purchase a Cricut EasyPress. However, this ultimately depends on whether you can afford to get it and if you will indeed use it often enough for it to be worth the purchase.

Standard vinyl

There are two main types of vinyl varieties: permanent and reusable. Of course, there are other types, but they are not as common or easy to locate. If you want to make things like automobile window stickers or if you intend to design teapots, mugs, dishes, and mailboxes, it would be better to choose permanent vinyl because this type of vinyl is more durable! You can also get yourself the Permanent Vinyl Starter Kit, which comes in many colors.

For items like mirrors and bathroom decals, it would be preferable to use removable vinyl. In such cases, you can also purchase for yourself a Reusable Vinyl Starter Kit in different colors. It's ultimately up to you! If you buy either type of vinyl, keep in mind that you cannot forget to get transfer tape. Many users often forget to get this and then later must go out of their way to buy the transfer tape, which can be a real hassle. So, make sure to purchase it early on to avoid wasting time.

Although you can choose to purchase the types sold by Cricut, Inc., this is not a necessity as there are hundreds of vinyl types and brands that are sold in the marketplace. Many people have bought types that weren't sold by Cricut, Inc. and were still perfectly satisfied with the quality of the vinyl they selected. In fact, it was also cheaper, which made it a much better deal, so take that into consideration when you are buying some vinyl.

4. Cardstock

Many people have cardstock lying around, and they normally shop using coupons or other discounts on Amazon or Daniels. It's good to have on hand as you will never know when an urgent situation may emerge where you may need to prepare something for an event or a loved one over a short period of time. As such, you will find that having some cardstock lying around is a real-life saver, so just make sure to buy some while you're outside and keep it stored in your closet for any emergencies.

5. Cricut Terminology

There are so many terms used in the world of Cricut. Some of the most common are:

Heat transfer vinyl (HTV):

iron-on vinyl

Removable vinyl:

This is a type of vinyl that is used indoors, especially in relation to stencils, temporary wall designs, and window clings.

Permanent vinyl:

This is a vinyl that is used for the outdoors and is consequently weatherproof.

Weeding:

This involves removing unwanted vinyl from any cut-out structure.

Mirror:

This is what users must do to guarantee that all iron-on projects come out properly! Not all projects need to be mirrored, as this step only applies to standard iron-on vinyl designs. At first, you may overlook this step. However, considering that vinyl is particularly pricey, you will want to be extra careful when working with this material to avoid messing up and throwing away this precious material.

Weld:

This involves combining certain materials together,

such as cursive letters in the event that you want them to be a single word. Move the letters next to each other and then press the "weld" option so that they can turn into a single piece. However, note that this process is irreversible, so make sure that this is a step you want to take.

Attach:

This involves grouping specific pictures, fonts, or other items together when they are on the mat and are being cut. Please note that this process is actually reversible.

Group:

This option also puts a few items together, for example, in order to keep track of them.

6. How to Start a Project with Design Space

In order to make projects for yourself or others, you must first have access to Cricut Design Space. People who have used this program find it to be quite similar to Adobe Illustrator. It can take a bit of time to adjust and learn how to use all the different icons that are included, but you will eventually get the hang of it after reading this guide. For example, if you were to make a donut in Design Space, you would need to follow a few steps.

First, utilizing the "shapes" tab, draw a circle. Then, change its color to pink, which will also be the color of the paper you will be utilizing. Please ensure that the line style that is selected is "cut."

Then, insert a second circle and resize it so that it is about one-third the size of the original circle. Then, move this to the center and change its color to white. Select all the circles, and then press the "cut" option, which appears in the bottom right corner.

After it is cut, you can remove the second circle so that a donut shape is formed.

By inserting a square layout, you can add a few sprinkles. Then, change the dimensions (using the small lock icon toward the bottom left side of the screen) and resize it so that it becomes rectangular. Proceed to duplicate this shape and rotate it until you have what appears to be a handful of sprinkles! Then, pick it and put all these forms together so that they can be more effectively managed. It is necessary to "fasten" them to the donut before cutting by pressing the "attach" button so that they all get printed correctly!

The Cricut will then presume that it has two distinct colors to print. Continue to load the slicing mat into the system and ensure that the dial is adjusted to the right cut settings (based on the material). Users will be instructed by the device about which shade to load first. In this case, you can load the next one until the first page is trimmed and keep working until the task is finished!

Start a new project

You will have two possibilities to start designing a project in Cricut Design Space.

1. Simply click on the latest design tile from the Home page.
2. Start a new project from your Home page.

On the Home page, select the "new project" tile to begin your project.

You should now see a blank canvas, where you can begin to work on a design.

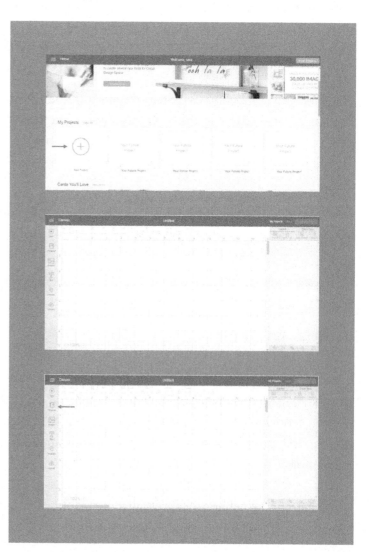

7. Saving the Project

If you begin a project and want to take a break and resume later, you will need to save it before closing to refrain from losing all your hard work. Alternatively, you can also just save it once you are done, although it's always a good idea to regularly save your project in case your device is no longer charged. Once you've saved it, you can find this project and access it again through any of your other devices where you have downloaded the Design Space app.

Phase 1

In order to do this, press the "save" button in the top right corner, which will allow you to either save immediately or choose the "save as" option.

The "save" option updates the previous project file so that all the changes that have been made so far can be accessed later.

The "save as" option allows you to save this version of your work as a separate file, meaning that you can access all the changes you have in this session in a new file. You will also be asked to provide a new title for this version.

Tip: It is useful to use the "save as" option to retain the current format of the project when making a new version.

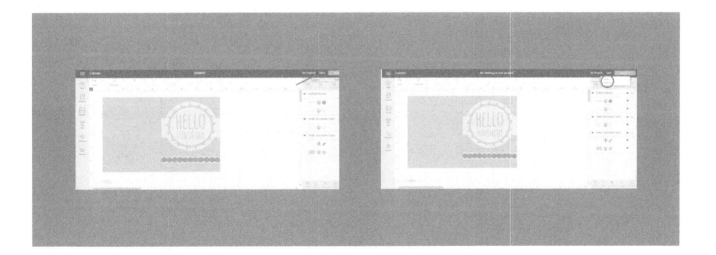

Phase 2

If you have never saved your project and you try to save it

for the first time, a small box will appear where you can "save" the design screen as is shown above. Enter the name of your project, then press "save."

Phase 3

After saving, users can go back to the design page. A notification will also inform you that the project has been successfully saved. Users can also see the title of the project on their Home screen. If you are already done designing your template, you can also proceed to start the cutting phase.

8. Viewing, Renaming, Deleting and Sharing Projects

In the Design Space, there are two different ways to access your saved designs.

1. On the Home screen
2. From the canvas

Option 1: On the home screen

Users can view all the currently saved projects in the first row of tiles shown on the Home screen. You can simply click on any of the design tiles to see the project's details. Alternatively, you can also open a single file or see all stored projects by pressing the "view all" icon.

Option 2: From the canvas

Stage 1

If you have the canvas open before you, press the "my projects" label to access all of your saved works.

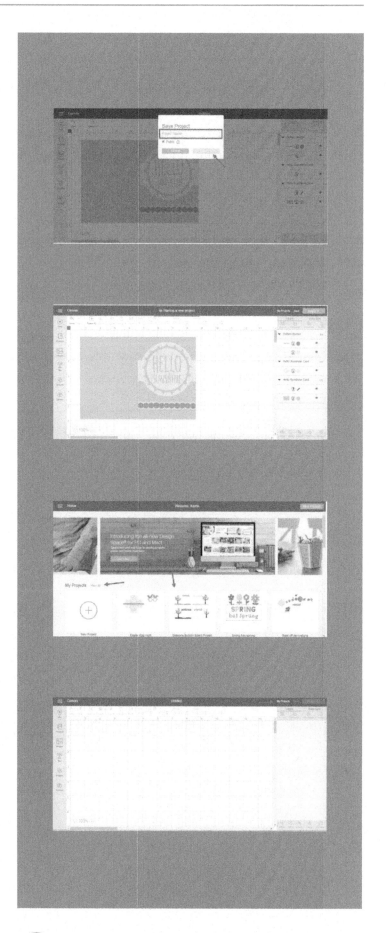

Tip: Users can also reach their projects by clicking on the "project" button in the layout panel, whereby you will have the option of selecting "my projects" from the drop-down list that appears.

Stage 2
Tap on the project tile you want to access.

Stage 3
It will open all of your projects and show you them in the form of large tiles. Here, you can access all your projects' information, while further having the option of modifying sharing requirements, renaming, deleting, or opening a project.

In relation to your formatting preferences and sharing options, we would recommend that you uncheck the "public" option to make sure your files are secure if you want to keep them private.

Tip: If you do decide that you want others to access your work, you can copy and then paste the link to your project and proceed to share it with your family and friends. However, you can only do this if you have left the "public" icon unchecked.

Renaming the project

Press "rename" to change the title of the project file.

Deleting the project

Press "delete" to remove a project from the library. You may be asked if you are sure to verify whether you indeed want to remove your file from your list of projects.

Opening the project

Press "open" to access the file in the canvas. Afterward, you can continue working on your project, or you may immediately proceed to the cutting phase.

Sharing a project

Cricut Design Space allows users to share designs with their relatives and friends.

Stage 1

To share a design, please ensure that your document has been saved first.

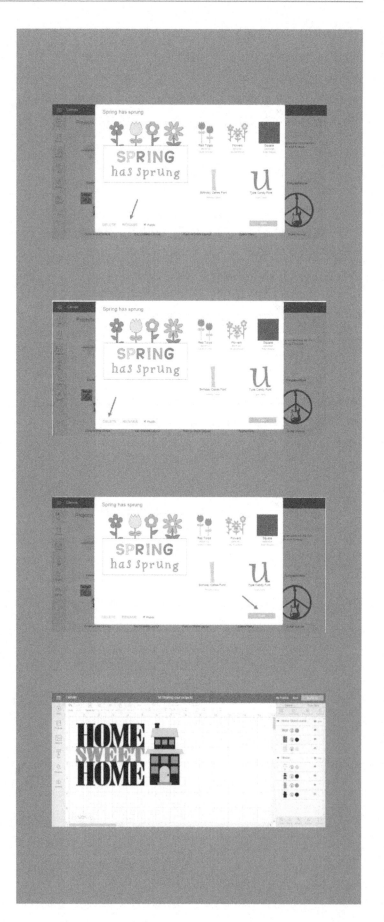

Stage 2

Once you have saved your file, check the details of the project to see whether you can share certain photographs and designs. This is important to ensure that you are not infringing upon others' intellectual property rights. This ultimately depends on whether you can tap the "public" checkmark that is shown in the picture.

Tip: If users want to limit certain programs or others from accessing their work, they should make sure to manually uncheck the "public" box.

Stage 3

Head back to the canvas. You can then click on the address bar of the project to access the project's URL. Proceed to copy the link by pressing the "Ctrl-C" keyboard shortcut key (for PC users) or "Command-C" (for those with a Mac).

Stage 4

After having copied the URL, you can paste it by pressing the "Ctrl-V" keypad shortcut (for PC users) or the "Command-V" shortcut (for those with Macs). You can also share the URL on your preferred social networking platform or via email.

9. Should I Replace My Cricut Explore?

Many users love their Cricut Explore machines. However, since the Cricut Maker has been released, they may consider replacing the former with the latter. Of course, it is important in general to weigh the pros and cons of each machine before making any major decision. In relation to the Cricut Maker, there are many pros because it can cut more materials and is also compatible with different blades and tools. The Cricut Explore Air 2 is also a great device to have, so your choice will likely depend on your budget, the extent to which you consider yourself an avid crafter, and the complexity of your projects.

If you are not looking to buy a machine for yourself but as a gift for a friend or family member, then make sure to consider the above-mentioned information. You should also think about which equipment and gadgets arrive with the unit, specifically in terms of cutting mats, accessories, and tools.

10. What Does the Cricut Maker Come With?

There are a couple of different colors in which you can purchase your Cricut Maker or Cricut device. Since this book focuses predominantly on Cricut Maker, the following information specifies the instruments that arrive in its packaging:

- Cricut Maker device
- High-quality fine-point knife and its drive housing
- Rotary blade and its drive housing
- Power cable and USB cable (to connect to a device)
- One pink 12 x 12-inch mat
- One blue 12 x 12-inch mat
- Fine-point black pen
- Instructional manual

Users will also receive:

- A few materials for a sample project.
- 50 project templates, 25 of which are sewing designs
- A one-month free trial to Cricut Access Service (for first-time subscribers)

Cricut has made it easier for beginners to try out a few projects by including a few blades and accessories with the latest models that are ordered. This is to enable everyone to get a feel for how the machine works before proceeding to buy more material.

The following section describes some other matters that Cricut users should be familiar with before operating their new machine, including in relation to Cricut Design Space.

Cricut Design Space

You may want to create a new Cricut username with your own personal email account. If you already have a username and password, please proceed to log in. Then, you will be redirected to the Home page. There, you can tap on the "new project" button, whereby you can start a new project from scratch. Later, you can come back to this page and access any files you began or completed.

If you cannot connect your laptop to the machine using Bluetooth, you can use the USB cable that came with your Cricut Maker. If you are using your iPhone or iPad, you may download the program through your app store. However, if you have an Android smartphone or tablet, you can proceed to the Google Play store. Then, proceed to install the app and login when you have completed all the necessary steps. The app itself will instruct you on how to make an account and access the main pages. In the old days, you could only link Cricut to a smartphone device through Bluetooth, so it's great that the system has become more sophisticated.

After users have downloaded the applications and signed in, they're just one step away from building their first Cricut Design! Once that is done, it is possible to proceed to cut the different projects.

11. Where Can Users Get Cut Files for Their Cricut Devices?

Design Space has a number of resources that can be used to create templates (which are named "cut files"). However, the best way to begin with your machine is to try out a template that has already been made in the Design Space. There are lots of sites from which you can access templates that have already been prepared, many of which are free and others that cost a small amount of money.

12. Accessing Cut Files through the Cricut Maker

There are two areas in Design Space through which you can access cut files: the "photos" section and the "projects" tab.

There is an "images" icon that can be selected inside the Cricut Design Area, which is located on the left side after you have pressed "new project." Tapping on this will take you to the Cricut Picture Library, where you can upload multiple templates into your project, reformat them if needed, and cut out any material. When you open the Design Space, you can immediately access all of your projects from the Home page. Within your projects, you can find some images or templates you want to insert into your project. You can paste them into the canvas and modify the design. If you are already satisfied with what it looks like and the dimensions, you can immediately press the "make it" option so that your Cricut Maker gets to work. As mentioned earlier, the picture repository and design library provide users with free files and those that need to be paid for. However, we mentioned earlier that you could use Cricut Access immediately when you sign up and get a new Cricut device. This provides users with the ability to download over 110,000 files for free, which is a really great offer. That way, for the duration of the month, you can use any templates that you find appealing. If you want to continue using Cricut Access, just purchase a subscription, and you can continue to use this repository.

13. Removing Cut Files from the Workspace

There are many Cricut users around the world that connect with one another online. In fact, many of them upload the files they have cut out using external apps and store them so that other users can access them. Several other different file forms can be imported and used in the Cricut Design Space. In general, the best form you can have is an SVG format, largely because SVG files are stored as projections rather than pixels. Etsy has a wide range of files that can be ordered from dozens, if not thousands, of creators. However, make sure that the pictures actually match your expectations by checking with the seller, as many inexperienced buyers make this mistake.

Design blogs are also another place where you can find project templates, in addition to numerous websites that focus on having a more productive lifestyle. There are some other places you can access such templates and files. For example, if you fill in a short form, you can get instant access to the "Crafter's Resource Collection" and download as many files as you like. Pinterest is another great online resource you can check out.

At some point, you can also move beyond always using other templates and files and progress to designing and printing your own with your Cricut Maker. This is a very exciting step for all avid crafters as it helps them get in touch with their artistic side and become more creative. Once you start creating your own designs, or even before this stage, you'll need to get some other materials with your Cricut Maker. Read the next section to get a clearer idea of what this entails.

14. What Materials Should You Purchase with the Cricut Maker?

Most artisans have workspaces devoted to their Cricut machines. This is probably a good idea as simply leaving your device on the kitchen table can clutter up your kitchen and annoy your loved ones to no end. In addition, when you begin purchasing other accessories, you will need a place to store them. That's why it's good to establish a separate location where you can work and also put your materials.
While you obviously can't purchase all your equipment at once, it's a good idea to generally know what is absolutely essential to have. This is because there are some accessories you can hold off on buying until later.

15. Important Cricut Accessories

Consider here the term "essentials" with a pinch of salt. Strictly speaking, there's little else users require but the products they need to carve. However, here are some items that most people realize they need pretty soon when starting to operate their Cricut Maker:

StandardGrip mat

This green 12 x 12-inch mat is one that users need to cut most of their materials, including thick cartridges and plastics. While it may seem odd that this is not included in the Cricut Maker package you purchased, this is because other mats can be more suitable to use when cutting light material. Once you have finished making a standard project with your starter kit, you can go and purchase this kind of mat for some of your other projects.

Cricut Fundamental Tool Kit

This includes a scraper, spatula, weeding gadget, scissors, and tweezers. This is a pretty essential purchase because you will often need many of these tools for more complicated designs as well as to clean your mat, which will have small scraps that can decrease its stickiness.

Other blades

One of the main distinctions between Cricut Explore Air 2 and Cricut Maker is the latest "Adaptive Tools Set" that comes with the latter. In other words, you have access to many different choices of knives, which makes it a worthwhile purchase.

Cutting materials

The authorized list of items that the Cricut Maker should be able to cut has over one thousand items on it. This list also doesn't even touch upon the products that can be utilized in relation to other resources. As such, depending on the project that you select, make sure to buy the materials you will need, such as cardstock, balsa wood, and paper.

16. Supply List Recommendations

We would highly recommend that you refrain from purchasing a number of blades and supplies that you may be unsure of whether you will need. Instead, try to find a few projects you would like to complete first, and then go ahead and buy the required materials.

When you first choose a material that you really like but don't have a specific design you want to use, at least be sure to purchase the right blade for it. In that way, once you have settled on a project, you should be able to cut the material. Otherwise, you may damage your blade and Cricut Maker.

17. Main Blades, Materials, and Accessories

Sewing

Your device comes with a rotary knife and a pink 12 x 24-inch FabricGrip mat. If you want to purchase a Cricut Maker and will be doing a great deal of quilting or sewing, you should make sure to also get the Cloth Applicator and Remover Kit.

Users can choose any fabric they want or currently have. Many of the designs that you find online may specify that you need quilting fabric; however, you can also just substitute this with almost any type of cloth. Before you try out your project, it's advisable that you practice a bit on some scrap pieces of fabric.

Paper crafting

The Cricut Maker arrives with a fine-point blade and a drive housing (casing), which users usually require with their blade. You can also get a scoring stylus and debossing tip. You can often use the StandardGrip mat or the LightGrip mat when you are making paper crafts.

In general, if you are interested in doing tons of paper art, it's just a good idea to get a few packets of various colored cardboards and a handful of printed cardboard or paper sheets. While it's good to have some additional colors, you shouldn't refrain from getting white and black sheets of paper!

Designing vinyl

Many people are inspired to purchase a Cricut machine because they are interested in creating vinyl products. If this applies to you as well, then make sure to get a small amount of vinyl-based on a particular project idea you have in mind and test it out. If it works out, then feel free to get a few vinyl rolls and store them in your cabinet at home.

18. The Cost Factor

The Cricut Maker is costly by itself. As such, if some kits or packs are out of your price range, do not feel worried about it. You can always come back later and purchase the items you need when you have a bit of pocket money to spare. However, what we would really recommend is to look for cheaper options online or perhaps in discount stores. That way, you won't need to refrain from buying the materials and tools you want.

19. Supplies Bundle

The "Basics Kit" (which is available in five color schemes) arrives with some essential tools that are needed by all users at some point, including:

- A range of cutting mats (green, purple, and blue)
- Scoring stylus
- Deep-point knife with drive housing
- Basic tools (i.e., a spatula, tweezers, scraper, and scissors)
- Black window-grip roll
- A collection of Cricut pens

Suggestions

If you already own a Cricut Explore Air 2 and want to get a Cricut Maker, you don't need to buy the Basics Kit as you'll likely already have most of the material that is included in it.

However, for first-time users, this particular tool kit can be pretty useful and will save you some time in searching for the individual objects you need. That way, you can also focus more on the materials you want to buy to cut in your spare time.

20. The "Everything Supplies Kit"

The "Everything Supplies Kit" (which comes in five color schemes) comes with everything users can use with the device on their own, including:

- Samples of apparel, felt, and leather
- Metal poster board
- Many forms of vinyl adhesive and iron-on prototypes
- Crimped cardboard
- Stencils
- Basswood
- Vinyl transfer glue or tape

Suggestions

Always get the "All Supplies Kit" if you do not have a clear idea of what sort of tasks you might want to undertake after you've checked out some interesting project ideas that were posted on Pinterest or other Cricut repositories.

Considering that much of this toolkit includes materials that can be cut, most users will still have to purchase some knives, mats, and gadgets. For example, if you want to cut your basswood, you will need a knife blade and a StandardGrip mat if you plan on cutting materials such as plastic, vinyl, and poster boards.

21. Specific Bundles:

Other major craft retailers may also offer special bundles or combinations of Cricut tools and equipment, such as Joans, which used to offer them in the past (for the Cricut Explore model). However, it's not so clear if such models also exist for the Cricut Maker as the only one that we have seen online is the Cricut Maker Stitching Essentials Kit.

22. Cricut Gadgets

We recommend that you don't go crazy when you get to the vinyl and plastics aisle at the arts and crafts store. Just make sure to get enough supplies to make a few projects. When you have a clear idea of what you're making in terms of the projects, go out and get a few new things.

If you may be wondering if you should get items like the BrightPad or EasyPress, we think it could be smarter to wait and see if you want to work with vinyl materials regularly. If this indeed applies to you, then it can worth it to buy these tools. Otherwise, it could be a good idea to wait until you find them being sold at a discounted price before purchasing them. In the meantime, it's enough to use a normal iron.

As far as blades are concerned, we would recommend that you begin using only two or three and add more as is needed. The following section discusses some Cricut blades in greater detail.

23. Are Cricut Explore Blades (and Equipment) Compatible with Cricut Maker?

Yes, all Cricut Explore blades are indeed compatible with Cricut Maker. Many of the users who have owned Cricut Explore devices realize that the blades can cut material in two different directions.

- The whole cutting mechanism is pushed down to cut the substance with the blade or marker before being released once it's done.
- The pad is then pushed forward and reverses the direction of cutting due to a group of static wheels that roll over the upper edge.
- The cover for the blade and casing rotate side-by-side due to a belt that extends across the length of the device's interior.

The three processes enable the blade, pen, or stylus being used to touch any place on the cutting pad.

The main improvement that has taken place in relation to the Cricut Maker would be that the blade now has a third dimension. Users will find that all the Cricut Maker knives and gadgets have a golden tip, whereby the Adaptive Tool Unit on the device includes a tool that allows the blade to spin as it cuts.

However, due to the device's design, blades that have no equipment at the top will still be fixed in a fixed position, which means you can still use them with your Cricut Maker. As such, no adapters are required, and users can even recycle their casing.

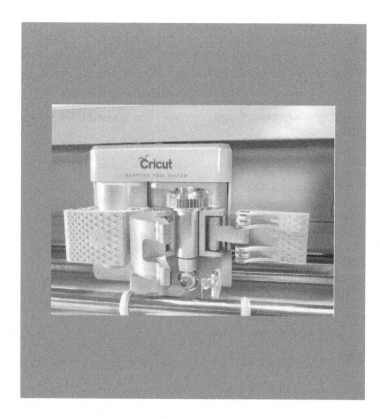

Are you trying to learn more about Cricut Design Space and don't know where to begin?

Starting your first activity or project can indeed be challenging. In fact, a lot of people don't really know what to look at or purchase because there are so many materials being sold in the aisles of craft stores. It's even daunting for a lot of experienced Cricut users!

However, in general, the best way to get accustomed to your Cricut Design Space is to start from the basics! When you finally know what each button and symbol can do, you can do a lot more with your device. Don't worry if it takes you a little time to get to that point – it's only natural!

Even if you are a bit tempted to leap from task to task, we suggest you exercise a bit of self-control and try to finish a project before beginning a new one. At the very least, don't go overboard and start multiple projects that you can't finish, as this will make it harder for you to learn what your Cricut Maker can do.

This book aims to provide you with a summary of the function of each icon and section of the Cricut Design Space canvas area.

As time progresses, you can start building more complicated projects and eventually expand your repertoire by selecting different complex icons and tools. If you're unsure about a certain tab or icon's function, then just click on the below description to read a little more about it.

The Design Space is where users need to work on and modify their designs. You can access and upload your own fonts and photos in this space but also utilize the exclusive images and fonts provided by Cricut through the image library or Cricut Access.

Tip: If you have skipped ahead to this chapter of the book without reading some of the earlier sections and you still don't really know which machine you should purchase, we strongly encourage you to turn back to the earlier chapter that discusses the different Cricut models that are out there. That section will clearly answer any questions you have and can save you some money to spend elsewhere, such as on your materials.

1. How Can Cricut Users Learn to Use Design Space?

The decision to invest in a Cricut machine is pointless if you're not willing to learn how to use Design Space to your advantage. How else are you going to make and cut out your designs?

Cricut Design Space is a fantastic platform for beginners, even if you do not have much knowledge or experience using other design programs like Adobe Illustrator. So, don't be intimidated by its sophisticated layout as it's really fairly simple to use.

On the other hand, if you have any experience with either Adobe Photoshop or InkScape, you'll find that using the Cricut Design Space is a piece of cake. Design Space is mostly used to touch up projects and produce at least a few patterned designs with scripts or fonts.

If users want any more advanced design templates, they will need to make their own prototypes or get Cricut Access, which requires you to pay for a subscription that allows you to use designs obtained from an extremely large digital library. You can learn more about that in this book.

When you log into Cricut Design Space and choose to create a new project or modify an existing one, you will need to do it from a browser called "canvas."

In the Cricut Design Space, the canvas is where you will do any necessary editing before beginning to cut your creations.

There are many other choices you can make and items you can use while operating your machine. However, don't stress about this as we're here on the sidelines, cheering you on!

In this chapter, you will soon discover what every individual icon can be used for in the canvas. To make it easier for you to understand, we're going to split the canvas into four main zones based on different colors:

- The top yellow panel – edit zone
- The left blue panel – insert region
- The right purple panel – layers section
- The green canvas region

2. The Top Panel of Cricut Design Space

The upper panel in the Design Space Canvas region is used for editing and organizing the different components of the canvas. In this segment, users can select what sort of font they want to use and can subsequently adjust its size, color, and so much more!

The panel is further split into two sections. The initial one helps users to save, tag, and eventually cut the designs. The one immediately beside it allows you to check and edit designs that are on the canvas.

Sub-panel no.1: Add a title to the project and then realize it

The whole sub-panel offers you a range of options, enabling you to double check your projects, save any changes you have made, and even realize your design through the "make it" button!

Toggle Menu   Project Name   My projects   Save Changes   Machine   Send to cut

Toggle settings

When users press this icon, another drop-down menu appears, which would indeed be very useful. However, it's not a feature of this canvas, which is why we will not go into it in very much detail.

From this section, users can move to the profile and update their picture. You can also use a few helpful and technological icons on this menu, such as calibrating your device, changing your blades, and updating the software of your Cricut model.

It will even help you keep track of your Cricut Access subscription (if you decide to get one, of course), your account information, and much more.

We suggest that you move your cursor over any icon that you are not familiar with so that you can learn its function. It might take you a little time, and you will notice that you will likely need to do this several times in order to eventually recall the function of each option in the Design Space. This is completely normal and is part of the learning process, so cut yourself some slack and don't worry about memorizing everything immediately. After all, learning how to use your Cricut machine should be a fun experience, not one that is stressful!

Tip: You can adjust the size of your canvas by using the zoom in or zoom out functions, which can be quite helpful if you have poor eyesight and want to check a particular detail on your canvas.

Project title

Since every project requires you to label it, make sure to describe the project accurately so that you can remember to find it later. This may become more challenging later on if you end up having multiple files that have been saved with very random names.

Users' projects

When users click on their creations, they will be guided to the library of items they have already made. This is really great because you might want to cut a design that you have previously made. However, you can also access designs you made but didn't cut yet, so it's not like you necessarily need to repeat the exact same project again and again.

Saving the project

This option is possible after users have made at least one change to their canvas region. We strongly recommend that people save their projects while working. Even though your work should technically be saved online, you never know when the browser may crash — so just get in the habit of saving to be safe!

Choosing a device

 Based on the type of device you may have, such as whether it's a Cricut Joy, model from the Cricut Explore Family, or Cricut Maker, you will need to specify this in the Design Space. This is really important to ensure that you are using the right features based on the machine type you own. While the Cricut Maker is the most versatile of the machines and can perform all the tasks that the other models can, this does not apply to the other models, which have more limitations. As such, if you have a Cricut Joy, you cannot select an option or tool that is exclusively used by Cricut Maker.

Cutting an object

When users are finished designing their work, they can proceed to press the "make it" button!

In the following image, you can see the design you want to finish up. The designs are split into mats that are in different colors.

That way, you can maximize the number of tasks that you want to cut from your screen, which is great if you're trying to do more than just briefly alter a design or image.

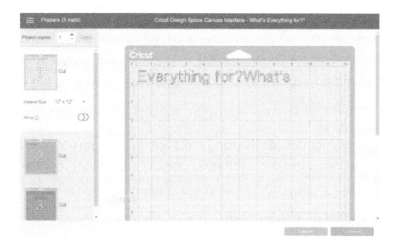

Subpanel no.2: Edit panel

This is a really helpful panel as it enables users to edit, organize, and manage fonts and photos in the canvas area.

Top Panel – Editing Menu

Redo and undo

People make errors even when they work. Selecting these tiny icons is a great way to reverse any step you didn't want to do or something that you changed your mind about.

Linetype

This option would enable you to "inform" your device about what equipment and blades to use.

Please keep in mind that based on the device that you have indicated are using, you will have various choices.

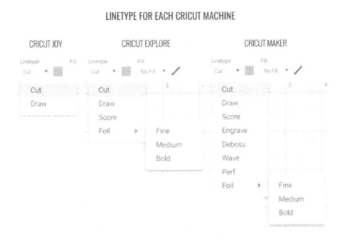

LINETYPE FOR EACH CRICUT MACHINE

For example, if you have a Cricut Joy, you only have two options: to cut your material or draw something. However, if you have a Cricut Explore model, then you have the two additional options of scoring or foiling something, which is pretty unique! This option, of course, also includes the previous two options of cutting and drawing. The Cricut Maker, in comparison to the previous two models, has a much wider range of choices. This is because the device can be used to cut, score, draw, engrave, wave, deboss, foil, and perf (perforate) your material.

Cutting: if users do not insert a PNG or JPEG picture to the canvas, "cut" would be the standard line form that most people use in relation to the canvas. In other words, it indicates that when users click "make it," the device will realize that project. For the cut method you have chosen, you will need to adjust the filling of these components. Then, you can change its color and make it look different before you cut the design. If you are still struggling with learning about the different types of Cricut knives and varieties that exist, please refer to the section of this book that discusses this in greater detail.

Drawing: you should be able to draw something with your Cricut if you want to make a certain kind of project! When you select this kind of line, you will be asked to pick a particular Cricut marker (as you will need specific kinds of pens unless they have a third-party adapter). Once you pick a customized style and design that you want your machine to draw, proceed to press the "make it" option.

Scoring: you can select the "score" option in your canvas, which is available on the vertical toolbar on the left. When users add this feature, all designs will be creased with the tool you are using, be it a scoring stylus or a scoring wheel. However, please keep in mind that you can only use the latter tool with Cricut Maker.

Engraving: this option allows you to engrave all kinds of materials, such as by making monograms on anodized aluminum or aluminum sheets.

Debossing: each debossing tip will enable you to personalize designs and produce stunning results, thereby taking your creation to a whole other level.

Cutting waves: rather than cutting straight lines like a rotary or fine-point blade, this method will enable you to cut out wavy lines. This option is really great because cutting out wavy lines is pretty challenging. Perforating: The perforation knife is a tool that helps you create short, evenly spaced lines to enable you to be able to easily rip apart or separate items like lottery tickets, vouchers, and greeting cards. As indicated earlier, this option is only available with the Cricut Maker, so you can't use the perforation blade with other models.

Foil: foil finish is one of the latest Cricut options that has been released by Cricut, Inc. Using this tool enables you to complete foil finishing tasks, which will make your designs much more attractive!

Users have the option of selecting different kinds of finishes that are good, moderate, or prominent finishes.

Fill

The fill tool is used for printing and filling out designs. You can only indicate if you want to fill out your design after you have selected the desired line type mentioned above. Afterward, you can also select the print type that you prefer, which can either be a certain color or pattern. There are a range of different colors to choose from, which is also really great because you can select some pretty cool colors.

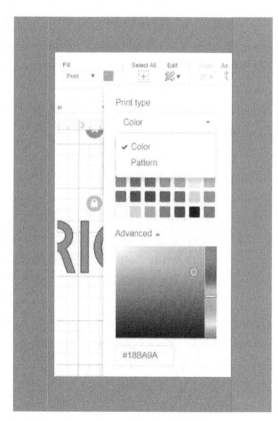

You can make hundreds of designs and decorations with your Cricut that will appeal to both young children as well as adults. In fact, you can even use your machine for professional purposes as well. If you are someone who enjoys crafts but does not want to spend several hours cutting out intricate designs with your scissors, you would surely appreciate having a Cricut machine do the work for you.

Once you have selected the desired fill choice you want, you can proceed to select "make it." If you don't select the "color" option and instead select "pattern," you can proceed to pick one of many different types of patterns. You can either make use of the available options or upload your own; it's completely up to you!

If you are thinking of making a Valentine's Day card for your crush or loved one, you can try to find a template from the thousands that are available through Cricut Access. Then, you can print and cut the design out, which will give you an edge over those generic Hallmark Valentine's Day cards. If you select one of those patterns, you can further edit it based on your needs.

Here, you can further change the scale, rotate the image, flip it (if you want) or adjust it further.

Selecting All

If you want to be able to make changes to all the images or designs you have on your canvas; you should use the "select all" button to make any additional changes.

Editing

This option will help you to cut (erase from the canvas), print (copy the same image or object, leaving the main one intact), and then paste (add the copied or cut items to the canvas region).

The edit option also has a drop-down button that can enable you to select the "cut-and-copy" or "paste" option.

Alignement

If you've ever used Microsoft Word or any other basic programs, you'll probably be familiar

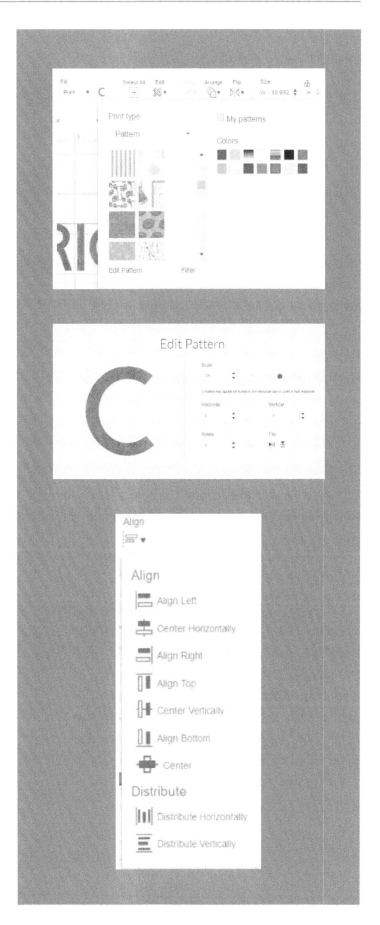

with the "align tool." In general, it's not too complicated to use as it can ultimately help you change the location of your object in relation to another.

This feature enables all designs to move in a certain direction in accordance with your preference.

Alignment to the left: when this feature is used, all components of your canvas that are selected will become oriented toward the left.

Horizontal center: when you choose this option, all items will be placed in the center of the canvas.

Alignment to the right: when users use this configuration, all components will be oriented toward the right.

Alignment to the top: this icon enables you to move all your components toward the highest point in the canvas.

Vertical center: this choice enables components to become vertically aligned. This is particularly useful when you are working on columns and want them to be coordinated.

Bottom alignment: this choice will move all of the selected material toward the bottom of the image or to one of the lowest points on the canvas.

Center: this is a useful icon that enables you to center multiple images or pieces on top of each other.

If you have three or more images or elements on your canvas and you want to make sure that the spaces between them are even, you can select the "distribute" icon. This is far easier than doing it yourself, which may even take more time and won't even be completely accurate.

Horizontal distribution: distribute the items horizontally with this option. The extent of the distribution ultimately depends on the designs that are the furthest on the right and left. This implies that the products in the middle shall be separated slightly so that the spaces between the images become even.

Vertical distribution: distribute the items vertically with this key. When you do this, the images or files that are furthest from the bottom or top will determine the extent of the distribution. This implies that the designs in the middle will be separated so that they are evenly situated between the images that are closer to the top and bottom.

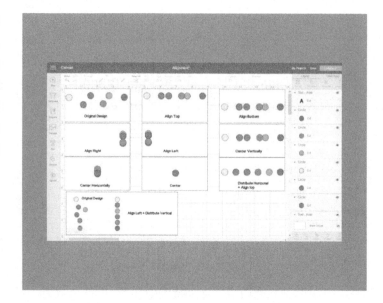

Arranging

When working with different pictures, words, and templates, anything you later add or insert into your canvas will be placed on top of your other images. Consequently, some of the design components must be rearranged so that they are either moved to the back or moved forward. This way, you can easily organize the images or designs you have on your canvas.

Send to back: this icon enables you to move one component so that it is behind all the other images on your canvas.

Move backward: this option allows you to move the selected object so that it is moved behind the image that comes before it. So, for example, if you are working with three images and the picture or element you have selected is at the forefront, it will be moved so that it is now in the middle of the three components. Move forward: this option allows you to move the selected object so that it is moved in front of the image that comes after it.

Send to front: this icon enables you to move one component so that it is in front of all the other images on your canvas.

Flipping

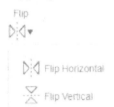

If you want to flip your image for any particular reason, you can also go about doing this quite easily! You can flip your image in two ways:

Horizontal flip: this flip will essentially serve as a kind of mirror image, which is useful when you're trying to create very specific designs. For example, if you want to create a pair of wings, all you'll need to do is design the left-wing or right-wing. Then, you can proceed to copy this image and paste it so that you have two versions of the same wing. Then, if you proceed to flip the second wing, it will become the mirror-image of the first, which saves you the trouble of designing the left-wing and right-wing separately!

Vertical flip: the vertical flip option is quite similar to the horizontal flip one, with the exception being that the mirror image of an object appears under it. This is quite similar to what you will see if you peer into the surface of the water.

Resizing

Anything that you want to build or type within Cricut Design Space needs to have a particular size. You can change the size of your object based on what will best suit your overall project.

A great option that exists is the ability to make your image smaller or bigger based on a specific ratio, which will not change if you select the "lock" option. In this case, you can increase your image by 0.5-inch increments, for example.

Rotating

The "rotate" option is also useful because you can select the angle you want when rotating a certain object. As such, you'll have greater control over the angle of rotation since you can specify it instead of just arbitrarily rotating your object.

Positioning

This box tells users where things are on the canvas when they press on a particular design.

They can shift the components around by deciding where an element should be placed in the canvas. This is convenient as it's a sophisticated tool. However, in truth, many users don't use it that often because they want to simply move on to other stages of their project design.

Font

You can pick any font you want to use for your projects by clicking on this section. If you already know which font you want, you can also type it in and use it directly.

If you have Cricut Access, you can use a range of additional fonts that have a small green "a" next to them to indicate that they require you to have a subscription. However, make sure to pay attention to this if you don't have Cricut Access because you will otherwise be required to pay for the font you have selected before you can submit your design to be cut.

Style

If users have selected the font of their choice, they can make further alterations to it based on their preferred style. Some of these options include:

Italic: This font is slightly inclined toward the right.

Regular: This is the default mode, which will not change the appearance of the font.

Bold: This option will make each letter appear a bit thicker.

Bold italic: This option will make your text or letters appear to be thicker while inclining them toward the right.

If you want to be more specific in terms of your design's appearance, you can further alter your font size, letter space, and line space.

Font size

You can manually adjust it by clicking on the up and down arrows beside the font number, or you may type in the desired font size directly.

Letter space

There seems to be very little or a lot of distance between every two letters in certain fonts. This option enables you to either increase or decrease the gap between letters quite easily.

Line space

This option enables you to adjust the space between lines in your paragraph. This is quite beneficial since users often struggle with adjusting the line spacing.

Text alignment

This alignment is different from the "alignment" discussed earlier, as this option applies to any text you have written.

The different kinds of textual alignments that exist are:

Left: This aligns a paragraph toward the left.

Middle: This aligns a paragraph toward the center.

Right: This aligns a paragraph toward the right.

Curves

This choice enables users to become extremely creative with their text!

Using this feature, you can curve your text using a small slider.

As you push the slider to the left, the text curves upwards. However, when you push it to the right, the text curves inwards.

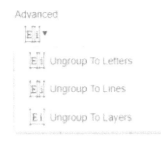

Advanced features

This is an advanced icon, which is the last one included in the "edit" toolbar that hasn't been discussed yet.

Don't be intimidated by the name of the drop-down menu. The options are not as difficult to apply as the name implies.

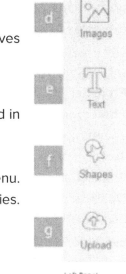

Left Panel

Ungroup to letters

This choice allows you to split each character across a single level or layer. You can consider this if you intend to change each letter.

Ungroup to lines

This choice is great and enables users to split a paragraph into separate lines. As such, if you write a paragraph and select this icon, you will have multiple separate lines that you can individually modify.

Ungroup to layers

This icon is the most complicated of all these choices. This choice is only accessible to multi-layer scripts, whereby these font styles are mainly available to Cricut users.

The multi-layer fonts are types of fonts with more than one layer, meaning that they're perfect if you want to have any shadow or shade around them.

In case you want to have the option of using a multi-layer font and do not need the layer to be added, you can select the text and then press "ungroup" to differentiate between the layers.

3. The Left Panel of Cricut Design Space

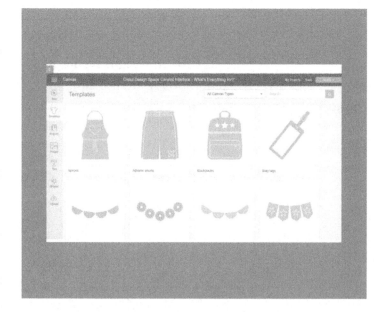

Through this panel, you can add shapes, pictures, and so much more!

There are seven icons shown in this panel:

New: you can select this to start a new project with an unused canvas.

Templates: this option helps you get an idea of the kinds of items you can remove. For example, if you want to iron vinyl onto an onesie, you can pick a design and see how it will look as a prototype.

Projects: you can try to find some ready-made projects to cut through Cricut Access.

Photos: select the individual images you want from Cricut Access and the cartridges you want to use for your project.

Text: tap on the canvas to add text.

Shapes: place all sorts of shapes onto the canvas.

Uploads: if you want to use your own photo or designs, make sure to upload them to Design Space so that you can further modify them. However, remember that if you do end up liking a design or font that is only available to users with a subscription to Cricut Access, you'll need to pay money to purchase it. As such, make sure you're willing to pay for the components you use from Cricut Access, or don't bother using them as you'll just have to discard the font or element you chose.

New

When you click on the "new" icon, you will see a window open that asks you whether you are willing to replace your project with a blank screen. As such, if you do want to be able to access the project you currently have open, make sure to save it before starting a new project from scratch. Otherwise, you will have wasted your time on your current project, which would be a real shame!

Templates

Templates provide users with a rough sketch or design that can be modified in the canvas. This great option differs from other design programs and allows beginners to get a head start on customizing their own designs. There is also a wide variety of templates to pick from, so we suggest you keep reading this chapter if you want to learn more about models and how they can be utilized.

The Projects

In case you find a picture or design that you already like and want to cut straight away, you can proceed by selecting the green "make it" icon in the top right-hand corner of the canvas. If you want to make a few changes to it before you cut it, that's also fine. It just comes down to what you want. Just make sure you don't press the "make it" option too hastily if you are not sure of the exact measurements of the object you want to create, as this can lead you to waste some of your materials.

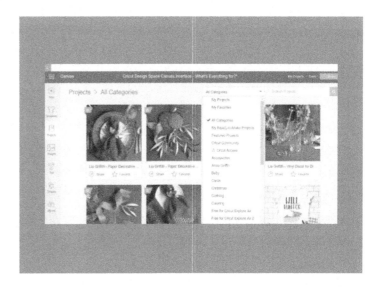

Tip: Several of these project options are available to those with subscriptions to Cricut Access. However, there are also a number of projects that most Cricut users can make use of, depending on the device they have. Therefore, make sure to select your model in the group drop-down list.

Pictures

You can use your own photos in the designs that you make in Cricut Design Space, as that will make your projects unique. If you want to find other pictures, you can also do so by looking for specific keywords, outlined groups, themes, individuals, locations, and events.

You can also choose to buy cartridges, which are collections of pictures that can be purchased individually. While some of them come with Cricut Access, many do not. Many of these cartridges are thematic, meaning you will find several pictures and designs relating to a particular idea, company, TV show, or cartoon characters, such as Disney, Hello Kitty, and Sesame Street.

Under the "outlined sections" icon, Cricut also has an unlimited number of pictures that are available for users to choose from and cut each week. You can also use different filters to find specific pictures you want.

Inserting text

Whenever users wish to write anything in a canvas, they will need to press the "text" option. From there, you can see a tiny window appear on the canvas that states "insert text here," which you should proceed to fill in.

Shapes

It is also important to remember that you can use shapes to improve upon your designs!

There are nine forms that you can pick select:

- Square
- Star
- Pentagon
- Triangle
- Diamond
- Circle
- Octagon
- Heart
- Hexagon

The final option you can add is not a shape but rather a "scoring line," which can help users indicate where creases in materials like paper should be made.

If you want to make a box or a card, using the scoring lines is a good idea.

Uploading

Lastly, you can upload files and photos with this option. There are so many designs that can be found online that you can use in your own projects for free, so make sure to check those out and upload them if you want!

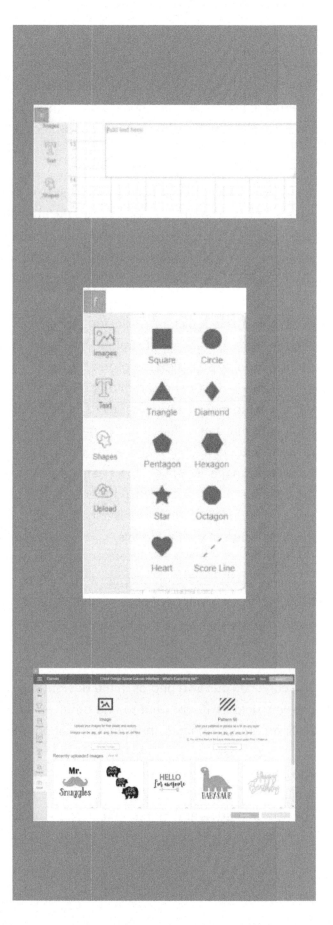

Moreover, many FREE expanding collections of printable designs and SVG documents are ready to be cut. For example, you can see some pictures in the image below that indicate how recently uploaded images will show up in your canvas. You can proceed to make use of these pictures from here.

4. The Right Panel of Cricut Design Space

For those of you who have more experience using Cricut Design Space, you may be itching to know more about the layers section mentioned earlier. In general, the layers refer to any single feature or layout in a canvas region.

Think of it in terms of clothing. When people get ready, they need to put on various layers of clothing to make up their outfits. This further depends on the day, time of year, climate, and type of outfit you want to wear.

For example, on a cold day, you will put on your undergarments, in addition to a pair of pants, shirt, sweater, gloves, neck scarf, and coat. However, on a hot day, you may just wear shorts and a tank top over your undergarments, especially if you decide to go to the beach or for a stroll in the park.

Similarly, when working on a design, based on the quality of the project you are modifying, you are likely to have multiple layers and styles that affect the design of the whole project.

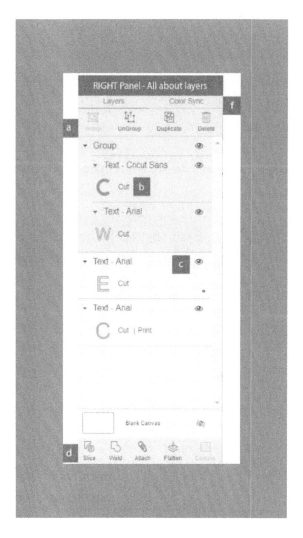

For example, let us assume that you want to make a Christmas greeting card. What will this card look like? Perhaps you may want to have a card that states "Merry Christmas" on it and further has a flower on it. The point, in this case, is that all the tiny drawings and components that make up the design constitute layers.

Some layers can be reconfigured, whereas other layers, such as PNG and JPEG photos, cannot be changed due to their format. Otherwise, they may be considered separate layers by themselves.

For instance, the text layer can be modified based on other layer types – or you may choose to combine multiple layers together to form a single one. Just keep in mind that if you do this, you cannot undo this step.

As you proceed to get accustomed to Cricut Design Space, you will learn more about what layers can or cannot do.

These adjustments can make life easier for you as it becomes easier to move certain elements or components across your canvas, thereby making it simpler to work on your project.

Grouping

If you tap on the "group" icon, you can use multiple layers to make up a complicated design.

For example, if you are working on designing an image of an elephant, you will likely need to add various other layers, such as the legs, eyes, feet, and trunk of the animal. If you want to introduce additional forms and text, you'll likely need to keep moving the elephant around your canvas a lot.

Thus, by moving all of the elephant layers together, you can try to ensure that it remains ordered and that nothing moves out of place as users keep changing their position on the canvas.

Ungrouping

This option allows you to ungroup certain layers that users have picked from the canvas or layers screen. You can use this option if you want to modify certain aspects of your work, such as the dimensions and font style.

Duplicating

This option would allow you to duplicate certain layers or patterns that you have picked on a layer's grid or a canvas.

Deleting

This choice will delete everything you have worked on a canvas or the layers screen.

Line type/filling

Each object in a layers panel would indicate what sort of line or filling users can use (such as cut, type, print, perf, and score).

Visibility of the layer

The tiny eye that shows up on each sheet of the layer grid reflects the transparency of the pattern. If users are not convinced if the feature looks acceptable, instead of removing it, you can move the small eye so that it covers the item.

Tip: By tapping on the layer and moving it, you can move a certain template up or down.

Empty canvas

Each "layer" helps users to adjust the color of the canvas, in terms of whether you are trying to see what a certain style looks like. What is great about this option is that you can further modify the shade and design of your project in accordance with your personal preferences.

Slicing, Welding, Attaching, Flattening, Contouring

The icons that users see here, which are slice, weld, attach, flatten, and contour, are essential! However, make sure to learn how to use them properly. For more information on this, read on!

The shapes shown in the below image show you the outcome of using these tools.

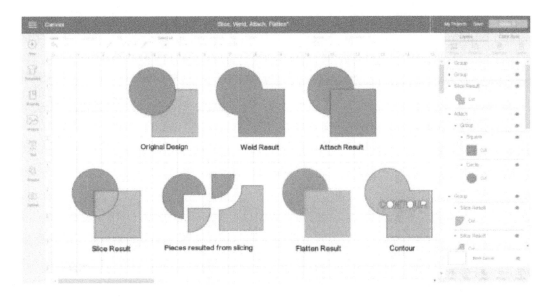

Cut, weld, mount, compress, and contour information graphics

As you can see from the image, the original shapes that were drawn were a pink circle and a green square. So what happens when you start applying these tools to the shapes?

Cut/Slice

This tool enables you to cut different components, such as texts as well as other components, into various styles. In other words, by using this tool, if you decide to cut or slice the shapes along the lines where they overlap, you will end up with four independent shapes, as can be seen in the image above.

Weld

The welding tool enables you to fuse two or three shapes into one.

When users select two shapes and click "weld," the two images will fuse together. Then, you will have an entirely new shape. The color of the item will be the shape that is in the foreground. As such, in this case, the new color of the fused shape is pink because the pink circle was partially on top of the green square.

Attach

This option enables the two shapes to become one shape, which is a bit similar to the welding option. However, the lines where the shapes overlap stay visible, meaning that they are simply attached to one another as opposed to becoming one indivisible shape.

Flatten/Compress

This feature is great to use when utilizing the "print" and "cut" options. In fact, when users adjust the filling from "no filling" to "print," the images will appear as if they comprise only one sheet.

Once you have set up your template, select the layers you want to print together as one and then press "flatten." This will help the pictures and shapes look like they have fused together so that the layers of a multi-layer image have become compressed into a single-layer printable picture.

Contour

The contouring tool helps users to cover unused parts of their template. However, this can only be used if the form or design contains components that can be taken out.

For instance, you can merge the original template in one form with a welding instrument. Then, you can write the term "contour" and cut that against the current shapes you have. Next, use the contour feature to cover the insides of the "O" and "R" letters.

Color Synchronization

The color synchronization tool is the last option you have on the layers column.

Each color on the canvas region reflects a different shade of ink. If the template has several shades of blue or yellow, are you sure that you want to use them all? You can feel free to adjust the color scheme based on whether you want to use more or less materials so as not to waste some.

Canvas zone

The canvas area is where you can view all your drawings and their components. It's really simple to use!

Canvas grid and measurements

The canvas region is a grid that consists of multiple small squares, which is important as it helps you determine the exact measurements you need so as to make the most out of the space you have.

You can adjust the dimensions from centimeters to millimeters and switch your panel off and on when you press on the upper grid and choose "settings." You have many options to choose from within the settings.

Choosing

Whenever users pick one or several layers, they often select the blue option, which can be adjusted from all four sides. The red "X" can be used to erase any layer.

The top right region will enable users to rotate the picture; however, if you need a picture to be at a particular angle, we recommend that you utilize the rotate option on the editing toolbar.

In this case, you can also activate the tiny "lock" to use only one ratio to increase or decrease the size of your object.

Inside and outside zooming

If users want to see their image in greater detail, they can zoom in. However, if they want to see it from a distance, they may zoom out of the picture. Both options can be done by clicking the "+" and ''-" symbols in the bottom left-hand corner of the canvas.

This chapter shows you how to make a few projects for beginners with the Cricut Maker model.

1. Cricut Paper Flower Decorations

Consider making a few paper flower bouquets! This isn't a very difficult task, although it requires a little bit of practice. However, when you get the hang of it, you will never need to buy any fake flowers ever again!

The website Abi Kirsten Collections has some beautiful hand-made flower templates that you can check out. If you try out this project and enjoy it, you would probably love to buy her book, which contains free templates and tutorials on how to make large flowers.

2. Greeting Cards

Creating greeting cards with Cricut machines is a great way to start out on your Cricut adventure! That way, you can avoid wasting money on buying greeting cards from Etsy or other online stores. In addition, most Cricut machines, including Cricut Maker, offer the tools needed to make such a project in the packaging. As such, we encourage you to try this out and to check Cricut Design Space for any other templates that catch your eye!

Cricut users have direct access to thousands of images, dozens of scripts, discounted items, materials, and apps through Cricut Access. However, even if you haven't bought a subscription to this library, you can still make use of a lot of different free images, templates, and fonts.

You can make use of these resources when designing your greeting card and they are very convenient for when you have to attend a celebration or event last minute!

3. Cricut Paper Designs

You can make many different paper projects using your Cricut machine. All you'll need is some cardstock that you can find at the neighboring craft store (i.e., Michaels, Walmart, Hobby Lobby, and Target). Otherwise, you can also order some of your paper tools and equipment online.

4. Cricut Domestic Cardstock Decorations

You can cut many different types of paper and use them to make some home décor. For example, if you want to make some decorations for Halloween, you can cut out paper bat templates with your Cricut Maker and hang them up in your home!

In this case, you can use Cricut paper bags to help make the main poster. You can also use heavy cardstock to make this design, as can be seen in the above image. You may also use your Cricut Maker machine to draw the text "I put a spell on you" on the main cardstock, whereby half the work will already be done! Once Halloween is over, you will surely end up taking down these holiday-themed decorations. However, make sure you don't throw them away as you can store and use them again next year!

The identical Cricut bats shown above are usually used as Halloween household decorations. During the fall of 2019, many people who decorated their houses in this way were complimented after they posted these pictures online! As such, you can even make your friends jealous of your crafting skills and cool house!

If you want to design something for Valentine's Day, you can also cut out a few paper hearts and stick them to your wall. Moreover, using your Cricut Maker, you can design several pink cushions! Instead of wasting your money by hiring an interior designer or buying several expensive household décor items, just make use of your Cricut to prepare your own decorations. You can also use your Cricut Maker to challenge yourself to recreate trendy furniture items that are, of course, way more affordable because you'll only need to buy the materials and dedicate some time to this endeavor.

You can also design some paper butterflies and stick them in your young daughter's bedroom beside her crib. This will help liven up her room and give her something to look at when she is going to sleep.

5. Foam Designs

Did you know that Cricut can also cut through foam? This book teaches users how convenient it is to use Cricut Explore to do this!

6. Foam Stamps

DIY foam stickers are some of the best Cricut Art scorers you can get! In fact, many of the most popular items that people have made with their Cricut machines are foam stickers. So, go ahead and try making one in your free time!

7. Personalized Trays, Tea Mugs, and Tins

A particularly popular project that many people enjoy trying out is personalizing porcelain or glass items, such as teacups, mugs, and containers. By adding a simple design to your plain glassware, you can make them fancy and much more attractive!

8. Customizable Cricut Latte Mugs

You can use this book regardless of whether you are a beginner or advanced Cricut user because all users enjoy using their machines to make DIY mugs! The book has included a free Xmas SVG guide to provide you with some holiday-themed suggestions and in-

structions on how to design a Cricut mug. Moreover, designing coffee mugs with Cricut isn't complicated! You don't need a lot of material to make these mugs! For example, if you want to draw a clover onto your cup for St. Patrick's Day, you'll only need to use some of your vinyl scraps.

You can also draw a heart with your Cricut machine and use it to put onto a mug to gift to your loved one on Valentine's Day

9. Customizable Plates

On Valentine's Day and other special holidays, you can use a "Love You Very Much" template and put it on a serving plate, pan, or cup to gift to your loved ones. However, you can also use the same cutout to put on a T-shirt, purse, or other clothing items!

10. Custom-Designed Body Wash Container

By using Cricut vinyl, you can create a customized glass body wash container. The two most important items you will need for this, aside from the container itself, are transfer tape and vinyl, so make sure to get those!

11. Glass Candle Jars

You can personalize these cheap glass jars and turn them into candleholders! You can find some great SVG template suggestions when you search for "great pumpkin pie" and "cozy weather" in the Cricut Access search engine.

12. Customizable "Greeting" Doormats

DIY doormats are really fun projects to make with your Cricut machine! You can make hilarious customizable doormats that make your friends and family laugh when they visit you.

In fact, if you wanted to make these kinds of mats and sell them, you could charge as much as $45 to $50 on Etsy for such an order!

With their unique style, these innovative mats are great projects to try out that will help you save (or even earn) money!

13. Valentine's Day Doormat

The designer of this "Love Shack" front doormat was inspired to make this after hearing a popular song on the radio! If you want to surprise your partner with a cute symbol of your love for one another on Valentine's Day, you might want to try this project!

14. Farmhouse Sign

Farmhouse signs are really great and easy to make. Many Cricut users have made these with old wood, foam sheets, paint, and cottage material. In other words, you can use a lot of material you already have lying around the house to design your own sign!

15. Foam Board Wooden Sign

These foam board wooden signs are great to make with your Cricut Machine. Instead of getting generic signs from Target, make your own unique ones and surprise your family members by hanging them up around the house!

16. Wooden Signs

If you want to make a unique wooden sign, you can get a piece of bamboo. If you have any that is left over from a previous project, you can use this. Otherwise, you can go check out the junk area of the local timber stores. Once you have gotten your wood, paint it and personalize it the way that you like. You can even add sawtooth hooks to its backside so that you can hang it up in your house.

You can also use other types of material to make such a sign, such as reusable plastic, which would enable you to redesign it when you get bored of the sign next year.

17. Cloth Portrait Cushions

Each year, when the holidays come around, designers try to sell expensive holiday-themed household items in the supermarkets. Instead of falling prey to these cheap advertising schemes, remember that you have your own Cricut machine and can make even nicer holiday décor.

You can do this for every season and then store the items you made for the next season. For example, if you make some Christmas themed pillowcases, you can put these away once December ends and use them again next year. This also applies to holidays like Thanksgiving and New Year's Eve.

18. Embroidered Pillows

Have you ever thought of designing your own pillows but were put off by all the sewing work involved? If you are an artsy person and have your own Cricut machine, you can use stencils to make some pretty cushions. Many people try this popular Cricut project, so you should check it out too! All you will need is some dense cardboard, your Cricut Maker, glue, a stencil, pillowcase, and dye.

19. Customizable Outdoor Furniture

Have you ever seen any customized outdoor chairs, such as those shown in this image? They look cool, right? Most people would love to have something like this but are not sure how to do this. However, for those of you with a Cricut, you can use some iron-on vinyl and give your chairs a makeover!

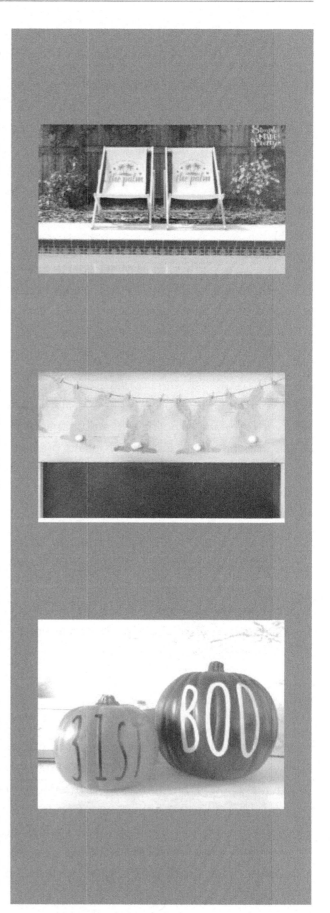

20. Felt Projects

When it comes to using felt, there are so many options! It's not always very cheap, so consider stocking up on felt whenever it's on sale!

21. Felt Bunny Banner

A great beginner project you can try out with your Cricut machine is to design a felt banner for the holidays! This will make your house look festive. In addition, it doesn't cost that much money to make and doesn't need a lot of time to be made.

22. Customizable Decorations

One of the best things you can make with your Cricut is a customizable design or decoration! For example, you can get some inspiration from Rae Dun's designs. All you'll need

are some materials, but it's ultimately up to you to further customize your designs in the way that you like!

23. Crafted Pumpkins

You can make a few crafted pumpkins, which are inspired by Rae Dun's designs. In this case, you would need a handful of tools as well as pumpkins to do this project. Aside from the supplies you'll need for this project, make sure to handle your pumpkins carefully so that you don't break them.

24. Specially Designed Easter Eggs

You can design a few Easter eggs with your Cricut Maker. You will just need a handful of white eggs and some essential Cricut tools.

25. Print and Cut Designs

Print and cut designs are great for those of you who don't want to spend too much time working on making your own. As such, if you have a busy schedule and need to wrap up a particular project, you will find that these kinds of ventures are worth trying out. In addition, if you're a beginner, you will also likely appreciate the print and cut projects a lot due to your inexperience!

26. Halloween Treat Holders

Halloween treat holders are quite easy to design with your Cricut machine. All you'll need to do is upload an accessible SVG document and follow the instructions you are given. Then, you'll have a delightful surprise to give trick-or-treaters over Halloween!

27. Cricut Customizable Beverage Koozies

In order to make a few exciting drinking koozies, you will need to use heat transfer vinyl! These are great gifts for kids, so if you're a parent or a teacher and want to inspire your students or children to behave better, you can make a handful and distribute them whenever they are being good.

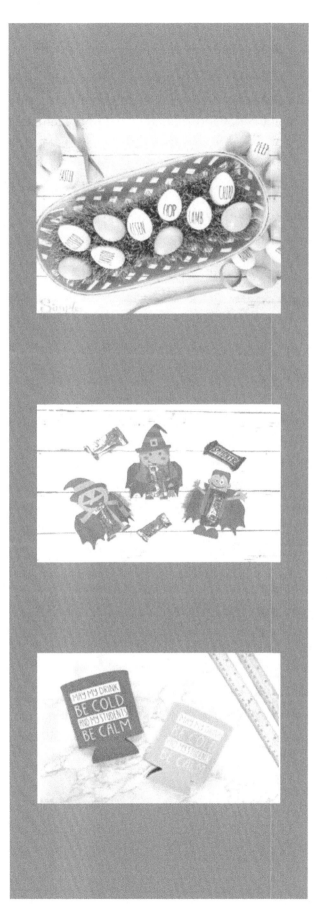

28. Wooden Treat Holders

These wooden treat holders are similar to the Halloween ones described above. All you'll need to do is use your Cricut to print and cut out these furry creatures!

29. "Print and Cut" Greeting Cards

If you want to try out the print and cut designs, you may use one to make a greeting card the next time that you are in a bind prior to an event!

30. Clothes (Totes, Gloves, Tops, and Boots)

There are some clothes designs you can try out with your Cricut Maker that aren't too complicated for beginners. For example, you can try to style items like T-shirts, pouches, shoes, and gloves!

Users can also make St. Patrick's Day Skeletons and Bone Sweatshirt using iron-on vinyl. What you'll need to do is import the file, adjust the width of the design based on the size of the T-shirt, and then iron the photo.

These "If you could read this" socks are a pretty funny and cute gift. You can customize them further and change what you write on the second sock, depending on who you will give them to.

However, they are still likely to be appreciated by the receiver because they are homemade! So, give it a try and see if your friends or loved ones would like them!

1. Christmas Presents for Your Neighbours

Do you want to prepare some Christmas presents for your neighbours? Bake some cookies and utilize your Cricut Maker to make a festive box for your treats! Your neighbours will surely appreciate receiving a beautifully wrapped tasty treat this Christmas.

This will also give you the opportunity to repay those next-door neighbours that always made it a point to stop by over the holidays to give you gifts or sweets. You can also establish a stronger relationship with them also perhaps find a way to get your children to mingle with the other kids in your neighbourhood instead of being glued to the TV!

If this gift idea sounds appealing to you, you can check out a few templates in Cricut Access to get some inspiration. Since this platform has so many designs for packages and boxes, you can likely find a nice design relatively quickly. You can even customize the box further depending on the season. For example, if this idea sounds appealing to you, why limit yourself to giving gifts during Christmas only? You can perhaps also give out some cookies during Thanksgiving or Easter. All you'll need to do is find a design or template that suits the season or holiday you have in mind!

1.1 Cricut Snack Package

Supplies

- Cricut Maker
- Silver cardstock or craft card for containers and present tags
- Colored pens
- Colored sheets of paper or cardstock for plastic covers
- Cellophane
- Poinsettia felt
- Glue
- Craft pearls
- Cricut Design Space pictures
- Cupcake holder
- Poinsettia home decorations
- Wildflower font (writing style)

Instructions

Go to the Cricut Design Space and search for the project template that matches the cupcake holder shown below. Once you find the template, you will notice that it has six sections. In addition, you will need four of these designs to build these two packages, which are the yellow package base, the pink window cover, the scalloped window lid, and the present tag.

Conceal the others (the green plain cover and the blue cupcake ones). Then, proceed to recreate the base of the yellow box and the sticker as you will need two of them. You can decorate them to complement the colors of the final design. Since light blue and red are trending this year, you can use these colors to make your design more festive.

Scoring stylus

You can use the scoring stylus to create creases along with the packages, as is shown in the dotted lines in the above photo.

You will also need a poinsettia photograph, such as a three-dimensional flower. However, you can cover the middle of the plant and the leaves, thereby selecting the two sections of the flower itself instead. This step should be replicated to create a purple flower and another red one to complement the colors of the final project.

You can then proceed to write out whatever you like on the tag, depending on the idea and emotions you want to convey to the receiver. We would recommend that you use the Cricut Wildflower font in two different colors using markers from the Cricut Absolute Pen Kit.

Before cutting, make sure that you re-sized all or most parts of your design so that the size is correct, depending on how many cookies you want to fit in your box. Then, proceed to cut out the papers using your Cricut Maker. Once it's been cut and scored, fold the edges to create the box!

Once you have folded the box, make sure to use some kind of glue or a tiny spraying adhesive to add a cellophane square to the top of the box to make sure your treats are visible.

Then, you can add the two flowers together and add three miniature handmade pearls in the center, using a bit of glue to make sure they stay there. Your neighbors will surely adore this sweet gift! If you want to make sure the lid doesn't accidentally open, you can use white lace to tie around the box to keep it together. Now, you're all set!

1.2 How to utilize the stencil blank to make a Cricut stencil

When it comes to individual craft tutorials, many users want to make decorative signs for their homes using Cricut. There are several ways to do this. In this case, we will show you how to create a stencil blank. Firstly, you will need a few supplies for this, which include:

- Crystal adhesive vinyl
- Plastic Cricut stencil
- Freezer paper

You can also make use of iron-on vinyl, which is even better!

In order to get started on this project, you will need to have all the materials ready. You can get these from the nearest craft store or on the internet! Here are some of the resources you need to make your Cricut stencil:

- Wooden frame design

- Adhesive tape roll
- Stencil blank
- Craft paints in a range of colors, like white
- Thin, stiff brush
- Sponge brushes
- Green StandardGrip or Purple StrongGrip mats
- Color trays
- "Merry and shining" SVG

If you only have a white backboard, you can proceed to color it. However, if you don't mind having a white backboard, then it's fine to keep it the way it is. Since this is a matter of personal preference, go with the option that you like.

Cricut stencil instructions

You can make this project in Cricut Design Space. Select the "upload" icon on the left and then attach the file shown below.

Press the "save" option.

Then, select the imported file you want and press "insert photos" to place it on the canvas.

Now, you may have given someone an individual stencil as a gift. However, if you want to teach your friend how to make a stencil, then he or she will need to utilize the stencil script and take hold of the inside of the letters attached to the stencil.

You can begin this process by tapping on the "shapes" icon in the design grid on the left and by clicking the square.

Then, adjust the size of the square to accommodate the desired frame. If you want, you can make it around half an inch bigger than the square so that you can glue the words onto the backboard so that it doesn't move. In this scenario, if your words are around 10 x 10-inches long, your backboard should be around 10.25 x 10.25-inches long.

You can also better coordinate the size of the square and image you have selected in this way. For example, if you want the square to be in the foreground, with the letters placed on top of it, then you should select the option in the toolbar that states "send to back" to achieve this (see the image below).

Now, you will be able to line up the picture and the rectangle. If you like, you can align the shape and the picture together so that the design turns out the way you want it to.

Now, you can proceed to cut out your design! This can be challenging for beginners, but there are generally two key points you need to know:

1. You should only cut two things at the same time (in this case, the picture and the square).
2. When you are done, you will have various cut-outs that can be seen.

Select both the square and letters together at once, and then select "cut" at the bottom of the layers panel on the right.

You can also see that the layers section has about three "sliced results": a dark version of the design, a grey version, and a stencil. Delete the first two results and keep the image of the stencil.

You can make additional changes to the stencil if you want. Even if you make a few mistakes, you can practice on a couple of blanks until you get it right. You may end up going through three stencil blanks until you get one that you like, but it's ultimately worth it to keep experimenting until you have the shape that you want. It's really the only way you'll learn! Once you have this down, you can proceed to the next step.

Cut the stencil

Click the "make it" option in the top right-hand corner of the canvas.

There seems to be nothing else to do in the "prepare" section, so you can press "continue." If you have a Cricut Maker, do set the dial to the customized option.

If you are working with either the Cricut Explore or Cricut Maker models, you can press the "browse all materials" option and then search for the stencil in the "create screen."

At the bottom of the tab, you will notice a green link to the resource settings, which will provide you with access to other options. Then, you can scroll to the bottom to the "stencil film" option and change it so that the pressure is set to 349 and the 3x multi-cut option is selected.

Then, press the "save" button. You will need to go backward and browse through your "all supplies" section before selecting the "stencil film" option. Place the stencil film on the mat and follow the instructions on how to insert it into the machine, in accordance with the flashing arrows that are shown. Then, click the flashing "C" button so that the Cricut can split the stencil film.

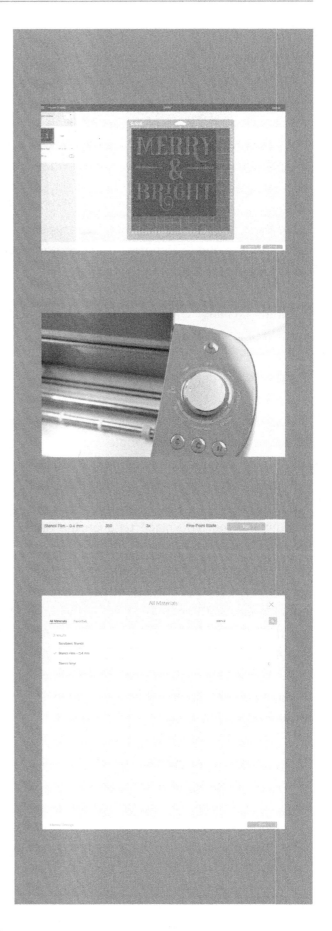

Double-check that the material has been cut

Before removing the mat from the device after it has been cut, double-check to ensure that the material was actually cut all the way through. Suppose it hasn't, press the "C" again so that it will be cut once more. However, you can't do this if you already pulled the mat out of the device, so be careful when cutting your material.

Place the stencil film on the mat. Then, position the mat under the object and press the flashing arrow to enable the mat to slide into the device.

Press the flashing "C" button and wait for the Cricut to split the stencil film.

Create a home decoration symbol

You can begin stenciling the sign now by taping the stencil to the interior of the photo.

In order to refrain from getting the paint colors onto the blank stencil in any unwanted areas, we highly recommend that you place tape on the areas that are not covered by the stencil. In this case, you can choose to paint the stencil area with white first before waiting for it to dry. Then, you can paint over the stencil again with the colors that you want to stick. If you choose to use these two coats of paint (white and another color), the paint may not stick properly to the canvas. As such, just be careful when you are weighing your options and be aware of the fact that this can indeed happen.

If you want to skip the step of adding white paint, you can proceed to paint the stencil directly with the color that you want. You can use sponge daubers for this step, whereby you will need to dip the tool in a bit of paint before applying it to the canvas and coloring the stencil. We advise you to use this method to prevent the paint from bleeding through the canvas.

You can then move on to paint the rest of the canvas with the other colors that you want.

Before the paint is dry, peel the tape off, and lift the stencil gently (to prevent the paint from sticking to the stencil).

It is quite possible that some of the pain in the letters may spillover onto the white canvas. In that case, you can use a bit of white paint to touch up any parts of the design where the paint has spread beyond the stencilled areas.

Once the canvas is fully dry, you can apply some poly gloss if you want. However, if you intend to keep this indoors, you may opt to skip this phase. Then, you will be fully done with your canvas, which is ready to be hung up!

2. Warm Cocoa Cup Present

Everyone loves a warm cup of cocoa. However, the next best thing you can gift a loved one or friend is an actual mug to be used to make hot cocoa. Read on to learn more about this!

This cup is easy to make with your Cricut machine. It also doesn't take much time to find a nice template, so we would recommend that you give this a try in your free time.

You can also use your Cricut Explore Air 2 machine if that is what you own. It's a great designing tool – and JOANN has recently launched an incredible color scheme of this model in cobalt blue!

2.1 Simple Christmas crystal gifts

What may be obvious to our readers is that Cricut users genuinely love their machines, with many owning various models and materials. One of the best things about this tool is that it has made the prospect of designing material so much easier. You can also involve your kids in your design projects to keep them busy, which will also save you the trouble of hiring a babysitter.

If you also need a simple gift that won't take you too long to make, this "cup of cheer" will admirably fulfill this function!

Aside from this particular object, there are so many other items you can make with your Cricut machine, including:

- Customized T-shirts and onesies
- Customized cooking gadgets and towels
- Decorative cottage signs
- Elegant, hand-made invitations
- Gift baskets and wrapping paper
- Mugs, goblets, and wine glasses

Let's start making one of those lovely mugs! In sum, it can take 10 minutes to set up and put together! This gift idea is for those of you who want to give something cute to your loved one but are on a tight schedule.

Supplies

- Cricut Maker
- A blue or green mat for cutting
- Transfer tape
- Three permanent vinyl shades
- Decorative ribbons (from any store)
- Weeding tools
- White mug
- Crinkled paper filler
- Hot chocolate ingredients

Instructions

Being able to upload your own creations to Cricut Design Space is another reason why users love their Cricut machines. In this case, you can find the lovely SVG "cup of cheer" file in the Design Space.

As indicated earlier, there isn't much that you need to do with this particular template. However, you must resize it to make sure that the file will fit on your mug, as you don't want it to be too big or too small. You can make it around three inches-wide, for example, by using the edit toolbar on your canvas. You can also adjust the colors if you are using various types of vinyl.

Then, cut it using Cricut. Use your scissors to cut out the different components of your design. Then, weed any extra material.

Make sure that the transfer tape is just a little bit bigger than the phrases. Then, remove the paper from the transfer tape and spread it across the writing, pressing the transfer tape to bind it to the vinyl.

The letters are meant to cling to the transfer tape. Then, place the vinyl on the mug and, beginning from the center, press the phrase to the mug. Peel away the transfer tape, leaving the vinyl on the cup! If it doesn't stick to the mug, press a little bit harder as it's meant to stay there. Repeat this step with the three hearts.

Place some paper filler in the bottom of the mug and then add all the ingredients needed to make hot chocolate, including dark chocolate, a small packet of marshmallows, and candy cane. The gift is now ready!

3. Cricut DIY Phone Case

So many things can be made with your Cricut model, including things that you probably never thought about actually making. In this case, you can also design a mobile cover to protect your phone instead of buying one. If you don't have a phone cover, this is the perfect opportunity for you to make sure your phone is well-protected at all times. However, if you do have one but have gotten bored of it, you can design a new one for yourself or for a loved one.

Supplies
- Cricut Maker
- Plastics/vinyl
- Phone-related cases
- Weeding tools
- Photos or preferred scripts used to make templates
- Acrylic seal

Instructions

The very first step you need to do is open the Cricut Design Space and the file you want. Then, cut the photo and weed it after making sure that the dimensions of the image are accurate and will fit your phone cover. Otherwise, you will need to repeat this step if you make a mistake.

Use a Cricut scraper to remove any unwanted vinyl, such as the white surroundings of the cat design shown in the image below. Once you have done this step, you may take out some transfer tape and apply it to the vinyl.

Then, use your fingertips or Cricut scraper to flatten the photo.

Lift your transfer tape carefully and gently apply it to your phone case.

If you like, you can further secure the outside of your smartphone cover with a modified podge translucent acrylic sealant. This will essentially ensure that your phone cover is waterproof, and that the vinyl will not get damaged.

4. Personalized Planning Organizer

A great activity you can do toward the end of a year is creating a calendar or agenda for the following year. This can help you stay organized to ensure that you can meet your university or work deadlines. There are also many stylish planners out there that are really appealing. However, if you want to have one that really fits your personality and is unique, you should make it yourself. After all, if you have your own Cricut machine, why not? To learn more about how you can make this and the supplies you need, read on!

Supplies

- Cricut Maker
- 3 large quarters of different patterns (from your fabric leftovers)
- A 7-inch-long zipper
- 2 elastic strings that span the planner's length.

Instructions

The very first step you should take involves measuring the size of your planner, as it should be 12.5 x 9.5 inches long. You should expect the final product to be about half an inch or so smaller than the planner.

When you have finished the calculations, sketch the different designs that you want to decorate your organizer with. When drawing, make sure to add 1/5th of an inch to each piece of fabric. Here are some of the different dimensions of the cloths:

Polka dot cloth:
- Slim 5.5 x 3-inch bag
- 12.5 x 55-inch front segment
- Scraps at the ends of a zipper.
- Two 115 x 2-inch zippers

From the dimensional fabric:
From the tissue of the shrub:
- 5.5 x 55-inch upper pocket
- 12.5 x 75-inch backside
- 4.5 x 35-inch lower pocket

Begin to make the organizer by adding a zipper. Using two pieces of the same cloth, cut out two 2-inch-long pieces of fabric. Then, attach a strap to either side of the zipper, whereby the zipper and cloth must be 12.5 inches as soon as the pieces are tied together. Then, fasten the two-inch-long pieces to each end of a zipper.

Stitch around each side of the zipper and then double-check that part to ensure that it is 12.5 x 3.5-inches long.

Then, you can proceed to work on the bags. Pick up the three distinct pocket segments. Press on the upper edge of all three pouches and then stitch the fabric on the spot. Next, press on the right side underneath the 4.5 x 5.5-inch-long pouch and stitch the fabric in place.

Place the pockets' lining near the upper pocket where you expect it to fit, making sure to leave an extra one-fourth of an inch of space to place the fabric. Then, turn the pocket and fasten it in position. You should stitch that pocket in place, as can be seen in the photo below, and stitch it over the pins. Now, turn the pocket inward and press on the crease.

Now, in the same fashion, add the second pocket. The final pocket does not have to be stitched in place in a certain order. Instead, you can add it before the whole organizer is completed.

Next, connect the zipper to the pocket.
Proceed to pin the last pocket in place. After this, pin the two 12.5-inch-long elastic strings to the organizer. Then, pin the back section down and make sure the zipper is fully unzipped, as this is what users are supposed to flip. Next, stitch all four corners together.

Flip the piece over and push the corners down. The final product is done!

5 Halloween Garland

These custom dollar shop burlap fall garlands are really great seasonal designs. The wreaths can be placed anywhere in your house. However, if you want to hang them in a place where both your family members and strangers will appreciate them, you can hang them over the knocker on your front door.

People often make these kinds of burlap ornaments for Halloween, so you'll fit right in with these designs. You can also add a few other designs, such as cardboard leaves, and reuse them during Thanksgiving. In other words, you can reuse your awesome garland for other seasons, so make sure not to throw it away when Halloween is over.

If you have a Cricut Maker, you can get to work!

Supplies

- Cricut Maker
- Straw ornament, pool noodle or foam garlands
- Quick printable sheet or customized adornments
- Burlap ribbon
- Glass head sewing pins

Instructions

1. Collect the materials you need.
2. Wrap a straw wreath in a burlap cloth.
3. Attach the edges of a ribbon to the base of your straw.
4. Cut out the printable design by hand or utilize your Cricut to cut them out immediately.
5. Use some pushpins to tie the flowers or bats to your wreath.
6. Attach your ribbon and put it up anywhere in your house!

People enjoy placing wreaths in different places in their houses. As such, you can hang your wreath over doors, cabinets, walls, fire pits, and photo frames.

6. Felt Unicorn Night Mask

A felt-made unicorn night mask is a cool unicorn event item, slumber party present, and gift for children (or adults) who like unicorns. You can check the following DXF, SVG, PNG, and EPS files to put this mask together.

Many avid crafters who have kids have made this gift for them to play with and generally appreciate. Kids especially like to role-play and often have a fascination with animals and imaginary creatures, including unicorns. Therefore, if you want to make your kid happy, this is a good project to work on in your free time.

You will need a Cricut Maker to create this project.

Supplies

- Cricket Maker
- Felt (two white papers)
- Felt (black, light pink, purple, hot pink, and yellow papers; you will only need one of each color)

Instructions

1. Collect all your materials first.
2. Access the SVG, EPS, PNG, or DXF file and upload it to your Cricut Maker.
3. Edit the picture and adjust the scale so that it is 8.5 x 7.65 inches long. However, you can change this depending on the size of the face of the person who will wear it.
4. After that, cut out the photos.
5. Organize the pictures and then stick them together to form one layer.
6. Position the elastic edges between the two clear layers' edges to make a band across the mask.
7. Fasten all sides together and allow it to dry. Alternatively, you can stitch the rim and tie it together to keep it intact.

Suggestions for cleaning: you can use a cloth to clean this product. Otherwise, you can also spot-wash it. Just make sure to be gentle with it to avoid damaging the material.

You can make this unicorn night mask anytime as it's not hard to put together. Moreover, it can take you a mere 5 minutes to make if you further use these materials:

- Glue (for fabrics)
- White elastic (the size of the child's head)
- Needle and thread or a sewing machine (optional)

7. Felt Christmas Fairy Lights Garland

Felt lights can be seen everywhere during the holidays as people often enjoy attempting to create a wreath that matches their colorful Christmas LEDs. Those who have a Cricut Maker can use it to do this project. You should only import PNG or SVG files to the Cricut Design Space, which you may then proceed to scale, cut, and compile!

Supplies

- Felt in different colors (i.e., red, blue, orange, yellow, black, and green)
- Color-coordinated threads
- Online printable pattern
- Sewing device
- Cricut Maker
- Filling (pillow stuffing)

Instructions

1. Cut out the shapes of small Christmas lights (specifically cutting out the front, back, and upper edges).
2. Stitch together the base and then start filling them with the lights.
3. Stitch the black pieces of fabric at the top of each light.
4. Split the black felt strips and stitch the edges together to create a long black "ribbon."
5. String the black "ribbon" through the small spaces at the top of each light to create the garland.
6. Stitch the edges of all the lights together as well as the black "ribbon."
7. Hang it up once it is complete!

You can make the Christmas garland as long or short as you want. It really depends on where you want to hang it up, as you can string it across your fireplace or directly between the two walls of your dining table. However, you can also create a particularly long garland that you can loop around your Christmas tree. Wherever you want to hang up

your garland, it is sure to look fantastic!

This homemade felt Christmas lantern garland is a simple creation that can be made with your Cricut Maker in no time! If you have a bit more time to spare

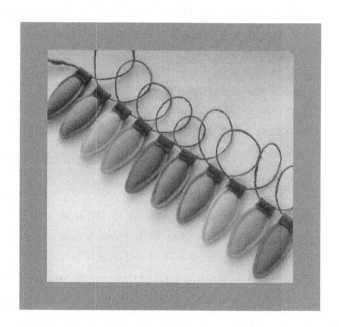

and you don't own a Cricut Maker, you can also just stitch it together by hand. However, if you want to keep practicing how to make projects with your Cricut machine, we would advise you to use it for this project just to get the hang of your device. You have nothing to lose and a lot to gain – in terms of experience, of course!

8. Customized Graduation Cap Present

Most students graduate high school and university by wearing a graduation cap. If you want to make one, you can do so using your Cricut Maker machine! Of course, if you want to make one for any other purpose, such as if you require one in a play you are acting in, then you can also follow the instructions specified below. Either way, we can teach you how to put one together in no time, as this isn't too complicated an endeavor!

You can use your Cricut Maker in addition to a few files you can find in the Cricut Design Space. If you have a subscription to Cricut Access, you can also check it out to see if you can find fancier designs there.

Supplies
- Cardstock paper
- Yarn
- Scrapbooking tape
- Printable gift box template
- Embroidery string
- Glue
- Cricut Maker
- Cricut party foils
- Scoring wheel or scoring system stylus

Instructions
1. Print the sample graduation cap present box design from a website online. Otherwise, you can try to find another project template through the

Cricut Design Space. You should generally use an A4 size format. However, if you want to make a slightly larger cap, you can also try printing these files on A3 paper.

2. Cut the prototype out.
3. To attach the two strips, add glue to the flaps of each prototype.
4. Fold the base flaps of the body's template backward.
5. Fasten the existing flaps of the body prototype together in order to form a circular shape.
6. Apply glue to the base of the flaps and place the base within the circular body.
7. Repeat stages three to five to construct the lid prototype.
8. Split 25 inches of thread into two parts.
9. Fasten another strip of yarn to the middle of the yarn.
10. Drag the coiled yarn downward to create the outline of the cap.
11. Then, cut the edges of the looped thread.
12. Tie that yarn to the split pin.
13. Place the split pin in the middle of the square-shaped cover.
14. Place the two covered templates alongside it.
15. Then, close the lid of the case!

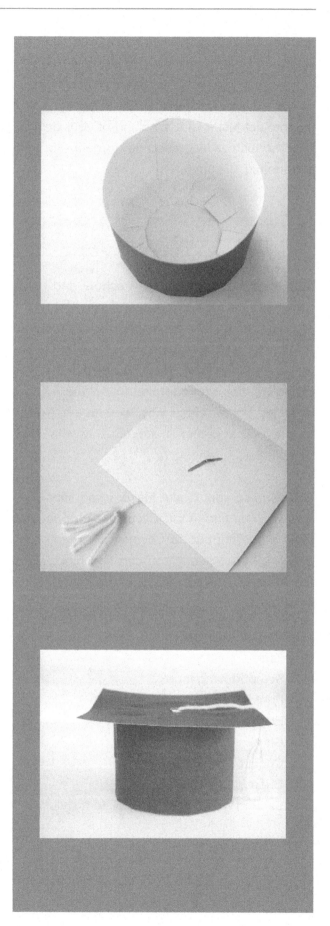

9. Christmas Decorations Inspired by Rae Dunn's Designs

There are so many decorations and designs that are inspired by Rae Dunn – that's why we have decided to include a few in this book! They're extremely popular and are quite creative as well. In this case, you can find a few Rae Dunn designs online or you may use designs by Pearl Simmons for other projects as these are also quite good. However, since this particular project focuses on Rae Dunn, you can google the Pearl Simmons designs later if you are interested! If you want to figure out how to make DIY decorations inspired by Rae Dunn's designs, read on!

Supplies

- Cricut Maker (or buy decals from any nearby shop)
- Transparent plastic decorations (purchased from the dollar store)
- Light craft paints
- Ribbons

Instructions

1. Place some white paint inside the plastic decorations and allow it to spread evenly, so that it coats the insides. Do not put too much paint as it otherwise might not dry, or it will take far too long.
2. Tweak the top part of the decoration.
3. Develop and cut out your photos using your Cricut or bypass this stage if need be.
4. Weed any leftover vinyl and stick the contact sheet to it. Then, transfer the pictures to the decorations.
5. Attach the ribbon and hang it!

Conclusion

Cricut is an advanced cutting device that offers users a simple way to cut out prototypes they like. As the most durable of the Cricut models that have been released into the market, we would highly encourage you to purchase a Cricut Maker if you do not have any of these devices. If you cannot afford to get a new one, perhaps consider buying one that is second-hand, as long as you're sure that it's not damaged and is in excellent condition, of course!

This book is a great reference guide for those with little experience and knowledge of the Cricut world. Beginners can learn a lot about how to use Cricut machines, the differences between the models, and how to undertake different types of projects. Most of the book is dedicated to explaining easy projects to beginners. It further contains multiple creative designs that you can work on for different occasions, including event decorations, holiday gifts, home decorations, and hand-made designs.

What makes Cricut machines so great is that the number of projects that can be realized is endless. There are also hundreds of materials that can be used, so you don't even need to get bored as you can just keep working with new materials! As such, we encourage you to continue experimenting with different materials and crafts for as long as you like.

Cricut Maker and the other Cricut models that exist also offer users many different opportunities for artists as well as professional growth. Through your Cricut machine, you can harness your artistic skills by trying projects that challenge you as well as developing your own designs. Moreover, if you enjoy creating very specific projects and are rather good at it, you can also market your skills to potential clients online. Of course, this ultimately depends on your motivation level and hard work as you cannot succeed in this kind of endeavor without a lot of determination. It could take a while to build up a client base, and once you have one, it would be better to avoid slacking off as this could negatively affect your business.

However, if you are not interested in working full-time in arts and crafts, then it can also just be temporary work to earn some pocket money. Either way, we expect you will have a lot of fun trying out different things with your machine. The point is that you should not limit yourself. Lastly, above all else, you should make sure you are having fun while you are making projects and try to make the most out of your experience!

3.

CRICUT PROJECT IDEAS

---

25 DIY Projects for Cricut Maker & Explore Air 2 to
Inspire Your Creativity. Step-by-Step Instructions
+ Tips & Tricks for Beginners and Advanced Users.
2021 Edition

Philippa Smalley

INTRODUCTION

Many complicated designs can be created using a Cricut machine. Everything began with the invention of this device, which functions like a printer but is capable of being used in multiple ways in any field.

A Cricut is a cutting machine which helps you to make amazing crafts from a number of different materials. To create 3D templates, greeting cards, and pockets, you can also draw, emboss, and create folding lines, depending on the style that you would like to have.

The process is quite easy. You start by drawing a template on your tablet or phone and then send this to your Cricut machine, which can subsequently cut out a particular design. The most important distinction between a printer and Cricut is that the former can only print out images whereas the latter can make 3D objects as well as other designs. A Cricut additionally has a dial on it that you can use to identify how you want a certain object to be designed. However, what makes a Cricut unique is that it can also often be used a lot like a printer. By sticking a marker in it, you can instruct the machine on how it should draw a template on paper, which can be a dream come true for many artists! There are also several tools on Cricut machines that you can use in relation to your cartridge library. Just search for the type that you need and then print it out. The blade that is mounted in the Cricut machine is a sharp one that can cut material in an exact manner. The cut-outs are impeccable at each corner as each edge is cut out exactly, as can be seen on the screen.

The Cricut machine also offers you endless possibilities to design material and create one-of-a-kind objects. Being creative is not limited to artists and craftspeople. The role of this machine is such that, if you know how to operate it, you can use it to literally make whatever you want. Hence, do not be discouraged if you are not an artist. Embrace your own ingenuity and create whatever you want. Purchasing a Cricut is a particularly good option for people who love craftsmanship and need to cut several objects.

01 A BRIEF OVERVIEW OF CRICUT MACHINES

Cricut machines are well-known for their ability to cut various materials, such as fabric, vinyl, paper, and cardstock for craft projects. It is a cutting unit that is a great tool in the arsenal of many artisans. It can be used to create a variety of different items, including cards and home decor, whereby anyone may use it. However, you cannot print material with a Cricut. All the new machines they have, with the exception of the Cricut Cuttlebug, can draw and outline items such as signs and forms.

Whether you are undertaking crafting or need to cut material, you might find having such a machine at your disposal to be useful. If you are an avid crafter and enjoy designing and decorating material, you will surely love having a Cricut machine.

Although other items, such as embossers and heat presses, are included in the brand, the term Cricut has become associated with die-cutting machines. If you are curious about what kind of a device a Cricut is, the answer is that it is a die-cutting machine that can be used anywhere, especially in homes for painting purposes, artistic projects, and journal crafting. In other words, it is an intelligent cutting machine that is recognized as the ideal entry point to the world of crafting with precision. One can also cut fabric, thin wood, and leather more easily with Cricut machines. You may have received a Cricut over Christmas or for your birthday that is still sitting in its case. If you are an avid crafter who is looking to make an easy product or you have seen intriguing projects on the internet, you may have wondered how such complicated designs are being cut. If you have also heard of Cricut but wondered about what it is, then you're in the right place because this book discusses it all and teaches you more about the fun stuff that Cricuts can make!

The Cricut machine and some of its cartridges can be used to make beautiful signs and event decorations by cutting out shapes and letters. Cricut machines have now become even more sophisticated since the launch of the earliest Cricut model.

Physical cartridges are no longer available as everything is arranged digitally so that each font or design on the device can be used. Most Cricut machines operate through Bluetooth or Wi-Fi, meaning that they can connect to a user's iPhone, iPad, or tablet. These Cricut devices are quick to use, flexible, and limited only by your imagination.

The three original Cricut cutting machines are also available in the market.

1. How Do Cricut Machines Work?

You don't need to be tech-savvy to use a Cricut. In fact, you only need to know the basics of how computers operate. If you know how to use computers, this won't be too difficult. For example, you will need to open online websites and sign in to the Cricut Design Room to organize the material that needs to be cut. If you have a mobile and want to use the app on the computer, then you must also be acquainted with how the software can be downloaded. If you are worried that you would not be able to learn how to use Cricut software, don't be discouraged. If you put a little bit of time and effort into this endeavor, you will learn how to use it quite quickly.

You should get to know more about the operating mechanism of the machines you own and how certain functions produce different results. A Cricut machine functions kind of like a printer in that it cuts out material based on what is shown in the form of a picture on a screen, which you can send to your Cricut via Bluetooth or a USB cable that links to the machine. It also includes a little screen that operates the cutting blade rather similarly to the nozzle of an inkjet printer. Just like how the nozzle is instructed by the printer on where to place the ink, the unit's device informs the blade about exactly where to make the cuts.

It's the same way the Cricut cutting machine operates for writing, scoring, engraving, or embossing.

The template is delivered to the cutting unit and the pen mechanically moves to write or draw. In order to produce something, numerous other tools will be commanded to function in a certain way. One may wirelessly link a Cricut to any computer, generate or import designs to it, and upload these designs to be cut by the Cricut machine. Cricut uses a software named Design Space (that can be accessed by MACs, cell phones, and devices that use Windows), which can help you to import machine-cut designs. A small blade (or rotational cutter instrument) is installed within each Cricut. You can then attach the material you like to a broad, 12-inch-long cutting mat until you have a template that is ready to be cut in Design Space. This can then be sent wirelessly to the Cricut machine from your phone and subsequently loaded into the system. Cricut machines will begin cutting projects with the click of a button.

With time, you will also figure out that there is so much more to Cricut machines than cutting material. In fact, a Cricut Community exists where you can be given suggestions by other crafters and obtain access to free tutorials. In general, crafters love to exchange tips and talk about how to make use of their Cricut machines. In the world of Cricut, the term "cartridge" is distinct from the kind used in the world of printing; it also explains why many people believe that Cricut devices can print.

There are two types of cartridges: physical and digital. The physical ones can be inserted into the machine. However, the digital ones can be ordered either from the Cricut Design Space or downloaded from a website. Cricut cartridges simply refer to a collection of fonts, images, or graphics or that one can buy and use forever. They are usually based on a certain concept such as "popcorn" or "Disney party," which are two examples of the wide range of themes and template designs that exist. Digital cartridges are accessible to the software after they are activated, meaning that physical cartridges will no longer be required.

2 Cricut Design Space

Cricut Design Space is a very user-friendly and convenient platform as it is easy to switch on and open the Design Room. While there are other crafting machines that use software, they can be more difficult to use and may take users several years to master. As such, many users find that they can become familiar with this machine in just one hour. It is also possible to see many already-made ideas, tutorials, and projects when one opens.

Design Space. However, you should not be overwhelmed; just make sure to click the + sign where "New Project" is written as this will present you with a blank slate.

Cricut Design Space is a web-based program, meaning that it looks like an ordinary website with a typical layout. The best thing about this is that while you are online and can move between machines and tablets, you can install the program at any point. In addition, some computers or tablets have an app for them. Thus, if you are, for example, waiting in your car, you can design anything and pick up right where you left off if you had already started a new project. You can also link any gadget to it through Bluetooth if you have a Cricut Maker. The already-made projects are very useful to use as they have the program loaded with certain files, templates, and demonstrations. This means that the whole design shows up on the canvas with precise notes, pictures, and supplies when selecting a project. You may personalize some of the projects as well and the measurements and colors can be changed according to your preference.

3. All Cricut Machines

It is necessary to note that Cricut devices are not to be used exclusively for paper cutting. They are built to cut a broad range of materials in unique ways, including vinyl, cover stock paper, and wood. The devices can also sketch and write with pens, score material for simple, crisp folding, and also cut all kinds of other material.

The Cricut Explore devices are the most popular types with three options to pick from. Any of these three devices may cut the same products and each has various functions.

The models preceding Explore Air 2 were the Explore Air and Cricut Explore One. In fact, the Explore Air only has one tool holder whereas the Explore One has two holders and can be connected to via Bluetooth. Although Cricut no longer sells this model on its official website, it is possible to purchase them used. Explore Air also has the same potential as Cricut Explore Air 2 (in terms of cutting, drawing, scoring, printing, and then cutting), but it's also twice as fast.

Cricut Maker: This unit is better than the Explore Air 2 since it is ten times stronger. It is possible to deboss, cut, score, and do much more with the Cricut Maker.

Cricut Joy: This is the newest unit issued by Cricut. It's compact and is able to cut and draw a wide range of materials. Even without the mat, Cricut Joy can be used to draw vinyl, cut, and iron-on material.

Other machines are also available, which includes the Cricut Cuttlebug. It is also possible to buy them on Amazon or other websites. However, they do not comply with the Cricut Design Space as the Cricut Craft Room's software has been shut down. As such, we don't advise you to buy the really old models.

4. Advantages of Cricut machines

You can cut and write at the same time

You can write and cut material simultaneously using a Cricut Explore One, which saves you a lot of time in terms of making crafts. You may also create folding lines for special projects, such as cases, cards, and other 3D items, by using the scoring stylus.

It's great for everyone

For beginners as well as experienced crafters, a Cricut is the most efficient and practical kind of crafting machine you can purchase. It is compatible with over 12 scoring, cutting, composing, and many other pro-level impact devices. For first-time consumers, hobbyists, and DIYers, such machines are quite flexible and inexpensive. In fact, Cricut is the most popular machine that can be bought by crafters.

It has one-click cutting settings

This gadget can cut more than 100 different kinds of materials, so you can easily click on the right setting with the Smart Dial and cut the material of your choosing without needing to adjust the blades.

It's very easy to use

The instructions are simple, and through Circuit's website, you can access the design software needed to build and make your crafts for free. This implies that without needing to update apps on each computer you use, you can work on your tasks anytime and from wherever.

One can make use of old cartridges

If you have bought several older Cricut models and still have some cartridges left, you can always use them for your Cricut machine, while keeping in mind that these machines run perfectly fine without them.

5. Disadvantages of Using Cricut Machines

They are not compatible with Android mobiles

Unfortunately, there is no smartphone framework that is compatible with Android tablets or cellphones because these devices do not allow you to use the Design Space app.

Pricing

You can buy the Cricut Explore One for about $149. However, a used machine can be bought for much less by those wanting to test one out before making a significant investment. There are some other cons related to specific machines:

Missing Wi-Fi connection

You cannot connect to the Cricut Joy using Wi-Fi. In addition, for certain people, the absence of a power button can be irritating.

Noise

Cricut Explore Air is louder than other models and the knife blade must be arranged differently.

Dimensions

There is only a small space that can be used for cutting in the Cricut Maker model, which can be rather limiting for avid crafters.

6 Projects to Do with Cricut Machines

There are a lot of different projects you can make with your Cricut machine through its ability to cut, draw, engrave, or score material. Here are some suggestions that you can try out for yourself:

- Designing a shirt
- Building a wooden logo
- Putting together garlands and decorations for parties
- Cutting out delightful letters and shapes for scrapbooking
- Creating personalized, crafted cards for any special occasion
- Making coasters out of felt
- Creating a vinyl sticker for your car's windshield
- Designing decals for your walls
- Creating gift-giving boxes made of paper and adding tags to them
- Labelling water bottles
- Making greeting and Christmas cards
- Designing monogrammed pillows
- Making leather jewelry
- Putting together Christmas ornaments
- Customizing your Tumblr mug
- Creating stencils for painting
- Labelling things in the house

7 Cutting different materials with your Cricut

There are hundreds of products that can be cut with this awesome device, some of which are:

- Sticker paper
- Plan paper
- Parchment paper
- Faux leather
- Vinyl (glitter, iron-on, removable and permanent)
- All sorts of cardstock
- Paper (corrugated)
- Thin woods (which can only be cut by the Cricut Maker)
- Metallic paper
- Textiles, fabrics, and much more

There are three types of Cricut machines that are currently available on the market: Cricut Explore Air 2, Cricut Creator, and Cricut Joy (this one just came out). Choosing which computer to purchase depends on what sort of project you want to complete as all devices come with free Cricut Design Space tools.

Cricut Explore Air 2

Of all the models, this is the version that we would encourage you to consider buying as it's the most common Cricut machine and can cut most materials needed for a number of DIY projects, such as cardstock, vinyl, paper and chipboard. With this unit, you can cut over 100 materials and also use it for writing and scoring.

Cricut Maker

In addition to cutting heavier or more fragile items, like leather, thin woods, and fabrics, this unit does all that Cricut Explore Air 2 does. With this unit, you can cut over 300 materials and use around 12 instruments for cutting, writing, and scoring. If you want to try out more complex products, we recommend this model.

Cricut Joy

For quick, regular DIY ventures, the newer Cricut machine, Cricut Joy, is a more compact machine than the previous two. It can cut material that is up to 5.5-inches long, meaning that you can also buy material that is up to 20 feet long. It can cut over 50 kinds of materials and use two cutting and writing devices. If you want to pay less for a Cricut and make simple projects like vinyl posters, cards, and tiny iron-on designs, we would recommend this gadget.

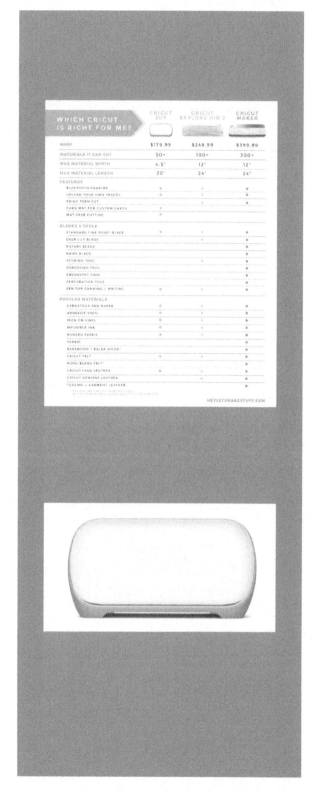

1. Cricut Joy

Cricut has unveiled its next cutting unit, Cricut Joy, on February 12, 2020. Cricut Joy, which is less than half the size of Cricut Explore, is a lightweight, tiny cutting unit. It is scaled down a little in comparison to other models in that it has a pen holder, a single blade, and is only able to cut material that is 4.5-inches long.

However, don't be deceived by its size as it has some new features, including mat-free cutting, which ensures that you can cut "smart vinyl" that is up to 20 feet long in a single go. Cricut Joy often has a card mat, making it very useful to create cards for all types of occasions.

For some crafters, the price of $179 may be a bit steep because of its limited abilities. However, Cricut Joy is great for making nearly all simple crafts with materials such as vinyl, stickers, and cardstock.

Cricut Joy's functions

This machine has a tiny blade, which is very impressive as it cuts materials from vinyl and paper while also using infusible ink to create countless projects on your phone or device using the basic Cricut Design Space application. You may also change the blade to write or sketch using a marker or pen. Either way, it's the fastest cutting machine we've ever used, whether you are making your own designs or selecting ready-made templates. Aside from a power cable, it does not even have any other cables or buttons that need to be switched on.

How to use Cricut Joy to make a DIY label
Active Time: 5 Minutes | Total Time: 5 Minutes | Difficulty: Easy

Supplies
- Tools
- Weeding tool
- Cricut Joy smart vinyl
- Transfer tape
- Cricut Joy

Instructions
- In the Design Space app on your device or phone, open a blank paper and then press the "Text" icon on the left-hand bar to add a text box.

- Write the text you want in the box. Once you have written down what you want, you may modify the font. For most of our work, we used Cricut Sans as this font is easy to read. You may also modify the size of the font or make the box's corners larger or smaller.
- Click on the "Make It" button
- When the screen prompts you, you only need to put it under the lines on either side of the box to load your vinyl into the unit. As such, all you need to do is let the machine do its job once you have built the sticker and inserted the vinyl. You can see how you can complete cutting and setting up the label based on the pictures shown below.
- In the Design Space, the "go" button is visible in the right-hand corner at the bottom of the screen once the vinyl is loaded. Press it and let the machine do its magic. The computer can unload itself when the process is over, and you don't need to do anything specific here.
- Remove the latest sticker off the cylinder of the vinyl with scissors. Then, beginning from the corner, strip away the extra vinyl so that you can see your sentences.
- To extract any leftover vinyl, use the Cricut weeding method.
- Cut a slightly bigger portion of the transfer tape than the phrase as you should use it to ensure that the sticker covers all of your bottle.
- Peel off and discard the remaining transfer tape, leaving the translucent grid sticky. Make sure that the letters stick to the tape and then place the tape on the word or label, gently rubbing it.
- Pick up the tape, which should show the letters, without taking off the backing (the white part).
- Press the new sticker to the bottle, push gently on the letters, and then peel back the transfer tape so that only the letters are stuck to the container.

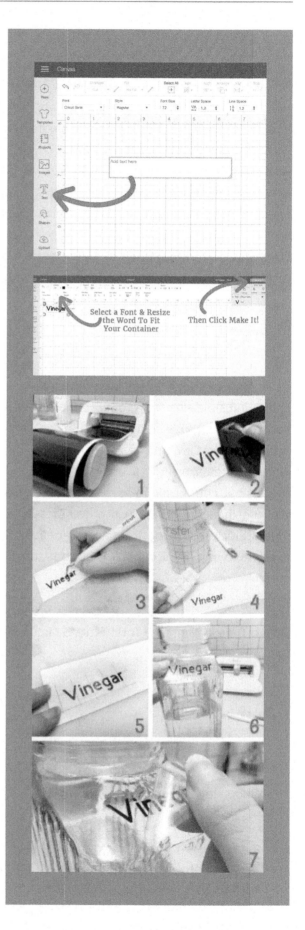

Can Cricut Explore Air 2 or the Cricut Maker's components be used with Cricut Joy?

The latest smart vinyl, which can be used without a mat, is the vinyl roll seen in the images shown. You will absolutely LOVE all the latest colors that have been made. You may use standard vinyl as well; you will only need to position it on the included pad. You can also use it on the smart iron without a pad, much like smart vinyl, or use the current stash along with the pad. You should also be mindful of the fact that the Cricut Maker's multiple blades and pens will not fit into the Cricut Joy's storage container. Cricut Joy is also incapable of cutting fabrics such as leather and timber to emboss the metal.

2. Cricut Maker

Cricut Maker is an excellent crafting machine that is similar to the Explore models to an extent, with the difference being that the former has been re-designed. It does everything that Cricut Explore does but is even more efficient. Cricut Maker cuts unbounded cloth (so you don't need a stabilizer, which you would need with the Cricut Explore line). It also cuts material quite evenly, including felt. You can also cut and design thicker items such as balsa wood and thick leather, which can be sliced by the knife blade. Using the scoring wheel is also great for all kinds of materials as it is a better tool than the scoring stylus.

The adaptive toolset of Cricut Maker has been designed with expansion in mind, suggesting that it was built to handle material or use resources that Cricut has not even released yet. It also has a dozen external testing equipment as this tool can do so much more when new instruments are released. This is the most expensive kind of model as it costs $399 on average, although it
can also be sold for $349. However, this device is ideal for you if you're a working professional who uses a lot of fabrics, an ardent paper crafter, a woodworker, or someone who just loves to sew.

Cricut Design Space and Cricut Access

Design Space is a software design kit and digital resource library that is compatible with various devices, including the Windows program that is used by many laptops. However, you can also purchase a subscription to Cricut Access, which enables you to access additional pre-designed projects, although you can also use one without the other. You may also upload a range of files and file types, including JPEG and SVG files and fonts as Design Space transforms them to either SVG "cut" images or "print and cut pictures."

Things to know before using your first Cricut Maker

You need a crafting workspace

The Cricut Maker is a large machine and to make use of it, you'll need a decent workspace. This is the perfect time for you to select a place you never knew how to decorate, such as a guest bedroom, a cozy closet, or a specific corner of your dining room, to turn into a workspace. Either way, all of your crafting equipment should be stored in one place to enable easy access.

Are you excited about the prospect of setting up your workspace? Here's a list of essentials you need to do so:

- A counter, a bench or a work surface, and a cozy chair (preferably one with wheels).
- A computer or laptop: It doesn't have to be very big, but it also shouldn't be too thin, so make sure not to store it on a ledge that's very high or low. A great place to keep it safe is on a rolling cart within your reach.
- Strong lighting: This is extremely important as you will need a good pair of glasses and a bright light after completing the tutorials and learning about weeding. The ceiling light is not going to be useful, so try installing LED lights in the workspace.
- Containers for Transportation. You may have wanted to start by getting a parcel or working on projects on an individual basis, thereby only purchasing materials as you go along. However, no matter what route you pursue, you will likely need a lot of extra storage space. To differentiate between your materials and equipment, buy some transparent containers and make sure to make labels with the newest Cricut Maker to mark the boxes so that you know their contents.

Try using disposable vinyl to get comfortable with the material

Someone who has never worked with vinyl will need a little longer to get acquainted with it completely. It's quite common to mess up the material, misplace your

cut-outs, and tear it. As such, if you want to begin getting comfortable with this particular material, you should start with disposable vinyl.

Be selective when you are first purchasing Cricut accessories and material

Cricut has several useful gadgets that come with the Cricut Maker, which can make creations much smoother and simpler while helping them appear more professional.

The BrightPad is the most well-liked add-on instrument, which is a rectangle-shaped lit box that people use for tracing. Using this tool can also make weeding a much easier task.

We also strongly recommend buying a "Necessary Package," self-healing cutting mat, and handheld trimmer.

You can re-organize and label everything in your kitchen

Do you recall all the cute container labels you've been eyeing since 2013? Now, you can learn to make some and personalize them as much as you want.

Let the Cricut party begin! You can print labels for transparent pantry jars and fridge drawers, whereby such labels are some of the best and easiest beginner projects you can make. The below image is an example of what you can do if you follow an online tutorial and decide to label everything in your closet or kitchen.

It can be useful to get additional cutting mats

Although you don't need these right away, after a few months when you have become acquainted with the device, you will need to purchase a few extra mats. This is because you will need to design material on specific mats with different colors and textures when you proceed to make intermediate designs. In fact, these mats will ultimately help you save time so that you don't need to restart the printing process once you strip the vinyl off the cutting pad so that you can use it during

some other time. We propose that you buy three to four normal mats and, at the very least, two strong and weak grip mats.

It is easy to get addicted to weeding
Since weeding is so soothing, you will need to get more weeding designs. Although it's an activity that requires practice, it's a great way to relax because it's like a game.

There are three production space fonts that you can use:

- Castellar, for a look that is classic
- Cheerful Shapes, which look appealing
- Rennie Mackintosh ITC Light, which gives you a new feeling

You can also make use of a Cricut BrightPad when weeding, which will make it much more enjoyable.

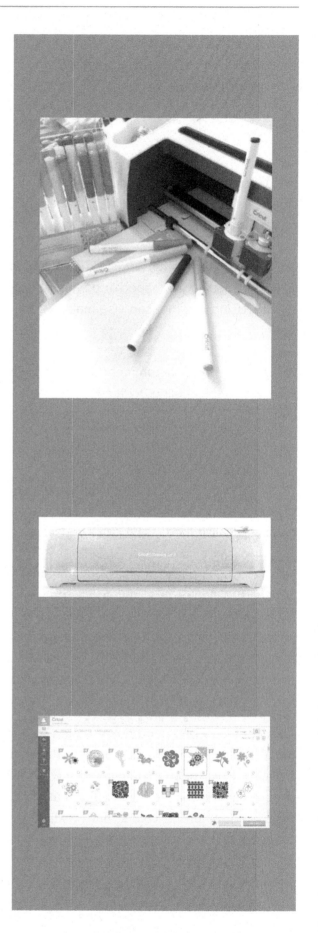

3. Cricut Explore Air 2

This is the Cricut Explore Air 2. At $299, we realize it may be out of certain users' price range. Fortunately, it's often on sale for as little as $179. It can cut plastic, iron-on, cardstock, fake leather or suede, Cricut felt, and over 100 other items and materials, which makes it an awesome device. While it can't cut some tougher fabrics that the Cricut Maker can, it's still a great machine for most crafters. Plus, it comes in a lot of colors.

It is the best option for most consumers because it cuts common materials, such as iron, vinyl, and cardstock.

Guide to work with Cricut Explore Air 2

Let's presume that you want to cut out some flowers to apply to a postcard that you are creating. First, click the "Insert Images" button on the left side. Now, type "flowers" in the search bar and browse through the photos. Then, select the one you like and press the green "Insert Images" button.

You may adjust the scale by moving the cursor to the bottom-right corner of the picture and selecting the flower you want to add to your template. Alternatively, you can press the "Edit" button and select your preferred size. The layer of the template may also be chosen and the color needs to be adjusted. Thus, while cutting, it is useful to keep in mind which vinyl or color paper to transfer on the cutting pad as any coordinating colors would be cut with the same content in your template.

Note: This is often an imaginative way to print and then cut your patterns. You can effectively select the pattern to be printed on your chosen paper and then cut it after choosing the colors and subsequently pressing the "Flatten" button in the layers tab. This enables you to modify elements to better fit your project.

Once you have the form you want, press the "Go" button. You should modify the desired number of project copies if you wish to cut more than one flower.

Then, repeat the process.

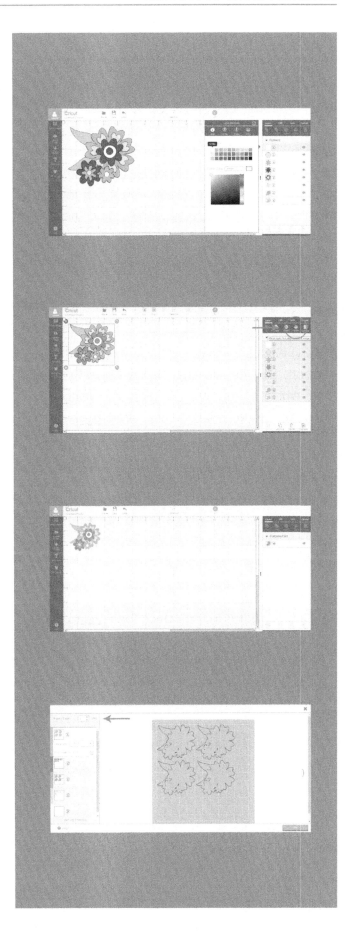

4. Cricut Explore Air

This device is no longer in stock but was previously sold by Cricut. Cricut Explore Air is not as useful as Explore Air 2, although it does have the two features that the Cricut Explore One has. It is possible to connect to it via Bluetooth because you don't have to link it to your laptop. In addition, it also has a secondary machine tool holder, meaning that it is possible to write and cut at the same time.

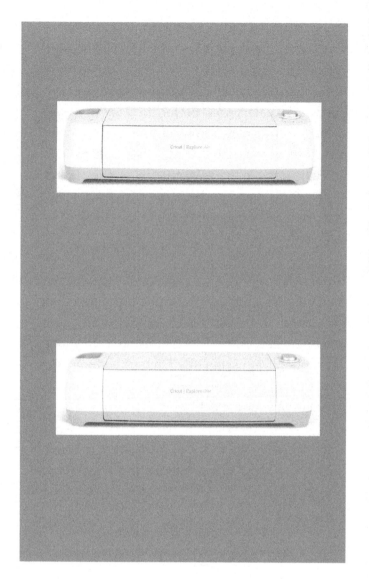

5. Cricut Explore One

The simplest and most economical device that is currently provided by Cricut is the Cricut Explore One, which offers all the Explore Air machine's detailed cutting, printing, and scoring abilities. You can also cut over 100 materials with this device. It does not offer the option of connecting to it through Bluetooth, which means that you need to link it to your desktop computer with a cable. It also doesn't have a double cartridge, meaning that you can't compose and cut (or rate and cut) with it.

Features

- It is a great starter machine for a cheap price
- It can cut or write on over 100 materials
- It has a fine-point blade which can be used to craft a broad range of products
- It can use a deep-point blade, scoring stylus, and other tools
- It offers apps for iOS, Android, Windows®, Mac®, and Design Space®
- It enables you to upload photos and fonts for free
- It is compatible with Cricut cartridges

The best 28 Cricut and concept room hacks that any beginner should recognize can help you stay organized and aid you in the Design Room. Having a Cricut machine is exciting and may even be a little daunting for a novice. However, whether you are a novice or a more experienced Cricut crafter, the following shortcuts and tips can help you stay organized.

• Differentiate between every mat and its uses

Many people have no idea that they can use mats for Cricut machines. There are many unique mats, each with its own characteristics. Prior to loading the materials into a Cricut machine, any content that needs to be cut should be placed on a mat. Then, the machine can cut the material based on your specifications. Although every mat has a sticky surface that allows the material to stay in a certain position, the type of mat you use ultimately depends on the kind of material you are cutting.

• Sharpen the blade against tin foil

By sharpening your blade with aluminum foil, you will prolong its life, potentially making it last three times longer. Remove it from the clamp to sharpen the blade and move the edge of the blade 10 to 12 times through the tin foil.

• Peel the mat from the material

Peeling the material (i.e., cardstock and plastic) away from the mat may be instinctual. However, it is usually easier to softly curl and peel the mat away from the object, which helps keep your product intact.

• Use a special plastic bag for the storage of vinyl

Using IKEA plastic bags to store vinyl is one of the smartest Cricut hacks that has become well-known over the previous few years.

• Begin making the projects included in the Cricut model you bought

You should complete the activities that are suggested in your kit as a way to practice, regardless of whether you are using the Cricut Maker or Easy Press. Before starting with lengthy projects, try using what is already present in the box and you will be satisfied.

• Use a lint roller to remove small scraps or glitter from your design or mat

You should be able to remove any tiny bits of leftover material using a lint roller, which is easy if you have a complicated pattern that is cut out on paper or vinyl. This trick also works well in your workspace by helping you collect any glitter powder.

• Learn to utilize a pen adapter to have more options than the Cricut pens

It's a really great thing that Cricut machines can cut and design material. However, you may possibly wish to use pens that were not released by the Cricut company. The great thing is that you can buy pen adapters if you possess an Explore Air 2 or a new version that can allow you to use virtually every pen brand, including sharpies.

• Use an empty nail polish bottle to store vinyl pieces

This is one of our favorite Cricut hacks, where tiny vinyl bits gathered while weeding can be stored in an inexpensive nail polish container.

• Convert a JPEG image to an SVG file with one click

If you're not able to create your own SVG files yet, consider converting one of your pictures so that it becomes an SVG file. This section will guide you through this process.

• To store all your Cricut supplies, utilize a pegboard

To keep your supplies sorted, pegboards are extremely useful. You should also have some empty wall space to put your pegboard on. You can order one through Amazon or pick one up from IKEA, which will make your art space much more organized.

• Store the blades in the Cricut

In case you were wondering whether you should remove or keep the blades in your Cricut machine, we would like to reassure you that they can be stored inside it so that they don't get dusty.

• Clean the mats with soft wipes

By wiping dirt away with baby wipes, you can breathe some new life into your used Cricut mats. Upon spraying a few coats of simple tack on the board, you can make your mat sticky again for 5 to 10 additional uses.

• Store the vinyl scraps in the magazine holder

Don't waste all your small vinyl scraps as they can be used in different ways. In the meantime, you can place them in a magazine holder to use again later. To quickly see what you must deal with, store the scraps in a plain magazine tray.

• Use a rubber band to keep the vinyl rolled up

You might have a lot of vinyl but are unsure of how to store it securely. In such cases, you can purchase and use rubber bands, which is a simple way to keep your vinyl rolls in the same place.

• Try to make SVG cut-out files in Inkscape for free

Wanting free templates and buying Cricut Access are great ways to get Design Room SVG data. However, how does this help you with your project? After all, you will need to envision your creation before making it with your machine. This is where Inkscape comes in, which is an open-source, free software downloaded from scratch to transform images to layered SVG formats in order to build SVG files.

• Keep your vinyl organized in wooden bins based on their types

It is necessary to keep track of the different vinyl styles you have, including adhesive, iron-on and textured types. As such, using bins can be a good way to store your material and enable you to identify it by form and name more quickly.

• To avoid uneven edges, use a straight edge to split vinyl

Vinyl can easily get wasted if you are not careful. Before use, trim your vinyl with a straight edge to remove excess material.

• Finding great SVG freebies

In blogs and through customary internet searches, you can find free SVG files for Design Space. For example, there is a huge vault at Abbi Kirsten Collections with just over 150 free SVG and printable models.

• When cutting thicker materials, utilize painter's tape

To prevent your material from sliding on the mat, use painter's tape as it is especially useful for chipboard and wooden projects and products.

• Use (HTV) iron-on vinyl on wood

On wood, you can use iron-on vinyl. To help you with this, Cricut also has a heating guide that is available. In fact, the heating transfer vinyl design can be even more useful than other adhesive vinyl, which is why it is a great alternative.

• Make slits in the transfer tape when pasting vinyl to the curved surfaces

How can vinyl be smoothly applied to a curved surface? This is a question that people have frequently asked. One technique, apart from practice, is to make slits on the sides around the transfer tape, which helps the tape to be removed when the pattern is being applied.

• Use cheat sheets

It can be hard to remember all Cricut terminology and how to use Design Space. Therefore, we recommend you use a cheat sheet glossary, which can be found and downloaded online.

• Utilize the storage carts for machines and materials

It's essential to store supplies and machines in specific containers. One of the best ways to do this is by using a moving cart for transportation.

• Make use of the printable setting guide

Similarly to the Design Room functions, it isn't easy to recall all custom or material settings. Therefore, we have written a free, helpful guide that comes with the Freebie Vault.

• On tumblers, use the iron-on vinyl with the Cricut EasyPress Mini

Cricut introduced a mini edition of the EasyPress in 2019, which is called the EasyPress Mini. It is a small gadget that is simple and convenient to use in that it also helps you put iron-on vinyl on your tumblers.

• To import designs to Design Space, use character maps

Installing fonts is one thing but practicing making a word appear is more complicated and requires a different talent. It can also take a while to learn to navigate those unique scroll letters using "character maps" or "glyphs" on your screen.

Go to the PC and "search" bar and then look for the character chart or character viewer.

To pick your font of choice, click the drop-down button.

Go through the fonts until the letter one that is needed is identified.

Click on and then copy it.

In the Design Room, paste the font template into the textbox.

• Search Cricut Design Space for freebies

Did you realize that Cricut shares a fresh package of freebies every single week that is accessible to everyone, including those without Cricut Access? You can find them by going to the "Photos" tab, clicking "Filter," and then selecting "Freebies."

• You should know where to find the best material

It may be time consuming and require a great deal of trial and error to figure out where to find the best priced Cricut products are sold. However, there are tons of blogs available that you can read to find some great products.

• Copy free fonts that are available on the web

If you haven't learned the power of downloading Cricut fonts for free yet, you sure are missing out.

• Too many types of vinyl are hard to locate

There are too many styles, textures and vinyl labels to remember where they are stored. Keep track of your vinyl scraps on a metal ring with the brand and style you have in order to easily locate your favorite type.

1. What's in the Cricut Packaging?

All you need to set up your machine comes with the Cricut device. In addition, you also get items such as sewing patterns, ready-to-make projects, and a free trial to Cricut Access. In addition, these are some of the other supplies that are included:

- All materials needed for one project

- Welcome manual
- Cricut Maker machine
- Premium fine-point blade and sheath (it is pre-installed in the B clamp).
- Rotary blade and drive housing
- 12 x 12-inch fabric-grip TM Mat
- Power adapter
- 12 x 12-inch light-grip TM Mat
- Fine-point pen
- Quick start guide
- USB cord

Please know that the quick swap tools, knife blade and all other accessories are sold separately.

2. Materials that Can Be Cut by the Cricut

What products can be used by Cricut machines? There are over 100 types of distinct materials that can be cut by these devices.

Many individuals believe that such machines can only cut paper or vinyl, although they can actually do much more than this. For example, the Cricut Explore machine can cut almost 100 unique materials and the current Cricut Maker has a rotary blade and a deeper knife blade that can cut much further than the average blade. For those who are just getting started, Cricut also includes a guide to the supplies and accessories that each Cricut novice requires, which are just useful to have and can be bought later if desired.

There are over 100 materials that can be cut and found from within the Cricut system. The Cricut Explore machine can cut almost any material, regardless of whether it is 2 mm thick or even thinner than that. Cricut Makers are particularly powerful machines and they can cut material that is approximately 2.4 millimeters thick.

Cardstock and paper

Cricut machines are perfect for cutting cardstock and paper although they do not only cut scrapbook paper. There are multiple types of paper that a Cricut machine will cut, including:
- Metallic poster boards
- Cardstock adhesive
- Boxes (such as for cereal)
- Cardstock
- Paper copies
- Flocked cardstock
- Construction paper
- Flocked paper

- Paper-embossed foil
- Freezer paper
- Flat cardboard
- Metallic cardstock
- Glitter paper
- Kraft board
- Glitter cardstock
- Kraft paper
- Metallic paper
- Parchment paper
- Foil poster board
- Paper board
- Pearl cardstock
- Paper grocery bags
- Pearl's paper
- Paper notebooks
- Pictures
- Shimmer paper
- Photo frame
- Rice's paper
- Wax paper
- Aquarell paper
- Paper scrapbook
- Solid core cardstock
- Poster boards
- White core cardstock

Vinyl

Vinyl is yet another excellent material that can be cut by Cricut machines. It is great for creating labels, stencils, decals, and graphics.

If you are interested in checking it out on the computer, these are some different types of vinyl that you can use with your Cricut:

- Metallic vinyl
- Adhesive vinyl
- Outdoor vinyl
- Printable vinyl
- Holographic vinyl
- Dry erase vinyl
- Vinyl chalkboard
- Matte vinyl

- Glossy vinyl
- Vinyl stencils
- Glitter vinyl

Iron-On

With your Cricut machine, which is also identified as heat transfer vinyl, iron-on vinyl is a great material to cut. In fact, you can customize tote bags, T-shirts, and other cloth products using vinyl iron.

- Neon iron-on
- Flocked iron-on
- Sparkle holographic iron-on
- Glitter iron-on
- Matte iron-on
- Printable iron-on
- Foil iron-on
- Glossy iron-on
- Metallic iron-on

Textiles and fabrics

A Cricut does a fine job of cutting materials. However, before cutting material, it's a good idea to apply a stabilizer like "Heat's Bond" or "Wonder Under." Such garments and fabrics can be cut with a Cricut Explore unit, although there are actually many more types of cloth that can be cut with the Cricut Maker's rotary blade, including:

- Faux leather
- Cotton
- Duck fabric
- Canvas
- Denim
- Felt
- Burlap
- Polyester
- Felt wool
- Faux suede
- Flannel
- Leather
- Silk
- Metallic leather
- Oiled cloth
- Printable Cloth
- Linen

Other materials

Besides paper, vinyl, and fabric, there are lots of different materials a Cricut may cut. These are a few other examples:

- Plastic sheets
- Foil adhesive
- Aluminum sheets
- Wood adhesive
- Balsa wood
- Aluminum foil
- Cork board
- Corrugated paper
- Foam craft
- Birch wood
- Duct tape
- Foil acetate
- Glitter foam
- Embossed foil
- Metallic vellum
- Printable paper stickers
- Plastic packaging
- Magnetic sheets
- Magnetic printable sheets
- Paint chips
- Stencil material
- Wood veneers
- Tissue paper
- Film wraps
- Vellum
- Wrapping paper
- Temporary tattoo paper
- Washi sheets
- Washi tape
- Cling film
- Soda cans

If you have a Cricut Maker, it can cut even more stuff as it has ten times the cutting power of Cricut Explore machines as well as a rotary blade and knife blade which helps more products to be cut. The Cricut Maker can cut material that is up to 2.4 mm thick as well as over 125 varieties of fabrics, including:

- Kashmir
- Chiffon
- Fleece

- Moleskin
- Jute
- Seersucker
- Knitted fabric
- Velvet
- Jersey
- Tweeds
- Terry Fabric
- Tulle
- Muslin

All the materials that can be cut by Cricut are mentioned here to make it easier for you to work with the material.

1. Fall Acorn Treat Box for Home Decor or Gifts

Have you ever held a bunch of scrapbook papers and gotten a giddy, bubbly feeling?

If you're in the mood to make a seasonal craft, you may enjoy making an acorn treat box. Read on to find out more!

Acorn treat box supply pieces

Although you might not have worked with scrapbook papers before, you may find that they are very fun to work with. If you want to try something new, feel free to dig through some of your old scrapbook paper supplies or those of your siblings. Don't worry if you cannot find or purchase all the papers that are mentioned below; it's enough to select a few fall-themed or colored papers that you like.

Supplies
- Orange chevron
- Tan chevron
- A 6 x 6-inch paper pad
- Polka dot paper
- Tan brown cardstock
- Fall sets including acorns (SVG)

On Hand
- Strong paper glue
- Cricut Maker
- Ribbon

Acorn treat boxes

Although this project may seem to be rather intimidating, it is actually much easier than you can imagine and the way to make it is quite straightforward. The most difficult thing to complete is to allow the glue to stick the curl on the sides so that the strain on the paper is lifted to an extent. You should be prepared to hold the fragments together for some time before they are stuck together.

You can fill your little acorns with gifts, use them as fall centerpieces, or fill them with sweets and share them at your workplace.

This particular project can be quite soothing, similarly to meditation, due to the calming colors and textures. If you spend a few minutes allowing your imagination to run wild, then your mind will be at ease. Feel free to make your own adjustments to the project so that it becomes more personal and unique.

2. Reusable Gingerbread House Centerpiece

This project utilizes white vinyl, Circuit's 2 mm craft chipboard, and a few red cardstocks. Although attempting to assemble the project is not very complicated, it may be slightly time consuming since several parts need to be cut out. In addition, the knife blade requires quite some time to shape each item, thereby requiring some patience.

Supplies
- 11 2mm-thick heavy craft chipboards
- Transfer tape
- Two white rolls of 12×48-inch Cricut vinyl
- Six sheets of vellum
- Blue painter's tape
- Red cardstock
- Gingerbread house side project file
- Gingerbread house front project file
- Christmas string lights

Other items
- Cricut 12×24-inch mat
- Cricut 12×12-inch mat
- Cricut fine-point blade
- Cricut knife blade for the Cricut Maker
- One sticky cutting mat
- At least one old cutting mat that is not sticky any longer.

Cut walls off of your gingerbread house

To cut off all the chipboard, you'll need the knife blade attachment. Make sure that both the front and sides of the gingerbread house are on the chipboards. The Cricut Design Room also has a limited number of shapes that can be cut be in one project file when building this house.

In addition, due to limitations caused by the size of the chipboards, it is necessary to cut the gingerbread house walls into tiny pieces and then piece them together to form a sturdy wall. You can change the project file size if you choose to make a smaller project.

Although regular mats can be used for the chipboard and cardstock, the 12 x 24-inch mats must be utilized for the vinyl.

After you finish cutting the chipboard, you should have:
- 11 squares containing two windows
- 1 tiny rectangle without cut-outs
- 2 rectangles comprising four windows
- 2 peaked roof pieces
- 4 large-scale rectangles
- 9 semi-circles of varying sizes
- 1 door

The front wall of the gingerbread house

The gingerbread house's front wall should have five squares, with two windows between each. One square with no windows or doors cut through it should also be made and placed near the bottom.

Although these walls will become very large once they are all glued together, you can place some shims along the seams.

Tape the seams together with any tape you have on hand while you have the front wall spread out on the table. While you position the shims over the seams and tape them together, make sure to create at least one vertical and one horizontal brace. The shims can also protect the walls and stand up correctly where the walls are assembled into the form of a house or box.

You'll want to put vellum over each window opening when the wall is flat. With these, you do not need to be precise as you can take a pair of scissors and trim the vellum to fit each frame's height, which can vary based on the size of the shim used for each window. Just make sure all the holes are fully sealed and then use transparent tape to hold down the vellum.

The back wall of the gingerbread house

There are six squares on the back wall with two windows or squares. Tape them together and add the shims for protection while adding the vellum to the windows.

Sidewalls of the gingerbread house

There are two parts to tape around. To support the four window openings and the roof, there needs to be a peaked top. The other one is going to become a rectangle with all four windows. The pointed section should be placed just above the rectangle. Then, tape them together again and add a shim that is horizontal. Add vellum to the windows.

The roof of the gingerbread house

The roof is comprised of four parts that you should tape together. However, you don't need to add shims as it's going to be okay on its own.

Gingerbread house steps

Glue together all the half circles based on a certain dimension by using a glue stick. When you are finished and they are all piled on top of one another, you will end up with what looks like steps.

Adding vinyl to your gingerbread house

Vinyl makes it easy to add gingerbread house style decorations. You need to turn them over after each of the walls is taped in order to place the vinyl on them once the other products are finished. This implies that you should place it on the table so that the untapped side pops up.

Vinyl on the windows

Moving the whole front of the gingerbread house at once is quite complicated and splitting it up into different sections can be the best way to add decorations. Use transfer tape to pick up the dots and add them to the chipboard around one pair of windows at a time. You can add a series of dots for every window in the building.

Vinyl on the front door

The front door of the gingerbread house should have vinyl decorations. To add it, you can just peel it from the carrier sheet and apply it on the frame.

To close the seams, add ricrac

The super-long ricrac vinyl bits can be placed horizontally around the house to shield the seams. You don't need a tape switch as you can just peel it and stick it on. In the gingerbread house, the shorter ricrac pieces go over the vertical seams. Do this for each of the walls. When you are finished building the house, you will have some very large bits of ricrac that go on.

Putting vinyl on the roof of the gingerbread house

You will need to use transfer tape to position the scalloped vinyl on the gingerbread house's roof. Before you put the vinyl on, make sure to fold the roof so that it is the same size as the piece of vinyl.

Assembling a reusable gingerbread house

In the order that they will be taped together, spread out your wall parts around the table: side wall 1, front wall, back wall, and sidewall 2. Then, tape each wall to the adjoining wall.

Pick up the walls, position them upright after all four parts are glued together along their edges, and then fold them so that the walls form a box. At this point, the house can stand on its own. Reach the last wall joint across the top of the package and tape it, as this must be on the inside of the box. After this final corner is taped, the house will stand on its own.

Use a hot glue gun (or a bit of glue) to attach the steps to the front of the house. Place some glue on the back of the door and push it across the front wall's steps.

Make your bows and place them between the front door and the windows

Fold the ends of the bow at the center and keep them there with glue. Then, wrap a tiny piece of red cardboard in the middle with a blue theme on the back.

Assemble the gingerbread house

Place the house where you plan to display it. Then, grab and drop a string of Christmas lights into the gingerbread box and switch off the light. We may choose to bring them in via the roof or through the back wall.

Fold the gingerbread house's roof and put it on top of the structure you have created. However, we left it unattached because we wanted to flatten the house and pull it out again next year.

Place a couple of the creative paper gingerbread houses in the space around it and then present your DIY reusable gingerbread house. This creates a lovely little village of gingerbread houses that flicker at night and is a particularly beautiful craft to make in preparation for Christmas.

3. Pineapple Vase Idea and Printable Tags for the New Cricut Scoring Wheel: A Back-to-School Teacher's Present

When the vacations are over, it's time for kids to go back to school. It's a common tradition to send your kids back to school every year with a gift for their teachers to start off their first day in an exciting way. This gift concept for teachers is cute and utilizes some awesome crafting materials to create it.

Teacher's gift and printable tags

We have created great gifts such as honeyed treats, dry erase markers, and highlighters in the past few years. A particularly lovely gift idea that teachers will surely enjoy is a pineapple vase alongside a few printable tags that are produced with your Cricut Maker and the latest scoring wheel, which is our favorite crafting product.

Paper pineapple vase concept with printable tags

The double and single scoring wheel is the newest adaptive tool added to the Cricut Maker model. What makes this project so easy to create is this little gadget. Making sharp lines and creases in DIY projects or with the initial (scoring) stylus with the Cricut Explore Air was far more complicated previously.

However, the Cricut scoring wheel's stylus can easily create folds along the designs, which makes it easier for one to make more creases in DIY projects.

Cricut Maker single scoring wheel

So, let's get started! Here's the guide on how to make a back-to-school pineapple vase with tags (printable):

Supplies
- Fine-point blade
- Cricut Maker
- Cricut mat
- Glue gun
- A delicate or small plant that looks like the leaves of a pineapple
- 12 x 14-inch Cricut cardstock
- Single scoring wheel
- Pineapple vase paper cut-out file

You can begin working with your Cricut cardstock and cut-out file. You can personalize it or if you are pleased with the dimensions, simply click "Make It." The vase we are making is around 7 inches tall and is ideally around the height of the plant. Design Space can inform you about precisely when this project's resources can be updated, and you can begin working with the single scoring wheel first as it is suitable for creating everyday items from thin paper as well as cardstock.

This will score all the lines, which require folding. Design Space can then tell you where the scoring wheel will meet the sharp-point cutter in order to cut out the design.

Cricut Maker

Use the Cricut Maker and the latest single scoring wheel to assemble the pineapple vase. You can also see how the two parts that the Cricut Maker scored and then cut were folded. All the directions for this fun task can be found here. It's really easy to make and fold all the sides!

How to make a paper pineapple vase with the Cricut Maker

The hot glue gun will glue the ends along with the paper vase created by the Cricut Maker. Then, you should start finishing the vase, and when you are done, it should be opened a little at the base. It would still be hot because it was glued to the bottom of the star section that was removed. Then, make sure to seal the final side of the pineapple vase together with hot glue.

You can use a little candle glass frame as the vase and place something slim but large enough to be put inside the vase that is made up of paper. You can then fill the paper pineapple vase with soil until it reaches the top and then you may proceed to insert your succulents.

Once the vase is complete, you can add a sweet tag to the succulent turned pineapple. You may open a file in a software program like Microsoft Publisher, Microsoft Word, or Photoshop after downloading the printable file. In order to make it better suit the vase, you can also choose to redesign the file. For the best output, make sure to print on photographic paper that is not shiny or white cardstock. Make sure to use hot glue to attach a wooden skewer to your tag and cut it so that it matches the plant.

4. How to Make 3D Paper Stars with the Cricut Maker

You might have thought of making flat paper projects as well as 3D ones. We want to show you how you can use the scoring tool to create 3D crafts with your Cricut Maker. We have some bright and attractive decorations in my craft room that we decided to use to liven up the area. This project was one we always wanted to try out!

Your Cricut is perfect for cutting; however, the addition of the scoring wheel is what we were the most enthusiastic about in relation to the Cricut Maker.

What is a scoring wheel?

The scoring wheel is part of the Cricut Maker's adaptive toolset that enables you to turn tools to score, cut fabric, create deep cuts, and so much more. The scoring wheel is perfect for getting sharp and smooth folds in order to add a score or fold lines.

What to make with the scoring wheel

- Boxes
- 3D structures
- Wall decor
- Cards
- Gift tags
- Jewelry

- Party decor

Supplies
- Cricut Maker
- Scoring wheel
- Embossed paper foil (deluxe)
- Space star file design

Design

Open Design Space to find the desired template. If you've never developed your designs before, it's very simple as we looked for a star form and then realized that we had to include scoring lines. You may add scoring lines by clicking on the shapes and then by choosing the desired scoring line through the toolbar on the left.

In the file, you can change the scale of the stars. Be sure to pick "detach" if you choose to alter only one star. Once you've finished resizing, pick and attach all the tabs, which will keep them on the same cutting mat by adding the stars together.

Scoring and cutting

We used a deluxe assortment of embossed paper foil for the first time due to the paper's consistency and patterns. With the deluxe file, we loaded the mat into the machine.

You may now want to obey directions in Design Space. Before inserting your pad, make sure to add certain items. You can now load your mat and press the flashing "C" button after you want to score side B. Do not unload the mat now until the Cricut is finished scoring. Then, you should swap the fine-point blade for the scoring wheel, at which point the form can be cut out by Cricut.

Weeding

To get the stars off the mat, scrape away the extra paper with the spatula tool.

Fold

If you look carefully at the stars, the indentations or "score lines" are noticeable. These lines help you find the spots where you can fold them. Then, proceed to fold the stars so that they become 3D objects.

It is so much fun to make these stars. Using the scoring wheel allows them to end up in this form; however, the foil paper's metallic feel and pattern make them look high-end and trendier. As such, they can be put up on your wall now.

There are a number of places where you can put these on the wall. We only used some low-temperature hot glue to hang them with some fishing line, which is another option that you have.

5. Succulent Paper Wreath

In the Design Room, open the "Succulent Paper Wreath" project. In addition to several leaves, all four of the succulent patterns are there. To make some changes, such as duplicating, resizing, and adjusting the color of the succulents for a number of the wreaths, press "customize" to go through the canvas. Press the green "Make It" button when you are done editing so that you can begin the cutting phase.

A variety of green papers made with Cricut

With several shades of green cardstock, you can create all the succulents. You can make a beautiful wreath by utilizing papers with varying patterns and shades of green. Place the document on a computer mat that is green or blue and insert it in the machine. Design Space will then guide you through the cutting process and once the project is complete, the mat will display which colors to remove. Each succulent is created a little differently, which requires a lot of steps to piece them together. We will guide you through each one to make it easier for you to alter and make unique designs.

Pattern 1

Perhaps the simplest one to make is this succulent pattern as there are five segments in the form of a star that are to be used, each in a different size.

To curl the sides and ends of each petal, use a pencil, some scissors or even your fingernails, similar to how you would curl a wrapping ribbon. These petals are easy to break, so be careful when curling them. It is convenient to hold the middle of the succulent in your opposite hand between your thumb and forefinger when curling the petals with your other hand in order to prevent the paper from tearing.

Stick the pieces together by placing a tiny dot of quick-drying glue between them, in the order of largest to smallest. Keep the succulent in the middle before the glue settles, then "fluff" the petals to make it look more like a flower. It's that simple, right?

Pattern 2

There are a couple more steps that you'll need to complete to create this succulent pattern, but it is still pretty basic. The succulent has 11 parts, each of which has three petals. Each size has two, apart from the smallest piece, which has three.

You should curl up the ends of the petals as you've done before. First, align each piece that is the same size as another and glue them together, offsetting the petals. Then, you should have one small piece leftover. Upon placing a small amount of instant glue in between each sheet, line the parts up again from the largest to smallest. Place the last small piece on top and press down on it until the glue dries. To make the succulent more voluminous, curl in and "fluff" the petals.

Pattern 3

This succulent is a little bit more difficult to complete. With a Y-shaped succulent petal, this succulent has seven separate parts that are different sizes. You will need to curl up all the petals' ends.

Begin with the piece in the middle with the circle and attach it to one of the straight-edged petals with a tiny quantity of glue. Then, line the piece up with the glued petal's upper top half. Keep the petals in place until the glue settles. Then, bend each of the petals downwards.

In the middle of the largest section, apply a drop of rapidly drying glue and place the layered piece of succulent on top. Wait until the adhesive is dry.

Then, place a tiny amount of quick-drying adhesive between each sheet, stack the remaining pieces on top, from the largest to smallest. Place the last small piece on top and hold it firmly until the glue sets the succulent in place. In order to improve the shape of the succulent, curl in and "fluff" the petals.

Pattern 4

This is not too complicated although it's the most time-consuming of the four patterns. It consists of 18 leaves and two segments with three petals.

First, you should curl up the segments with the three petals. Then glue them on top of each other while offsetting the petals.

Set this piece aside. Then, use scissors to cut a slit that is half to two-thirds of the way up the leaf's narrow side instead of curling the individual sections of the leaf.

Add a little dab of glue and the ends of the leaf will overlap. This will help the leaf feel more like a cupped petal. Repeat this step for all the leaves.

To create six sets, glue three of the same-sized parts together in the middle.
Then, pack the sets with the petals being offset from the largest to smallest, putting a little bit of glue between each layer. Place the last small piece on top and press down gently until the glue dries.

Rolled flower

We made a few basic flowers to go on the wreath as well. To make it pop, we recommend using a color that stands out next to the green. Everything looks amazing in pinks, purples, and yellows, so you can check out a few paper flower wreaths if you want some inspiration in this matter.

In the tip of the quilling tool, slide the ends of the flower piece and roll the paper up.

When you have come to the center or end of the flower design, gently extract the quilling tool's flower. Place a drop of quick-drying glue on the center and fold it over the rolled paper bottom. Hold it in place until the glue dries as it will otherwise unroll quickly.

Make a bunch of flowers to fill any empty spaces in your wreath and set them aside.

Glue the components of your wreath together
Gather all your flowers and paper succulents together. Glue each succulent onto the wreath with a glue gun.

Close-up paper succulent wreath
Glue additional leaves and flowers to cover any hollow spaces in the wreath. It is a great decoration for the late summer and autumn, with the best thing about it being that you don't have to worry about keeping it alive.

6. DIY Wooden Frame Clock

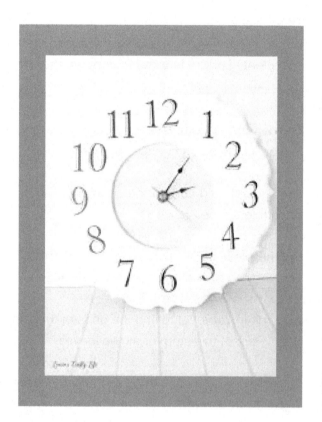

Rearranging your living room can be a really refreshing experience as it can increase the amount of space in the room and give you a chance to move around items that you are using. You can also set up a nice clock over your TV, if you don't already have one in your room. If you're not sure how to do this, read on!

Guide on how to make DIY wooden frame clock

We had a digital clock which you could see from the sofa because our living room furniture used to face the opposite way. However, after we reorganized the room, we could no longer see the clock easily. Instead, it would be easier to change its location so that it is above the TV on the wall so that it is more visible, which will also improve the room's decor.

Supplies
- Wooden frame
- White chalk paint
- Paint brush
- Paper scrapbook
- Craft knife
- Clock kit
- Number stickers

- Cricut Maker
- Vinyl

We had an incomplete decorative wooden frame to start with which was just laying around, so we decided to use it for this project. Paint the frame with any paint you like or stain it. In our case, we used some white chalk paint.

Wooden panel painting

We installed the clock mechanism as the case dried out. By marking a line from one corner to another, we used the strong chipboard that came with the frame and found the middle. Using a craft knife, carve an X into the chipboard. Then, move the clock up across the back of the material.

Find a chipboard and insert the center

To build a square for the assembly to fit into, use your craft knife to remove any excess chipboard. To make space for the clock assembly, cut your scrapbook paper so that it matches the size of your chipboard. Then, add it and adhere to the following directions:

- Use a craft knife to cut an X
- Cut a few squares to assemble the clock
- Using the directions given, assemble the clock pieces
- Insert the image frames into the installed clock

We didn't want an entirely blank clock, so we wanted to use our Cricut machine to cut out some vinyl numbers in the Imprint MT Shadow font.

- Use Cricut Explore Air 2 to cut out the clock numbers
- Use transfer tape to place the vinyl numbers on the clock
- Prepare the wooden cover with the numbers for the clock
- Connect the back of the wooden frame to the rest of the clock

Due to the complicated font that was selected, we cut out each word, weeded the vinyl, and then used transfer tape to add the numbers. We just roughly estimated where to put each number, although it was a little simpler since there are 12 points on the frame. We inserted the chipboard in the clock assembly and added that to the framework until all the numbers were on the frame.

In relation to our current living room setup, this DIY wooden frame clock is great as it matches a lot of our wooden furniture. You can also easily add a stenciled pattern, modified podge paper, or fabric to your picture so that it better matches your decorations.

7. Personalized Vinyl Balloons

Supplies
- Balloons
- Vinyl
- Cricut Maker
- Weeder tool
- Tape
- Scraper

Develop your template in the Design Room

You can use the "Baby Johnson" font, which is quite simple and pleasing to the eye. We added and resized the two lines of text to fit the balloon without needing the text to wrap around its circumference.

Cut the vinyl and weed any unwanted material

You can then use the duct tape on top and remove the remaining transfer tape and backing. If you are worried about adding a wider template to the balloon and fitting the bent side, split the design into several parts.

Remove the support and align the balloon with the pattern

Push down on the pattern gently so that it sticks to the balloon. Then, slowly remove the transfer tape from the balloon and your template.

Repeat this for each balloon you want to make

You can customize four balloons in the baby shower. The other three were easy to finish until we successfully completed making the first good balloon.

The last thing we did was replace the standard ribbon with the leaf ribbon that we cherished, which made the balloons look a little fancier.

Lessons learned
- Trim the transfer tape near your layout as using an unnecessary amount of transfer tape means that it will bind itself to your balloon and need to be removed, which can also pop the latter.
- Use a Cricut brand of transfer tape as other types of transfer tape can be too sticky and may cause the balloon to burst. Make sure to also use this type for the other four balloons so as not to face any problems.
- Slowly and carefully remove the transfer tape to make sure the balloon will not pop. It's important to take it slow so that it doesn't burst unexpectedly.
- Apply vinyl to the balloons shortly before the party begins as latex balloons deflate over time. Otherwise, you will need to make some last-minute adjustments if you apply the vinyl too soon.

- If you follow these instructions, the balloons are sure to come out perfectly and the vinyl lettering will look very professional. As such, they are sure to help create a nice atmosphere for your party.

8. Cricut Key Ring

This key ring design project is very fast and simple to complete. The Cricut Maker makes it particularly easy to cut and it saves lots of time by drawing the seam on it. Cricut Design Space has many amazing patterns that you can use instead of individually purchasing a template and cutting out all the parts as the pieces will all be cut and numbered for you.

www.sewwhatalicia.com

Supplies

- Pattern
- Webbing
- Key hardware ring
- Cricut Maker
- Pink fabric mat
- Fabric marker
- Fabric

Directions

- Place the right side of the fabric down so that the marker is on the opposite side of the fabric. Use some water to rub the marker away if you've already put it right side up, with the marker showing on the piece.
- To prevent it from staining and falling out of the keychain's side, place a tiny piece of tape around the sides of the webbing.
- To click the seams below, use your Simple Press. Cut a stripe of HeatnBond so that it is the very same size as the piece of fabric. Then, push the edges under it and place the webbing on top of the fabric.
- Consider using a colorful piece of yarn while you are stitching to provide some contrast.
- When you have put the webbing inside, use needle-nose pliers to close the ring.
- Try utilizing your favorite fabric to make them!

These are great presents for family members, teachers, and just about everyone!

9. How to Use Vinyl Lettering to Make a Wooden Sign

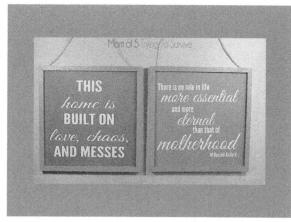

Folk-art multi-surface and outdoor acrylic paint can be used for this project. The indoor or outdoor house paint that you purchase from the nearest hardware store can also be utilized. If you tape it up very well, you can also use spray paint.

Using your Cricut Maker, you can cut out the designs you want. In this case, you can use Cricut permanent glossy vinyl, which can be cut very easily by this particular Cricut model.

Supplies

- Wooden sign
- Vinyl lettering
- Acrylic paint
- Sponge brush
- Painter's tape
- Paper plate (to paint)
- Sealant (optional)
- Permanent vinyl
- Weeding tool
- Transfer tape
- Scraper tool
- Paint for wooden sign

A wooden sign with vinyl lettering will require the above-mentioned supplies, including a Cricut Maker, vinyl, acrylic polish, a sponge brush, and a wooden label.

Painter's tape

Place the tape on the inside of the edges of the canvas to avoid painting over it. Painter's tape is particularly useful in this case and if you have a hanging string, you can also proceed to tape it to the back of the wooden sign.

Paint the panel

Place a bit of paint on a paper plate and paint your board's inner square with your sponge brush. Leave it to dry. You can use one coat of paint as this is usually enough. However, you can go ahead and paint a second layer if you think it will improve the overall look of the panel.

You should paint the redwood frame with acrylic paint and a sponge brush.

Remove painter's tape

Remove the painter's tape when the paint has dried and add more tape to cover it when painting the border. Remove the painter's tape from the edges of the wooden sign.

Then, place some painter's tape on the wooden sign to outline the area that should be painted.

Paint the frontier

Paint the border with your sponge brush. You can start with an inside layer and then make your way to the surfaces of the top and outside layers. We painted two coats because it was a lighter color, which prevented us from seeing the texture of the wood under the paint. Leave it to dry. Then, remove the tape and paint the rim of the wooden sign grey with a sponge brush. Then, cut and add the vinyl letters.

Download file

Using these quotes, download a free SVG file by filling out a form, and then import them into the program for the cutting unit.

Cut and resize the board

You can now resize it so that it suits your board. If you have a Cricut and want to use a 12 x 12-inch mat, note that your material can't be longer than 11.5 inches. Alter it until you get the size you want and cut the quotation from the vinyl using your Cricut Maker.

Remove excess vinyl using the weeding tool

In order to remove all scraps, use your weeding tool, which will constitute the insides and outsides of the letters. The only thing you'll have left is the quotation. Then, proceed to separate the quotation from the vinyl on your wooden sign.

Apply the transfer tape

On top of your quote, you need to add some transfer tape, which you should cut so that it frames your quote. Then, hold the transfer tape with both hands so that it forms a U-shape. Then, make the center of the vinyl lettering touch the lowest point of the U-shape.

Next, gently lower one of your hands to apply the transfer tape face down. Use your hands to even out the transfer tape from the center to the end and rub it gently.

Proceed to rub the scraper tool along the surface of the transfer tape before removing the vinyl that is attached to the tape so that the paper backing can be peeled.

Use a scraper tool to remove the transfer tape so that the vinyl letters stick to the latter.

Peel the paper off

The paper backing should be gently peeled off. If some sections do not stick to the transfer tape that is still hanging on the paper backrest, try the scraper method again.

Then, proceed to peel the paperback off of the vinyl quotation.

Apply the board quote

You should take a look at the board to see where you want to place the quote. In this case, you can also use a measuring tape to determine the exact dimensions of the board before applying the transfer tape accordingly. You can also use the scraper method to rub it all over the quote after placing it on the board and waiting for it to stick to the latter. You may use the scraper tool to gently massage the transfer tape and vinyl quote.

Peel off the transfer tape

Remove the tape at a 45-degree angle in a steady movement to refrain from removing part of the quotation as you will want it to stick to the board. If it is sticking to the quotation, place the transfer tape down immediately and rub it some more with the scraper tool if you have come across a piece that is falling off when you are peeling the transfer tape.

Seal the quote

Sealing the quote is an optional move. In case you will place the board inside, you may refrain from doing this, especially if you are using permanent vinyl. However, you can also seal the quotation with something like Mod Podge or a UV-resistant spray sealant if the board will be placed outside in an exposed area.

10. DIY Custom Manicured Gloves

These custom DIY gloves will be perfect to place in your friend's stockings over Christmas. You could even pick the patterned vinyl iron-on that better reflects the style of the person receiving the gift. It will make it look like they've just had a manicure any time they wear them. If you make several pairs of gloves, you can also wear the fingernail design that matches your mood.

They are gloves that look like you have stylish painted fingernails. As such, with fabric gloves and textured iron-on vinyl, you can create and establish a new fashion trend.

Making these custom gloves is easy and they are well-liked by a lot of crafters because you get to customize the "manicure." They will also be a great present for members of a sporting or dance team. As such, you can make several in bulk and gift several pairs to others. For the squad colors, you can also match the colors of the gloves with patterned iron-on vinyl.

You can use this concept to mend iron-on vinyl holes or you can also apply iron-on vinyl to sneakers to make "toenail shoes." There are truly a lot of fun creations you can make with your Cricut Maker, as long as you have the motivation!

Supplies
- Fabric gloves
- Cricut Maker
- Patterned iron-on vinyl
- EasyPress or iron
- 0.5 x 0.75-inch SVG ovals

Directions
- Cut out ten ovals from the textured iron-on vinyl with your machine.
- Weed the ovals and cut each one out.
- Place the ovals carefully on the tip of each glove's fingers.
- Follow the patterned iron-on vinyl guidelines to iron it onto the gloves.
- Once the textured iron-on vinyl cools off, remove the backing.
- The ironing may cause the gloves to shorten somewhat. However, they'll return to their original size once they are worn.
- Wrap them in some gift paper and give them to your friends, family, or teammates!

11. How to Make Iron-on Vinyl Napkins

Parents often send their kids to back-to-school parties as a treat.
In order to prepare for these, you can make a few iron-on vinyl napkins that will help set the mood! It's also a great opportunity for you to experiment with a few different materials.

Supplies
- Cricut Maker
- EasyPress Cricut or iron
- Iron-on vinyl Cricut
- Paper napkins
- "Hello School" in Design Space cut-out file

Make sure you have enough space to make your design while attempting to create the paper napkins. Be sure to add to the template what you intend to put on the napkin so that they turn out to be the right size and are not very ugly. Before committing to a concept, consider making a few on a trial-and-error basis.

Directions

- Start by opening Design Space and finding the cut-out file for "Hello School" or opening another file you want to add to the paper napkins. Make sure you measure the length and width of the area you intend to apply your iron-on to in order to enter its measurements into the Design Space.
- Remove your cut-out file similarly to how you would use your iron-on vinyl. Cut your paper using the Cricut Maker and weed the leftover vinyl.
- Get your preheated EasyPress. We did a little testing to see what temperature could be applied to a paper using the Cricut EasyPress printable temperature guide. Since these are napkins made of paper, heat them for 30 seconds at 280° F.
- Apply pressure to each napkin for 15 seconds in order to ensure that they are no longer damp and to heat them so that they stick to the iron-on vinyl.
- Place the iron-on vinyl on the napkin and hold it down for 30 seconds. Allow it to cool for about 15 seconds before removing the protective layer.
- Turn the napkin upside down and press on it for 30 seconds again. Now, you will have a personalized iron-on vinyl napkin to use for a picnic, meeting, or special event.

12. DIY Rustic Wooden Sign

This DIY rustic wooden sign is ideal to make if you have the materials lying around, especially because it's rather easy to customize.

Skill level

You will need to have some basic skills to make this sign. However, only three simple steps are needed to make this rustic sign. If you have it finished at your home renovation shop, you won't have to cut out the wood yourself or you can also choose a used sign as your foundation. The rest involves drawing a design and placing it on the sign.

Ski Salt Lake wooden sign

If you have some extra pieces of wood, you can make this by following a template and modifying it to make the board more attractive. In our case, the rustic DIY sign turned out wonderfully!

Customized wooden sign

There are three steps you can take to make this wooden sign, which are:
- Select a surface

- Stain the surface
- Pick and apply a graphic
- Seal it (optional)

Stage 1: Choose a surface to prep the rustic sign

- You will need to find the correct board(s) that will act as a surface before you get started on the process of making your wooden sign as you have a few choices.
- You can go to a home renovation store such as Home Depot and pick a fresh wooden base. They can also cut it for you or you can dig through their scraps to find the size that you want. It doesn't matter what kind of wood you pick, but a good option that is readily available is pine.
- You can also check out the discount store to see if there's anything you can purchase from there (maybe by sanding or painting over the top of a board).
- Ask if you can use scrap wood that is left behind or is unused at a building site, such as within a community in which new houses were constructed, where they often have lumber bins.
- You can also check online through websites like Freecycle or Craigslist, where people in your region may offer to give away piles of lumber for free.
- Once you have gotten your board, you can begin this project.

Ski Salt Lake DIY sign

Supplies

- The wooden board
- Material to stain wood or paint
- Cricut Explore or a Cricut Maker
- Vinyl

Stage 2: Staining/painting

- Try to find brown or black spray paint
- You may want to purchase paint to apply to the top if you are working with a stained wooden surface. Using blended black and brown paint that is mixed with water, you can stain your rustic sign.
- Before you begin, test the color on the back of your board to know whether you will like the look or if more water should be added. If you go to the home renovation shop, you may also buy paint in the color you want. However, make sure to pay special attention to the sale section. For a fraction of the cost, you can also buy wood that was returned at such stores.
- By wiping a rag across it, you can stain your wooden board.
- Rub it with a rag and then wipe it off with a clean rag until you have determined the color that you want. The way that you can stain the board depends on how dark you want the color to be. The longer you will keep it on, the darker it will be. However, if you're not sure how dark you want it to be, just clean it with a rag and wipe it off. Then, wait for it to dry and see if you like it. You can always add a few more layers if you think it is too light. If you have also acquired a used board, you will have two options:
- Sand the board to remove the finish so that you're left with a blank wooden surface.

- Paint with filler over the surface (like this one) and stain or paint over the surface afterward. You're not going to be able to see too much of the wooden grain so this might not be the best choice. However, if you don't want to be able to tell that the board is made of wood, you can follow this option.
- Wait for your rustic sign to completely dry.

Stage 3: Add a vinyl decal

Cut out the Ski Lake City quote. You'll want to pick and print the template based on your vinyl preference if you have a cutting machine. There are some lovely ski mountain designs. As such, you can cut these out or choose the terms and city names that you prefer when making your sign.

You may wonder what you should do if you do not have a cutting machine. Well, this problem can be easily solved by ordering a personalized vinyl decal on Etsy, where hundreds of stores are willing to print the template of your dreams for you in the exact size that you want.

Depending on what you are seeking, we also suggest that you find a template that suits your style and interests. For instance, if you want to have a style that uses images of mountains, search for a "mountain vinyl decal."

If you find a supplier, make sure to ask if the vendor is willing to customize your order so that you can have the size you want.

Another suggestion is that you can enter groups like "Cricut for Dummies" on Facebook, where you can ask whether any Cricut users in your vicinity would be willing to lend you a hand.

Adding a vinyl decal to a piece of wood

Use painter's tape to put the vinyl on the wood once you have your desired vinyl decal in your hands. You should then add a strip of painter's tape over the top of your letters and use it to lift the stickers so that when you set them on the surface, they will stay in the right place.

We suggest investing in some vinyl transfer tape to do this if you intend to create a few rustic signs. It is very easy to pick up designs and move them to a surface with some transfer tape. In addition, having lines will allow the positioning to be more accurate.

Stage 4: Sealing (optional)

Using a frame, build a rustic wooden sign, and then add a vinyl decal.

If you decide to utilize a transparent acrylic product like Miniwax or Polyacrylic, the rustic sign can be sealed. It's not going to adhere to the vinyl, so that's all right. The painted wood is the part that you should seal.

Although you may not need to seal the board, it is the perfect way to protect it from drying out if you live in a dry climate. You should also use a sealant if you want a shiny or satin finish.

Once your DIY wooden sign is done, allow it to dry for 24 hours until you hang or display it.

13. DIY Puzzle Piece Necklace

Make a tiny puzzle piece pendant as a gift for someone unique. This particular design can be used to make a set of accessories as long as you get in touch with your creative side.

Supplies
- Cricut Explore machine
- Cricut Design Space
- "Puzzle Piece Necklace Adventure" designed by Jen Goode
- 12 x 12-inch StandardGrip Cricut® tangle
- White cardstock
- Glue (i.e., Aleene's Clear Gel Tacky Glue)
- Glitter
- Necklace chain

Directions
- Print and cut out the puzzle pieces following the on-screen directions.
- Do this until you have 4 to 7 pieces. You can also select the thickness you want based on how it will look when worn around a person's neck.
- Remove the center of the puzzle pieces.
- Layer out the pieces and place some glue between each layer before pressing down to ensure that your layers will stick together. Wait for it to dry.
- Apply the glue to half of the puzzle piece and apply a bit of glitter to it.
- Seal the entire pendant with some Mod Podge or another sealant if you'd like.
- Thread it through an accessory chain.

14. Free Buffalo-Patterned Printable Plaid Banners

For your fall and winter decor, you can make a black-and-white buffalo plaid banner. This will look amazing with your Christmas decor – or you can alternatively use a red-and-black buffalo checkered banner.

To spruce up your holiday decor, download a free printable buffalo checkered pattern in two different colors. For your fall and winter decor, the black-and-white buffalo plaid banner will look fine. With your Christmas decor, the red-and-black buffalo checkered banner will look fantastic.

These are particularly easy to make. Once you are done with them, you can hang the banners wherever you like. For example, you can hang the black-and-white checkered banner over a wide chalkboard or even over the mantle of your fireplace. Some other good suggestions include placing the banners over the headboard or footboard of your room, window, mirror, or front door. The possibilities are endless!

You may also want to create a particularly long banner, which is completely fine. Just make sure to pick the free printable design that you want. Please note that the "Easy Rendered Beautiful" cut-out that is available on Design Space cannot be re-sold or distributed as this is illegal.

If you want to make an autumn-themed banner, you can easily find any supplies you are missing at the dollar store.

Two colors can be selected in the digital file:

- One black-and-white buffalo checkered banner
- One black-and-red buffalo checkered banner

Supplies

- Cricut Maker
- Free printable design
- Heavy white cardstock
- Scissors
- Twine or ribbon
- Hole puncher

Directions

- Gather your supplies.
- Print the banner based on the desired number of flags.
- Cut out every banner.
- Punch holes in the tops.
- String twine through the top of every flag.
- Hang and enjoy!

This banner and home decor is pretty easy to make as you can find any missing supplies at the nearest dollar store.

15. Halloween doormat

Supplies

- T-shirt
- Iron-on
- Tools
- Cricut Explore or Cricut Maker
- Weeding tool
- Cricut EasyPress
- EasyPress mat
- StandardGrip mat
- DIY football tee cut file

Directions

- Gather your supplies.
- Open the DIY football tee cut-out file in Design Space.
- Resize the image so that it is the correct size for your
- shirt.
- Mirror the image before cutting it.
- Cut the image out of the iron-on material.
- Remove all excess iron-on material from your image with the weeding tool.
- Preheat the EasyPress to the correct setting found in the Cricut Heat Guide.
- Press the image onto the shirt following the steps in the heat guide based on the type of iron-on material used and the fabric of your shirt.
- Flip the shirt over and press on it from the back.
- Follow the heat guide in relation to whether you should do a warm peel or cool peel and remove the carrier sheet at the correct time based on the fabric type.

Notes

Don't forget to mirror your image.

Follow the settings in the Cricut Heat Guide to obtain the best results.

How to make a "Welcome Halloween" doormat using a free SVG file:

Supplies

- Cricut Explore
- 12 x 24-inch Cricut mat
- SVG file (get it free or make and design your own)
- 12 x 24-inch cardstock
- Plain doormat
- Fabric paint
- Stencil brush
- Gloves
- Painter's tape

Guidelines

- You will need a basic doormat, stencil brushes (you can find a set of these at your local craft store), waterproof fabric paint, painter's tape (you can buy it at your local craft), and a stencil.
- Save the SVG file to the Cricut Design Space and upload it. Adjust the size of the picture according to the doormat size, which should be about 21.1 x 9.8 inches.
- Cut and weed the picture while removing any part of the image that you don't want. In this case, you can remove the letters that are inside. To make your stencil, you can use strong cardstock or stencils.
- Use painter's tape to protect the picture on the doormat. We had to position a few letters, such as "o," "r," and "a," rather carefully and placed a tiny piece of painter's tape behind each to protect the mat. When painting certain places, you will need to be very patient.

- To paint inside the picture, use paint and a stencil brush. Wear some gloves and pin the sides down using your hands. For any job you are doing at home, we recommend that you use gloves.
- To show the completed project, scrape off the vinyl stencil straight away. You don't want to leave the stencil on there for a very long time as the cardstock can stick to the mat. You should fill in any empty spot with a black sharpie or with some paint.
- Let it dry for 24 to 45 hours before putting it outdoors so that it doesn't get covered in rain. This is because fabric paint must be completely dry in order to become waterproof.

16. Make Vinyl Stencils

A nice project to make is vinyl stencils, although they can be difficult to craft. Nonetheless, making wide vinyl stencils is a great Cricut project and you can also use them in different locations, like children's bedrooms.

Supplies
- Cricut Explore Air 2
- Vinyl
- Sander pallet
- Brushes and paint

Directions
- The very first step you will need to do is to prepare the pallet for painting on whichever surface you want to use. You can instantly discover that in Design Space, large templates are difficult to cut and finish all at once.
- The best thing you can do in this case is prepare one section of each style and remove any middle parts. Then, the picture can be applied to the square shapes and cut into pieces on a suitable cutting pad.
- At this stage, once you push the "Make It" button, you cut out the pattern, select your equipment, and use the machine in different stages. You can place this on the surface you're utilizing and piece the different parts together with each line. Then, after piecing everything together, you will have created one picture.
- Then on the vinyl, trace the line and paint the initial design. You should easily draw the first one and then paint the inside of the second set of stencils. You must have the layout done at this stage. Remove it very carefully when you are finished.
- Then, you'll practically be done! Since it is a project, larger stencils can take a bit of time to complete since you will need to use multiple designs at once. However, you'll be able to build everything you need in Design Space as it will help you get the look that you want.

17. DIY Girls Bedroom Home Decor

Two years ago, we relocated from a two-bedroom apartment in the city to a four-bedroom suburban house. Naturally, our kids got their own bedrooms because there was enough space so that they wouldn't need to share one room anymore. We also wanted our daughter to choose the color of her room. At that point, she was only four years old – so you can imagine what color she wanted. About a year ago, she asked if she could paint her room purple again since it was her latest favorite color. Finally, we agreed to let her redesign the room, which ended up being quite pretty.

After our daughter relocated to a pink room with all-pink furniture, we didn't want to buy all the latest furniture in purple. Once we realized that she was still attracted to teal blue shades, we agreed to combine teal, pink, and purple styles together, which made her room pretty colorful.

Supplies
- Yarn
- Cricut Explore
- Purple curtains
- Cardstock
- Existing bedroom decor
- Paint

We agreed to paint her walls in three colors, which are "Valspar Pantone Sheer Lilac," "White SW Eider," and teal. We painted only one of her walls lilac because she wasn't really a fan of the color anymore. A simple way to test out a color is to paint a small corner of a wall and step back to see if it matches the furniture and other items in the room. If it looks nice, then you can proceed to paint the whole wall.

We colored the shelves white so that they matched the current bedroom furniture (as the walls were painted white originally). The racks belong to Ikea.

We also got her a few wall decorations hooks in a couple of colors. However, the color she ultimately preferred was teal, which we found in Ikea, and looked quite nice in general.

We painted a few different decoration pieces on the side tables and desk (including a pencil holder, vase, and wooden trays). We also got her some nice curtains that complemented her room decor.

We chose some photo frames from the dollar store and decorated them in purple, teal, and pink. We also painted her chair and the legs of her desk the same shade of purple as the wall. We found the chair on Craigslist (it was a bar stool swivel chair with shortened legs) and the curtain rods were purchased from

Target. In addition, we got the night light from Home Depot and the teal curtain links from Michaels. We also colored a purple stool blue, which can be seen in front of her dresser.

Cardstock

Decorations: We used the Cricut Explore device to cut many butterflies using pink, purple, and teal cardstock into various sizes. To bind it to the wall, we used double-sided tape. In order to apply a polka dot design to the walls, we used the Cricut Explore machine in order to cut out a few circles in pink, purple, and teal cardstock. To stick them to the walls, we used double-sided tape. In a color template, we grouped the dots together and then put them on the walls.

Thread used

We also used yarn we purchased from Michaels to produce many pink, purple, and teal pom-poms, which we added to the white-colored duvet. We had also bought the duvet cover and vintage pillowcase from Target.

How do you select the correct paint shades?

We all face some difficulties when trying to find the best colors to paint the house. It can be overwhelming to choose the correct shades of paint when trying to redecorate or do a home makeover, especially because there are so many "whites" and "greys."

Each house is unique as some houses' entrances look extremely different from those of others. It ultimately depends on how the house was designed as well as how much effort you put into making your property look attractive. It's really up to you to spruce up your place and put some extra effort to design it. If you are an artistic person or appreciate crafts (which is something we assume since you have purchased this book), we encourage you to go the extra mile to make your home stand out.

Paint vs. peel and stick wallpaper

Stick and peel wallpaper has recently become very common as not everybody wants to or owns the instruments needed to make Shiplap walls. If you are looking for peel and stick wallpaper, you can find it at Goal, Home Depot, Amazon, or online.

There are a variety of styles and colors that can be found and purchased. If you want to test them out before putting them up on your walls, you can also place them on your wardrobe, shelves, or bookcase to see if you like the design. If you are thinking of where it would be ideally placed in your house, we would recommend trying it out in your dining room or even in the kitchen as this can help you refrain from damaging your walls due to cooking stains.

As such, if you don't want to worry about cutting faux timber, shiplap, or tiling, using peel and stick wallpaper can be seen as a cheap option to give your house a new look. However, before doing this, we strongly suggest that you read about this and look for wallpaper designs that will match the decor of the room that you decide to put it in. Otherwise, you may choose a style or design that isn't very attractive, which is definitely something you want to avoid!

Inexpensive home hacks that can raise its value

If you have an unlimited budget and want to really invest in renovating your home, this will surely be more expensive. However, it can also be worth it if you have the means, largely because you will acquire your dream home in this way. Otherwise, if you ever decide to move because you have, for example, gotten a better job, you can sell your house for a higher price as the renovations should have increased its overall worth.

18. Free Printable Thanksgiving Tags

Thanksgiving is just a few weeks away and we are excited about taking a family trip to the countryside. If you want to use a little bit of color, like navy, pink, and purple, you can change up the typical Thanksgiving decor that is used in many homes. Using such banners can make this holiday season feel even more festive.

As part of your table decorations, you can create a few "Thankful" leaf tags to use, although you also have the option of using them in different ways. You can upload, print, and cut them out to use as place cards, unused labels for Thanksgiving dinner, or even as decorations.

Pink printable leaf tag

These bright leaf tags can be printed out on either white cardstock paper or printable vinyl. You can also print them out on navy or orange-colored cardstock. You will then need to cut them out with your Cricut machine.

How to use Thanksgiving leaf printable tags:

- You can import the PNG version of the file and then print and cut out the tags with your Cricut machine.
- Place the layout on the canvas, adjust the size so that it is about 6.75 x 9.25 inches, and then cut out the boundaries.
- Print the tags. In order to do so, follow the on-screen directions and then put it on your Cricut computer. The computer can do a "kiss cut" if you are using printable vinyl as the stickers can then peel off. You can cut through them if you decide to use cardstock.

Print peel and cut printable Thanksgiving tags

You can add the colored cardstock to the vinyl stickers.

Thankful printable stickers on cardstock

Proceed to trim the stickers using scissors.

On cardstock, cut out the printable thankful vinyl labels

Use a mini hole punch to finish them by inserting a hole in the string.

19. Iron Material on Shoes with the Cricut EasyPress Mini

By making another canvas called "sprinkle shoes," you can test out your EasyPress Mini and see if you can iron material onto your shoes and make them look fancy!

This involves using iron-on vinyl on a colorful backdrop and adding a spray pattern to white shoes.

Supplies
- White shoes
- EasyPress Mini
- Iron-On vinyl
- Cricut Explore or Cricut Maker
- StandardGrip green mat
- Cricut EasyPress mat

In Cricut Design Space, prepare the file that you want. Then, cut the strips you want to add to your shoes, selecting the different desired shades. You can use the traditional colors of pink, purple, and brown or any other color of your choosing. It's also up to you to determine the size of these strips.

Once you have created the design you want, select the "Make It" button in the upper-left corner.

Click the "Mirror" option for each layer that is shown. While this is not necessary with the colored strips, it can be nice to actually try to iron them on so that each shoe is a mirror image of the other.

Instead of selecting the "Everyday Iron-On" setting on the panel, make sure to pick the "Cardstock" option. This will help ensure that your project won't get weeded and it'll also make it easier to put your strips on your shoes. Utilizing this "cut through" method is particularly helpful for such applications so we would highly recommend it!

Cut the iron-on

On your cutting mat, put your iron-on face down, and cut the material you want using your Cricut Explore or Cricut Maker.

When you are cutting, apply some extra pressure and you can also place some glitter to the sheets if that is desired.

Set the EasyPress Mini setting to medium and wait for the temperature to increase. Place a balled-up sock in the shoe in order to be able to press the machine onto the shoe while preventing it from caving in. Keep pressing on it for 22 seconds or until the strip gets stuck to the shoe. Make sure that the machine only touches your shoes and not your hands as it will otherwise burn you. You should also refrain from doing anything to the shoes' rubber soles.

To attach the strips to the shoes, use the EasyPress Mini. When you've attached all the strips, cut all the carrier sheets and you'll be finished.

20. DIY Leather Earrings

When you want to make leather earrings, you will have plenty of choices. In fact, you can buy leather material and different types from your favorite art shop or online via Amazon.

There are a lot of different types, including some that are thicker or lighter than others. However, you can choose a few that are light or others that are stiff. In addition, several faux types of leather are light and look fantastic as earrings.

It's more about what you want your earrings to look like. If you have wondered whether you will need plenty of materials, rest assured as only a select few are required, such as leather or faux leather, ear wires, and jump rings.

Of course, you can also add cool charms to your diamond earrings to add a little extra flare or you can even use iron-on vinyl on the ends. You only need a few supplies to start with and you can then create many quirky and pretty earrings.

Supplies
- Faux leather fabric sheet
- Wire earring jewelry
- Jump rings for jewelry

- Pliers
- Cutting machine (preferably a Cricut Maker)
- Leather cut-out files

Directions

- If you want to make some earrings, we would recommend that they be 1.5 to 2 inches long or so as dangling earrings are typically more attractive and noticeable than smaller earrings.
- Place the leather in your cutting machine. You should normally use your fine-cutting blade when you are cutting faux leather. Make sure to use your deep-cutting blade to cut out the real leather or your knife blade if you have a Cricut Maker.
- Adjust the material settings to garment leather and tooling leather while using your knife blade, which should be clean and sharp or unused. Refrain from using a dull blade as this will not effectively cut your leather and it can also make uneven cuts, which may require you to use another strip of the material.
- Open one of the jump rings with the pliers and thread it into the earring's opening. Close the ring of the hoop and repeat this step with the second earring. Do this for a single jump ring if your pattern has two holes drilled at the ends. Then, proceed to fold the two holes and thread your jump ring through them.
- Use your pliers to loosen the wire loop and then attach the leather to the jump ring. Close the circle with your pliers and repeat this step with the second earring.

21. "Enjoy the Little Things" DIY Hanging Canvas

The expression "Enjoy the Little Things" is particularly appealing and resonates with many people. This is why it is considered to be a popular phrase and is often downloaded from the Cricut Design Space. Indeed, we often get caught up in our daily routines, which can prevent us from enjoying simple joys, such as a cool, refreshing glass of lemonade in the summer or the smell of fresh-cut grass.

When intending to decorate your house, you may opt for soft hues and earthy colors. However, you can also decide to try out some other colors, including raspberry, which will brighten up your summer decor and make your living room much more welcoming. If you are not sure if you want to put a colorful banner, such as the one shown in the picture, in an open space in your home, you can also give it to your daughter as it could look really nice in her bedroom.

You can also use an unbleached cotton canvas to create this gorgeous wall design that only requires a little bit of stitching. You can also use the same canvas material to make crafted Christmas canvas decorations, a hand-stenciled storage ottoman, or a stenciled chevron table runner. Have you ever wondered what other projects you can make using this inexpensive and flexible canvas material?

Supplies

- Light or heavy ½-yard canvas (i.e. 100% cotton Army Ducks canvas)
- Printable banner template on six sheets of 8.5 x 11-inch paper and tape
- Fabric scissors
- Long 16-inch piece of driftwood or stick
- Sewing machine with matching thread
- Cricut's Design Space "Enjoy the Little Things" pattern
- template
- Cricut Maker
- StandardGrip Cricut mat
- Everyday iron-on vinyl (raspberry)
- Weeding tool
- EasyPress 2 machine
- EasyPress mat

Preparing the banner

Print out the design of the banner on six 8.5 x 11-inch stock sheets. You can tape the records together to create a full pattern. The cut line will be roughly 24-inches high and 15-inches long when it is unfinished. Place the paper template on top of the canvas and use a pair of fabric scissors to cut out the canvas. Remember to also clip all the notches and remove them from the pattern of the cover.

Sew a single straight stitch that is half an inch long from the edge around the entire perimeter of the canvas. Then, proceed to fold the banner's top edge over by half an inch on the backside, using the notches as a reference. To create a hem that is 3 inches high, fold the top hem over once again.

At the beginning and end of the stitch line, stitch the folded hem together to ensure that a backstitch is added, which will enable you to place a piece of driftwood or a branch through the wide hem, which looks a bit like a tube. The sewn banner should be about 21-inches long and 15-inches wide.

Adding the "Enjoy the Little Things" decal; Cricut Maker usage

Upload the "Enjoy the Little Things" pattern prototype from the Design Space.

To cut out the vinyl, follow the instructions on the screen.

To change the pattern, click "Customize."

Tap on the outline of the box and select "Uninstall." This project does not require that part of the pattern to be replicated.

Tap on the sentence and change the dimensions so that they are 11.5 x 11.1-inches high.

Select the "Make It" option.

To change the direction of the lettering, press the "Mirror" toggle icon.

Finish cutting out the vinyl by pressing the "Continue" button.

Pick the iron-on option that you want from the list of material choices that are offered to ensure that the unit is cut by the right blade.

Directly place the raspberry iron-on vinyl on the Cricut mat with the polished side face down.

Insert the ready-made mat in the Cricut machine and press "Launch."

Note the clear-cutting lines on the vinyl and then remove the mat and peel off the vinyl when the machine stops moving.

Peel away the excess vinyl, leaving just the decal portion to be pressed. You can then use the weeding method.

Adding the "Enjoy the Little Things" decal; EasyPress usage

Position the mat on a flat surface and lay the banner on top of it.

Turn the EasyPress 2 on.

Check the reference guide and adjust the temperature and time that is applied by the unit to the vinyl and content being used.

Test this step on a scrap piece of vinyl first. We noticed that while the reference guide suggests that you apply the vinyl at a temperature of 340°F for 30 seconds, you can also use a higher temperature.

You can also apply the machine to the canvas for 5 seconds initially to brace the fabric for the vinyl while also preventing it getting creased. Then, place the decal in the middle of the prepared canvas.

Press the iron down on the vinyl that is on the canvas. Since the EasyPress 2 is smaller than the decal, you will need to press different parts of the vinyl with the machine.

Turn over the canvas and press down on the backside as well.

Allow the vinyl to cool until the plastic portion can be carefully peeled off.

Hanging the canvas

To create a frayed-edge look, draw on any loose canvas threads around the cut edges. Then, insert the driftwood into the wide hem.

Tie a bit of twine to both ends of the hanging driftwood. String some big wooden beads together and tie them to the front of the hanging canvas panel. You can then put this up on a fuchsia-colored wall.

22. How to Make a T-Shirt with the Iron-on

You can learn how to create customized T-shirts with your Cricut Explore or Cricut Maker. This is actually one of the main reasons why people buy these awesome machines!

To have the best possible and long-lasting results, there are three main processes that every custom T-shirt should undergo.

2 SVG files should be used in this project:
- BABY LIFE #tired mom
- MOM LIFE #the best life

Since all files are similar, you can choose the ones you like best in the Cricut Design Space while further customizing your shirts to make them more unique.

Nevertheless, regarding the transfer procedure, all files should be used. For the "MOM LIFE" file, you can use the EasyPress 2. For the "BABY LIFE" file, you can use any household iron.

Let's begin the project!

Supplies
These are the supplies you will require to complete the project:
- Parchment paper and a small towel
- Long-sleeved, black T-shirt
- Cricut Explore or other Cricut machines
- EasyPress 2 or any house iron
- Light-grip or normal mat and sharp-point blade
- Heat vinyl transfer or white iron-on
- Weeding instruments

Cricut machine directions (Design Space)
- Upload files. Press the upload link found on the panel (shown on the left side) in the canvas section. You can take a look at the picture below as a reference before uploading a pattern or an image. Then, you should pick the SVG file you want.

Choose the recently added SVG file and then press the "Insert" button. As you click on the Insert button, check the file inside the Design Space. You can also change the size of the file so that it will fit the selected T-shirt. It is also possible to resize it by selecting all the components, changing the length and width of the selected region in the edit screen, and pulling down the lower-right corner of the selected area.

When editing the size, there is something crucial that you will have to do as all the components must be linked. In addition, all the layers should be selected, and you can then choose "attach" at the bottom of the panel to make sure that when you select "Make It" that all the words will stay in the correct order as shown on the canvas.

One of the easiest things to do while making a T-shirt pattern is to use templates to better visualize a concept. On the left side of the area of the canvas, you can see a model named "template." When you are selecting the template, you can better visualize the design, which is really helpful.

You can use a classic T-shirt in this case, further changing the size to small and the color to black because those are the colors you should use for the original design.

To send your design to your mat, click on the "Make It" button once you have attached all the layers and are happy with the way your design looks.

- Mirror the image and make it. You are getting closer to finishing the project, so just be a little patient as you will soon be rewarded! You will be prompted to begin the cutting process after clicking the "Make It" option.

However, you must click the "Mirror" option that is located on the left panel area for iron-on or HTV projects. You need to do this because you are cutting it upside down. Therefore, if you forget this essential step, your design will turn out incorrect (see the below image).

IMPORTANT: Don't forget to place the mirror image ON your design

Choose your materials

At this point, we have just explained that all the steps will either work with the Cricut Explore machines or the Cricut Maker.

Cricut Maker instructions

Upon browsing all the materials that Cricut has to offer, select the type that you want. If you have already marked your favorite, you can select it more quickly.

Cricut Explore Air 2 directions

Since you will use HTV, a very popular material, you need to move the smart set dial to the Iron-on option, which is shown on the Cricut Design Space screen.

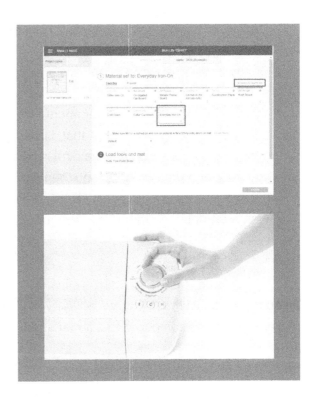

You should follow these steps to cut your design to perfection:

- Place the iron-on vinyl down on the shiny side of the mat, which is particularly essential. You will not cut the vinyl if you place it the other way and will instead cut the transparent material to which it has become stuck to. You can gently use the scraper to smooth out the vinyl on the mat if the material seems to have any bubbles.
- By tapping the small arrow on your Cricut, you can insert the fine-point blade and mat into the machine. Then, go ahead and press the "Make It" button so that the magic can happen!
- When your design is cut, Cricut Design Space will inform you. You may then proceed to unload your mat to weed out any scraps once this occurs.
- Weed all of the unwanted components of your design. To make sure you removed all of them, we recommend that you check the image again.

Transfer the T-shirt to the vinyl

You can now proceed to transfer your design to the T-Shirt after doing all the above-mentioned steps in Design Space (as well as cutting and weeding).

You can use a standard household iron and EasyPress 2 for your "BABY LIFE" file.

Also, something else you should keep in mind and is worth mentioning is that before you press them, Cricut recommends that you pre-wash your items without fabric softener. If you'd like you can also use the first EasyPress model. The temperature that should be applied to cotton clothes that will have material ironed on them is 330° F. As such, go ahead and preheat your EasyPress.

- Once your EasyPress is preheated, transfer your design to remove some of the wrinkles and press on the area for about 5 seconds.
- Gently apply pressure to your design for about 30 seconds. As you can see, when using a medium-sized press, some areas can be overlapping.
- You can press on each side for about 30 seconds, which is fine when you are working with the regular iron-on, so don't worry about that. However, if you're working with iron-on foil, try to ensure that no areas overlap because this material is quite delicate. Hence, make sure to turn the T-shirt around after you are done pressing on it and then lightly apply pressure to the back for about 15 seconds to finish the process.
- Wait a bit until enough of the design has cooled off before peeling it off while it is still warm to the touch.

Learning experience:

If you have an EasyPress Mat, we advise you to use it as it allows you to press the garment against the heat more lightly when compared to a firmer surface.

Place a towel between the front and back of your T-shirt or beneath it. If you don't use a towel or mat with your EasyPress machine, you may need to apply some more pressure to the front with a regular household iron or a transfer iron-on.

- Preheat the regular iron at the highest heat. Meanwhile, place a towel through the onesie. You need to make sure that your design is smooth and even across the area that you plan to iron.
- Get rid of any wrinkles and press wherever you want your design to be located for about 5 seconds.
- Place and cover your design with a thin cloth or parchment paper.
- Apply some pressure on half of the design for about 30 seconds and then proceed to vertically press on the right side for another 30 seconds. Press the top half of the design horizontally for about 30 seconds and then the bottom half for another 30. Turn the onesie around and press on its back for another 30 seconds (with the parchment paper on top).
- Wait a bit until enough of the design has cooled before peeling it off gently while it is still a bit warm to the touch.

23. How to Use Cricut to Make Felt Flowers

Did you know that you can use your Cricut to cut felt? You can easily learn how to use your Cricut to cut felt and make felt flowers, which is a particularly great project to do in the springtime.

Supplies
- Cricut Air Explore 2 or Cricut Maker
- Cricut felt samples
- Cricut mat
- Glue gun

- "Free flower" SVG file
- "Leaves" SVG file

You can use Cricut felt as it doesn't require a deep-cutting blade and it has been used effectively by a lot of crafters. You can then proceed to build a new project and then download the SVG to your artboard. Then, press the "upload" icon at the lower-left corner of your toolbar and pick your desired SVG file. Save your choice, click the "Design" button, and then insert the file. Then, re-size your flowers. Now in order to make sure that your flowers are unique, we would recommend that you choose to make them a few different sizes. In order for them to remain shorter than what you are cutting, remember that the flowers rollback.

Customized cut settings

Now that you have determined the exact size of your flowers, make sure that your dial is set on the desired setting on your Cricut Explore Air 2. You should be able to customize the material as your device attaches to your Cricut. In the search bar, press "Browse All Materials" and choose "Felt." Then, load the mat and proceed to cut your flowers.

This is a really simple project. Once you have removed your Cricut mat from your flower spirals, you can plug in your hot glue gun. It is now important to note that you should begin with the outer edge of the spiral, add some glue to it, and continue to roll the felt. Every quarter of an inch add a bit more glue to create the bud or the flower's center. Start to roll it more loosely when you have gotten through about three-fourths of the material. This would make it easier to make the flower's exterior edges appear like they are in bloom.

24. How to Style a Coffee Mug Using Cricut

Suppose that you are using a Cricut device to design DIY mugs. This is a really fun and creative project to work on because you can make it for yourself and your significant other or gift it to your loved ones, such as your married siblings, parents, or grandparents for Christmas. It's also quite easy to make for those without too much experience with Cricut.

To produce this DIY, you'll need a Cricut Explore machine. In the Cricut Design Space, you will only need to upload the desired SVG or PNG file and then adjust its size, cut it, and apply it. Keep in mind that these Cricut mugs must be hand washed as they cannot be inserted into the dishwasher. If you do give these mugs as Christmas gifts, then make sure to attach this as a note so that the mugs don't become ruined as the hot water used by many dishwashers can dissolve the vinyl you used. Hence, it's best to hand wash them with lukewarm soapy water.

Supplies
- SVG file
- Cricut Explore
- Red permanent vinyl
- Tape transfer
- Coffee mugs
- 12 x 12-inch Cricut mat

Directions
- Gather your supplies.
- Use the Cricut cutting device to cut the desired image. The mug images are approximately 3 x 2.5 inches, but this should ultimately depend on the size of the mugs you have.
- Apply the tape to the cut-out picture, peel the vinyl back, and press the image onto each mug.
- Peel the transfer tape back and you should be finished.
- Once you have completed this project, you will see just how easy it is to design and customize coffee mugs with your Cricut machine. You should definitely try this Christmas project and download the free SVG file.

25. Tiny Leather Journal Using the Cricut Maker and a Pen Holder Clasp

This is a great homemade present, but you should make sure that it's made of a high quality. The Cricut Maker is particularly awesome because it will cut fabric, leather, wood, faux leather, chipboard, and so much more.

Supplies
- Cricut Maker
- Scoring wheel
- Fine-point blade (included with machine)
- Cricut faux leather (silver or blue based on preference)
- Small Cricut iron-on foil
- Cricut EasyPress 2
- EasyPress Mat
- BrightPad Cricut
- Cricut tools
- Normal cutting mat
- Protective iron-on Cricut sheet

- Mini composition books
- Cement glue rubber

The scoring wheel is marvelous because it makes a deep, smooth line that is ideal for folding material, even faux leather. Using forms, grinding, and welding processes, you can build this yourself and then put the faux leather on the Cricut mat face down. The project doesn't need to be mirrored.

Place the scoring wheel in the holder by slipping the mat into the machine. Then, proceed to detach the scoring wheel and substitute it with a fine-point blade. During this process, do not remove the mat. Simply replace the blade and press the "C" button. It can cut the shapes easily and you can then extract them from the mat.

Cut some of the iron pictures into the vinyl. The photos only ought to be 1.75-inches long or less. Heat your EasyPress 2 up to 300°F and then put the iron-on journal cover on the EasyPress mat. Cover it with a plastic layer and press on it for 15 seconds with the EasyPress 2. Let the iron-on cool off and then peel the carrier layer back. Then, you can use the rubber cement. Print out a faux leather scrap piece that will mask the slits of the journal. Then, on the back of the journal cover, add some rubber cement and remove the top side. Don't use glue on the piece between the slits.

Just let the rubber cement dry and use the smaller part to cover the slits. Next, place rubber cement on the top and inside the journal cover. Let it dry and then line up and press on the leather. Then, add some more rubber cement to the back of the journal and place the leather inside. Do not place any rubber cement between the lines indicated. Instead, allow the rubber cement to dry, then line it up and push it together.

To keep the journal in place, press down on it firmly, which enables you to later re-use the leather. Now, fold over the top flap and insert a mini or normal-sized pen through the loop. It's particularly useful to add the pen because you cannot use a journal without one. Moreover, this project only takes 15 minutes to create with your Cricut Maker. That makes this the perfect gift to insert into a friend or loved one's stocking for Christmas. Otherwise, feel free to make one and carry it around in a pack. Whatever way you want to make use of this Cricut project, we guarantee you will love it! It's extremely useful and is quite classy due to its use of leather. You should never underestimate the value of having a notebook or journal at hand to take notes in or to jot down an idea that comes to you while you are at the office. We highly recommend that you test it out for yourself!

In sum, this chapter has presented you with several amazing project ideas to try out and experiment within the privacy of your own home. Instead of wasting money by buying gifts for your friends and family in the holidays, you can invest in a decent Cricut machine and a few materials and make a lot of cheap, customized gifts for your loved ones. Moreover, homemade gifts are always far more meaningful because they require more effort to be made and designed. Unlike gifts that are ready-made, homemade gifts are also particularly great because you can make sure that they really suit the personality of the receiver. Paying others to customize gifts for people you care about is an added expense that can be avoided through the purchase of a trusty and reliable Cricut machine, which will last you several years.

Another benefit to having a Cricut machine is that you can dedicate your time to getting in touch with your artistic side. If you have a knack for making pretty or creative things, you can do something that you enjoy as well as potentially sell your products or designs to others who want to buy customized items. As such, Cricut also provides you with the opportunity to begin your own business venture. In addition to a small amount of money for startup costs and materials, the only other things you need to have are determination and time. However, if you don't want to start your own business from scratch, you can just make and sell certain arts and crafts on the side for some additional pocket money. This is also pretty useful for university students, people who are in between jobs, or those who are looking for part-time work that isn't too stressful or demanding.

With your Cricut machine, a world of opportunities opens up to you and you can choose whether you want to use it to make personalized items for yourself, family, and friends — or to alternatively start your own business or earn some pocket money on the side whenever you need some extra cash. Either way, you should capitalize on this by trying out the projects in this book and then expanding further to make your own unique designs.

4.

CRICUT EXPLORE AIR 2 MASTERY

The Unofficial Step-By-Step Guide to Cricut Explore Air 2 + Accessories & Tools + Design Space + Tips & Tricks DIY Projects for Beginners & Advanced Users!

Philippa Smalley

Introduction

The Cricut kingdom is yours to discover. You may have received your machine and are unsure of what to do with it, or you may be afraid to take it out of the box. Do not be worried. It is for this purpose that this book has been published. It's expected to be a fantastic experience, with limitless possibilities as long as you have a fantastic computer to work with.

You have several options as a crafter, and the possibilities of a Cricut are endless. The Cricut can be used in a variety of ways, whether you're a scrapbooker or a business owner. It's a brilliant way to work as a skilled craftsperson while also finding a tool or companion to help you pursue your passion. Cricut has created an amazing tool with advanced cutting capabilities that allows you to sculpt, create, and bring all of your beautiful art ideas to life, which is fantastic news for anyone who works with crafts.

Understanding what tools and gadgets the Cricut can accommodate during the planning phase can save you time and headaches. Because the Cricut is versatile, it can be used for a variety of materials at any point during the project.

This book contains Cricut projects and is intended for beginners. It will teach you everything you need to know about the Cricut method, as well as how to make the most of it. We'll go over all of your personal information so you can get up and running with your computer in no time.

1. What Is Cricut and How Does It Work?

A Cricut is a smart electronic machine for cutting. It represents a cross between a plotter and a laser cutter (with the help of a knife). Since it substitutes what we can usually cut with the help of either scissors or a knife, a Cricut machine helps one to build projects with amazing precision, encouraging unprecedented pace and consistency. You may subscribe to their design library, pay per job, or upload your own files and artwork.

This tiny powerhouse delivers a smooth crafting environment like we've never seen before. Since infusible ink heat exchanges are indefinitely infused onto the base content, the advent of infusible ink goods has become a game-changer. They last for the lifetime of the project. There will be no flaking, peeling, rotting, or wrinkling – ever.

2. Models of Cricut Machines

The Cricut family actually comprises of three separate Cricut models. You can order them either from Cricut's website or on marketplaces such as Amazon. On eBay and Craigslist, you will find some older ones. However, I would not recommend them since they are more challenging to procure.

Cricut Joy

Cricut Joy is a tiny cutting machine that's half the size of Cricut Maker and Cricut Explore, making it suitable for those who don't have a dedicated crafting area. It's a little easier than the other Cricut machines, with only one blade and a pen holder. But don't be confused by its diminutive size. it has some exciting features.

Cricut Maker:

This is Cricut's most recent release. It comes with a new collection of blades that were developed especially for this model to enable for the cutting of harder materials including leather and even wood. It's the family's most influential member, in my view.

The Explore Family

These were once the most common, and each version has its own collection of features:

1. Cricut Explore One:

This computer is the first in the Explore family. It is strong and only has a single tool holder.

2. Cricut Explore Air:

This machine allows you to cut and sketch at the same time because it has a dual tool holder. It also introduces Bluetooth compatibility to the mix.

3. Cricut Explore Air 2:

This version has the same functionality as the previous model (Bluetooth communication and a dual tool holder), but it is twice as fast and a bit less noisy, according to certain users.

Cricut Cuttlebug

This is the initial Cricut machine. It is a hand-operated die-cutting system that helps you to emboss and use metal dies, unlike the other devices. It's portable and small, but unlike its larger siblings, it's not electronic, and has no storage space or automated function.

3. Which Cricut Machine Should You Get?

The rule of thumb is that it all depends on the fabrics you choose to cut. If you just intend to use the device for paper crafts and vinyl, you might get away with only the Cricut Explore family. The Cricut Maker is the system to use if you want to cut thicker materials such as leather, chipboard, or fabrics without stabilizers. Both of them are fantastic, but the Cricut Maker's extra cutting power takes the cake when it comes to the range of materials it will cut.

4. Differences Between Models

Cutting Power

The cutting power of the Cricut Maker and the Air 2 (Cricut Explore) is the most significant difference between the two. The Cricut Explore Air 2 has a cutting force of 400 grams, whilst the Cricut Maker boasts 4,000 grams. Yes, that's right. The cutting strength is ten times higher.

So, in terms of crafting, what does it mean? It means that, with that much strength, you can cut much thicker materials than paper and cardstock, like wood, acrylics, leather, and more. If we had to make an analogy, the cutting strength of each machine might be compared to the strength you use when cutting veggies. If you're splitting a cucumber in two, you'll need far less pressure than if you're cutting a fresh potato in half.

New Technology

Coupled with the improved cutting strength, modern techniques were added that can only be used with the Cricut Maker. Almost all of the blades are kept in position by a modern technology named QUICK-SWAP, which enables you to simply click the instant button on the top of the flexible housing, snap the chosen tip into position, and get creating. Press, swap, and carry forward.

Framework of adaptive tools

This device is the primary difference between the Cricut Maker and Cricut Explore Air 2. They said that the latest blades were developed explicitly for it, so what exactly is it? The blades' trajectory is still regulated by the integrated tool system technology. It governs the strain so that you can cut products of varying thicknesses and densities. It's also why the Cricut Maker is ten times stronger than Cricut Explore Air 2.

5. Cricut blades, and how do I choose the right one?

Before you start, there is something you should know, particularly if you plan on cutting hard material. There are actually several blade types and three other carving tools accessible online for larger devices (Maker and Explore).

Rotary blade

This blade is capable of cutting through any form of cloth. And, unlike when cutting cloth with the Cricut Explore Air 2 (where the fabric must be stabilized first), the movement is different when utilizing this cutter. When chopping, the blade rolls rather than dragging. As long as you use the fabric mat, you're good to go.

Scoring wheel blade

As the name suggests, a scoring wheel blade helps you to score sheets to create sleek folds. This method is particularly helpful for someone who wants to score regularly because, unlike the scoring stylus, it was developed with the adaptive tool framework in mind. Consequently, it exerts ten times the pressure.

Knife blade

This is used to cut items as thick as leather, thick chipboard, balsa wood, and acrylics.

Perforation blade

The simple perforation blade allows flawless tear-offs and makes easy-peel a pleasure, including for bent forms – no folding needed.

Wavy blade

In one easy move, the wavy blade adds whimsy to every straight-edge project. Iron-on, acrylic, cloth, and cardstock creations will all benefit from a decorative edge.

Debossing tip

For a beautiful impact on foil-coated paper, poster board, shimmer paper, basswood, foil cardstock, and other fabrics, use the rolling debossing ball.

Engraving tip

Use plastic, metal, leather, and other materials to engrave professional-looking, customized text, logo-types, flourishes, and embellishments.

1. Getting the Cricut Explore Air 2 Up and Running

When you complete the system initialization, the machine is automatically connected to the account. Follow these instructions:

For use on Windows and Mac operating systems:

1. Switch on the machine by plugging it in.
2. Use the USB cord to attach the unit to your phone, or pair it with Bluetooth.
3. Open the internet and search for design.cricut.com; then go to setup.
4. Get Design Space for laptop and download it.
5. Sign in or build a Cricut ID, then configure the new machine by following the on-screen directions.
6. When you're asked to make a test cut, you'll realize the configuration is complete.
7. During system initialization, the device is registered automatically. Reconnect your system, go to design.cricut.com, and select setup or pick New Device Setup from the Design Space menu (account), and follow the on-screen instructions if you did not finish setup when you first linked the computer to the device.

IOS and Android:

1. Switch on the machine by plugging it in.
2. Use Bluetooth to link the Android or iOS computer to your Cricut unit.
3. Get the Design Space software and install it.
4. Open the software and sign in or build a Circuit ID if you haven't already.
5. Pick System Configuration from the menu.
6. To complete initialization, pick your computer model and follow the on-screen instructions.
7. When you're asked to make a test cut, you'll realize the configuration is complete.

2. Realistic Recommendations

You may be scared when you first get your Cricut Explore Air 2. You won't know where to begin so that it may remain in the box for months. But later, once you are familiarized with the machine, it could be one of your favorite hobbies.

I'm not one of those individuals whose every project comes out wonderfully – in fact, plenty of them end in tears or are eventually discarded because they aren't worth completing. But, over the years, I've learned a lot, and I hope that this book can be helpful to all of you who are getting started and need a little extra support.

3. What Kinds of Materials Can You Cut with Cricut Explore Air 2?

You can use the Cricut Explore Air 2 to create designs. It will cut a range of fabrics, including film, cardstock, acrylic, iron-on (thermal energy vinyl), vellum, sticker paper, faux leather, and cloth. In addition to creating and writing with markers and pens, the Cricut Explore Air 2 has a helpful score function that will elevate your project. This machine will also inspect and cut materials.

4. Cricut Explore Air 2 Unboxing

Let's double-check that you're not missing something. If you are, return the Explore Air 2 to the shop you bought it from or contact Cricut Help for a prompt exchange. If you have something extra, consider it a great reward.

The following items should be included in your package:

- Accessory adapter and silver pen (pre-installed)
- Vinyl samples and cardstock
- USB and power cords
- Cricut cutting mat
- Instruction manual
- Cutting blade (pre-installed)

Remember that, since there are various packages (Premium Vinyl, Ultimate Package, Complete Starter Kit, Tools Kit, Vinyl Starter Kit), you can receive several extra parts.

5. Cricut Explore Air 2: Insider's Guide

Now I will show you the main features of Cricut Explore Air 2, which are all very useful. The screenshot below depicts the initial Explore Air, but the interface is similar. Look at the wonderful mint finish.

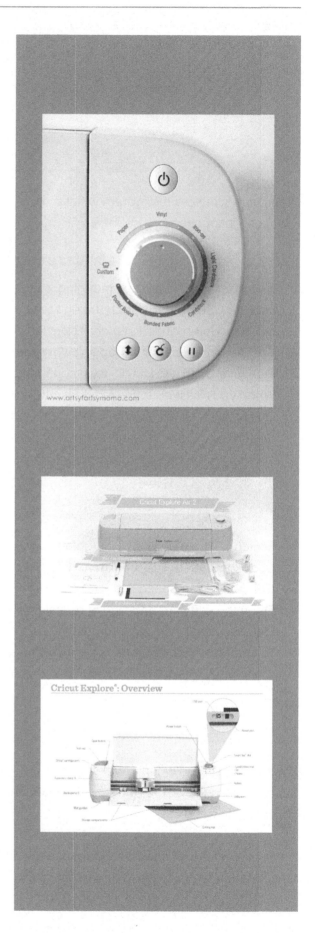

Cricut Explore Air 2 overview in depth

Tool cup

This carries markers, scissors, and other small objects.

Accessory clamp A

That's where the accessory connector is pre-installed, and you can use a pen to draw instead of cutting. It may also be used to carry scoring knives.

Blade clamp B

The blade is already mounted. This is where you can look if you really have to fix it or cut vinyl pieces.

Accessory storage compartments

The Explore Air 2 comprises two storage compartments in addition to the tool cup. Knives, additional blade housings, and the accessory connector are held in the smaller compartment on the left. It has a magnetic strip that prevents replacement blades from rolling about. Longer tools/pens may be stored in the wider compartment.

Smart set dial

To pick the item you'll be cutting, turn the dial. It's fun to transform, and it shows you which items you may cut in 2x quick mode.

Mat for cutting

This is how we insert the majority of our materials through the Cricut machine. It's adhesive, which helps keep your stuff in place.

A quick reminder about the blade and attachment clamps: to detach the blade/accessory clip, just open the lever and take out its metal housing. The blade is on the inside, and the top has a little plunger. You use your finger to push down on it to show the needle, which sticks out magnetically. If you decide to repair the razor, simply take it off and fix it. To use a pen, easily select accessory clamp A, place the pen inside, and close the clamp. Then attach your computer and load the appropriate drivers.

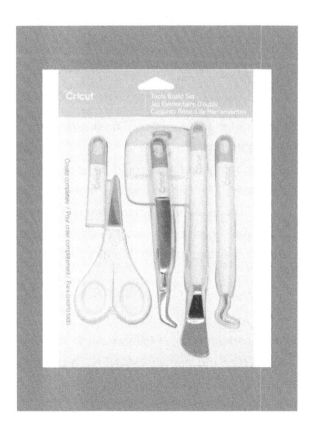

6. Basic Set of Cricut Tools

This is a set of valuable resources available directly via Cricut. It contains the following items:

Scissors

A type of cutting tool (self-explanatory).

Tweezers

They are reverse grip, meaning you press the handle to unlock it and then loosen it to lock it. It's great for keeping items together until they dry, as well as other little tasks.

Scraper

Used for dealing with vinyl and washing the cutting mat, this is a must-have.

Spatula

To cautiously lift items off the cutting mat, use this tool.

Weeder

It aids in the removal of vinyl from its liner or even the removal of small portions.

If you don't already have these tools, it is recommended either purchasing the Cricut kit or Explore Air 2 kit that includes them. If bought as a pack, these should cost about $15.

7. Cartridge Filling and Unloading

What are Cricut cartridges, and how do you use them?

Cricut cartridges are themed samples of pictures and fonts, such as the beach, Halloween, or springtime. Each picture collection costs between $5 and $30 and may involve hundreds of images, fonts, or ventures. The cartridges in the initial Cricut devices were plastic, and you had to insert them into the cutting machine to use them. These cartridges, or picture sets, can now be connected to one's Cricut ID and accessed online via Cricut Craft Space (The Expression series) or Cricut Design Space (The Explore series). You may also buy automated cartridges to gain access to collections of photographs without needing to work with plastic cartridges.

Do you need to use Cricut Explore Air cartridges?

That's no longer the case. Thank Cricut for removing the need for cartridges in the different Cricut Explore models and the Cricut Maker. The initial Cricut cutter and Cricut Expression series were built to be standalone devices that could be used with actual data cartridges that didn't need a device or an internet connection. The Expression machines may be used for the free Cricut Design Space program, but photographs purchased from Cricut cartridges are still restricted. Cricut also offers a range of cutter versions that do not need cartridges. So, if one has a Cricut Maker or Cricut Explore and doesn't want to worry about cartridges again, you can skip this stage.

Cartridges for the Cricut Explore Air 2: How to Use Them

Cartridges must be connected to the Cricut account in order to be viewed digitally with Design Space while used with Cricut Explore Air 2. A Cricut cartridge may only be related to one Cricut account. Connecting a cartridge is PERMANENT: it cannot be undone or moved to another account. Before connecting the cartridges, make sure you're signed into the right Cricut account.

1. Open Cricut Design Space on a Windows or Mac device by heading to cricut.com/design. The phone/tablet apps do not allow you to connect cartridges.
2. Check to see if the Cricut Explore is charged up and attached to your device.
3. Pick "Link Cartridges" about midway down the menu by pressing the menu icon in the top left corner (it looks like a hamburger: 3 horizontal bars).
4. From the drop-down screen, select the Cricut machine.
5. Place the cartridge in the space on the left side of the Explore cutter, just above the tab "Open", when prompted.
6. The green "Connect Cartridge" button will glow until Design Space has identified the cartridge. To attach your cartridge, click the icon.
7. Configuration space will show "Cartridge attached" until the cartridge is connected to the Cricut account. You may now begin connecting your cartridges, display the cartridges, or close the cartridge connecting dialogue and return to Cricut Interface Space by pressing the X at the top right corner.

In Cricut Design Space, how do you locate the cartridges?

Cricut Design Space makes it simple to view your connected cartridges and purchased images.

1. In the Design Space, open the Photos window by pressing the "Photos" icon on the main menu to the left of the open canvas.
2. There are three clickable terms across the top: Photos, Divisions, Cartridges. To see a catalog of all the cartridges available, go to "Cartridges."
3. To display just the cartridges you currently possess, go to the top right of the Photos window and pick "My Cartridges" from the "Filter" menu. This will refer to all cartridges, both free and purchased.
4. If you've bought or posted specific pictures, be sure to find out the Pictures tab as well.

What exactly is the distinction between traditional and wireless cartridges?

Physical cartridges are plastic cartridges that comprise themed collections of photographs that you manually inject into the cutting device. Physical cartridges should be used by loading them into the computer and picking and manipulating the pictures with the keyboard. You may also use Design Space to connect such physical cartridges to the Cricut account. Once you've connected your devices, you'll be able to view digital copies of cartridges in the editing app (online) right away, hold the physical cartridge, and, at the very least, take a couple of images of the front and back. If you have difficulty accessing the connected cartridges, and need them to be resynced, Cricut Help can request these images as proof of ownership.

Digital cartridges are customized collections of photographs that can be purchased digitally and instantly viewed from Cricut Design Space. Nothing will be delivered to you and nothing will need to be inserted into the Cricut cutter as they don't have a physical component. When you're linked to the internet and signed into Cricut Design Space, you can use this for some of the most recent Cricut machines.

Advantages

Cartridges are a crafter's dream come true. Making your own creations from scratch can be a lot of fun, but gazing at an empty canvas and not knowing where to begin can be overwhelming. You can quickly find motivation through cartridges, which are arranged by every holiday or style you can think of. Cartridges are a fun and fast way to get started producing your own vinyl decals and greeting cards without needing to spend hours perfecting the pattern.

You will find a plethora of step-by-step instructions for creating prototypes with cartridges online. When you're first studying how to operate a Cricut, these are perfect. When you're just starting out, there is a lot of stuff to remember, and tutorials make learning a lot simpler by removing the guesswork. Take a look at this adorable fox head produced with the cartridge of 3D Animal Heads:

Each cartridge's photographs have been carefully chosen and selected. Many creative designers have invested a great deal of time and money into making cartridges just for you. You should be assured that the pictures and fonts will be of a good standard and will fit well with the Cricut.

In the Library of Cricut Cartridge, there are nearly 500 cartridges. Each cartridge includes a collection of photographs and creations that can be modified and coupled with various artistic features to create a broad range of designs. You will always find one that looks perfect with the project you're working on because there are so many forms, patterns, and fonts to choose from.

Cartridges are actually a great deal. From the base photos on a single cartridge, you can build hundreds of different designs. If you're afraid that the Cricut cartridge range is becoming too pricey, commit more time to play with the cartridges that you already possess and exploring their artistic ability.

Keeping a physical set of Cricut cartridges may be a perfect place to get ideas for future designs. You should remain off the monitor and look via a physical library with the cartridge set to locate something to create.

Drawbacks

The biggest drawback of the cartridge scheme, previous to the Cricut Explore sequence, is that you were confined to what appeared on the cartridges. This is no longer a drawback for the newest Cricut units, as cartridges are now fully optional. You can also use your own templates or import free SVG files from the internet.

One big flaw is that you can only connect one Cricut account to a cartridge. If you collect cartridges as a gift or purchase them on eBay or at a thrift store, they can already be connected to another account. Cartridge binding is final, and you can't alter the account they're connected to. And be cautious not to be duped into getting cartridges that aren't compatible with your unit.

After purchasing a variety of cartridges, you may feel obliged to stay with the Cricut label, or even a specific device. This is awesome for Cricut apps, but not so much for the crafting and DIY cultures. You can't freely share your ideas with anyone if you use cartridges, which is one of my favorite facets of designing new projects. Instead, use plain old SVG images, which can be conveniently exchanged and imported into modeling applications for other cutter brands, such as Silhouette Studio.

The cartridges aren't compatible with all Cricut devices. Without the internet, the Expressions can use cartridges. You must connect the cartridge to the account in order to use Cricut Explore Air 2. And there isn't even a cartridge slot on the Cricut Maker. If you choose to use photos from all of the old cartridges you have used with a Maker, you'll need to buy the Cricut Cartridge Adapter. Alternatively, you might borrow a friend's Cricut Explore to complete the task.

8. Defining The Machines' Latest Firmware Update

How can you figure out what firmware update your computer is running?

For optimum efficiency, Cricut suggests that your machine's firmware be upgraded to the most current edition. This section will supply you with the most current firmware update for all Cricut machines.

1. Log into Cricut Design Space and make sure your Explore or Maker device is turned on and attached.
2. Pick "Upgrade Firmware" from the account menu in the top left corner of Design Space.
3. n the pop-up display, pick the computer from the drop-down chart. It will take several moments for the program to identify the computer.
4. Once your computer has been found, you will either be informed that the firmware is updated or asked to download any available upgrades.
5. The following are the most current firmware versions:

   - 1.091 Cricut Explore
   - 3.091 Cricut Explore Air
   - 5.120 Cricut Explore Air 2
   - 2.095: Cricut Explore One
   - 4.175 Cricut Maker

Design Space on a Windows or Mac PC can be used to check the firmware of the Cricut Explore and Maker. At this time, the Design Space Android or iOS App does not support this functionality.

Cricut EasyPress 2

1. Make sure that the Cricut EasyPress 2 is switched on.
2. Click and hold the Temperature, Time, plus, and minus controls at the same time.
3. On the screen, you'll see the firmware version.

9. Cricut Explore Air Machine's Fast Mode and Its Usage

How can you use Fast Mode and what is it?

Cricut Explore Air 2 and Cricut Maker machines have a feature named Fast Mode that helps you to cut and write up to two times faster than later Cricut Explore versions. This functionality is accessible on Explore Smart Set Dial for the Iron-on, Vinyl, and Cardstock content settings (Vinyl to Cardstock+). The details of the speed contrast test can be found here.

- Go to the Cut display when you're about to write or cut the project.
- If you've chosen compatible content, you'll have the option to use Fast Mode.
- To enable Fast Mode, simply click or tap the switch next to the "on" button.

When using Fast Mode, computers can make a quiet noise. This is completely natural and nothing to be worried about.

For Mac and Windows:

For Android and iOS users:

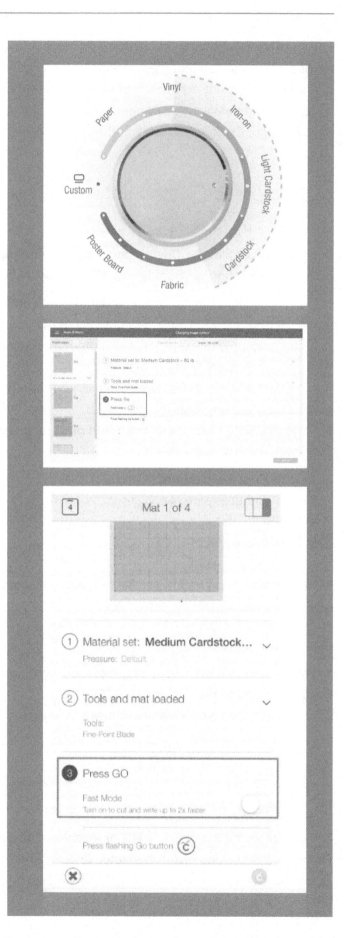

The below is an example of a sample speed measure.

10. Pros and Cons of Cricut Explore Air 2

As I previously said, this unit, like every other cutting machine on the market, isn't flawless. Let's go into the key advantages and disadvantages of this quick yet powerful cutter.

Advantages:

The way it looks
Mint green, gold, baby blue, and a soft pink are the four colors available for this device. You can choose a color that complements your workstation.

Cutting speed
The majority of the design and compartments on this system are similar to those on the Explore Air, but it is quicker. The Air 2 also has wireless network capabilities.

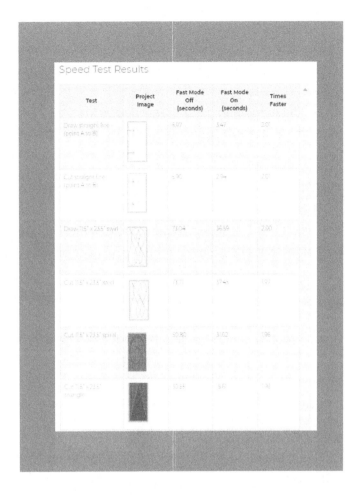

This device quickly picks up the wireless signal. This ensures you can submit a large number of tasks to it and it will take care of the lot for you.

Plan to be checked
If you are a newcomer, you'll love the fact that this workhorse comes with a test assignment. You may also watch extensive instructions on how to use this cutter online.

Cost-effectiveness
If you are looking for a cutting machine that's new, reliable, and inexpensive with a strong reputation, look no further than this Cricut model. It offers outstanding value for money. The Explore Air 2 costs less than $300, which is far less than the Maker. The Maker is around $150 more costly than the Explore Air 2.

Mat of good quality
Unlike many other cutting machines on the market, the Explore Air 2 does not have an issue with slipping mats. It does, however, have a nice mat with a unique design.

Cutting capacity

The cutting strength of Air 2 is 210g. It's not quite as heavy as the Maker's 4kg. However, it is still a respectable statistic. The standard blade will cut surfaces up to 1.5mm wide.

All you have to do to get a sharper cut is load the deep cut blade and you will be able to cut items as dense as 2mm. About 100 separate materials can be managed by Explore Air 2.

Bluetooth compatibility

This functionality adds to the machine's versatility for smartphones, iPads, and PCs.

You won't require cables to print designs and images from your tablet or phone if it has Bluetooth. This is one of the cutter's greatest features, in my opinion.

Disadvantages

There isn't an Android version

Cricut created an iOS version but didn't create it for Android users, which is ridiculous.

If you're keeping up with the latest news, you're definitely aware that mobile phones are dominating the industry. Hopefully, Cricut will address this issue and release an Android version as well.

Software for beginners

Cricut, in some opinions, could encourage consumers to use third-party apps. While the current program is free and easy, experienced crafters may find it to be too simplistic.

Cricut should also concentrate on refining its applications in terms of graphic design. It isn't strong enough for this. If this is the case, users can try out an alternative.

Some Cricut models are loud

The Explore Air 2 is not a distracting cutter. It is, though, significantly quieter than the Explore Air. While this is not a major concern, it is worth noting. It could bother you if you're extremely sensitive to noise. Otherwise, the Explore Air 2 is a great choice if you want a cutting machine that is both fast and inexpensive.

11. Creating the First Concept with the Cricut Explore Air 2

Now let's have a look at how to create a sample project using the items that arrived with your Cricut machine.

If you followed the "New Machine Setup" guidance earlier, you could see a pattern on your computer screen. If you can't find the style you're looking for, go to design. cricut.com. Choose New Machine Structure from the list button at the top left corner.

The provided demo cardstock, notebook, cutting pad, and silver pen will all come in handy. If your cutting mat still has the protective coating on it, remove it now and put it aside for future. If you're not using it, it should be left to cover the floor.

1. Place a sheet of grey cardstock on the cutting mat and start cutting. Mark it up evenly on the pad only with textured hand facing up. It should be centered just below the Cricut emblem in the top left corner.

2. Place the mat in the machine and turn it on. Place the mat in accordance with mat guides; here's an example of how it should look. When clicking the load/unload buttons located on the right side of the unit, keep the mat squarely against rollers. The symbol resembles a pair of double arrows.

3. Put a silver pen in the slot. A is the accessory clamp that you can open. Remove the pen lid and put it in the housing tip-down just before the symbol on the pen vanishes. Lock this clamp as quickly as possible. To avoid losing the cap, put that on the bottom of another pen when cutting.

4. Press the Go button after checking the design on the mat preview screen.

5. Set the dial on your machine to cardstock.
6. The machine's "C" icon should be blinking. To begin the template, press it and wait for the miracle to happen.

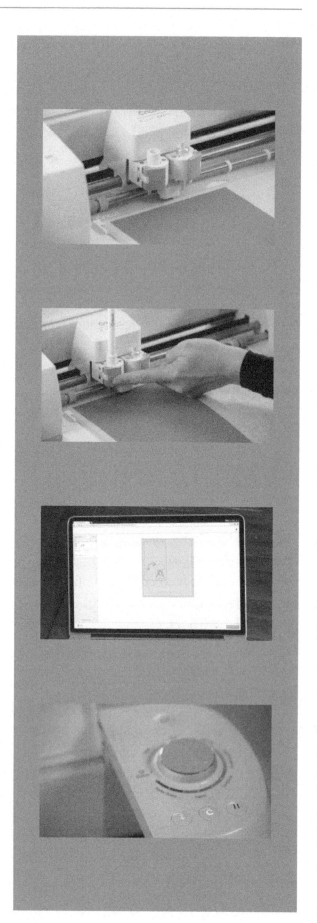

7. The mat could be unloaded. Click the load/unload icon and remove the pen until the job is completed. Normally it is stored in the accessory compartment, but if you want quick access, there's also a convenient bin on the machine's left side.

8. Curl the edge of the cutting mat up against you and position it face down on a clean board. To make things smoother, continue curling the mat up while you draw the material away from it.

9. Fold the card in half with a crease down the middle. Place the blue paper within the grey card in the same way. If you like, you can use glue to secure it.

10. The finished product should look like this:

1. Pairing with a Bluetooth Computer

With the Cricut Explore Air 2, you can cut wirelessly. To pair it with the machine or mobile device, follow the instructions below:

To connect wirelessly, the Cricut Explore Air 2 needs a wireless Bluetooth adapter.

Windows

1. Ensure the Cricut Explore Air 2 is switched on and next to your monitor (about 10-15 feet). Make sure the wireless Bluetooth transmitter is inserted if you have a Cricut Explore Air 2.

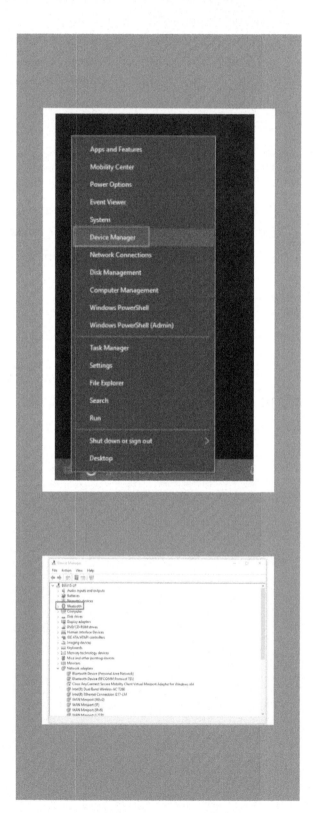

2. Bluetooth is accepted by the majority of devices. Right-click on the Start button and pick System Manager to see if your machine is Bluetooth-enabled.
3. Your device is Bluetooth activated if Bluetooth is displayed. If not, you'll need to buy a Bluetooth dongle, which is a USB device that enables your machine to connect with other Bluetooth devices.

4. Quit the System Management software.
5. Choose Settings from the Start menu.
6. Pick Gadgets from the drop-down screen.

7. Make sure Bluetooth is switched on, then pick Add Bluetooth on the other device.
8. Push the Bluetooth button and wait for the computer to accept the machine. Choose the machine from the drop-down screen.
9. If you're asked for a PIN, enter 0000. After that, choose Connect.
10. Your Cricut Explore Air 2 machine is now linked to your Windows computer.

Note:

These guidelines and screenshots are for Windows 10. If you require assistance for a particular Windows operating system, ask Member Care and use one of the methods mentioned below. It's common for Cricut Explore machines to appear in the list. If you have several Cricut machines, use the system code to locate the one you wish to combine. This can be seen on the serial number sticker on the end of the machine.

Mac

1. Ensure the Cricut Explore Air 2 machine is switched on and next to the device (about 10-15 feet).
2. Make sure the wireless Bluetooth transmitter is wired in.

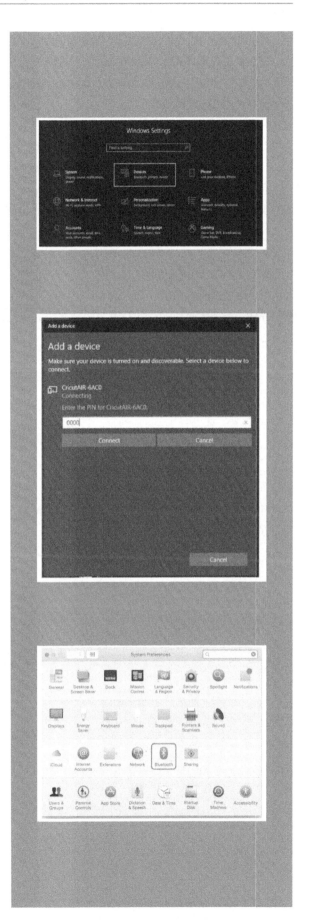

3. Bluetooth is accepted by the majority of devices. Open Apple Menu, click Device Settings, and search for the Bluetooth alternative to see if your Mac has Bluetooth compatibility.

4. Press the Bluetooth icon to access the Bluetooth panel. If Bluetooth is switched off, press the button to activate it. Choose the adapter/Bluetooth module from the drop-down display.

5. Make sure the machine is switched on and within 10 to 15 feet of the smartphone or tablet. Make sure the wireless Bluetooth transmitter is inserted if you do have a Cricut Explore Air 2.

6. Go to Settings then Bluetooth.

7. If Bluetooth is switched off, press it to activate it. Your Bluetooth system will now be visible.

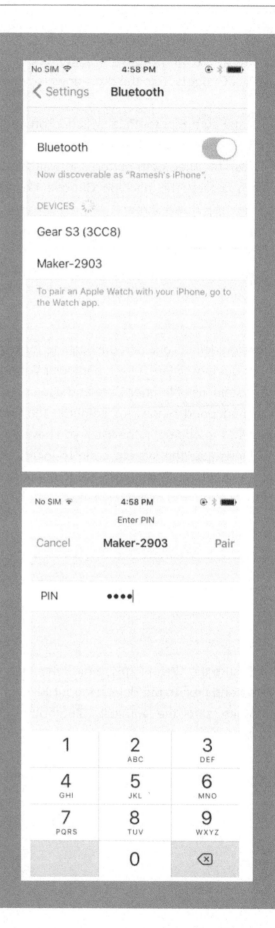

8. Select the adapter/Bluetooth module from the drop-down display (the name of the adapter is printed on the packaging materials.)

9. Type PIN 0000 when asked, then tap Pair.
10. The pairing process is now complete. When the software is interacting with the device during a cut, the Mac device does not always display "Connected." It's common for Cricut Explore devices to appear in the list as Audio. If you have several Cricut machines, use the system code to locate the one you wish to connect. This can be seen on the serial number sticker on the end of the machine

Android

1. Make sure your Cricut Maker or Cricut Explore is switched on and within 10 to 15 feet of the smartphone or tablet. Ensure the wireless Bluetooth transmitter is inserted whether you own a Cricut Explore 1 or Cricut Explore Air 2.
2. Go to Settings, then Bluetooth.
3. If Bluetooth is switched off, press it to activate it.
4. Select the Bluetooth adapter module from the drop-down display (you will find the name of your adapter in your packaging materials.)
5. Enter PIN 0000 when asked, then press OK.
6. The pairing phase is now complete.

Notice that the menu navigation can differ depending on the manufacturer and the edition of your Android device. For further details, please check your Android device's manual or message Member Care using one of the methods mentioned below. It's common for Cricut Explore machines to appear in the list as Audio. If you have several Cricut machines, use the system code to locate the one you wish to combine. This can be seen on the serial number sticker on the end of the machine.

1. How Do You Use the Cricut Explore Air 2 to Upload Images?

There are so many options for this; I'll teach you how to upload photos of your own in Cricut Design Space right now, and you probably wouldn't believe how simple it is. Designing your own photographs and templates in Photoshop Elements and then importing them into Cricut Design Space to be cut is one of my favorite activities to do with Cricut Explore Air 2.

To start, go to the left-hand side and press "UPLOAD Photos." Then, on the right, press the blue "UPLOAD File" icon. Press "BROWSE" once you've arrived at this screen. It can control the computer's files. Go to the picture you want to share and select it. To open your picture, right-click it and select "OPEN." You'll be able to make improvements to the picture until it's in Cricut Design Space. Choose the most suitable picture form for the task. You may pick "SIMPLE Picture" for this image and then press Proceed. In Cricut Design Space, one can now delete anything that you don't wish to be permanent. You render all of the white space clear by tapping on it. Then you can hit the Proceed button. Since one may like to save the photos as cut photographs, you may choose "SAVE IT AS A CUT PICTURE." Then you hit the Save button. The picture is now available in the image files that you have imported. It's at the bottom of the list. With the ability to upload photos of your own in Cricut Design Space, the possibilities are infinite, and I love how quick it is.

2. Cricut Design Space Software

Did you know that Cricut has an app? Cricut Design Space can be downloaded and used on an Apple or Android smartphone. Many people choose to build on their iPad or phone, then link it to a Cricut cutting machine.

How to use Cricut Design Space

So, let's talk about the software and what you should do with it. If you need support getting started with Cricut Design Room, here is a guide to getting started with Cricut Design Space.

Canvas

The canvas in Cricut Design Space corresponds to the panel you're working on. Simply press one of the two "new project" buttons on the Cricut Design Space home-page to begin a new project. This will expand the size of the canvas. Now it's time to let the imagination run wild.

How to zoom

On the bottom left corner of the canvas, there are zoom in and out buttons.

If you press the - or + buttons by 25 percent, the Design Space zoom will increase or decrease. You may also want to zoom out and see the whole picture if you are conducting on a project on a broad scale. Simply press the zoom out (-) button until you reach the desired size.

Click the zoom in icon (+) to enlarge the picture and you will see the smaller details. To zoom in to the portion you need to see, you may need to drag the screen up or down with your mouse.

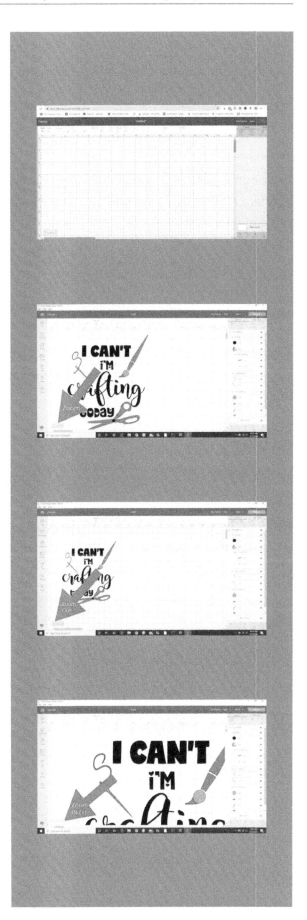

Key buttons on the canvas

The key buttons are located on the left-hand side.

New:

Create a new project.

Templates:

Utilizing the templates to see if the idea can fit on different items is one of my favorite aspects of the canvas. To get a clearer idea, you can quickly adjust the color and scale of the models.

Projects:

Displays all Cricut Design Space projects.

Images:

This is where you'll find all of the images eligible for purchase through Cricut Access, as well as the ones you've posted.

Text:

Fill in the blanks with text and choose a font from the drop-down menu.

Shapes:

Many of the simple shapes and the score line are used. By mixing forms, you will design a variety of designs.

Upload:

Choose a .png, .svg, or .jpg file from your device and upload it.

Purchasing one thing at a time

If you don't want to sign up for Cricut Access yet or you still have a number of connected cartridges, you can always buy files one at a time. Once you've purchased a file, it never expires, and you can use it on whatever project you want.

Once you cut the file, Cricut Design Space can ask for payment. Set up the payment system on the left-hand side under "Account Settings" (click the three horizontal lines).

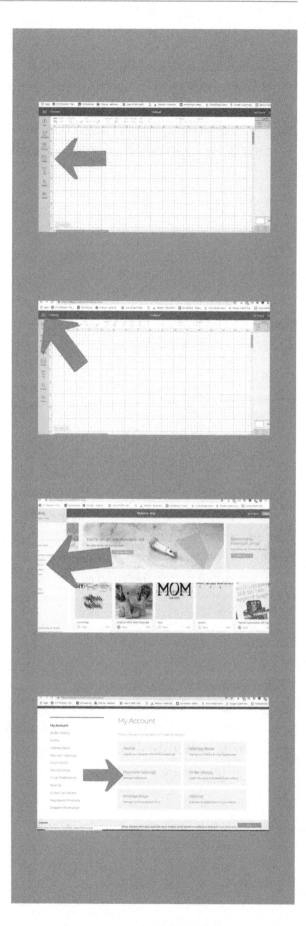

Filters

In Cricut Design Space, narrowing down what you are searching for saves a lot of time. You may use the filters to narrow down the search for things you've uploaded or items accessible in Cricut Access if you're looking for a particular text or image. This is definitely the tool I use the most when looking for photos. Filter by uploaded, Cricut Access, free, and so on.

Upload your own files

I create a lot of things with photos that I upload. This is the place to go if you want to create absolutely one-of-a-kind personalized gifts and decorations. Cricut Design Space makes it simple to import and cut out images saved on your screen, or to use print and cut.

A word of advice when uploading photos: if you are selling something, make sure the images you use aren't copyrighted. You can look up the rules governing copyright infringement on the internet. Disney is a massive corporation! If you're selling something with the Disney logo on it, proceed with caution. Don't get me wrong: a Cricut will help you launch a great craft company, just make sure you follow the rules.

Preview/Prepare screen

Cricut Design Space recently modified the overview or prepare panel, which I really like. Before you cut, you can now switch things about in the preview screen.

While the Cricut software tries to preserve as much content as practicable, you can find cuts with wide blank spaces in between them. Most like having the choice of manually moving other cuts through certain spaces.

Inside the Prepare screen, you can also switch items to various mats. Click on the picture, then on the three small dots. You'll see the words "Move Object" appear.

All of the multiple mats will appear until you click on Transfer Object. To adjust the image, click on the mat or color you want to change. It will change to the mat on its own.

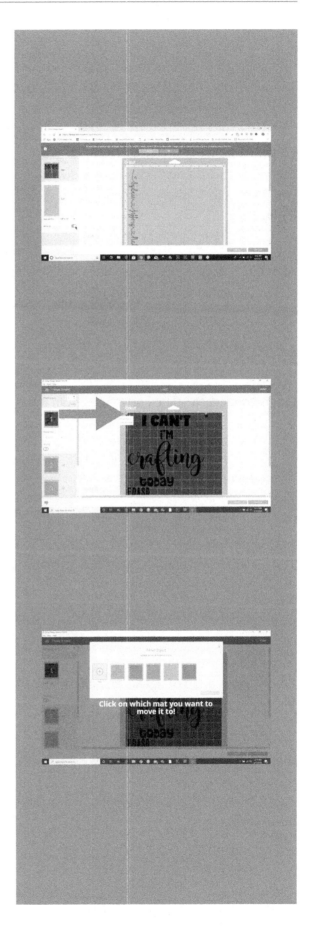

All editing tools

Cricut Design Space editing tools are surprisingly easy. These are also the pillars for creating your own designs.

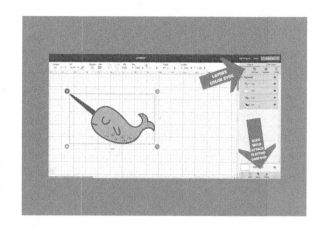

In Cricut Design Space lower right corner

• Slice

Cut pictures from collections of individuals or objects into slices. To render split letter monograms, use this method.

• Attach

Attach text or pictures to the canvas so they cut out just as you like them.

• Weld

Weld cursive text together such that there is one single line with no tails. Weld objects together to create a single object.

• Contour

Erase unnecessary lines or images from the outside or inside of the graphic.

• Flatten

To print a file, flatten it together. Here's what you need to know about print and cut, as well as the latest offset feature.

In Cricut Design Space upper right corner

• Layers Panel

The Layers Panel allows you to see all of the photos' layers. To hide or display those layers, click the eye.

• Color Sync

Count the number of colors on your canvas. Drag and drop objects in this column to make them the same color.

Whew, that's a ton of details and information, but once you have played with the Cricut app for a while, it'll become second nature.

3. Cricut Design Space Features Comparison

The following table illustrates the availability of Cricut Design Space features across Design Space platforms:

FEATURE	ANDROID APP	IOS APP	WINDOWS/MAC
Attach	✓	✓	✓
Contour	✓	✓	✓
Bluetooth compatible	✓	✓	✓
Cut and write in one step	✓	✓	✓
Writing style fonts	✓	✓	✓
Flatten to print	✓	✓	✓
Machine setup	✓	✓	✓
Slice and weld	✓	✓	✓
System fonts	✓	✓	✓
Print then cut		✓	✓
Offline		✓	✓
Photo canvas		✓	
Smart guides	✓	✓	
SnapMat		✓	
3D layer visualization		✓	
Image upload	✓	✓	✓
Pattern fills			✓
Templates			✓
Curve text			✓
Knife blade cutting			✓
Link physical cartridges			✓
Community (projects, profiles sharing)		✓	✓
Offset			✓
Project collections			✓

4. Cricut Design Space the Most Powerful Program

You must build the Cricut designs if you are thinking about doing this. You do this with PC tools. Cricut Design Space falls into play at this stage. It is the most commonly utilized and realistic application for producing this form of project. It is, though, one of the more costly – and it does not include any of the functionality you need.

Firstly, a deeper look at Cricut Design Space

"Cricut Design Space is a companion program for the Cricut Maker and Cricut Explore machines that allows you to design and cut wirelessly. Design projects from scratch or search the Cricut Image Library for thousands of pictures, predesigned Build It Now projects, and fonts. You can view your projects and photos anytime you're motivated since the software is cloud-based and connected through your devices. To imagine the idea on a real-life backdrop, use the built-in camera. Then, using your Cricut Maker or Cricut Explore machine's wireless link, cut your designs."

Features

- Use the Cricut Explore and Cricut Maker cutting machines to design and cut DIY designs.
- Choose from the Cricut Image Library's more than 50,000 images, projects, and fonts, or use your own pictures and fonts for free.
- Edit and upload your own images.
- Use images and fonts downloaded to your computer to design and cut without the need for an internet link.
- Predesigned cuts can be made quickly and easily. These are called Start It Now projects.
- Create home and party décor, cards, and invites, scrapbooking, jewellery, fashion, and children's crafts, among other things.
- Cut a range of products, such as paper, vinyl, iron-on, cardstock, poster board, cloth, and also heavier materials like leather.
- Use your device's built-in camera to place and imagine your designs against a real-world backdrop.
- Log in with your Cricut ID to view your projects and photos, as well as to make transactions on cricut.com or in Design Space more convenient.
- Wireless capability via Bluetooth (a wireless Bluetooth adapter, which is sold separately, may be needed).

As a consequence, searching for a Cricut Design Space substitute is completely legitimate. Even if you already own a Cricut machine, you may find that some of the alternatives are even more useful. Whatever you choose to build, we're certain that one of the Cricut Design Space substitutes below won't let you down. Continue reading to find out more about them.

Sure Cuts A Lot

After Cricut Design Space, this is the most common alternative. And it's because it's compatible with a broad variety of Cricut machines, including the standard Cricut to the Craft ROBO, the Silhouette, and even the Wish blade – to mention a couple.

You'll be able to sketch, model, color, and modify a number of items in order to make the most fascinating drawings. At the same time, it helps you to translate arbitrary pictures into die-cut templates, resulting in even better performance no matter what you're seeking.

Sure Cuts A Lot is easy as pie to use and comes with a slew of special functions that you won't find with most systems.

Here's a rundown of the numerous features and advantages which Sure Cuts A Lot provides:

Simple to Use

When you use Sure Cuts A Lot, the first thing you'll notice is how easy the interface is. You won't have to waste hours studying how to use the program because it makes it easy.

Around the edges, you'll see a range of choices for adjusting the color, brush thickness, stroke softness, and more. You can also focus in on your projects to allow more detailed edits. You'll have no trouble constructing even the most complicated designs due to the layer method.

Furthermore, you have the possibility of customizing the worktable's appearance to meet your needs. When it comes to files, you can arrange them as you like and store them in special directories with customized names for later usage.

There's nothing to worry about when it comes to utilizing Sure Cuts A Lot.

Strong degree of compatibility

It is a software that operates on almost any machine. It is compatible for both Windows and Mac and offers full support. It also operates with more than 30 separate Cricut devices, which is amazing.
You can even align the computer you're using with the app. You should pre-set fabrics, knives, and other crucial considerations in this manner before printing something.

And, sure enough, you can use your favorite measuring method to make things operate everywhere in the world. This app will not let you down, unless you use centimetres, millimetres, or inches.

Extra plugins and features

If you choose to make creative prototypes with the most thrilling Cricut performance, a large variety of plugins can come in handy. These plugins are also compliant with the majority of Cricut machines, which provides another level of convenience.

Advantages

- Provides full design and interface power
- Compliant with the bulk of die-cutting devices and computers
- Automatically updates with maximum support
- Offers a lot of plugins and additional functionality

Drawbacks

- Certain functionality does not work on Mac computers
- You can only operate on one task at a time

Make The Cut

Make The Cut, or MTC, is another third-party application framework you may use to modify die-cutting designs. It has all of the same features as Cricut Design Space, including optimum design features and excellent system usability.

Making The Cut has it all, from editing shapes and producing special patterns to incorporating exciting effects and even naming the Cricut template.

The real gain arises from its willingness to operate with a large collection of files. As a result, it not only offers superb editing but also unrivaled usability. Another gain is the length of time it has been on the market, making it a highly prestigious and trustworthy choice.

Want to hear more about what it has to offer? Some of its qualities are as follows:

Convenient editing

There's nothing you can't do with this app. Free-hand drawing, shadowing, node editing, auto-tracing, and external font installation are all available. You may also use the jigsaw design framework, the lattice design feature, and the additional pre-set design elements as required.

You can convert even the most complex template into a vector direction that can be die-cut using the Pixel Trace method and the graphic capability it includes. You may also print some form of a message on the photos utilizing the TrueType font framework.

If you love extra-useful apps, you won't be disappointed with this one.

Compatibility at the next stage

Another feature of this application is that it can be used with nearly every die-cutting machine in existence. It can operate with a Gazelle, Wish blade, Roland, Craft ROBO, and others. It is still the best choice available, even if it does not work with Cricut machines.

At the same time, it helps you to operate with a number of files. Working with PDF, JPG, SVG, AI, EPS, and PNG files would be a breeze. At the same time, it fits great with OTF, EPS, TTF, PS, AI9, GSD, and WPC files imported from other apps.

The compatibility that Make The Cut provides is literally unrivaled.

Fast and well-made

It doesn't end there; this is one is the fastest systems you will find. If you'd like an app that operates easily and takes minimal effort to use, this one will do.

At the same time, you will get sufficient assistance and little to no mistakes. Although other applications may abruptly shut down, this one will continue to function even when running on the most complicated and challenging designs.

Advantages

- Editing suite with loads of features
- Compatible with most die-cutting devices
- Outstanding compatibility with a range of file formats
- A dependable and fast method

Drawbacks

- Not compliant with Cricut machines
- Reliability problems for Mac machines

Inkscape

Inkscape, unlike the former two apps, is open-source software. That ensures you can have it for free and get all of the latest functionality. That means you can do anything from drawing, layering, cloning, and transforming to importing, rendering, and exporting files with full support.

There's also a special vector route scheme, which helps you to construct icons, charts, lines, and text layouts, as well as import and modify the most intricate works of art.

As an open-source application, you should expect excellent help in all fields, as well as a variety of tutorials and guides to turn to when required.

Since Inkscape provides so many features, I wanted to bring it all in one place for you:

Powerful editing

Inkscape's editing tools are, to put it simply, incredibly strong. There's almost nothing you won't find complicated.

If you choose to fill shades, for example, you can pick from solid, linear, blurred, or gradients. At the same time, you may alter the visibility of lines and colors when inserting whatever form of text and fonts you want.

There is also embedding, vector graphics, optional tracing, raster sources, and more. And, sure enough, you can openly move, rotate, scale, and skew designs. Despite the fact that it is an open-source application, it contains all you want and more.

Excellent import and export

Another important bonus is the freedom to export and import every type of file with no limitations or problems. Inkscape supports a broad variety of formats, including SVG, PDF, DXF, sk1, PNG, EPS, OpenDocument Drawing, and even Postscript.

You can also use the XML editor to modify and monitor files in real-time, deal with command-line choices, convert files to various formats, and more. The best aspect is the ease and flexibility it delivers, which makes it a piece of pie to finish without mistakes or time-consuming procedures.

The maximum degree of compatibility

Finally, Inkscape has the greatest compatibility in the industry for die-cutting design software. It can operate with Linux-based programs, Windows PCs, and Apple macOS desktops with no issue.

Everyone has outstanding compatibility and provides the same functionality with virtually no limitations or restrictions.

Advantages

- A feature-rich editing framework that can be used for any reason
- Compliant with nearly all layout file formats
- Linux, Windows, and macOS are all supported
- You won't have to spare a penny to use it

Drawbacks

- In big projects, the editor has a tendency to lag
- The interface is a bit complicated to use

Studio Silhouette

To bring our list to an end, we must discuss the Silhouette Studio. This is a textile design and embroidering method, not a die-cutting program. However, it acts in the same manner as the previous ones.

The efficient editing system, as well as the top-notch modeling capabilities, are what render it such fantastic software. You can make tiny designs with a lot of layers and edits, as well as bigger designs with many more products, without noticing the difference.

The software is quick to use and compatible with virtually every machine.

Would you like to hear more about Silhouette Studio? Here's some more information regarding its features:

Outstanding file integration

We all like design tools that help us to interact with a range of files. That is just what Silhouette Studio provides.

TTF and OTF files, GSD and GST files, and also STUDIO and STUDIO3 files, can all be imported. That's not even taking into consideration the numerous picture types, which vary from PNG to JPG, GIF, BMP, and TIF. Another significant benefit of this system is the ability to import from CorelDraw and Adobe Illustrator/Photoshop. You can also store the designs in PDF, SVG, and high-resolution JPG files. These functions, though, are only included in premium versions, which entail additional installation and activation.

Editing methods that aren't available everywhere else

Once you've imported an image or project, you can start using the awesome tools it has to offer. It has it all, from the Sticky Notes and Pop-Up maker, which allows you to stamp exclusive stamps on the designs, to Font Management software Warp, Trace, and even the Glyphs system.

With the Rhinestone tool, you'll also have access to a unique editing feature. It will allow you to make one-of-a-kind rhinestone elements and integrate them into your designs for outstanding results. You can also position them wherever you wish for a more appealing appearance.

Functional for all machines

It doesn't matter which Cricut machine you have or which platform you choose to mount it on; Silhouette Studio is compatible with virtually all of them. There's no reason to be worried with the compliance of operating systems such as Windows and macOS.

Although the installation can be a little complicated for those who are inexperienced with computers, it is still easy. You may even switch to the premium models in a matter of minutes without facing any performance problems.

Advantages

- Works well for a large variety of file formats
- Provides efficient and practical editing software
- Cricut and other die-cutting devices are extremely compatible
- Works well with other crafting and editing tools

Drawbacks

- Some services are paid
- Downloading and activating apps may be challenging

Final thoughts

As you can see, seeking an alternative to Cricut Design Space is not challenging. There are a number of choices to pick from, and they all have excellent features to bear in mind. It's all up to you. Choose the right one based on my limited recommendations and make sure it suits the specifications. Then you'll be able to enjoy fantastic Cricut designs without wasting any time or hard work looking for the perfect tool.

I hope you are able to find a better substitute to Cricut Design Space. Select one of these now and let the imagination run wild with fantastic Cricut designs. You won't be sorry.

5. New Updates and Features Coming to Design Space

Below is a list of all new (or soon to be added) features on Design Space, including innovative new additions like Offset (yes!) and Project Collections. I will be introducing several of the new features in the immediate future; this is only the beginning. To learn more, continue reading.

- Offset
- Project Collections
- Education videos in Design Space
- Kerning
- Thickness of pen on canvas
- "My Project" search
- Profile search
- Faster image and text load
- Copy and paste between projects

When will you be able to use these latest features on your PC? The majority of the latest functionality mentioned above have already been implemented. Over the next few weeks, Offset and Project Collections will be accessible.

Offset

To make the designs stand out, use the offset option in the desktop app to add stylish outlines to shapes, groups of items, or text. This popular design technique gives personalized stickers, T-shirt designs, cake toppers, and other items a professional look.

Collections of Projects

On the desktop app, you can easily sort projects into custom files so you can locate the project you want, whenever you want it. You can name the collections anything you want – T-shirt Designs, Paper Flowers, Custom Orders, and so on.

Education videos in Design Space

Within Design Space, you'll find links to beneficial how-to and tutorial videos. These quick tutorials will help you discover new functions, brush up on the fundamentals, or simply improve your artistic abilities.

Kerning

Kerning is a literary aesthetics strategy that requires changing the distance between two characters. You may want text to be nearer or further apart depending on the design; now you'll have further control over the look you're going for. Keep an eye out for when this latest function becomes accessible.

Thickness of pen on canvas

You may now display the template on the canvas with thicker or thinner pen and marker tip sizes to get a better idea of how your layout would appear.

"My Project" search

Find individual tasks you've stored in My Projects quickly.

Profile search

Find your favourite Cricut Community members and their joint ventures in a matter of seconds.

Faster image and text load

Text, huge images, and complicated projects are now loading more quickly. The canvas' code has been rewritten to boost efficiency, including its ability to manage larger, more complex files more easily! Learn more on how to load images and text quicker.

Copying and pasting between projects

You can also copy and paste design components from one Design Space canvas to another. Simply copy and paste the target entity (or set of objects) onto a new or current Design Space canvas. Use the Copy and Paste commands, use your own keyboard shortcuts, or the Edit drop-down display.

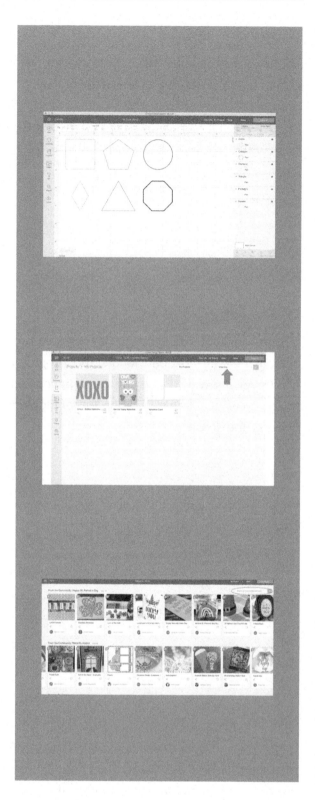

You may be wondering whether your Cricut Explore Air 2 is still useful in light of the latest Cricut Builder and Cricut Joy releases. Please, learn everything there is to know about this powerful cutting machine by trying out these awesome DIY designs.

The Cricut Explore Air 2 is a versatile cutting machine that can be used for a variety of tasks. With three distinct blades, it can cut over 100 different materials. You can create a wide range of products.
Check out some of the projects you can create with your Cricut Explore Air 2 right now. Both of these designs were cut with a Cricut Explore Air 2. As you will see, there are a range of fabrics and projects to choose from.

1. Leather Notebook Cover Crafted by Hand

This leather notebook cover was made with the Cricut Explore and synthetic leather. It is re-usable.

If you keep a journal or a file, or if you don't, you must take notes regardless of how many warnings you have placed on your computer.

Journal articles and documents are distributed in a range of ways and can be used for a number of various reasons. To-do list notebooks, bullet papers, spiritual journals, and travel journals are the most popular notebooks. A travel journal is a popular notebook concept, to which you can add ticket stubs, photographs, and notes as a keepsake.

If you enjoy a beautiful notebook cover, this project is for you. To learn how to make a custom-made recycled leather notebook cover with your Cricut, start with a cheap writing book from the dollar store or a thrift store.

Supplies

- Faux leather
- Blade with a deep cut
- Cricut Explore Air 2
- Easy Press Mat
- Vinyl
- Tweezers
- Sewing machine
- Iron-on vinyl

Instructions

- You can use genuine or faux leather to make this DIY journal cover. Since faux leather is smoother, it is easier to cut with a Cricut.
- Before cutting, put the leather smoother screen on the mats and fit the template. This will prolong the life of the cutting pad.
- Another option is to use transfer tape to cover the leather's fuzzy side and place it on the cutting board with the transfer tape facing down.
- Check that the leather is securely fastened to the cover. Lock the leather to your mat with painting tape or masking tape.
- Use a brayer to firmly press the leather against the cutting pad thus ensuring that it is securely fastened.
- Move the white stars to the side of the coaster bar if you're using real leather; otherwise, they'll indent the leather.

1. Gather the required materials.
2. Open the model space file in your window (recollect to mirror all your pictures).
3. Place the leather's good side down on the cutting pad. Delete the prototype from the mat you downloaded and cut it off.
4. In the design space, join any designs you choose to use to decorate your leather journal cover. Place the iron-on vinyl on the cutting mat with the positive side down. Place the pattern on the mat after printing it.
5. To iron on the leather, use an EasyPress and a mat.
6. Alignment: position the tiny bits on the ends of the wider cover wrong side up. For a 1/8-inch seam allowance, sew the sides together.
7. Have fun placing the notebook inside the leather cover.

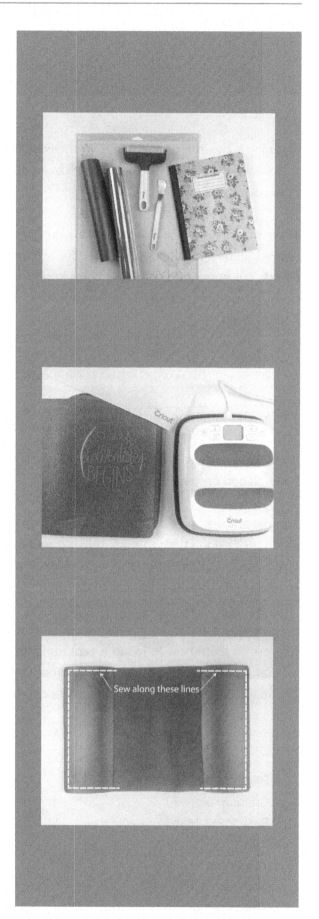

2. Cheer Mug

One of the most common projects you can build with your Cricut Explore Air 2 is a mug.

Supplies

- Green/blue cutting mat
- Cricut Explore Air 2
- White mug
- Weeding tool
- Three colors of permanent vinyl
- Hot chocolate ingredients
- Transfer tape
- Ribbon for decoration
- Crinkle paper filler

Instructions

1. Use the Upload feature in the Design Panel on the left of the canvas to upload it to Cricut Design Space. The file would need to be resized to fit the height of the mug, and the colors can be adjusted if you're using various vinyl shades.

2. Cut it out with your Cricut; unlike iron-on vinyl, regular adhesive vinyl does not need to be repeated (HTV). Clip and weed out any undesirable material from your images.

3. Cut a sheet of transfer tape to the dimensions of the slogan, peel back the transfer tape paper, place it over the words, and then burnish the vinyl.

4. Line up the slogan on your mug and begin clicking your decal in the center. After you've extracted the transfer tape from your vinyl, it should adhere to your cup. Rub it in a bit deeper if it doesn't.

5. Half-fill the mug with paper filling before incorporating all of the hot chocolate products, such as hot chocolate mix, mini marshmallows, and a candy cane.

3. Ink Tote Bag Cricut Infusible

Supplies

- EasyPress 2 Mat
- Cricut Explore Air 2
- Cricut Standard Grip Mat (Green)
- Ink Blank Tote Bag Cricut Infusible
- Heat press or EasyPress 2
- Cricut Infusible Ink Transfer Sheet
- Butcher paper
- Tweezers
- Tape (heat-resistant)
- Lint roller
- White cardstock

Instructions

Since infusible ink isn't normal in Cricut products, you'll need to adopt a specific technique to achieve the best performance. You don't want to wreck your dream, your EasyPress pad, or your sanity in the process, and making an error isn't cheap.

1. Make a sketch

Create your bag pattern in Cricut Design Space first, and, if this is your first project, start with something simple like this humorous "World's Okayest Adult" badge.

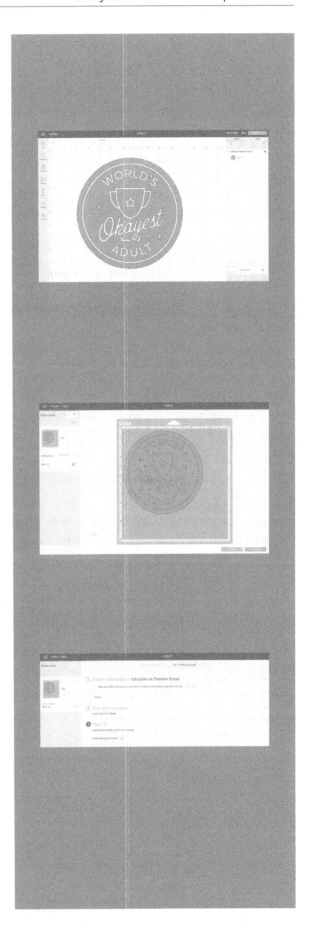

Making the picture 9x9 inches (though if you're using medium Easy Press 2, you'll have more wiggle space along the edge if you make it closer to 8.5x8.5 inches). Pick "Make It" in the top right corner.

Pick Infusible Ink Transfer Sheet as the substrate in the Render panel (search for "ink" using the Specific Material set on the dial of the Explore), then use a fine-tipped cutter.

2. Cut out the prototype with Explore

Put the filler side of the Infusible Ink Transfer Sheet on a green cutting pad. I used a Cricut brayer to smooth out the mat even further. As you can tell, the transition coating is a very light brown, almost off-white. But the ink does lighten when heated, as you can see.

Write it out and cut it out after that.

3. Weeding with Cricut Ink Infusion

The Infusible Paint, which is similar to a double sheet of paper, is made up of a paper ink sheet with a thin paper covering. After the first wash, I had to handle the second coat with tweezers despite getting a lot of weight on my weeding hook.

4. Have your Infusible Ink Tote Bag ready

Until you begin the transfer, pack your tote bag by putting the EasyPress Mat inside and covering it with a sheet of white cardboard. The white cardstock will help keep your EasyPress mat clean if it bleeds, and it can be saved for another infusible ink project.

Remove the mud and dirt from your tote bag with a lint roller to ensure a seamless transfer. It's a bit lighter and smoother than a conventional canvas tote since it's constructed of polyester rather than cotton.

5. Temperature and heat time settings

The EasyPress 2 is by far the most practical way of heating infusible ink, but you can still use a heat button. The EasyPress 2 will tolerate temperatures up to 400 degrees, while the original EasyPress can only accommodate temperatures up to 350 degrees. You can use the original, although the picture will be less colorful, according to Cricut.

The period and temperature for infusible ink on a tote bag, according to Cricut's Heat Settings Guide, is 385 degrees for 40 seconds; nevertheless, a few people complained that their transfers were always boring at

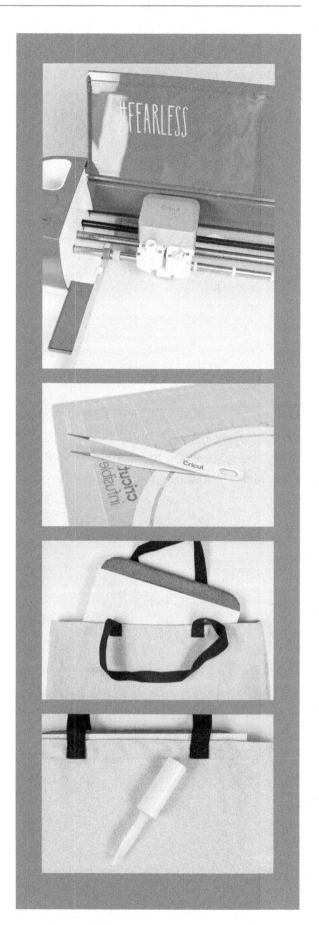

that temperature. One explanation is that the EasyPress loses a little heat as it reaches the cool bag and Easy-Press mat, resulting in a temperature of less than 385 degrees for the entire 40 seconds.

6. Transfer Cricut Infusible Ink with the EasyPress

To start, cover the blank tote bag with the butcher paper that comes with the transfer tray. Pre-heat the bag before applying the turn to help compress the surface and dry the humidity in the package, then allow to cool completely after 15 seconds of pressing. It's worth noting that the temperature fell as soon as I moved onto the cooler bag and mat.

To stop the switch from moving and blurring the corners, move it as little as possible and hold the button down for 40 seconds.

Allow time for the turn to cool before picking it up; it will not adhere to one's clothing.

After zooming in, you can see how deeply the ink is embedded in the tote bag's fabric.

4. Paper Flowers

Tissue paper florals are easy to produce, affordable, and time-saving. Cardboard flowers take longer to create, but when done correctly, they look elegant. I recently came up with a basic method for making large paper flowers.

You can learn a couple other tricks and tips when developing and testing this model that made the process even simpler, so I figured I would share them with you.

Supplies

The below are colors used:

Teal flower
- Mexican Poppy
- Navajo
- Turquoise Mist

Pink flower
- Mexican Poppy
- Arroyo
- Flamingo
- Coral Cream

Instructions

1. Here's where you can get the big paper flower design

https://heyletsmakestuff.com/giant-paper-flowers/

It includes an SVG file for cutting the flowers with any Cricut or other cutting device, as well as a PDF guide for hand drafting and cutting.

The SVG files can be sliced to whatever size you choose. They're large enough to make a flower that's almost 2 feet tall. If you'd like to create smaller models, you may do so. Reduce the file size to around 6 inches tall for the larger flowers, resulting in a 12-inch crop. Each of the teeny-tiny ones are 4 inches wide and produce an 8-inch flower.

2. Assembling the huge paper flowers

When you've finished cutting out all of your parts, you'll find that each petal has a cut running down the middle. To add dimension, replicate the bottoms of each petal with a little art glue. It doesn't matter how much the flower petals overlap; what matters is that they are all the same height.

Glue all of the petals together until they're dry to create the flower. Begin by gluing a loop to the top of the circular template, with the largest petals at the bottom. Apply the second coat after the first has dried, and so on until the flower is fully sealed.

Rather than supplying hand-cutting patterns, the most effective way to extend this flower-making method is to use a Cricut or another cutting machine.

Since the sample bits can be cut so precisely that they seem to be fully complete, it's ideal for quickly accomplishing tasks like this. Through changing the sizes of your sample pieces, you can quickly alter the scale of your floral design.

3. Best Glue for the flowers

Dry tacky glue is a good option for large paper flowers. It dries easily but not quickly enough that you can't make improvements if your petals aren't well arranged to begin with.

4. Organize a production line

Quick-dry tacky glue, as previously mentioned, is suitable for assembling these flowers. Apply a dab of glue to each of the six to eight petals that are lined up in parallel. Keep them together after that.

5. Extra hands and Wonder Clips are the same thing

Now, I put these flowers together first, then stayed with the same petal until the glue was dry enough to set it flat. As a result, each flower took about four days to develop.

You may also use Wonder Clips, which simulate a crowd of tiny friends pushing the petals together around you. Simply secure them with a clip and leave them to sit for a while. They leave a small indent on your paper, but the highest point covers everything except the inside page. Hold the three center sections between the fingers until the glue sets if the indentation bothers you.

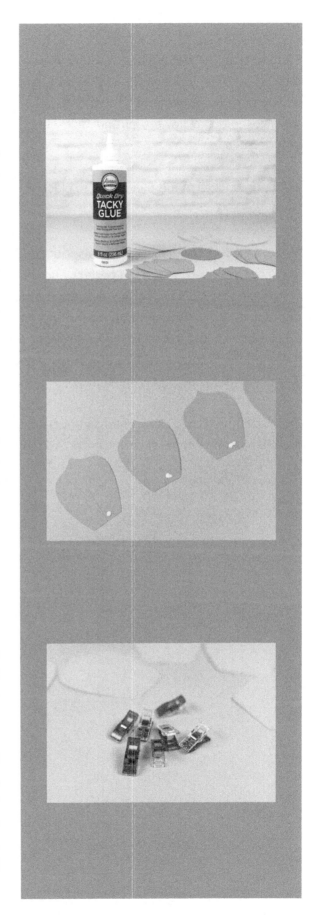

6. One layer at a time should be your focus

Starting from the bottom and working your way back is best. Then, until it dries, put a layer on top and secure it with a bowl or a bottle of glue or craft paint. You don't have to hold the flowers as the glue sets, unlike the Wonder Clips.

Continue until all of the pieces are in place.

7. It does not have to be flawless

Make an effort to match the petals, but don't worry if they're not precise. You're not perfect, and neither is life. There are six petals on the two outermost sides, five on the two center layers, and four on the two smallest layers. There are just three right in the middle. As a result, there's no way to ensure that they're evenly dispersed on each sheet, starting on the first side.

That's all there is to it. Both of these brief pointers add to the intimidating nature of large cardboard plants.

5. Make a Pillowcase for Yourself

Design a DIY color-your-own-pillowcase package for a party so that each child can make their own. Each child can paint and build their own naming outlines, which are constructed of vinyl or iron-on. Followed by recoloring the cloth with permanent cotton markers or waterproof markers.

A birthday party was recently planned for a group of nine-year-olds. They all got dressed up, and painting pillowcases was their favorite afternoon activity (aside from eating birthday cake). Each girl received a pillowcase with her name in ironed-on vinyl lettering. They were then given fabric markers and told they could paint and draw anything they wanted.

Supplies

- Cricut EasyPress Mat
- Cricut Explore Air 2
- Iron-on vinyl (black)
- Pillowcases
- Fabric markers
- Machine for cutting

Instructions

1. Create with a Cricut
In Cricut Design Space, type your name. Cricut Sans Illustration is a fantastic outline font that comes with Cricut Control, but you can use any other font on your screen.

2. Patterns for cutting
The Cricut Explore Air 2 can be used to cut out sketches. It's important to bear in mind that the document can be duplicated. You should iron the vinyl until you've weeded it. A transparent plastic sheet should be placed at the top of the design.

3. The ventilation system
Place the pillowcase over the heating pad after the EasyPress has warmed up. Iron on the vinyl pattern after

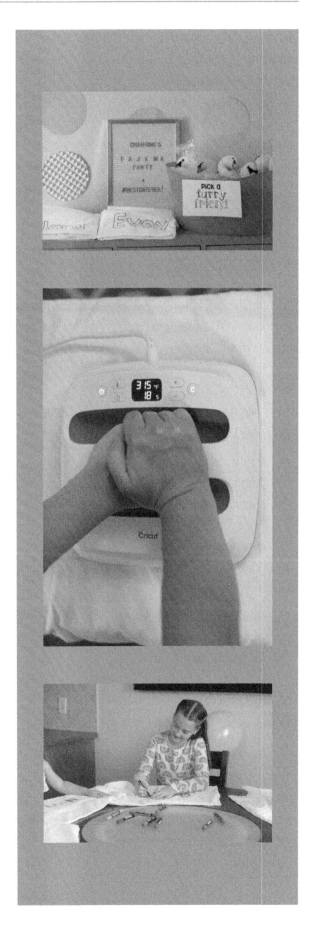

warming the pillowcase with the EasyPress. Heat your material according to the Heat Configurations Guide and peel as instructed.

Place a sheet of cardboard within the pillowcase before you're about to color to prevent the markers from leaking from front to back. You may want to cut it out and slip it in ahead of time to make naming simpler. The most enjoyable aspect is painting.

6. Painted Wood via Adhesive Vinyl

One of Cricut Explore Air 2's greatest crafts is the home decor sign. The majority of people enjoy it, and there are many ways to do it.

Supplies

The Wild Rose kit comprises almost all you will want to complete this project

- Pink adhesive vinyl
- Cricut Explore Air 2 (Wild Rose)
- Black adhesive vinyl
- Transfer tape
- Weeding tool
- Scraper

You'll also require the following items

- Paint brush
- Wood sign
- Clearcoat white paint

Instructions

Learn how to apply vinyl to furniture.

1. Make a symbol

If you'd like to paint the sign on raw wood, sand down the rough areas; the finer the wood is, the more it can adhere to the vinyl. The best piece of advice is to begin with the best wood you can afford.

After that, apply at least two coats of color. After that, let the sign dry for at least 24 hours to enable the paint to cure.

2. Begin the Design Room submission process

You'll need the Cricut Design Space file to make this build, which you can get here. https://design.cricut.com/#/design/135107376"

3. Reduce the size of the project

Resize the symbol using the scale function in the Edit Toolbar at the right, based on the height of your label. Since this picture allowed the words to fit on a single black vinyl sheet, and combining them would have made it larger than 12 inches, I didn't enter two black words.

4. Create a vinyl cut

When the project is the correct size, click the "Create It" button in the upper right corner. Production Room will prompt you to cut the two vinyl shades. Since this isn't iron-on vinyl, don't copy that portrait. Place your

sheet on top of the vibrant side of your vinyl. Then place it in your Cricut and cut it out with the flickering C.

5. Get rid of your vinyl recordings

Use the weeding process to remove the "negative" vinyl after the project has been cut. Weeding is the act of eliminating any of the pieces of a picture that aren't being utilized. After that, cut out the bits and see how they'll appear on your sign.

6. Apply transfer tape to the picture

While using transfer tape, it's best to position the cut vinyl face up first, then cover it with the tape. When operating with larger pieces, however, it's more popular to start with the transfer tape sticky side up, then the cut vinyl face down. This encourages you to use bigger pieces of transfer tape, which may also be staticky.

Burnish the vinyl onto the transfer tape with the scraper. If at all possible, split the words (I had 2 words on a single sheet of transfer tape in this instance). The vinyl will adhere to the transparent transfer tape as you peel back the white carrier film.

7. Place the vinyl in a straight line on your sign

Place the vinyl on the project and transfer the tape. Check it is in place before you start burnishing.

8. Boost the symbol's visibility

Burnish the words on your wood sticker with the scraper.

9. Peel the transfer tape from the project

After that, the transfer tape should be stripped forward. Burnish it again if it doesn't stick (which may be tough on some painted wood). You may have noticed that, although the vinyl adhered well to this specific sign, other activities took more work, and that one has to use the weeding device to help free the vinyl from the transfer tape and transfer it onto the sign.

10. Finish with a clear coat

Apply a transparent coat to the project if appropriate. ModPodge Ultra, a smooth and solid-drying mist, is strongly recommended.

7. DIY Cricut Teacher Mug

Supplies

- Weeder
- Transfer Tape
- Standard Grip Mat
- Cricut Explore Air 2
- Cricut Permanent Vinyl

Instructions

1. We will begin by learning how to create a logo in Cricut Design Room.

2. Click "customize" when you've unlocked the template in Design Space, and you'll be led to the project page, where you can edit it. You'll see the screenshot of the "best teacher ever," and also the monogram used, that you have kept in the file for comparison, but you can erase now if you like.

3. Type the letters you want to use with the monogram using the type function. If you modify its font to Monogram, each letter will appear three times in a design. It may sound strange, but it's just what we need right now.

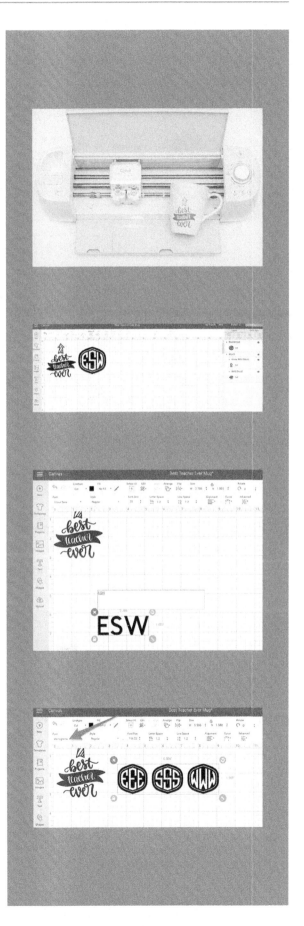

4. Ungroup the letters by selecting them and clicking "ungroup." You will be able to modify each letter individually as a result of this.

5. Exclude the first letter from the rest of the letters. To distinguish the first word from the other two, we will just use the slice function. Create a square with the shapes tool and position it within the first word, up to a black boundary between the first two characters.

6. The slice tool is then used to isolate the first word from the others. Click "slice" and then in the bottom right corner to choose the square and letters.

7. If you press and move the shapes, you will see that the two icons were cut to make new shapes, one of which has a split first letter for our monogram. Remove the extra shapes produced and also the remaining two letters while retaining just the first letter form.

8. Repeat the procedure with the next letter group, except this time slice the letters twice, one on either side, with a rectangle.

9. Remove the extra shapes once more, leaving just the middle letter.

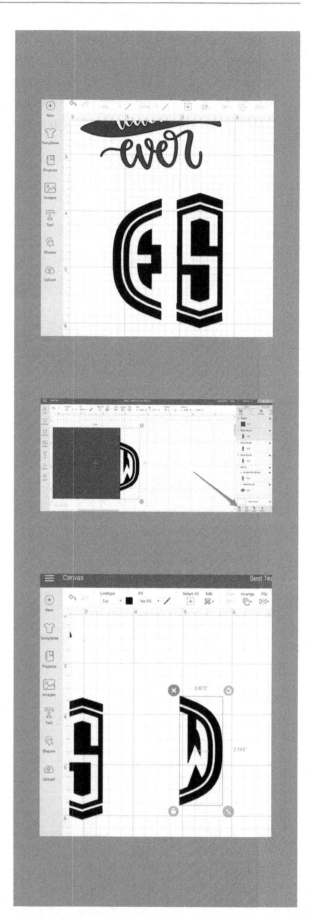

10. Repeat for the third letter group, this time just keeping the letter on the right side.

11. After that, we will need to combine all three mono-gram characters into one. From the align slot, choose "center vertically" and choose all three. This will guarantee that the characters are correctly balanced before we slide them horizontally together.

12. It's best to get full balance by zooming in with the plus icon in the bottom left corner of the frame. Switch the horizontal orientation of the letters with shift key (to lock motions to the horizontal direction) until they're precisely matched.

13. Select all three letters and press "weld" in the lower right until they're all in place. This was a bit finicky because, after the letters were welded, they would sometimes be disturbed by a very small margin, which did not look good. If this occurs, undo the weld, pick all letters again, and then use the align feature to select "align vertically."

14. After the monogram and the "best teacher ever" icon have been welded, we will resize them to suit the mug.

15. Now that you know how to create a logo in Cricut Design Space, it is time to cut the layout from permanent vinyl with our Cricut Explore Air 2. You will be led to the cutting screen after pressing "make" in the upper right corner. We don't need to copy the pattern as we would for iron-on because, if you're using one color of permanent vinyl, all designs can be cut from the same mat.

16. Load the vinyl into the unit by placing it on a regular grip mat (ensure that the machine is equipped with a fine-point blade). To transfer the file to your machine, follow the on-screen instructions, and make sure you pick the right material to be cut on either your machine or on the screen.

17. Allow the machine to do its work, then unload the mat and trim the designs.

18. Remove the negative vinyl with a weeder (make sure you're cutting the correct pieces with the monogram style – I did mine backward with the very first piece I cut, which would have been perfect except for the border section, so I had to cut a second image).

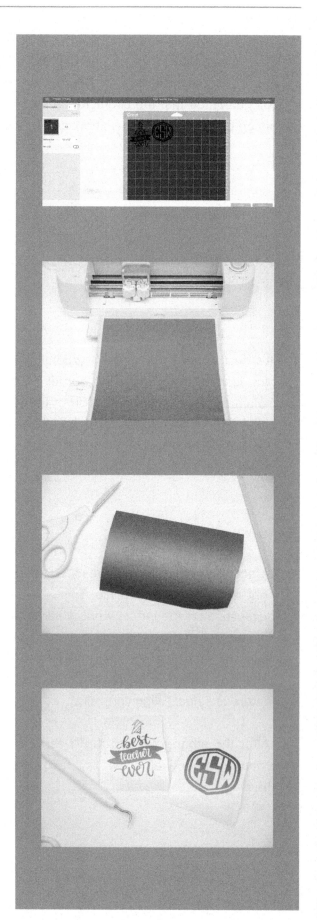

19. Cut a sheet of normal transfer tape slightly bigger than the vinyl designs (you don't want to use a heavy grip).

20. Remove the transfer tape's paper backing and put it on the "best teacher ever" pattern, following the grid lines to hold it straight. Make sure the transfer tape is securely stuck to the vinyl with a scraper.

21. Slowly strip the vinyl's plastic backing away, making sure that both of the vinyl parts adhere to the transfer tape. I had to use tweezers to replace the small insides of the Es because they wouldn't remain in place.

22. Starting in the center and steadily rolling outward on each side, put the design on the mug as desired.

23. To adhere the design to the cup, use a scraper to tightly push all areas of the design.

24. Peel the plastic away from the pattern slowly, making sure the vinyl is very well adhered.

25. Repeat the procedures above with the monogram pattern on the mug's opposite side.

You did an outstanding job. You should start designing them for all your favorite teachers now that you know how to create a monogram in Cricut Design Software for your own monogram teacher mug.

8. Vinyl Sticker

You'll learn how to design vinyl decals of your own, stickers, wall art, and window decals with this guide. With transfer paper, vinyl may be transferred to any sleek substance (ceramic, glass, or a wall). Better adhesive-backed vinyl is needed for rough surfaces. Don't worry; I'll clarify the variations below, as well as when you can utilize a cutting mat and when you shouldn't.

I'll assume you are using the Cricut Explore Air 2 and Design Space for this guide, but the same rules apply to other machines and apps.
Let's get this party underway.

Using the Cricut Explore Air 2 to make your own vinyl decals

Supplies

- Cricut Explore Air 2
- Vinyl (matte/removable Oracal 631 or glossy/semi-permanent Oracal 651)
- Tape for transfer
- A mat for cutting (optional)
- Cricut Tools Basic Package or Cricut Design Space Basic Set
- Tweezers
- Scraper

Instructions

Making the initial cut

Take a quick glance at your vinyl if you haven't already. The vinyl you'll need is normally comprised of two portions: the vinyl itself and a paper liner. It appears as follows:

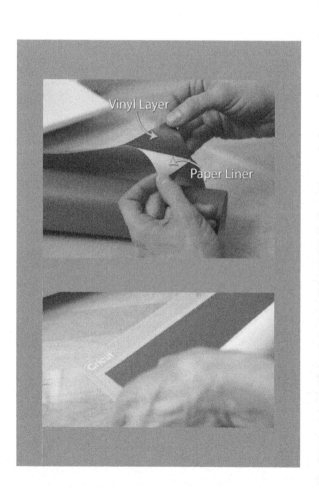

1. Plan the design ahead of time. If you need help loading a concept into Cricut Design Space, visit their YouTube channel, where they provide a good course.
2. Put your vinyl face down on the cutting sheet, with the paper lining facing the mat.
3. Put the mat in the machine and pick Vinyl on the smart set dial. Your machine will be designed to remove the vinyl and not the backing paper.

4. Press go (the C icon beneath the dial).
5. When your cut is done, extract the vinyl from the mat.
6. Weed away any residual vinyl film from the photograph. To make this easy, you could use tweezers or a Cricut/Silhouette hook tool.

Putting the cut vinyl to work

1. Clean and dry the sleek surface where the vinyl will be mounted eventually.
2. Draw a line where you like the design to go. If you're working on a wall, you can use a stage.
3. Calculate the size of the picture and cut a piece of transfer tape to match.
4. Peel the transfer tape's liner.

5. Put the tape over the picture using the orientation grid.

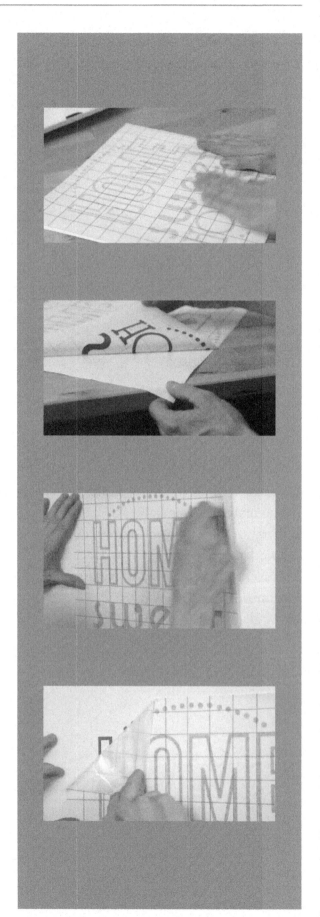

6. Smooth out any air bubbles that might have formed.
7. Peel the liner away from the vinyl portrait. The transfer tape will hold the vinyl in place.

8. Carefully put the transfer tape and picture on the item/wall, lining up the grid.
9. Press down tightly on the picture from the middle to the edges until it is fully flat.

10. Peel the transfer tape away from the surface one corner at a time.

That ends our process. The first period is often the most difficult; you typically need to test with a demo the first few times you attempt something different, and then you are flying solo a week later.

In the next few paragraphs, I will go through the most common errors and offer suggestions in the hopes of speeding up the process for you. Following that, I will go through numerous forms of vinyl, which types to stop using, and which is better for each use.

Some tips

- Move the transfer tape away from the picture at an angle of 45 degrees before replacing it.
- Instead of removing the tape rapidly, rock it steadily and softly.
- If the tape refuses to remove the vinyl, just reapply it to the surface and strongly push it down again.
- Cut the transfer tape at a slower speed if the design is thin.
- If you're working on a large image, recruit the help of a friend.
- When adding vinyl to rough surfaces, use strong adhesive-backed vinyl.
- Whether you're using iron-on, heat transfer, or t-shirt vinyl, make sure the picture is replicated in Design Space or it can come out reverse. This is also useful when adding vinyl to an internal window to guarantee that it reads accurately from the outside.
- Even though the vinyl's paper filler requires it to be fed directly into your unit, it's always a smart choice to use a mat for cutting for more accurate performance.
- Try new things.
- When using adhesive vinyl, don't peel off the paper backing until it's time to put it on the cutting mat so it can stick.
- Use outdoor vinyl on vehicle decals.
- Cricut has a fantastic video guide about how to use glitter vinyl.

9. How to Make Complex Stickers

Print then Cut is a Cricut Design Space feature that lets you print your designs before cutting them out with your machine. You should instruct your printer to Print. Then Split in two directions. The first is to adjust the Fill to Print choice and pick a color or template. The second approach is to use the Flatten feature at the bottom of the layers row to flatten the layers. Don't think about this during the design phase for better practices and zero frustrations; it would just stress you out. Simply add your forms, text, and pictures, then flatten the entire thing (you will learn this in the step-by-step tutorial.)

Note:
While you go through some Print then Cut topics in this section, bear in mind that this is a really strong method.

Producing Cricut Stickers: Computer and Settings

When designing stickers with your Cricut, there are two things you must always bear in mind.
The first is in terms of scale. Only templates ranging up to 9.25x6.75 inches may be printed and cut. So

double-check the measurements before submitting the project to be cut, or you'll get a message that the picture is very big.

Another factor to think about is the limits of your machine:

- Use colorful paper (that isn't too busy) and shiny white materials if you have a Cricut Maker.
- When you're using an Explore printer, use white paper with a matte finish.

Create Stickers with your Cricut: A Step-by-Step Guide

Now that you've worked out what your system wants, it's time to learn how to create stickers.

Supplies

- Cricut Maker/Explore Air 2
- Sticker paper
- Printer
- Razor with a fine point
- Pad with a light grip (blue)

Note:

If you still have Cricut sticker sheets, consider saving the Print and get it printed at Staples or Office Depot. Alternatively, if that's too much work, grab the other one. It is true that time is capital.

Putting Together a Technique

Since you can create stickers out of the text, pictures, forms, and pretty much everything in Design Space, you may feel overwhelmed and unsure where to begin.

So, in order for you to enjoy your sticker-making experience, I have invented a "frustration-proof" process.

The following are the steps we'll take:

1. Design a layout (by adding different shapes)
2. Introduce a splash of color or a template
3. Attach text and pictures to the page
4. Flatten and double-check the dimension
5. Cut the stickers with scissors.

Note:

Bear in mind to save your job while you're away from your Cricut. It takes a long time to make, and Cricut doesn't have any backup choices.

Step 1: Build a sticker sheet pattern in phase one

Since we can only print and cut in sizes no larger than 9.25x6.75 inches in Cricut Design Space. It is recommended to insert a checklist so you can keep track of your space and make a sticker sheet style.

To use as a reference, install a 9.25x6.75-inch rectangle. To incorporate the guideline, go to the left-hand side of the canvas and choose the square option from the shapes menu. Then go to the menu settings at the top of the canvas and press the little square in the center to enable proportions (while also selecting the rectangle).

Then type in 6.75 on W (width) and 9.25 on H (height). Shift the line type color to white after reformatting the rectangle to make it simpler for you to see the design.

Many of the shapes you may use for your stickers are seen in this illustration.

Insert the shapes you like for your stickers after you've built your guide. You can pick from nine different Cricut choices. You can use cubes, hearts, rings, stars, and triangles in this tutorial.

Now we must populate our guide with a number of different shapes. Don't forget to enable dimensions so you can build whatever rectangle you want.

Tip 1

To keep your shapes and all the other shapes you're applying to your sticker template coordinated, use the align option. Pick the components you want to align, and then use the multiple options to align them the way you want. In most instances, Core and Distribute can be used vertically or horizontally. But go ahead and give it a crack. You'll make a few errors while you're still getting used to it, but once you've learned it, there's no turning back.

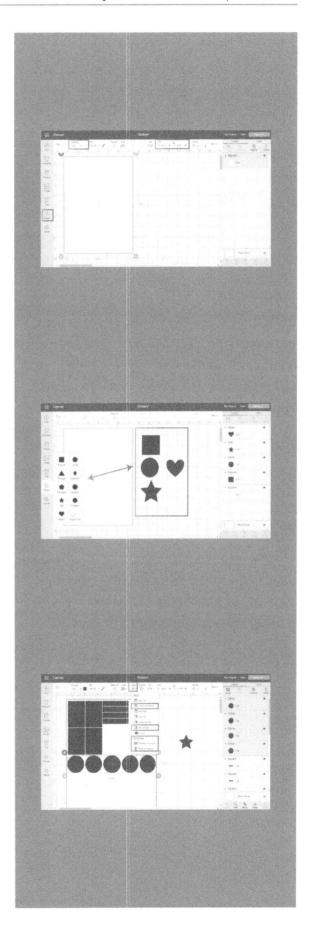

Tip 2

Make a number of figures with your stickers. For a step-by-step plan, see the picture below.

- Draw a rectangle and a triangle (the triangle must be flipped upside down).
- Connect the triangle to the rectangle's edge. They must be entangled (just a notch).
- To build a new component for our stickers, select all shapes and weld them together (the Weld icon can be found at the bottom of the Layers Panel).
- Rotate your stickers to match your style.

Continue to incorporate shapes of various sizes and let the imagination run wild. At the end, the stickers will be adorable. You must erase or hide your guide until your layout is complete. Please ensure to do this; if you don't flatten the labels, they won't cut.

Now pick all of the shapes and shift the line type color to white; this will make you see what you're doing next more clearly.

Step 2: Add colors and patterns

It's time to spruce up your stickers with some color. Don't think about line type or Print then Break, as I said earlier. We'll get to it later. You may select a strong backdrop or a design to add color to your sticker.

Make the stickers a strong color

Adjust the color box next to the line type environment, located within the side bar of the canvas field, to the feature you want to color. If you choose advanced, you will be able to see a larger variety of colors and use a code to scan for a particular hue.

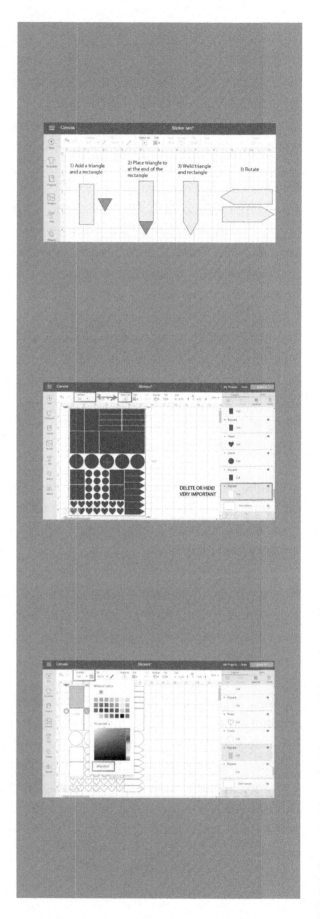

Tip

To adjust the color of several shapes at once, hold down shift on your keyboard while clicking on all of the items you want to change; this often helps for patterns.

Add patterns to Cricut Sticker

Patterns are backgrounds for stickers and other Print then Cut projects. You may pick from a vast selection of them. Cricut used to charge for them, but they're now online, so take full advantage of them while you can.

Explore new patterns for Cricut Stickers

Adjust the fills of the shapes you would like to change for Print, then tap on the color box for this choice and select Pattern for Print Form. There are several patterns to pick from. When you've discovered the pattern you'd like to use, don't hesitate to check the editing choices.

Patterns can be quite tiny at times. The size and horizontal orientation are the two aspects that normally can be adjusted. All of the adjustments made to a pattern will be displayed on a small preview as you adjust it.

Step 3: Fill in the blanks with text and photos

To add code, go to the left panel of canvas and press the Text icon. If you're not sure how to edit text on Cricut Design Space, check out any tutorial on this topic.
Once you've applied all of the colors and designs to your stickers, type in the text you intend to use.

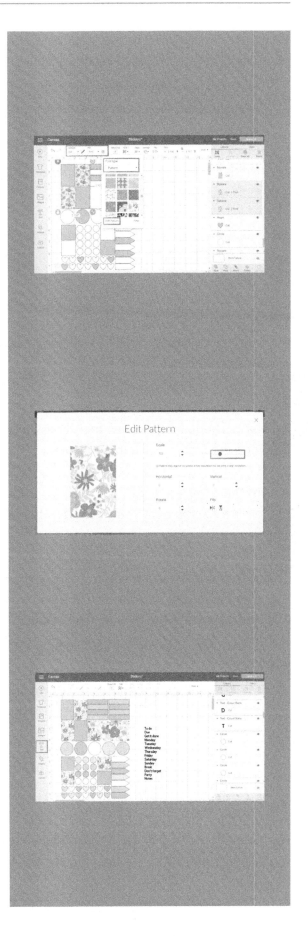

Fill in the text you'd like to use on your stickers.

Here are several samples of various sticker sheet types:

- To-Do / Due / Have It Finished / Days of the Week / Reminders / Don't Overlook / Essential / Break / Appointment...
- Enjoy life / Pool Day / Break / Dance / Holiday / Date Night / Snowboard Day / Ocean Vibes / Breakfast / Girls Night Out...

Place the text on the shapes you would like them to be once you've typed it in.

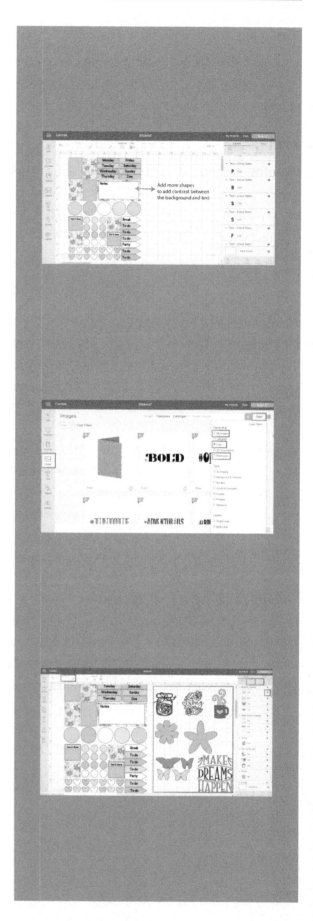

Creating Cricut Stickers is one of my favorite activities to do because you can personalize the text to suit your tastes and life in general, which is something you wouldn't be able to find in a normal shop.

Tip

Add more shapes if necessary to establish a comparison between the patterns and the document.

It's now time to start applying photos to your stickers. On the layers side of the canvas, press the Photos button.

To find free photos, use the filter.

You may either upload your own photos or use images from the Cricut Library. They do have a subscription, but if you're like me, and prefer free things, filter photos and choose:

- My Pictures (look at the ones you've submitted to the program)
- No expense
- Purchased (your machine will have a set of free images)

Fill the canvas with pictures

It is suggested to add one at a time and then resize them because if you do it all at once, the canvas would be a nightmare.

Remember that while dealing with pictures, they can be clustered together and have varying colors and sizes. As a consequence, you'll need to ungroup them in order to adjust the colors and sizes of each individual unit. To suit the sticker sheets, you may need to change the proportions.

Step 4: Double-check the scale and flatten it

We're going to get into serious territory now.

Note

If you have the Checklist we used at the outset, uninstall it immediately.

When you're done with your stickers, pick everything on the canvas (that's part of a sticker sheet) and press the flatten choice in the Layers Panel's bottom left corner.

Don't fail to flatten your job.
Our stickers, as you'll see in the screenshots below, are very distinctive. All are on one sheet, and the blade can cut into all of the shapes' outlines.

Flatten out the result

When you're ready to cut, go to the upper right corner and press the "Make it" icon, at long last.

Now, let's have a peek at these cuties and see what we can do with them.

Step 5: Print your Cricut Stickers and cut them out

The view you'll get when you start chopping is seen in the following screenshot.

As you can see, I made full use of the limited room – sticker paper is costly, so make the best of each square inch.

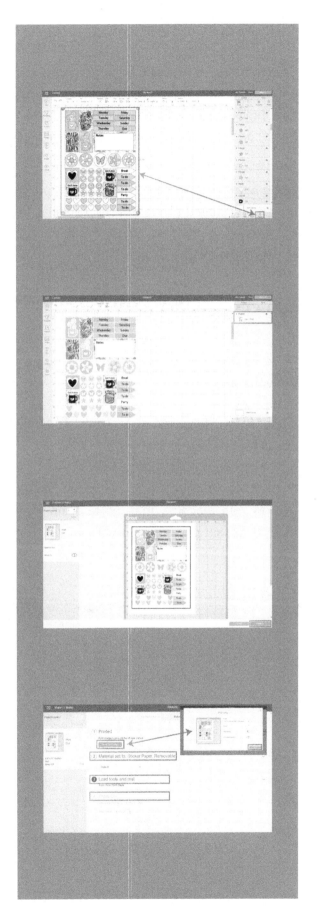

To begin choosing materials, press Continue.

Check that all is in order before clicking the next icon (this is how the printed copy should be put on your mat). To submit the project to the printer, first press Transfer to Printer (leave all of the default options on) and then print.

WARNING:

While printing on the sticker paper, ensure you print on the correct side. If you're not sure which side of the paper the printer prints on, check it with a normal sheet of paper marked with a circle.

Load mats and equipment after printing your sticker cover.

Once you've printed, you'll need to pick the sticker paper you'll be using.

If you have a Cricut Maker, go to all of the materials and check for "sticker" to limit the performance.

If you have a Cricut Explore, first change the smart set dial on your machine, then go to template space and pick the sticker paper you want to use.

Load mat

Unload mat

Remove from mat

Let's switch to real-life pictures now.

Attach fine-point blade and put an already printed sticker paper onto your mat, load it into your computer, and click the blinking Go button on your system after choosing the materials. See the magic unfold right in front of your eyes.

When Design Space says the cut is over, unload the Cricut mat and then remove the sticker layer.

That concludes the guide. You can use these lovely stickers to schedule your tasks.

Cricut stickers created with form models

I've provided six different layouts for you to choose from for your designs. Press mostly on yellow buttons to open them, then save them to the device, and upload them into Cricut Design Space.

They come in a range of shades, but please try to customize them using the techniques. Sticker models may be uploaded to Cricut Design Space.

Login into Cricut Design Space and press the Upload button on the Layers Panel to upload your idea. Second, pick the image from your device by clicking on "Upload Image."

Sticker layouts may be submitted to Design Space.

The template will appear under recently updated photos until it has been uploaded. Pick it and then choose Insert Photos from the drop-down screen.

To edit each shape individually; first, pick the file, and then press Ungroup.

Ungroup the shapes so that you can modify them separately.

Here is a curvy pattern. To add text to it, simply follow the measures illustrated in the screenshot below.

Text may be applied to wavy forms.

Take a peek at this.

Isn't it striking how odd it appears? To create a new tone, try to use a range of colors and pictures.

It really is more in the vein of beach and mermaid stickers.

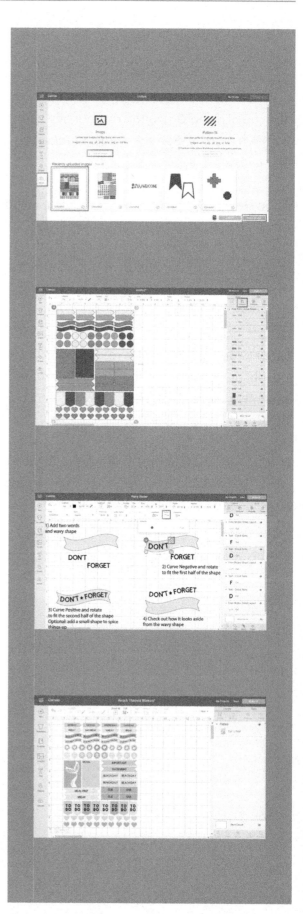

Adjust the colors and give the format a fresh look.
And, in case you're interested, here are the picture and color codes:

- Blue, Peach, Yellow, Purple
- Cricut Font / Cricut Sans, as well as Simple Shapes

You may also use the same shape to build a whole website. They are good for naming your papers, or you could just use them as an incentive scheme if you have children.

They're stunning, aren't they?

You may adore how bright and lovely they are. Don't you think so?

Hearts, stars, and flowers (#M3F100) were used as photos.

Use only patterns for the backdrop and free Cricut photos for this sticker sheet. You should also use your own quotations.

What are your thoughts?

Congratulations, you've perfected the craft of Cricut Stickers!

Did you notice that a single Cricut post takes about fifteen hours to complete? It's crazy.

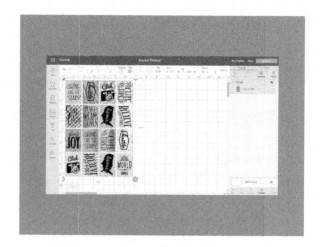

5.

CRICUT DESIGN SPACE FOR BEGINNERS

The Unofficial Step-by-Step Guide to Cricut Design
Space with Illustrations, Tips and Tricks, and
Original DIY Projects for Explore Air 2, Maker, and
Joy!

Philippa Smalley

CRICUT DESIGN SPACE FOR BEGINNERS

Introduction

The Cricut Machine has so far revolutionized the DIY world. Enable your imagination to run wild as you play and build with the cutting-edge Cricut Machine. With the Cricut Design Space's innovative fonts and templates, you can construct everything your imagination can dream up.

Isn't it true that everybody likes crafting? You can be very inventive and hands-on, but as time passes, you'll start searching for something different to challenge you and take your crafting to the next level. The Cricut machine seems to be the absolute favorite thing, with several machines, materials, and accessories available. It is a home die-cutting machine used for several arts, crafts, and ventures, such as scrapbooking and textiles. The Cricut is the best art and crafts cutting machine on the market and this book offers advice on the Cricut for beginners, starting from how to print and cut, to which sort of mats to use while crafting. The Cricut machine and Design Space software come together to create the design quite comfortably if you want to make something from scratch or start with ideas that have already been built. Design Space's readily available projects are perfect when you want to choose something and get started straight away. There is a range of choices to choose from, with guides, cut-ready templates, or material lists. All one has to do is follow along. Starting a concept from scratch is a wonderful way to learn, explore, and express your imagination. Design Space provides you with various images and fonts to use as building blocks in your design work.

Design Space is the free design template application at the heart of the Cricut experience. Design Space has been crafted to be easy for those who are just getting started with crafting but advanced enough for more experienced users. You'll start with a canvas when you begin a new design, where your concept will be laid out. Take images and fonts from those in the library and edit, orientate, paint, and scale them until you have a pleasing composition.

Pick your products, and Design Space will assist you by recommending the necessary equipment (such as blades and pens) for the job. When asked, load your mat and equipment, and the computer will take care of the rest. When you're done, carefully remove the cuts from the mats and assemble. It isn't easy to relax when you're just getting started. Setting a target to learn one new skill during your Cricut journey is a smart idea.

A Cricut is a cutting machine that can cut various materials, such as cardstock, paper, and vinyl, for art projects. One can also cut leather, thin wood, cloth, and more with certain Cricut machines. You also can cut balsa wood and even thicker materials with its knife blade if you've got a Cricut Maker cutting kit, and you will be able to cut even fabrics and crepe paper with a rotary cutter. Furthermore, you can also do engraving, perforation, debossing, and wany lines with the latest tools for Cricut Maker. The cutting machine of Cricut will help you make stuff like:

- Personalized mugs and tumblers
- Banners
- Cards
- Stickers
- Earrings and other jewellery
- Custom T-shirts
- Paper flowers
- Keychains

1. How to Make Your Cricut Setup

When the user takes Cricut out of its box, it will be closed just like in the image. Cricut Explore will look a bit different; however, most operations seem to be the same on both machines. Find a place near a socket for your Cricut, so you can conveniently plug it in.

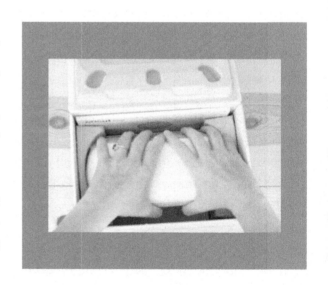

Also, make sure to leave sufficient clearance for the cut mats on the front and back of the Cricut machine because the mats move through the machine while Cricut is cutting the project.

The mats are 12 or 24 inches long for big ventures. But depending on the mat you're using, you're going to need a further 10 to 20 inches of clearance for the back of the Cricut.

There are two cords inside the box:

- One string has a square end and another USB end. This is the cord you need to connect Cricut with your computer. If you're planning to connect through Bluetooth, just leave this cord in the box or another secure location in case you need it. When you're using the cord plug, insert the square end into the Cricut Machine's right rear and the other USB end into a desktop computer.

- The second one is the power cord. The edge of the circle plugs into the back of the Cricut on its rear right and the end of the plug into the outlet.

Now that the Cricut is set up and ready to go, let us now set up Design Space and use it to check on how to use Cricut.

2. How Does the Cricut Machine Work?

One can wirelessly attach a Cricut to a computer system, build or import designs to it, and then upload them for cutting to Cricut. Cricut offers Design Space (applicable for Windows, Mac, and smartphones) that allows you to build and import machine-cut designs. A tiny blade (rotary cutter, pen, or scoring tool) is installed within the Cricut. You can mount your desired material over a 12-inch broad cutting mat if you have a design ready to cut in Design Space, deliver your design to Cricut wirelessly, and then load your material into the machine. With the click of a button, the project will begin cutting.

When you're new to cutting machines or are switching from another machine brand, you're probably wondering how hard the learning process is to catch up with a Cricut machine. It's fairly easy and divided into the following simple steps.

Move 1

Bring the machine out of the bag. As described before in the initial analysis, Cricut Explore Air comes wrapped in a carrying bag. Keep it inside the bag when not in use to keep the dust away from the machine.

Move 2

Plug in and open your machine. Connect the power adapter to your machine and then to the outlet. Use Bluetooth to connect Cricut Explore Air to a tablet, but if you've got a Cricut Explore One or just want to attach it to a laptop or desktop via USB, you'll need to connect a USB cable. Click the left button labelled "Open" to launch the machine.

Move 3

Switch on the machine. Click the power button on the right side to turn the machine on.

Move 4

Connect to Cricut Design Space. As described earlier in the series, Cricut Design Space is cloud-based software that you use to design projects and interact with the Cricut machine. People must use the New Machine Setup when they're a completely new user.

Move 5

If someone is a current user and using Bluetooth, they can connect to Cricut now.

Move 6

Pick a project to build or customize or plan your project. If you log in to Cricut Design Space, you can browse for a project, search for ideas before creating your new project, select one of your current projects, or develop a new project.

Move 7

Pick from Smart Set Dial. Rotate the dial so that the point on the pressure-setting dial faces the material you want to cut, compose, or rate. If your material is not specified, click "Custom" and pick the material from its Design Space drop-down menu.

Move 8

Mount the cutting mat. Place the material upon the cutting mat. Follow the guidelines in Design Space to load the cutting mat. Click on the flashing load button (up/down arrow on the right side of the machine). After placing the mat in, the machine guides it so that it loads correctly.

Move 9

Push the Cricut button and let the system work. If "Go" in the Design space is pressed, the Cricut button on the machine will start to flash. Click it to get your project underway. The Cricut will begin to work. Design Space will alert whether one needs to change blades, mats, or pens for a project.

Move 10

Remove it and congratulate yourself! Once the project has finished writing, cutting, and scoring, you will be reminded through Design Space and blinking lights on your machine to pack up the cutting mat. Just use the same up and down arrow button that you used to mount the mat to unload it. Get your idea off the mat, and you're free to enjoy it.

If it feels too overwhelming to pick your first project, note that your Cricut will come with materials and directions to get the project underway. And there'll be an online Service Center (which has a whole segment on new machines) and a free toll hotline to help out if you're lost. If you're searching for an in-depth lesson, check out Craft and Create with Cricut Explore on Craftsy.

3. What Are Cricut Legacy Devices?

Legacy devices no longer sold include Cricut Personal, Cricut Gypsy, Cricut Expression, Cricut Expression 2, and Cricut Cake. These machines are no longer sponsored by Cricut.

Cricut Personal

The Cricut Personal machine was designed to operate as a standalone machine with the initial Cricut cartridges.

Cricut Gypsy

The Gypsy was a personal portable design device for use with the Cricut® Personal, Cake Mini, Cake, Expression, Expression 2, and Imagine machines. It helps you to store the content of the Cricut® cartridge, plan it with that content, and then attach it to the Cricut® to cut.

Cricut Expression

The Cricut Expression Machine had some incredible features. The AutoFill and Quantity functions are a couple of favorites. They enable you to cut multiples of the same picture so that a batch of invites, location settings, party favors, or other projects could be produced easily. A scoring tip was included.

Cricut Expression 2

It was constructed as a standalone unit. The LCD touchpad and Cricut® cartridges helped you to build projects without being attached to a computer system; therefore, a computer was needed to upgrade the machine's firmware.

Cricut Cake

Cricut Cake was specially designed in such a way as to cut edible stuff, including gum, paste, and more. It was built with components made of food-safe material.

4. Currently Available Models And Features

The original Cricut Explore One, Cricut Explore, and Cricut Explore Air have been discontinued as well. Those very same three Explore machines are still endorsed by Cricut and operate with the latest version of Cricut Design Space.

Current models include:

Cricut Explore One

This machine is no longer available from Cricut but can still be found second-hand. The most simple and economical machine currently offered by Cricut is the Cricut Explore One, which has most of the Explore Air machine's precise cutting, printing, and scoring abilities, and one can cut the very same materials (there are well over 100).

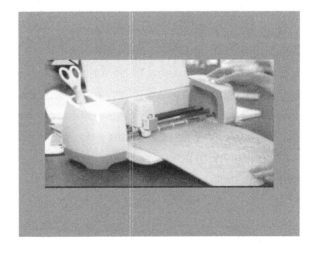

The Cricut Explore One will be a perfect match if you're hunting for something like a craft cutter that's quick to learn. This DIY system has effective cutting, ranking, and writing technology, retailing at just below $200. In addition, the opportunity to cut hundreds of different materials is featured.

Looking for a die cutter to cut patterns/images that are on your phone? The Explore One has got you covered.

What's more, the whole machine is a beast as it can cut various materials, from leather to vinyl. This is due to the way the German carbide luxury blade is used. This is a very strong blade designed to cut items that are light- to mid-weight. Also, the blade is exceptionally resistant to wear and breakage, allowing it a long life.

Features

- That being said, the Explore One cannot wirelessly operate. It does not come equipped with Bluetooth functionality, which means that to transfer images; you will need to attach cables.

- It tends to come with a user-friendly interface that helps you, via smartphone, PC, or tablet, to easily design your project.

- Smart Dial Set is a revolutionary feature for material selection. As long as you operate the machine correctly, it comes out right with predetermined default settings that help achieve optimal results. The positive thing about this function is that it removes the need to manually change speed, depth, and pressure.

- Integrated compartments for storage designed creatively to contain the work objects as much as reasonably possible. These will be perfect space savers if you're trying to keep the office clutter-free.

- Standard grip cutting mat has been customized to fit various kinds of materials for crafting. They have a strong grip and the strength to keep the material tightly in place, making it easy to remove. The multipurpose mat is of top quality and has the capacity to make flawless image cuts.

Cricut Explore Air

It is a wireless gadget that can cut the paper, fabric, and more. It functions with the existing application for Circuit Design Space. The above machine is no longer functional but can still be found to be used by Cricut. Cricut Explore Air seems to be a downgrade from Air 2, but it does offer the two things the Cricut Explore One doesn't have. It has been made Bluetooth-enabled, so one doesn't have to plug it into a device, and it also has a secondary tool holder so that one can write and cut at the same time.

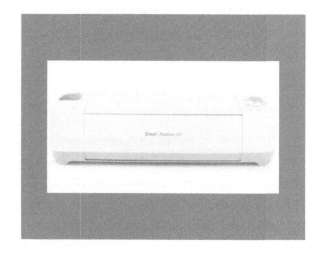

Features

- Explore Air has all the same features as Explore One and others. It has Bluetooth connectivity which guarantees that you use it wirelessly. Particularly for those who like to build on their phones, this is a big plus. Similarly, the wireless device replaces the need for wires. This helps to keep the office clean for a long time.

- Besides, the Explore Air has a holder for the Double Tool. What's that? you may be wondering. Well, this holder enables the ability to cut and write at the very same time. Therefore, you don't have to buy the tool adapter.

- However, this machine excludes the rotary blade. For all sorts of fabric, the rotary blade is better suited. Therefore, a lack of it is a big deal, especially for those seeking a machine for technical use. As you know, for trimming thicker items, this sort of blade comes in very handy. So, while this is a great DIY machine, it is better suited for scrapbooking and other light crafts activities.

- Not only are .jpg, .bmp, and .png files accepted by the machine, but also .dxf and .svg. This is the sort of freedom you need to drive your creativity to the max as a designer.

- Have you ever wanted to get a machine which would allow you to make accurate cuts from a quarter-inch to 23.5-inches? This is where Cricut's patented Cut Smart Technology comes into the picture. The revolutionary technology operates via a hybrid motor system designed to improve blade control. You enjoy far greater control over the types of cuts you can manage at any given moment when combined with the Smart Dial Set feature.

- This machine can also be monitored by an iPad app, in addition to its wireless capabilities. So, all your designs can be handled on the go. For example, to maintain your designs, you could even capitalize on free time spent on the subway, waiting rooms, traveling by plane, and so on. And, when you are back in your office, deliver the designs to the cutter. So, this not only helps make it easier to have the machine around but also saves time.

Cricut Explore Air 2

It cuts two times quicker, a minor modification from the Air. It is available in various colors and fits well with the current application for Circuit Design Space. At $299, however, the Cricut Explore Air 2 may be out of some users' price range. Fortunately, it's almost always on offer, sometimes as low as $179.

It can cut vinyl, Cricut felt, iron-on, suede/faux leather, cardstock, and more than 100 other items. This is an awesome workhorse machine. It cuts the same thicker materials as the Maker can, making it a great machine for most crafters. Furthermore, to match your craft room, it comes in a lot of colors.

Features

- It has a cutting force of 4,000 grams. When it comes to the use of die cutters, the pace is a great concern. With twice the cutting power as the Cricut Explore Air, this machine is ideal for a busy crafter. You may potentially use it to launch a small enterprise, but it might not be strong enough to do heavy-duty business jobs, of course. In that sense, when you're about to make every minute count, you only need to pick the Fast Mode. Else, if you don't need to rush to get stuff done, you should use the standard mode.
- The software it uses is Smart Dial Set.
- Technology is known as the Adaptive Tool System.
- It weighs about 16 pounds.
- It is 24 x 9.5 x 9.5 inches in size.
- It has a scoring stylus and Cricut pens.
- It is available in colors like pink, mint, black, red, blue, and many more.
- Bluetooth wireless technology is undoubtedly one of Cricut's coolest features to be added. With Bluetooth technology you have the ability to deliver amazing cuts remotely. This technology, of course, only works while you are next to the printer, but it definitely helps a lot. It simplifies the process of installation like never before.
- The moment you have an Air 2, you can access Pen Pals font and Lipstick Lettering font for no extra cost. For creative designs, the Pen Pals font is fantastic, while the Lipstick Lettering font is useful when boldness is required. Can you imagine designing and using your custom-made font for all your artistic projects? Well, maybe Air 2 is the sweetest choice you will ever make, particularly if you want to get creative.

Cricut Maker

Released on 20th August 2017, the Cricut Maker machine is used with Design Space, a cloud-based, online program. It does not run autonomously. An internet connection is needed while using Design Space on a laptop or computer.

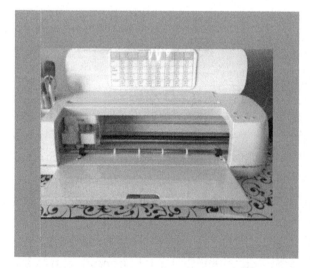

You can use the offline functionality in the Design Space app on an iPhone or iPad in order to use the machine and Design Space even without internet access. The Cricut Maker is an adaptable unit with adjustable cutting and scoring features. It may look pretty similar to the Explore series machines, but it has undergone a makeover from the bottom up. It is capable of performing each and every task that Cricut Explore does, along with additional features.

By using a relatively small rotary blade, Cricut Maker helps to cut fabric that has not been bonded (so users do not require any stabilizer as with another line of cutting machines designed by Cricut). It also nicely cuts felt, so this is the machine you'll need to produce felt crafts.

Products that are slightly thicker, such as thick leather and balsa wood, are often cut with a knife blade. By using a scoring wheel, it will score all kinds of materials (from its Scoring Stylus setup).

There were four new tools revealed in July 2019:

- The wavy rotary tool
- The engraving tool
- The perforation tool
- The debossing tool

The Adaptive Tool System of Cricut Maker was designed with the goal of advancement in mind, implying this was created to work with tools that Cricut has not even considered yet! They also have a couple of additional testing tools; so, as new tools are launched, this machine can do even more.

Throughout the Cricut line, the cost structure is $399, often $349 for a limited period. So if you're a professional crafter who likes to use a range of items, a sewing enthusiast, an ardent paper crafter, or even a carpenter, the above machine really is for you.

Features

- It has a cutting force of 4,000 grams. But in crafting terms, what does that mean? It means you can cut much thicker materials, not only paper and wood, but leather, cardstock, acrylics, and more.
- It weighs about 24 pounds.
- Technology is known as the Adaptive Tool System.
- It has a dimension of 22.6 x 7.1 x 6.2 inches.
- The software it uses is Cricut Design Space.
- New instruments developed to be used specifically with the Cricut Maker are connected to the updated cutting power.
- QUICK SWAP is the latest technology that carries these blades and helps you to easily push the quick-release tab at the top of its flexible housing, snap the preferred tip into place, and make it happen. Press, flip, go.
- It has a scoring wheel, scoring stylus, and Cricut pens.
- It includes colors like blue, rose, and champagne.
- It has a material width limit of 12 inches.
- The maximum length of materials is 2 feet.
- It has compatibility with more than 300 materials.
- It has 12 tools for cutting, debossing, writing, engraving, and scoring.
- It has a free design app for Windows®, iOS, Mac, and Android™.
- Connectivity is by Bluetooth.
- Performs with the home printer to print and then perfectly cut out the printed image.

Blades for Cricut Maker

Rotary blade

It can cut cloth of any nature. And now the motion is fixed, unlike when cutting cloth with the Cricut Explore Air 2. where you'll have to steady the fabric first while using the blade. The blade rolls and does not draw when slicing. Now you are all good as long as you use the cloth mat.

Perforation blade

The simple perforation blade allows flawless tear-offs and quick peel-aways. Even for patterns with curves, there is no need to fold afterward.

Scoring wheel blade

As the name suggests, this scoring wheel blade helps to score paper to make smooth folds, and it is particularly useful for someone who often needs to score. The scoring wheel was built with Adaptive Tool System in sight, unlike the scoring stylus, thus it delivers ten times the pressure.

Knife blade

This knife blade seems to be the group's game-changer blade. It reminds one of an x-acto blade, the instrument used to cut incredibly thick materials such as acrylics, leather, thick chipboard, and balsa wood — the sort of projects you might make just about as large as the imagination.

Wavy blade

In one easy move, it adds whimsy to every straight-edge project. For paper, iron-on, acrylic, and cardstock creations, simply apply a festive edge.

Engraving tip

Write professional-looking, customized text adornments in brass, monograms, plastic, flourishes, leather, and more.

Debossing tip

The rolling debossing ball provides free rein to customize a beautiful effect over various materials like foil poster board, glitter paper, basswood, coated paper, foil cardstock, and more.

Cricut Joy

Introduced 12th February 2020 and accessible March 2020, it is a simpler, lighter version of 5 x 8 inches, but weighs less than 4 pounds. In the Cricut product range, Cricut Joy adds two new features which are not present elsewhere. The Joy is capable of cutting single designs up to 4 feet long and repetitive cuts up to 20 feet with specialty accessories and materials.

Cricut Joy, only around half the size of Cricut Maker and Cricut Explore, is a lightweight, small cutting unit. This is pared down a little with a single blade and a pen holder like some other Cricut machines. The width of the cut is 4.5 inches.

And don't let its size fool you – it has some exciting new features! It has two big mats for free cutting, which means one could cut up to 20 feet of "Smart Vinyl" in just a single attempt. There's also a card mat in Cricut Joy, making it extremely easy to make cards for all kinds of functions. Cricut Joy is great for nearly every single one of your simple crafts, including vinyl, cardstock, iron, vinyl glue, writing labels, etc. For many crafters, the price range of $179 may be quite high, particularly because most of the functions are a bit restricted.

Features

- It has a material width limit of 5.5 inches.
- It has two tools for cutting and writing.
- The maximum length of materials that can be used is 20 feet.
- It weighs just under 4 pounds and therefore can be accommodated anywhere in the house comfortably. This will be a huge help for you if you don't have a lot of space or if you enjoy traveling with your Cricut.
- The introduction of hundreds of new items came along with the Joy launch! New mats, fabrics, and tools that can be used with the Joy are available. Smart Materials is one which I want to point out. It comes in Smart Vinyl, Writable Vinyl, and Smart Iron-On.
- By using these Smart Materials, we can cut such materials without the mat. Smart Materials can cut up to 20 feet. One may make multiple cuts approximately 20 feet long and individual cuts up to 4 feet long. And all of this is without a mat.
- It is compatible with more than 50 materials.
- Using the latest Cricut Joy Card Mat, we can design cards easier than ever using the Insert Cards.
- It can develop labels by using Cricut Joy pens.
- It has a free design app for Windows®, iOS, Mac, and Android™.
- Connectivity is by Bluetooth.
- It tends to work for quick custom cards along with Card Mat.

5. Considerations Before Buying the Best Cricut Machine Model

Are there certain machines that are capable of doing the same thing? Yes, other alternatives can be found out there, which can do to some extent what the Cricut does. There are two other main brands on the market that also cut a wide selection of materials and therefore have decent feedback; those are Silhouette America and Brother.

6. What Is the Best Cricut I Can Get?

Cricut Maker is the newest update, and they have come up with several tools that make it incredibly easy and much more fun to cut and craft.

7. Which Model Do I Need to Get?

It depends largely on which materials you are looking to cut. If you just intend to use the machine for vinyl and paper crafts, then the Cricut Explore will be quite enough for you. The Cricut Maker will be the right machine if one needs to cut tougher materials such as chipboard, leather, or fabrics, despite the stabilizer. Both of them are incredible, but when it comes down to the materials that it can cut, the extra cutting strength of the Cricut Maker WINS.

8. Which Is the Best Cricut?

The one that satisfies these three things is the best Cricut you can get:

- Is affordable.
- Can cut the materials you need.
- Leaves you able to buy materials with the spare money.

9. Is the Cricut Too Expensive?

I am going to give you a heads up right now that, yes, a Cricut machine can be pretty expensive. There are really decent prices to be found if you look at any of the earlier machines. The Cricut Cuttlebug seems to be the least expensive model, a small but efficient die-cutting machine, and the most expensive choice for their new update is The Cricut Maker.

10. Accessories

What other Cricut accessories do I need?

This is a challenging question that relies largely on the type of products you choose to deal with and cut. While the Cricut machines are diverse and interesting, to actually make things work, you will have to use them with the right tools. If you have some of the Explore Family Machines, for example, and would like to cut fabric, be sure that you have:

- Standard grip mat
- Backing material
- Bonded-fabric blade

On another note, you can use this tool whenever you would like to cut fabric with the Maker, or you could go for a rotary blade and a fabric grip mat.

With the fine point blade (the blade which tends to come with every machine), as well as the standard grip mat, the most popular and lightweight materials can all be cut.

But things are going to get so much better when you explore and be more aware of the machine and the materials you use. There are several different sets to choose from. The most popular, however, are indeed the Basic and Essential Tool Sets.

11. What Do We Mean by Cricut Mats and Which One Do I Need?

Cricut Mat

The surface used in order to cut particular materials is a Cricut Mat. They come in 2 sizes: 12 x 12 inches and 12 x 24 inches. The Cricut Mats are adhesive, and you're better off using varying degrees of stickiness based on the substance you're going to cut. And so-called grips, too. Mats are elastic, which is very useful since you can bend them to bring out projects that otherwise are hard to remove.

Protective Cover

There will always be a clear cover on the new Cricut mat that covers its surface. I install this as a component of the mat (you don't need this cover for either of the projects), and when you remove it, it will subject the mat to dust and other debris.

Outer Mat

There is no grip (or stickiness) on this part of the mat, and you can also see the name of the mat you are dealing with and the dimensions, including both centimetres and inches.

Inner Mat

The sticky part is the inner part of the mat, and that's where you place your projects while cutting them. The inner section of the mat is separated by squares of 1x1 inch; this is very useful as you can see where your material is at all times.

There are actually four kinds of mats for both the Cricut Explore and Maker:

- Standard Grip (Green)
- Light Grip (Blue)
- Fabric Grip (Pink)
- Strong Grip (Purple)

Each of the four Cricut Mats has pens and Cricut Tools.

There are three distinct mats in the Cricut Joy:

- Card Mat (Blue) – designed to render cards that are cut out.
- Light Grip (Blue)
- Standard Grip (Green)

Cricut Joy Mats are relatively small, like 4.5 x 6.5 inches and 4.5 x12 inches. When you're just starting out, the right mat for you would be the Standard Grip. The stronger the grip, the heavier the material you can use. For example, those who use a Light Grip mat can cut normal and thin paper, but if you are intending on cutting a heavier material such as cardstock, you're better off with a Strong Grip Mat. It seems that every machine comes along with a Standard Grip Mat. Before purchasing them, make sure that you read the product description.

12. Why Is There a Variety of Cricut Mats?

Cricut cutting mats are optimized in such a way that they allow you to cut a variety of materials easily. Each mat has a different grip level of stickiness as well as color to help identify them.

They are available in 2 varying sizes:

- 12 x 24 inches
- 12 x 12 inches

Try keeping the covering clear when storing it and, if necessary, use a scraper to clean off excess parts and a spatula for removing cut pieces and maintaining the mats in the best shape.
Light Grip mat (BLUE)

It is suitable for lightweight materials which can be operated with the Cricut Maker and Cricut Explore family like:

- Vinyl
- Thin cardstock
- Construction paper
- Printer paper
- Vellum

If you put a thin material over a thicker grip mat, separating the mat's material would be almost impossible.

Standard Grip mat (GREEN)

It is ideal for a wide variety of medium-weight materials. This mat can be used with the Cricut Explore family and Cricut Maker:

- Iron-on
- Embossed cardstock
- Vinyl
- Pattern paper
- Cardstock

The most popular and inexpensive one is the Standard Grip mat. Typically, it comes with every Cricut Machine purchased.

Strong Grip mat (PURPLE)

It is optimal for heavy products, so it can be considered for the family of Cricut Maker and Cricut Explore, and is ideal for:

- Magnet material
- Leather
- Glitter cardstock
- Fabric with stabilizer
- Chipboard
- Thick cardstock
- Poster board

Often, grip strength is not sufficient when using a hard material like balsa basswood. Use a painters' tape to attach the material to the mat in such situations.

Fabric Grip mat (PINK)

It is a special mat that combines enhanced density and strength with a light adhesive suitable for a wide range of fabrics. This mat was designed to be used with the bonded fabric blade or rotary blade.

With the Strong Grip Mat, the most popular materials one can cut are:

- Fabric (bonded)
- Any sort of Cricut Maker and rotary blade fabric

Cricut Joy Mats

With the Cricut Joy, there is no need for a Cricut mat for materials marked with the word 'Smart.' Other materials, such as cardstock and standard vinyl, require a mat to be cut, however.

Three various kinds of mats are available for the Cricut Joy.

- Card Mats are used with insert card. Your paper can also be used and cut to the same size as the insert cards.
- Standard Grip Mat
- Light Grip Mat

The design should not be greater than 4.25 x 6.25/11.75 inches while cutting with the mat (blue or green). And the design should not be bigger than 4.25 x 6 inches while using the Card Mat.

13. How to Clean and Care for Cricut Mats?

It's very important to take good care of the mat and ensure that the cuts are nice and smooth. You'll pro-long the lifespan and save money in the long run by giving your mats some extra attention.

Here are a few of the easiest ways to do this.

- After any use, cover it.
- You could expose your mat to lots of dust and dirt by removing the cover, and this will help in making that mat less sticky with time. Don't ever discard your protective cover.
- Cover and put it aside any time you're finished with the cutting/removing process.
- Using the right materials for Cricut Mats.
- Each mat is built use with various materials. When it messes up, you will have a tough time getting them removed. For example, you can have a hard time trying to scrape off the material if you put light materials over the purple mat, so this will bring more wear and tear to the mat.
- The very same refers to the way to remove discarded product from the mat. Be cautious and try to gently to remove elements. The mat can also ended up being scratched.
- Clean the mats often.
- The mat can lose its grip over time due to a build-up of materials on it, which can mean it's time for you to substitute it.
- Try cleaning it until you get a new mat. There are different ways to clean them.

14. Cricut Blades

- Regular blades
- Deep-point blade
- Fabric-bonded blade

Blades to be used for different projects:

Two things can impact your Cricut blade choice: the kind of Cricut machine you have now and the type of project you are considering.

Greeting/holiday cards

One can cut paper with the simple or premium fine-point blade, and you will require the stylus for folding the envelopes.

Vinyl graphics/decals

The fine-point blade works well for thinner vinyl, and one may go with the deep-point blade for thicker vinyl.

Projects for fabrics

Use either a bonded blade for fabrics with a rigid backing or a rotary blade for delicate fabrics.

Wooden models

For creating animal figures, wooden aircraft, ships, or any other wooden designs, pick the knife blade, which conveniently slices through the wood.

Jewellery/dog tags

You'll want the knife blade to cut through sheets of aluminium for these tasks and the engraving tip to incorporate names and personal details.

Cricut Design Space is a web browser program that allows for browsing hundreds of pre-designed projects and creating your own on the desktop, tablet, laptop, or phone. Around 400 fonts, 75,000 images, and over 800 "make it now" predesigned projects are available in Cricut Design Space. All of "make it now" tasks have already been completed; all you need to do is click "Go."

1. What is Cricut Access?

If you don't have a Design Space subscription, you'll pay around $1 for every image you use and $3-7 for buying each "make it now" task. It'll essentially be an "a la carte" service. You'll choose what you desire and pay for it. Cricut Access is a service for those of you who despise paying for stuff. Cricut Access gives you free access to a large number of images, cartridges, fonts, and "make it now" projects.

How does one know what one is getting?

It depends on which Cricut Access membership one chooses, but don't worry, they're all fantastic.

Monthly

- For $9.99 per month, you'll have unlimited access to almost 400 fonts and 75,000 images. There's no need to pay a la carte for every font you want. You also gain accessibility to the Premium Membership support structure for swift assistance whenever you need it, and unrestricted use to around 30,000 Cricut images, including special ones.
- A discount of 10% on most orders on Cricut.com, as well as 10% off licenced images.
- Finding Cricut Access images is a breeze, thanks to the handy little green flag that informs you about all the fonts, images, cartridges, and projects that come with its membership.

Annual

The next level of membership is annual registration. It includes the same benefits as the monthly subscription, but one can save by paying for a year in advance.

Also, with the yearly subscription, you get access to about 400 fonts that seem to be ready to use on the Cricut machine, access to priority user support for faster help whenever you need it, unlimited use of around 30,000 Cricut images (including unique ones), 10% off all fonts, images, and ready-to-make designs, as well as 10% off all Cricut.com products.

Premium

All of the same benefits as those of the monthly and annual subscriptions, plus extra perks like FREE shipping on orders over $50. You'll want to get a membership if you plan to buy more than a few designs per month or if you regularly order items from Cricut's website.

A green colored "an" will appear in the top corner of a Cricut Access premium membership if it includes an image, project, or font.

If you have a Cricut Access account, a green Cricut Access logo will turn on. It says "Subscribed," so if one has an Access account, one can get items without paying any additional fees. You can still buy the designs if you don't have an entry card, but it will charge an additional fee.

When the Cricut Access licence comes to an end and the user does not wish to extend it, the user will no longer have Cricut Access images available through their account. Even if you have the Cricut Access Discount, all purchased images, fonts, or creations will remain in the wallet because purchased templates are yours to keep. If the user does not want the Cricut Access subscription to automatically renew, then contact Cricut to cancel it.

What may one miss out on?

Some images, fonts, and projects aren't included in the Cricut Access membership; however, keep in mind that one gets 10% off any Design Space items one would usually have to pay for oneself.
The Cricut Access membership may not allow you to take the 10% discount when renewing your membership.

How much does it cost?

There seem to be two choices available:

- Paying $95.80 for the entire year at once, which works out to around $7.99 per month; or
- Paying $9.99 per month with the choice to discontinue any time.

Regardless of which option one chooses, one will have unrestricted access to a wealth of content and plenty of reasons to get crafting.

2. Cricut Design Space for Beginners: the Software

- Move to Cricut.com. Tap on DESIGN in the upper-right corner of the page.
- You'll be asked to sign up while you're on the design page. Click on "Creating a CRICUT ID" if you do not already have an account. Fill in your details on the next screen. The email address you type in will now be the ID.

- You will then be brought into Cricut Design Space once the green button is pressed. And that is where the magic takes place! Make sure that this page is bookmarked on your toolbar so that it can be easily accessed.
- This won't make the home screen look just like mine. "My Projects" pops up first because it has an image of every project I have. When you begin to make projects, yours will too.

3. Cricut Design Space Canvas Guide for Learners

If you do not know how to use Design Space, investing in Cricut is pointless because you'll need this program to cut every project.

Cricut Design Space is an ideal tool for beginners, in my opinion. If you don't have any familiarity with other design programs like Photoshop or Illustrator, you will notice that it's very simple, even if it looks daunting. And on the other hand, if you ever have preview experience, such as Adobe Creative Cloud applications or Inkscape, you'll see that such software is fun. Design Space, with Shapes and Fonts, is largely about refreshing the projects and designing minimal designs. You will need your designs or Cricut Access if you're after something sophisticated.

After you log in to your Cricut Design Space account and want to launch or edit a new project, you will be doing everything from the window called **CANVAS**. In Cricut Design Space, the Canvas area is where you make most edits before you cut the designs.

In this guide, you are about to discover what every single icon in the Canvas is for. We are going to be dividing the canvas into four categories and four colors to keep all of that in order and easy to comprehend:

- Top panel: yellow (editing area)
- Right panel: purple (layers panel)
- Left panel: blue (Insert Area)
- Canvas area: green

4. Top Panel of Cricut Design Space

The top panel is for editing and placing objects on the canvas. The font you want to use can be selected from this panel; you can change sizes; align styles, and much more.

The panel has been categorized into two sub-panels. The first one helps your tasks to be saved, named, and eventually cut. And now, the second will allow you to monitor and edit stuff in the canvas area.

5. Sub-Panel No. 1

Name the project and cut it

This sub-panel lets you navigate profile projects from the Canvas and even sends your finished projects to get cut.

Toggle menu

If you press this button, the entire menu will slide open again. This menu is a handy one. You can go to your profile from here and change the photo.

Through this menu, you can do many useful and practical things, such as calibrating the machine, blades, and upgrading your device's firmware. You can also track your Cricut Access subscriptions, account information, and more. You can adjust the visibility and measurement of a canvas through the settings option. To discover all that Cricut Design Space has to offer you, click on every link.

Project Name

All projects initially have an "Untitled" title. After you have inserted at least one element (image, text, etc.), you can then label a project from the canvas area.

My Projects

When you click on "My Projects", you'll be routed to the library containing items you've already built. This is perfect if you want to re-cut a successfully made item. So, there's no reason for you to ever have to replicate the same project.

Save

After you've inserted one feature into the canvas area, that option will be enabled. I propose that when you are done, save the project. If your browser fails, the time and effort go with it, even though the app is on the cloud.

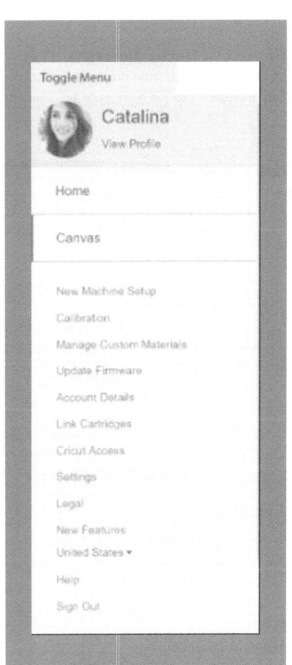

Maker, Explorer, Joy

We will want to pick either the Cricut Maker, Joy, or the Cricut Explore Machine based on the model of machine you have; that's very important because you will find Cricut Maker's features only accessible on that specific machine. So, you won't enable the tools that are for the creator if you've got a Maker and build with the Explore button on.

Make it

When you are finished uploading the files and ready to cut, press "Make it". Just below there is a snapshot of what you can do. Your project is split into mats as per the colors of the project. From that window, you can even increase the number of actions to cut; this is perfect when planning on making multiple cuts.

6. Sub-Panel No. 2

Editing Menu

It's incredibly helpful, as it allows editing, organizing, and coordinating fonts and photographs on the Canvas field.

Redo & Undo

Even while working, we can make silly mistakes. These buttons provide a perfect way of correcting them. Click "Undo" anytime you make something you do not like or make a mistake. Click "Redo" if you unintentionally delete stuff you didn't mean to delete or change.

Line type and Fill

This choice will tell your computer what equipment and blades are supposed to be used. Depending on the machine you have bought and chosen in the top panel (Maker, Joy, Explore), you will have various choices.

Line type

This option will then tell one's machine which tool you want to use for cutting the project. For now, there seem to be eight choices (Cut, Deboss, Draw, Perf, Score, Engrave, Wave, and Foil).

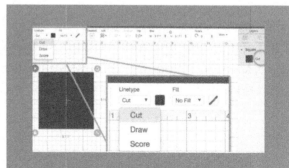

If you've got a Cricut Maker, all choices will be open; if you have an Explore, you will be able to Cut, Draw, Rate, or Foil; if you've got a Cricut Joy, only Cut and Draw will be accessible. Below is a more in-depth description of each tool.

Cut

If you upload a .jpg or .png image to the Canvas, "Cut" would be the default line type that almost all of the elements on canvas will have, which means when you press "Make it", the machine will remove those designs. With the Cut option, you can also modify the fill of certain components. This converts into the various colors of materials you can use when cutting the projects.

Draw

If you'd like to draw on your projects, you can do this with Cricut. When you select this line type, you will be asked to pick one of the Cricut Pens you have (you either have specific pens or a third party adapter). When you choose a specific style, the layers on the canvas area will be highlighted with that of the color of the pen you selected. With such a tool, when you press "Make it", instead of cutting, the Cricut will write/draw. This choice doesn't color the designs.

Score

The score seems to be a more potent variant of the scoring line positioned on the left panel. When you add this attribute to a layer, most of the designs will be displayed as marked or dashed. The moment that you press "Make it", the Cricut will not cut, but rather it will score the materials. For such designs, you would need to have the scoring stylus or scoring wheel – but remember a wheel only operates with the Cricut Maker. If you have questions on what materials you require, I recommend you read this book. It's the definitive guide for you to understand which accessories and materials you truly need.

Engrave

Enables one to engrave various kinds of materials. For instance, one can build monograms onto aluminium sheets and anodized aluminium to expose the silver underneath.
Deboss
Such a tip will drive the material in, and it will make stunning and intricate designs. The debossing tip would enable you to customize the designs to quite a new level. Just imagine debossing a lovely gift box with roses, hearts, stars, etc.

Wave

Rather than cutting in straight lines just like rotary and fine-point blades, this method can produce wavy results on the final cuts. Having curved lines in Design Space is very difficult, but this method can be useful if you like these kinds of results.

Perf

The perforation blade is indeed a tool that helps to cut the materials in thin and uniform lines to produce perfect and crisp tear results like those you have used in tear-out cards, raffle tickets, coupons, etc.

Foil (new)

Foil is the latest Cricut tool and it helps you make amazing foil finishes on projects, along with the help of the Cricut foil transfer kit. While using this line type, you have the option to pick between nice, medium, and bold finishes.

Fill

The fill option is primarily to be reserved for the printing and patterns. It'll only be allowed after you have cut as a "line type." "No Fill" means it won't be printing something.

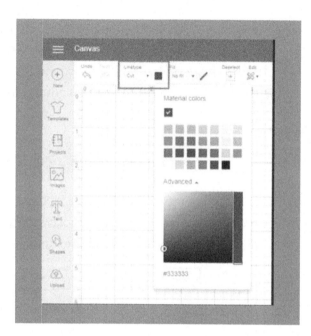

The print is by far one of the best features Cricut has as it helps you to print the designs and then cut them. This really is fabulous, and frankly, that is what inspired me to get a Cricut in the first place. Anyway, getting back to the printing option. Once the Fill option is activated, after you press "Make it"; you'll submit your files to a home printer and allow your Cricut to do all the heavy lifting (cutting).

Another amazing choice for the Print Type is the Patterns. Use Cricut's options, or upload any of your own; you can insert a pattern to pretty much any layer. Creativity is one's limit! One can make a gorgeous card from an already generated pattern via Cricut Access (membership, not free) or just your own. And after that, print and cut at the very same time.

The Fill option ONLY fits with Cricut Maker and any of your Explore Family Machines (it is not compliant with Cricut Joy).

Select All

When you're about to transfer all of the elements within the canvas area, you can struggle to pick them one by one. Select all so that all of the items from the canvas get selected.

Edit

The Edit function has a drop-down menu. This icon helps to cut, copy (copy the item, leaving the existing intact), and paste (cut elements upon the canvas area) things from the canvas. The cut and copy choice will be enabled when you select one or more items from the canvas. The paste option would be activated if you copy and cut something.

Align

If you already have previous knowledge of other graphic design systems, you will likely understand how to use the menu. If you are not familiar with Align Tools, let me tell you something; Align Menu is something you'll want to learn to perfection.

This feature requires all of the designs to be aligned, and by choosing two or more components, it is enabled.

Align Left

All elements should be aligned towards the left by using this configuration. Where other elements can pass towards will be determined by the furthest entity to the left.

Center Horizontal

This option would horizontally align the items, fully centering text and pictures.

Align Right

All of your elements are aligned towards the right by using this configuration. Where other elements will pass will be determined by the furthest entity to the right.

Align Top

This choice aligns all the designs you have chosen with the top. Where the other elements will pass will be determined by the furthest entity to the top.

Center Vertically

This option will vertically arrange the items. Columns are convenient, and you want them arranged and aligned.

Align Bottom

This choice aligns all the designs you have chosen to the bottom. Where the other elements can pass is predetermined by furthest unit to the bottom.

Center

When you press "center," one arrangement against another is centered, both horizontally and vertically. This is especially helpful when you try to center text in a shape like a square or a star.

Distribute

It's time-intensive to do everything on your own if you want the same distance between elements, and it's not 100 percent right. The Distribute button can help you out with that. You should have at least three elements selected for it to be allowed.

Distribute Horizontally

This button will horizontally distribute the components. The length of distribution will be calculated by the furthest left and right designs; this indicates that the middle objects will be divided between the farthest left and right designs.

Distribute Vertically

This button will vertically distribute the components. The length of distribution will be calculated by the furthest top and bottom designs; this indicates that the middle objects will be divided between the furthest top and bottom models.

Arrange

The latest creations you bring to the canvas will still be at the center of everything when you deal with various images, text, and crafts. Some of the components of the design, though, ought to be in the back or front. You can arrange the items very conveniently with the arrangement option. A nice thing about this function is that the software will know what object is in the front or back, and Design Space will trigger the available options for that specific element as you pick it.
What are the options that you get?

Send to back

It will transfer the element selected to the back of the composition.

Move Backward

This option moves the chosen object just one step backward. Suppose you've got a three-element design; it's going to be like cheese in a sandwich.

Move Forward

This option shifts the element one step forward. Usually, if there are four or more items you have to organize, you should use this option.

Sent to front

This choice will start moving the chosen element towards the front.

Flip

In Cricut Design Space, if you need to represent any of the designs, this is a perfect place to do it. There are two possibilities:

Flip Horizontal

This will horizontally represent your picture or design, kind of like a mirror. As you attempt to create left and right patterns, this is helpful.

Example: You're creating a few wings, and you have the left-hand side already; you could copy and paste that left wing with Flip, and voila! You've got both these (left and right) wings now.

Flip Vertical

This will flip the designs vertically, like a reflection in water. This choice is perfect for you if you would like to produce a shadow effect.

Size

In Cricut Design Space, anything you build or type has a size. You can adjust the element's size by yourself from the element (when clicked over). However, this choice would encourage you to do so if you require an object to get a precise measurement. Also, the little lock is something important. The proportions are still locked when you increase or decrease the size of an image. You inform the program that you do not want to retain the same dimensions by clicking on this tiny lock.

Rotate

Rotating an aspect, like size, is something you'll have to do from the canvas area but easily. Most designs, though, have to be turned at a particular angle. I suggest you use this feature if that's the case for you. Otherwise, you're going to waste too much time trying to angle an aspect the way you would like it to be.

Position

When one clicks on a particular design, this box tells where the items will be in the canvas area. By deciding where you would like the element to be placed on the canvas, you can move the elements around. It's convenient, but it is a more complex tool. Truthfully, I do not use it much because the alignment methods I described above help me get around better.

Font

You can pick any font you wish to use for your projects whenever you tap on this panel. You may filter these and check at the top edge of the window for them. If you have Cricut Access, you can also use the fonts which are marked with little green A. If you do not have Cricut Access, however, make sure you use fonts available to your device; else, when you transfer your project for cutting, you will be charged.

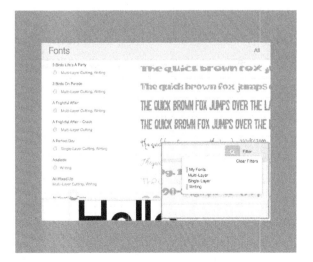

Style

There is the option to change the form once the font is selected.

A few of the choices that you've got:

Regular

It is the default configuration, and your font's appearance will not change.

Bold

The font can be made thicker.

Italic

The font would be tilted to the right.

Bold italics

The font would be thicker and slanted to the right.

Font Size, Letter, and Line Space

I can't express how good these choices are, particularly the letter spacing.

Font Size

From here, you may change it manually. Typically, I only change the font size in the canvas area.

Letter Space

There is a significant distance between each letter in certain fonts. This choice would allow you to very significantly decrease the space between letters. Seriously, it is a game-changer.

Line Space

This alternative fixes the space between lines in a section; this is very helpful because I often generate a single line of text since I'm not comfortable spacing among lines.

Alignment

This alignment seems to be quite different from the "alignment" I have explained above. That is the choice. For paragraphs, these are the alternatives you've got:

Left

Position a section to the left side

Middle

Position a section towards the middle

Right

Position a section to the right side

Curve

This choice will encourage you to use your text to get extra creative! You can curve your text with this feature. The easiest way to practice it is by attempting to play with a little slider. It will curve the text upwards as you push the slider to the left, and when you move it to the right, it will bend the text inwardly. Note: if you slide the slider fully towards the left or right, the font will create a circle.

Advance

The last choice here on the editing panel is Advance. Don't be confused by such a drop-down menu's name; when you understand what all of the choices are about, you can see that they're not that difficult to use.

Ungroup to Letters

This option helps split each letter into such a single layer (I'll explain more on layers later); use it if you intend to change each character.

Ungroup to Lines

This choice is extraordinary and allows you to distinguish the individual lines of a paragraph. Type the paragraph, then press Ungroup to Lines, and you've got it; new lines you may change individually now.

Ungroup to Layers

The trickiest of all these choices is this one. This choice is only valid for multi-layer fonts; such fonts are applicable for Cricut Access or individual purchases.

A multi-layer font is indeed a sort of font with more than just one layer; if you'd like to have any shadow or color around the letters, these fonts are perfect.

What if you'd like a multi-layer font and don't need the extra layer? To split every single layer, simply select the text and then press Ungroup to Layers.

7. Left Panel – Install Shapes, Images, and More

You can change all of the designs with the help of the top panel (which I have described in detail above).

So where do the designs come from? The Left Panel of Cricut Design Space. This panel is all about adding shapes, photos, projects ready to cut, and more. You are going to add together all stuff that you will cut right here.

It would help if you understood something fundamental; whether you have Cricut Access, Cricut Pictures, and projects ready to cut, Cricut fonts come at a price. If you need them, before cutting your project, you may have to pay.

To determine whether you need Cricut Access or not, check earlier on in this definitive guide I put together for you. Seriously, it is a life changer.

Now we've had a little glimpse of what everything is about in this panel, let's see what happens when you press the icons.

New

A notification will be received at the top of the window whenever New is clicked, and if you are still operating on a project, you will be asked whether or not you would like to replace the project. It is always wise to save all the updates from the latest project if you plan to redesign the project; otherwise, you'll lose all the effort. A fresh and unused canvas will then open so you can get started after you save.

Templates

Templates help you envision how the project will work on a specific surface. This function is really out of this universe.

This app is wonderful if you choose to add a personal touch to fashion pieces, to choose sizes and various styles of clothes. Plus, they have several different categories from which you can pick.
Note: templates are only for visualizing. When you finish planning, nothing would be cut yet but you will have the idea ready for cutting.

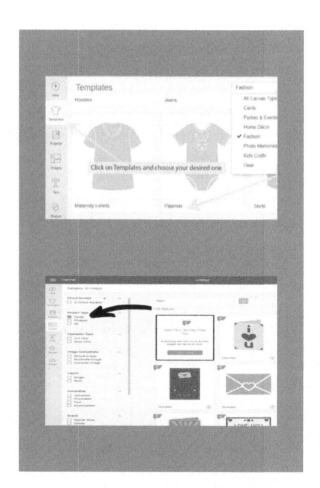

Projects

If you want to cut things straight away, then you need to click on Projects! You can configure it until you pick your project; tap on "Make it", as per the cut instructions.

Tip: For Cricut Access members, plenty of the projects are available, or you can buy those as you go. Based on the machine you have, there are many tasks available to you to cut. Scroll to the bottom of the drop-down menu for the categories and pick the device you own.

Images

Images are amazing to bring your creations together; you can produce an interesting effect and appearance to the crafts using them.
You can search by keyword, categories highlighted, subjects, people, locations, instances.
Cartridges are a set of pictures that you'll have to buy separately; some come with Cricut Access, and cer-

tain ones don't (labels such as Disney and Sesame Street are not included in Cricut Access). Every other week, Cricut seems to have free pictures to cut under "Highlighted Categories". A more efficient filter will emerge whenever you click under the category. You can limit the search even more with this filter. I suggest you play around with these filters, so you find images more efficiently.

Text

You will have to tap on text whenever you choose to type in the Canvas area, then a small tab that says "Add text here" will appear over the canvas.
With this wonderful guide I have put together, discover how to edit text like a pro.

Shapes

It's important to be capable of using shapes. You can produce easy and less complex projects with them, as well as intricate ones.
You can choose from eight shapes:

- Pentagon
- Square
- Triangle
- Hexagon
- Octagon
- Heart
- Star

The last choice is not just a shape but an awesome and efficient tool known as Score Line. One would use this option to score and fold the materials. The Score Line will be your best friend if you want to make boxes or cards.

Upload

This is the last one.

You will be able to upload the files and images by using this option. There seem to be many of these on the internet; a lot of bloggers can make projects free.

8. Right Panel - All Related to Layers

Let me give you a little insight into what a layer is, before clarifying what each icon on the Layers Panel is related to.

Layers define each specific pattern or layout in the canvas region. Consider it like clothing; you have several layers which constitute your outfit when you get ready, and the outfit could be basic or complicated based on each day or time of the year. So, the layers will be skirts, tops, gloves, coats, socks, boots, etc. on a cold day; then you'd only have a single sheet for a day at the beach, a swimsuit. A design is also the same; based upon the size of the project you're working on; you'll have multiple layers that shape the whole project.

Let's imagine, for now, making some Christmas cards. What's this card going to have? Perhaps a Merry Christmas note, a tree, the card itself, and probably an envelope too. The issue is that there are layers of these tiny delicate designs and components that are related to the project. Many layers could be altered; however, certain layers, such as .png and .jpg images, cannot. This is due to the file's or layer's existence. For example, a layer for text may be transformed to other layer style, but you will lose the right to edit the text if you do that. You will learn more about using layers as you read on.

To get a good grasp on the concept of a layer, let's take a look at each icon on the right panel and see what they're about.

Group, Duplicate, Delete, and Ungroup

Be sure to explore these settings as they can make moving items across the canvas area much simpler.

Group

To group the layers, tap here. When there are several layers which construct a complicated design, this comes in handy.

Let's assume that you operate on an elephant. The elephant would most likely consist of various layers (the torso, eyes, neck, trunk, etc.) Whether this is an .svg or cut file, if you need to add extra shapes and text, you'll have to move your elephant around a lot on the canvas. Therefore, make sure that it remains organized by arranging all the elephant layers so that when they're carried across the canvas, nothing should be out of place.

Ungroup

This choice ungroups all clustered layers that are selected on the layers panel or canvas area. If you do find it necessary to edit (size, font style, etc.) a specific layer or component in the group, use this option.

Duplicate

This option duplicates the layers or layouts one has chosen on the canvas or layer panel.

Delete

This choice will delete all items from the layer panel or canvas that you selected.

Line type/Fill

Each object on this layers panel shows what sort of line type or fill one can use (Cut, Wavy, Write, Perf, Score, Print, etc.).

Visibility of Layers

The tiny eye on each layer in the panel reflects the transparency of a design. Instead of removing an aspect if you're unsure if it looks right, press the little eye to cover it. When something is hidden, the eye has a cross on it.

Tip: You may move a specific design on top of or underneath a layer by clicking on it and dragging it; this is similar to the Arrange option (front, back, etc.).

Blank Canvas

If you are looking to explore how a certain style looks with a specific hue, this "layer" helps to change the color of the canvas. When used in combination with the Templates tool, the strength of this setting is unlocked so you can change the tone and choices of the design itself.

Slice, Flatten, Weld, Contour, and Attach

These methods are highly useful, so make certain you learn how to use them properly. You can use the graphic below to provide a short rundown of what they're all about.

Slice

For the purpose of cutting patterns, text, and other components from various designs, the slice tool is great. You will see how the original image is split up when choosing all shapes and clicking on "slice". To represent whatever the final result was, I copy-pasted the "slice end result" and afterward separated every one of that came from slicing.

Weld

This welding equipment requires two or three shapes to be fused into one. You will see how I achieved an entirely new shape when I chose both shapes and pressed "Weld". The color of the new form is determined by the sheet behind, which is why it is pink.

Attach

Attach is identical to surface sorting; however, it is more efficient. You can see how the layers changed color after picking all shapes and pressing "attach" (determined by the back layer). These forms are linked, however, and the connection will stay after I put it in place and submit my project for cutting.

Flatten

This tool offers additional aid for printing and then selects the Cut Fill option; this applies to only one layer if you adjust the fill when there is no fill. What if, though, at the time, you decided to do so in different shapes? When you're finished with the design, press "flatten" and then pick the layers you would like to print as a whole. When you're through with your template (you won't be able to undo this until you've exited your project), pick the frameworks you've built and want to print in general, and then press "flatten".

In this situation, the component would become a print and then cut out the template, which is why it no longer has a dark border (which the blade may go through).

Contour

The Contour tool is used to cover undesirable aspects of the design, and it is only used where a shape or design contains features that can be omitted.

For example, I used the weld tool to merge the actual design into one shape; so I typed within contour concept and cut it over the latest form, hiding the innermost portions of the letter O and also the inner portion of R by using the Contour tool.

Color Sync

The layers panel's last choice is Color Sync. Each color depicts a different color of the material on the canvas zone. If you have several tones of blues and yellows in your style, are you sure you want these? If just one hue of yellow is needed, such as in this situation, simply drag and drop the color to be deleted into the one you want to retain.

Canvas Area

Many of the designs and components are shown on the canvas. It's fast and very intuitive to use.

Canvas Measurements and Grid

A line separates the canvas region; this is perfect as you can imagine the cutting mat for any tiny square one would want on the grid. Finally, this will assist you in getting the most of your available space.

When you click over the top panel toggle, you can alter the dimensions from inches to centimetres, switch the grid on and off, and then choose Settings. (At the start of this guide, you can see the toggle menu). A window along with all the options will open.

Turn the grid off and on

The selection appears blue if you pick one or more layers, and then change from any of the four different categories. The red X is for deleting layers. The upper right corner helps to spin the pick.

When there is an increase or decrease in the size of a layer, the lower right key of the pick, known as "small lock", retains the size proportionally. You get different proportions by tapping on it.

Zoom Out and In

Finally, by clicking the – and + symbols on the left side of the canvas, you can view it on a greater or smaller scale (without altering the actual size of the designs).

9. How to Use a PDF File in Cricut Design Space

1. Select Cricut Design Space and choose New Project from the drop-down menu.
2. The simplest way of converting the PDF to a CDS-compatible format is by using a PDF converter.
3. Select Upload Documents from the menu.
4. There will be a new window open. Locate and open your PDF.
5. You'll note that your file is being converted.
6. The new file is available for download. It'll show up here as a zipped file. The file must be unzipped.
7. Return to CDS and choose Upload.
8. Choose the option to upload photos.
9. Select Browse.
10. 1Choose the PDF that has been converted.
11. 1In the upload image window, the file will appear. Even though the photos have been converted to .png, you will notice that there is always white around them. We'd end up with a big rectangle if we cut during this stage.
12. We need to get rid of the white pieces, so pick complex and then proceed.
13. To use the magic wand, simply click it. Then, click on the white area.
14. The white will be fully removed.
15. You may also use the eraser tool to get rid of any unnecessary bits. When you're satisfied, press preview.
16. Examine the shapes; each will have a cut line. Continue by pressing the enter key.
17. Choose Print, cut, and then save at the end.
18. Your file has now been added to the library. Pick it and paste it in.

10. Cricut Design Projects that Are Entirely Free

Cricut Design Space, which can be accessed from any computer, has a plethora of free projects and images, featuring gentle baby blocks. When in the Design Room, click left on the objects, then select "Available for Cricut Builder." One could also find more than 50 free pictures each week by pressing the "Videos" button on the left-hand side and then the "Categories" button at top of the screen.

.svg files and designs can be viewed online. Cricut Design Space has a limited number of free designs, but you could still also search online for "doc-inset holiday of preference - SVG data" to find more.

11. Significant Differences Between the Cricut Design Space App and the Cricut Design Space Desktop

Despite the fact that the Design Space App is completely functional and allows you to do pretty much everything you can imagine, there are some features that are only available in the desktop edition.

- Select All
- Curve Text
- Advanced
- Patterns
- Templates

Is there any distinction between the iPhone and iPad versions of the Design SpaceApp?

Fortunately, the difference in the two choices isn't significant. Imagine having to learn two different apps at the same time!

The only minor difference seen between iPhone and iPad apps is SPACE MANAGEMENT. It is noticeable on the top panel (Home – Canvas – Make). On the iPad, the names are always visible; however, on the phone, you may see a rectangle organized into three equal parts. They both, however, reflect the same thing.

Keep in mind that most of the time, when you tap on something, the menus are very long, so you'll have to scroll on the phone – and sometimes on the iPad – to see all of the options.

Due to the limited amount of space on a phone, the layers button can be deactivated repeatedly as you click on other features. On the iPad, the layers button can be kept visible at all times.

12. Design Space Is Getting Some New Features

Below is a list of everything new (or soon to be added) to Design Space, including other exciting new features such as Offset and Project Collections.

Offset

To make one's designs stand out, one can use the offset feature in the desktop app to add decorative markings to text, shapes, or collections of objects. This famous design technique gives custom T-shirt designs, stickers, cake toppers, and other items a professional look.

Project Collections

On the desktop app, one can easily arrange projects into custom folders so that one can find the desired project, whenever needed. You can name these collections the way you want – T-shirt Designs, Custom Orders, Paper Flowers, and so on.

Kerning

Kerning is a written aesthetics approach that involves changing the spacing between two characters. One may want text to be closer or further apart depending on the design; then you'd have more control over the aesthetic you're be going for. Keep an eye out for when this new feature becomes available. Design Space features educational videos

Within Design Space, you'll find links to useful how-to and tutorial videos. These quick tutorials will help to learn new features, understand the fundamentals, or simply improve creative abilities.

Thickness of Pen on Canvas

 One can now preview the design on the Canvas using thicker as well as thinner pen and marker tip sizes to get a better idea of how your project would appear.

Profile Lookup

Discover your favourite Cricut Community contributors and their shared projects in a matter of seconds.

My Project Lookup

Discover unique projects you've saved into My Projects quickly.

Fast loading of images and text

Text, big images, and complicated projects are now loading more quickly. Canvas' code has been rewritten to increase performance, along with its ability to manage larger, more complex files more quickly.

Transfer data between projects by copying and pasting.

Users can now copy and paste design components through one Design Space Canvas to another. Simply copy and paste the required object (or collection of objects) onto an existing or new Design Space canvas. For using the Copy and Paste commands, use the preferred keyboard shortcuts keys or the Edit dropdown menu.

1. Making of Pencil Case along with Patterned HTV Vinyl

Supplies

- Cricut Maker
- Canvas fabric (12×12 inch square)
- Zipper: 9-inch zipper
- Cricut maker/another cutting machine
- Patterned HTV vinyl/ iron on
- Heat press/iron
- Sewing machine and thread

Instructions

1. The thickness of the fabric should be the same as the length of the fabric —and your zipper. Cut your fabric to a certain length equivalent to that of the zipper, which is 9 inches. You can limit the height to whatever you want. Then cut out canvas fabric with scissors.
2. Place a 12×12 inch piece of cloth canvas over a fabric grip map, press it downward with a brayer's help, and cut it over with a rotary blade set to canvas.
3. To mount the zipper, push down almost a 1/2 inch just at the top of every rectangle, and then pin the right sides together. Then use a zipper foot and sew a basic line stitch along the length of a zipper, followed by a second line stitch about 2 millimetres away and parallel to the first.
4. Here, the pressed seam is on the inside.
5. Then repeat the procedure on the other side.
6. Open the zipper!
7. Now face the right sides together and pin around the three sides.
8. Stitch with a 3/8-inch seam allowance around all three edges, raising the presser foot here at the corners, and hence flipping the material about 3/8 inch from the edge. Trim the sides and corners diagonally close to the stitching to prevent bulky corners.
9. This is a step that can be skipped. If you like to protect the corners, just do a zig-zag stitch all around. Delete any stray threads. The canvas will unravel a bit at the edges before coming to a halt where there is stitching. If required, cut some of the excess canvas material there under the zipper flap.
10. The zipper bag will now be flipped right-side out. Take the corners out of the zipper opening with your hand. Push the corners out with something (not pokey scissors!) to make a smooth rectangle. It should be ironed clean.
11. That concludes the zipper pencil-case portion. Let's finish it off with a patterned HTV vinyl! In Cricut Design Space, you can make any cut you want. Line up the name script over the splash graphic, pick

both, and then select the slice tool in the bottom right corner.

12. Cut the name out of the picture CDS.

13. Pull the two cuts off and then delete the name by tapping on it.

14. Now you are left with a cut-out image.

15. Tap it. Select the mirror button. And after that, set cut over patterned iron-on.

16. Place the colored side down, cut it out, and then weed the excess vinyl out.

17. You may use an iron instead of a heat press. Set the oven to 300 degrees Fahrenheit, wait for it to warm up, then press the pouch to remove the moisture before folding it in half and press again now to have a center-line crease. To have the center, fold down the patterned HTV vinyl in nearly half. Press the two together for 15 seconds.

18. Remove the backing from the plastic. With a Teflon cover, click once more. Flip it over and click on the word if you have anything for the opposite side.

19. To ensure it is smooth and adhered, cut the backing, and press it again with a Teflon sheet for around 20 seconds.

That's it!! Adore the look of Cricut's patterned HTV vinyl! What would you do with it if you had it?

2. Fabric Tassels

Fabric tassels are simple to make and add a lovely handmade touch to any party setting. Do you want to make things easier? This is how to start making fabric tassels using Cricut Maker.

Maker's rotary blade makes cutting fabric a breeze – essentially; it's a tiny pizza cutter that cuts across the fabric like butter. It's fun to watch and it makes fabric cutting for small tasks like this a breeze.

Supplies

- Cricut Maker
- Pink Fabric Grip Mat (12 x 24 inch)
- Brayer (optional)
- Fabric (12 x 18 inch rectangles)
- Cricut Maker with Rotary Blade
- Hot Glue
- A file of Cricut Design Space

Instructions

1. To begin, open the file generated in Cricut Design Space by clicking on it. It's essentially a rectangle with several parallel lines cut into either side of it. You'll be taken to the Prepare screen after clicking "Make it" in the upper right corner of the canvas. Don't make any changes at this stage; so click next.

2. After that, pick your fabric. Pick cotton here as the particular. Cricut Design Space switches the type of blade to rotary blade automatically. In the Cricut's housing, position the rotary blade.

3. Place the fabric on the mat of your Cricut unit. Since there is no "direction", in this project, you can use the fabric right side down or up. Smooth out the fabric by using fingertips or a brayer – I prefer to have the brayer for keeping the oils on fingers away from the mat adhesive.

4. For cutting, place the mat inside the machine and press the blinking button. The rotary blade on the Cricut will precisely cut out fabric to make your tassel.

5. Remove the tassel from the fabric mat. Keep the extra fabric square that will be left around the whole edge. In a moment, we will use a scrap from it as well.

6. You might note that this cut is a little too "shreddy", as the fabric is cut directly across the grain, which may result in some long threads. Trim the worst offenders, but don't think about the rest – the idea of fabric tassels is to look a little shabby chic in the first place.

7. Put the fabric over a table, face down. Begin rolling your fabric from one of the uncut ends. As you get further, untangle the fringe, attempting to keep the roll as secure as possible. Roll until you have a funnel that has fringe at both ends.

8. Then fold it in half to form a loop.

9. Protect the tassel with a dab of hot glue and a piece of fabric from above. Check to see whether a strip of ribbon or twine could still be fed through the loop you made, and now you're done.

3. Box of Valentines from the Birdhouse

Use Cricut Maker to make this beautiful birdhouse Valentine card package and fall totally in love with how it will turn out.

Supplies

- Cricut Maker with Rotary Blade, Fine-Point Blade, and Knife Blade
- Fusible Fabric (polka dot red color)
- Cricut Chipboard/ Damask Patterned Chipboard
- Silver Glitter Vinyl
- Stainless Adhesive Foil (Red)
- Pearl Premium Vinyl (Permanent and Pastel Pink)
- Watermelon True Brushed Premium Vinyl (Permanent and Neon),
- Cricut (6×7 inch size) Easy Press 2

Since this cute small chipboard birdhouse is among one of Cricut Design Space's "Build It Now" designs, the design process is about as simple as creating the birdhouse project file and cutting.

Instructions

1. Cut mat number 1 from the chipboard as well as mats with damask pattern from over a really heavy-duty chipboard with the knife blade and a tight grip mat.

2. The display in Design Space will show you how many passes the cut will take and how much time you have left. After you hit the 75% mark (and after each additional pass), I suggest pausing the machine to check if the cut is complete.

3. Then use a blade with an extremely fine point in order to remove the foil that is adhesive, permanent luxury vinyl, and some glitter vinyl after chopping the chipboard parts.

4. For cutting fusible fabric for scalloped tiles of the roof, turn to the rotary blade. Scalloped edges and polka dots are two of my favorite things in the world, so one cannot get enough of this adorable combination! The Adaptive Tool System of Makers makes flipping between tools a breeze, allowing one to cut it all from thick chipboard to fine cloth without missing a beat.

5. After you finish cutting all of the bits, start weeding out the adhesive vinyl with the preferred hooked weeding tool. It's without a doubt my favorite hand tool. Such a red stainless brushed foil is highly desirable and gleaming.

6. Cautiously apply the vinyl onto the tops of the chipboard pieces, making sure the edges are neatly spaced.

7. 7. Use Cricut Easy Press to add fusible fabric to that same chipboard piece to accessorize the scalloped roof tiles. Please note that Cricut doesn't suggest using the Easy Press with chipboard and fusible fabric in the Interactive Reference Guide, but I have noticed that it works great.

8. 8. Use a double layer of parchment paper between the fabric and Easy Press 2, and then adjust the temperature to 300 degrees for 30 seconds. Since the chipboard begins to warp when exposed to sunlight, immediately put pieces under a heavy book to cool, and now, they come out perfectly.

9. The key reason to choose fusible fabric over some other material for the roof tiles is that fusible fabric is a sturdy and versatile material that will fit well with a "hinge". For the card box's roof to open and close use the Easy Press 2 to iron on an additional strip of fusible fabric right down the middle to tie the pieces together, and put the two top roof tiles with a bit of space in between to allow for folding.

10. Start laying out and assembling the birdhouse panels as per the instructions here in the project file once all the components have been painted with vinyl and fabric.

11. The Neon Watermelon Vinyl is a smoother, ribbed "rushed" surface with a transparent consistency that allows the damask chipboard pattern to shine through.

12. The pieces marked with the yellow arrow in the picture above are created from textured chipboard and coated in Neon Watermelon Brushed Vinyl – the main distinction is that the brushing on the fence piece runs vertically. In contrast, it runs horizontally on the pentagon piece, giving each piece a unique way of catching the light. The pieces can appear light pink and metallic at times, or they can appear far more red-toned and display the pattern more strongly at others. Isn't that amazing?

13. It's time to put the birdhouse together once almost everything of the panels is put together and when the glue has dried.

14. The parts match together neatly and accurately since the outlines of the side panels are now all slotted through box dovetail joints. During assembly, apply a narrow line of glue towards the corners and on the roof.

15. Choose to glue the right-hand side of the roof straightforwardly to the birdhouse and build an "of panel" for the left side, which could extend on this hinge to create the hinged roof.

16. The rooftop slope is edged as well, making it easy to see how far every other roofing layer will be glued down. I fixed each layer to the birdhouse and placed a glue strip for each layer to ensure that it was firmly and safely attached.

17. When reaching the top-hinged plate, only glue the right side down, leaving the left free to go up and down.

18. Glue each one of the left-sided roof parts to each other. Use the roof notches as a positioning guide to create a unified solid roof panel that can be opened or closed — using clothespins to keep the bits together until the glue dries is a brilliant idea!

19. That's it! The finished Valentine birdhouse is adorable and will be a perfect addition to my Valentine's Day decorations.

This birdhouse has many varying layered components, and I adore it because I used various vinyl materials for every layer, and you'll see the detail of each one. Stainless foil brushed metallic and glitter vinyl bring various levels of sparkle and glow to the project. Also, the birdhouse looks different from every angle as the light strikes the materials in unique ways.

However, the hinged roof is my best feature! With a moving roof, this adorable birdhouse can also be used as a Valentine card or treat box filled with sweet treats and love notes. I am curious to know how yours turns out if you plan to make your own.

1. Pantry Organization Tags with Smart Labels

Supplies

- Cricut Joy
- Cricut Smart Labels
- Cricut Joy Pen
- Mason jars/food storage containers

Instructions

1. Enable the Joy Pantry Labels cut document on your Cricut machine. Pick the labels you want to make by pressing Customize. Cut them down to the size you want for your storage containers. Make it happen by clicking "Make it."

2. Follow the on-screen directions to load a pen and a stack of Cricut Smart Labels here with the Cricut Joy. The words and design will be written by your Cricut Joy first. The machine will then ask you to reload your cutting blade so that it can remove the labels. Unload the machine once your labels have been cut.

3. Weed the smart labels by removing the stuff from around them and then leaving the labels on the paper backing. Remove the paper backing from your labels and stick them to your food storage jars.

4. And that's it! Using the Smart Labels and Cricut Joy, organize your pantry in minutes.

2. Greeting Cards for the Living Room

Supplies

- Cricut Card Inserts
- Cricut Joy Pen
- Cricut Joy
- Cricut Joy Card Mat

Instructions

1. Open the cut file "You're Cute, But I Am not Lion." Let it happen by pressing "Make it."

2. Follow the on-screen instructions. Place a card over the card cutting mat with the inner side of the card

within the pocket and the front of the card against the adhesive side of the mat. Put the card mat in your Cricut Joy. You'll be asked to load the Cricut pen first, and then you'll be asked to reload the cutting blade into the machine after you've finished writing.

3. Note: If you find cutting this pattern very difficult, look to see whether the card is cut all the way through it before unloading the mat; if it's not, press the "try again" key, and the Cricut Joy will cut your card a second time. For the first portion of the next pass, where everything is writing, leave the blade/pen holder empty, and then load it when it is ready to cut.

4. Remove your card from your mat and carefully peel it away. Any cut bits of paper which didn't fall out should be removed. Tuck a card insert into the card.

5. And that's it! You've made a charming lion card perfect for Tiger King himself.

3. Cricut Joy Cards

Supplies

- Cricut Joy tools
- Cricut Joy
- Cricut Joy pens
- Cricut Joy insert cards.
- Cricut Joy card mat (If you're using it, make sure the plastic coating is removed)

Instructions

1. The first move is to look through the "free for Cricut Joy" section for a card you want to create. Create it by pressing the "Make it" button.
2. It'll provide you with a sneak peek of the card upon the mat. Click the "Go" button.
3. Then you'll have to embed a card insert into the card mat. Launch the card and drift the back side in between the mat and the plastic guide. Slide the card here so that it butts up against both the top and side.
4. Fold the top of the card down and press it against the mat.
5. Pick insert card here from the material on the tablet or device.
6. Withdraw the blade housing from the clamp and place the pen in its place, as per CDS's instructions.
7. Set up the mat when Design Space asks you to. Simply position it in front of the rollers, and the system will begin to roll it in (there are no buttons to press!).
8. The computer will verify that it is inserted straight, and then a cut button will appear on the CDS screen. Move it and see what happens.
9. The Cricut Joy will then pause once the pen is finished drawing, and CDS will enable you to install the blade. Start by removing the pin and secure it in the blade housing with a clamp.
10. This will cut the rest once it has been detected. Cricut Design Space will then pause, and a screen will appear with an unload button. It'll unload if you click it!

11. Pull the front of the card away from the mat with care. If the cut-out sections do not stay on the mat, remove them from the cardstock. After this, slide the card off.
12. One of several background cardstocks should be inserted through its slits in the corners. There's no need for glue!

It's finished! So easy and adorable.

4. Wall Decals

Instructions

1. Making wall decals is also a breeze with the Cricut Joy.
2. Use Cricut Access to find a bunch of lovely dog silhouettes, size all of them to under 4.5 inches long, and cut all of them out at once (to about 4 feet).
3. Open the app and use the Bluetooth configuration to attach it to the phone, choosing Cricut Joy as your machine.
4. When instructed to load, use a foot stack of Smart Vinyl and put it directly into the machine. There's no need for a mat!

5. Trace the vinyl all the way in before taking out all of the adorable wall decals.
6. Once cutting is done, an offload request from CDS is clicked on, and the vinyl unloaded.
7. The excess vinyl is pulled and weeded out since there were several terms, just one of the images required to be applied with transfer tape.
8. Grab a portion of transfer tape, remove the backing, and adhere it to the image. Then I scrape it down with a scraper.
9. After that, cut the vinyl backing and you'll be left with the picture here on the transfer tape.
10. Press the picture around one of the drawers and then scrape it down after. The transfer tape is then peeled away.
11. Then peel off the remaining dog wall decals and place them wherever you wish. For a dog lover, this is a cute and basic wall decor idea.

1. Burlap Fall Wreaths from the Dollar Store with Free Printables

Supplies

- Cricut Explore
- Straw Wreath/Pool Noodle/Foam Wreath
- Glass-Headed Sewing Pins
- Burlap Ribbon
- Free Printable

Instructions

1. Gather your materials.
2. Burlap cloth is wrapped around the straw wreath.
3. Attach the ribbon ends now to the straw wreath.
4. Cut out the free printables by hand or using the make it now connect on the Cricut machine.
5. Attach flowers, bats, and the moon to the wreath with push pins.
6. Tie a ribbon around it and hang it any place in your home!
7. Wreaths are among my favorite ways to add color and texture to a room in our home. Wreaths are hung on walls, shelves, doorways, the fireplace, and portrait frames.

2. How Do You Make a Cricut Coffee Mug?

Supplies

- Cricut Explore
- Permanent Vinyl (red shiny)
- Cricut Cutting Mat (12 x 12-inch)
- Transfer Tape
- Svg File
- Coffee Mugs

Instructions

1. Gather your supplies.
2. Use your Cricut device for to cut the .svg image (or your own image); after this, weed the image.
3. Based on the size of your mug, you may change the size (3x 2.5-inches usually).
4. Adjust the transfer tape to all of the weeded images, scrape away the vinyl paper, and firmly tape the image onto the mug.
5. Remove the transfer tape, and then it's done.

3. Here's How to Create Farmhouse Signs From a Dollar Store

Supplies

- Dollar Tree Foam Board (black and white foam boards)
- Wood Stain
- Box Cutter
- Gallon Paint Sticks x5
- Tacky Glue
- Hand Saw/Circular Saw (could also use in Home Depot)
- Paint/Vinyl (optional)
- Rope (optional for "scroll" version)
- Cricut Explore

Instructions

1. Gather your materials.
2. Start by removing the curved edge from the paint sticks by cutting them. Then cut the paint sticks with a saw at home, but Home Depot has a free cutting station in the molding section where you could just cut them and then buy them. To make a typical sign (one with all four sides framed), cut one paint stick in half.
3. Wet the paint stick through, staining it. I used Briar Smoke stain.
4. If the stain is dry, measure the sign's size and cut out the foam board using the paint sticks as a reference.
5. After the paint sticks are cut, cut out the foam boards based on their height; the big sign is 17 x 25 inches in dimension. The large sign measures approximately 19 x 8.5 inches, while the small sign measures approximately 11 x 9 inches.
6. Cut each foam board with a box cutter. To prevent cutting the surface you're working on, put another foam board underneath it.
7. Apply the paint sticks to the top and bottom of the same foam board (while making a "scroll" sign) and all four sides (if creating a conventional sign) with tacky glue.

8. To hang the "scroll" sign, use tacky glue and a staple gun to tie the rope at the end. If you're making a four-sided frame, you can hang the sign with a photo frame hook or perhaps a saw tooth hanger. Alternatively, remove the hook and position it on a table.

Hope you enjoyed making a Dollar Store Sign.

4. How to Create a Teacher Koozie at Home

Supplies

- Cricut Explore
- Iron/Cricut Easy Press
- Blank Koozies (pre-made, various colors)
- Cricut Iron-on Lite
- Ironing Board/Cricut Mat

Instructions

1. Gather your materials.
2. Using Cricut Design Space, download the .eps, .svg, .dxf, or .png file.
3. Based on the size of one koozie, resize the picture.
4. Using a mirror image, put the shiny face down on the mat before cutting the images.
5. Disable the image.
6. For ironing the koozie, choose iron or Simple Press. At 250 degrees, just keep the Easy Press for around 5 seconds. It just takes a few minutes.
7. Add a drink or just give it to the teachers as is.
8. This idea for a teacher appreciation gift is brilliant. Who doesn't like a nice koozie?
9. These cute DIY teacher koozie gifts, including Fee SVG Split File, make excellent end-of-year gifts or teacher appreciation gifts.

6.

CRICUT JOY MASTERY

The Unofficial Step-By-Step Guide To Cricut Joy +
Accessories & Tools + Tips & Tricks + DIY Projects For
Beginners & Advanced Users!

Philippa Smalley

CRICUT JOY MASTERY

Introduction

If you're planning any DIY wedding, you've most certainly heard the words "Cricut" & "Vinyl" so several times that you've lost track! Perhaps you're new to DIY & have always enjoyed dabbling in different projects but never considered yourself a "professional craftsman" with all the necessary equipment & skills. Through all wedding Instagram accounts, Facebook groups, & online articles, you can't help but notice this.

So, what exactly is all this about? Is spending money on such items as a component of your wedding preparations a fair investment & a desirable cost? Is it more convenient to buy finished pieces and pre-cut vinyl via a third-party vendor?

You'll discover what a Cricut is, how to use one, & what you can do with that for a wedding DIY. Yes, and before you get into the details, it's pronounced as Cricket, but not Cricut.

Well, let's get started!

If you've got a professional model, Cricut is a brand for a system that may cut various materials, notably paper, vinyl, cardstock, & textiles. It works with an internet app named Design Space that lets you buy, upload, or create templates for the Cricut to do cutting for you. Also, it includes a 'print & cut' feature that allows you to create a model on a regular home printer & then cut that to size using the Cricut machine. In combination with cutting, you can purchase additional Cricut tools which enable you to draw in beautiful calligraphy, perforate score, or lines, engrave or emboss complex patterns.

There are many kinds of Cricut Machines globally, each with its own set of characteristics, features, advantages & disadvantages, cost analysis, etc. All of which you'll learn about in detail in the following chapters. Cricut Joy has been the newest member of the Cricut cutting machine family. It's Cricut's smallest sophisticated cutting machine (it's just 8.5 inches wide, 5 inches deep, & 5 inches tall), so it's extremely light, easy to store, & ideal for travel. Don't be fooled by its tiny size; it has some real cutting-edge features that will enable you to produce like no one else within the Cricut family.

Cricut Joy, like all Cricut machines, cuts & writes, but this does it using a variety of tools & materials developed especially for its tiny size. Everything for the Cricut Joy is good, small, but more relevantly, it is designed for eliminating fuss & frustration even when maximizing ease & flawless results.

To be fair, everything for your Cricut Joy has been uniquely designed.

Everything: mats, supplies, pens, blades, charging cable... Although you can cut down various materials to suit mats of Cricut Joy, any Explore blades/Maker, tools, markers, mats, & so on can't be utilized with your Cricut Joy. Always check that your "Cricut Joy" is properly labeled on the box to ensure that what you're working with is suitable.

For your creative endeavours, a Cricut is a tool that can cut various materials, including paper, plastic, & cardboard. Certain Cricut machines can slice thin wood, fabric, silk, and other materials.

A Cricut machine allows you to cut & create amazing designs from items you never knew existed. Depending on the framework you have, you may draw, emboss, or create foldable lines to make 3D masterpieces, gift boxes, frames, & so on.

A Cricut is a great weapon for those who love creating & need to trim a lot more things.

1. How Cricut Machines work?

You can connect a Cricut to a computer over a wireless network, create or save designs on your desktop, & then transfer them to a Cricut to cut. Design Room (for electronic devices, Windows, and MAC) is a Cricut program that allows you to create many imports machine-cut patterns. Within your Cricut is a tiny cutter (or pen, rotary blade, or measuring instrument). You may place your chosen item over a 12" thin cutting surface, wirelessly upload your plan to your Cricut, & then put your product inside your system once you've completed your design into Design Space. As you click trigger, the project began to split.

2. Can Cricut cut Fabric, Wood, and Leather?

Yes, many Cricut machines can cut silk, fabric, & even wood, in combination with vinyl, cardboard, & plastic. 1.3 Are Cricut Machines Hard to Use?

3. Are Cricut Machines Hard to Use?

Cricut machines come with a comprehensive online tutorial & a wide range of additional Cricut tools, making them relatively easy to use. Both Work Room & the Cricut tool are designed to be simple to use, and they don't require much graphic design knowledge (however, this does advantage if you would like to build your projects from scratch). There's a sequence of photos & designs in the Design Room of Cricut that you may buy as a proposed model. Some are unrestricted, while others are purchased for a nominal fee.

4. More than 50 things you need to know

Below are Some things to keep in mind when purchasing a Cricut.

1. Do I need a Cricut?

The Cricut is indeed a cutting device & a dream come true for many artists out there. You will use this for many things, such as interior design, card design, and so forth.
Do you have the ability to create, & do you encounter yourself in a situation where a significant quantity of material has to be cut? If you answered yes, a Cricut would be very beneficial to you.

2. Are there other technologies that can do a similar thing?

Absolutely. Many alternative options can do most of the similar functions as the Cricut.
Two additional well-known brands on the market continue to provide diverse materials and have received a positive response.

Companies like Brother & Silhouette America are examples of this.

3. What Cricut Machines are available out there?

There still are three different Cricut Device models to choose from:

i) **Cricut Explore Family:**
These are the most well-known devices, with three initial choices to choose from. Although all three machines may cut the same items, each one serves a different purpose.

- **Explore Air and Cricut Explore One:** Were the initial Explore Air 2 versions? The 1st only featured one tool holder, although the 2nd had two & a Bluetooth connection.
- **Air 2 Cricut Explore:** This has similar functionality to Explore Air (drawings, cuts, ratings, prints, & cuts), but that's twice as simple to use.

ii) Cricut Maker:

It's a more energy-efficient machine as compared to Explore Air 2, allowing you to shatter with 10 times the amount of energy. With Creator, you may break, Refill, rate, & do a lot more.

iii) Cricut Joy:

It's the most recent device from Cricut. It's teeny-tiny, yet it can slice & draw a wide variety of resources. Cricut Joy easily breaks & draws fabric & iron-on without a mat.

4. Is the Cricut Device too Expensive?

Let's initiate by acknowledging that a Cricut machine might be quite expensive.

However, keep in mind that it's possible. It's because all of the other initial machines will show you that they are quite inexpensive & that you'll get going right away.

The cheapest option is the Cricut Cuttlebug, a tiny but powerful die-cutting machine, while the expensive option is the Cricut Maker, their newest product.

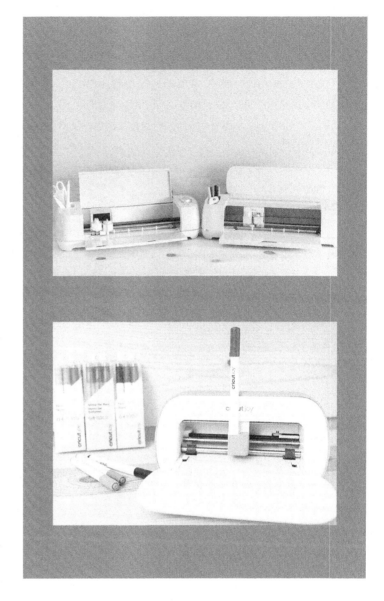

5. Is the Cricut Profitable?

This is very dependent on your preferences, goals, & financial situation.
If you just do crafts once a year, you won't need to have a Cricut. A Cricut is definitely worth the money if you like designing & creating things.

You should still view things through each of your objectives' lenses. Why am I making this investment? Since life seems to be all about achieving objectives, every decision you make should be based on those aims.

Is purchasing a Cricut going to influence you & make your life easier, saving you money and time while also improving your life to more enjoyable?
If you said yes, Pull the Switch.

6. What is the top Cricut I can acquire?

The best Cricut to buy is one which meets these three requirements:

- That's the one that customers may purchase.
- The one that allows you to split the things you desire.
- One which will leave you with additional funds to purchase supplies (frequently overlooked).

Ultimately, what advantage is a more expensive gadget if you can't afford to buy the basic materials with which you run it?

If you've not bought a device & are interested in cutting wood & cloth, it is thought that investing some money now & purchasing more resources & equipment as required is a better idea.

7. Can I modify my Cricut machine?

Let me tell you stuff: if you already own a Cricut machine, you are a rock star.

Are you considering a change? I'm aware of the situation.

After purchasing an Explore Air 2, You felt inept, assuming that all of the teachings were now for the Developer & that you could just upgrade.

Isn't that absurd?

Can you fix your phone, car, & other modern devices yearly? Certainly not. So, until an expert has given one, he will continue to do so unless he has exhausted all possibilities & are able to develop new methods. You won't be updating your phone.

So, how are things going with you?

Would you want to be forced to upgrade only to obtain the most recent version? Or are you attempting to upgrade because your old PC is no longer functional?

Assume you choose the second option & have the financial means to do so. Thank you for being a member of the Cricut Builder community. You will undoubtedly find that machine to be an excellent fit for your requirements.

8. Will you tell me where I can get a Cricut?

A Cricut may be purchased from a variety of sources.

It's famous at Michael's & JOANN, among other art stores. It's also available at a lot of Wal-Mart stores. Consequently, if you want to get started on the task, you must drive there.

9. Is there ever a deal on the Cricut and Cricut Materials?

Yes, absolutely.
Cricut has items available almost half the time.

The majority of them are available throughout vacations, but a few are available for significant occasions. Only a few supermarkets regularly run big deals. You've probably seen a lot of these on social networking sites.

10. Best Cricut sales and deals?

If you wish to get a Cricut immediately now, go to the official website of the company. Simply said, they offer better pricing on hand.

There are some excellent deals on bundles, gadgets, & equipment.

11. What components can be cut down with Cricut?

This amazing machine will cut potentially hundreds of different components; here are those few examples:

- Corrugated Paper
- Metallic Paper
- Sticker Paper
- Cardstock of all types
- Textile & Fabric
- Vinyl Paper
- Thin Woods
- Plan Paper
- Faux Leather

12. Where can I buy Cricut materials?

Materials may be purchased from a local design store. In the same manner, a Cricut would be used.

You were astounded by the sheer number of options available on the Internet. Through Amazon, you will purchase hundreds, though not thousands, of items.

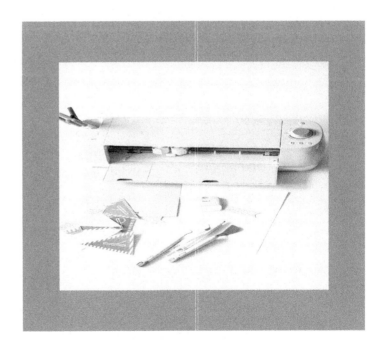

The Cricut store also offers some intriguing items, so they just promote their brand. On the other hand, Michaels is a popular location to buy supplies; many people are strolling around the isles & it is easy to waste time (plus money) there.

13. How much do Cricut materials cost?

Cricut materials may be very costly, depending on the jobs you select to cut. As a result, one may get a machine which will assist them in obtaining cutting materials.

If you're not using the money to divide additional components, buying the Cricut Machine is pointless. There's not any snow in Florida; it's like buying tire chains. Are you able to comprehend all I'm saying?

It's amazing how little things add up. Basswood, for instance, might be too expensive.

You start by focusing on paper & work your way up. Paper is an excellent method to learn how to use the machine, & if you screw up, it's only paper. However, if someone makes an error, it isn't a major issue.

14. Should I use non-branded items for a Cricut machine?

You don't have to limit yourself to Cricut products. Hundreds, though not thousands, of amazing materials, may be found online and at your local craft store.

There's little question that as time goes on, more options will become accessible.

15. Cricut mystery box, and how does it work?

So, each month, Cricut releases one Mystery Box. This box contains a plethora of exciting things, and you've no clue what they are. It's a treat unless you receive the box.

The greatest part about this deal is that you'll get more bang for your buck. Though if you bought any one of the package's items alone, the price would be considerably greater.

They will run out at some point. As a result, make sure you receive this one at the beginning of each month. Alert: Cricut hasn't been releasing mystery boxes regularly.

16. What is the Cricut Adaptive Tool System, and how does it work?

A Cricut Adjustable Machine is a distinctive & helpful tool found only in the Cricut Builder. This function controls the trajectory & speed of a blade at specific phases. This technique is so advanced that this can adjust the pressure of the blade to match the parts you're working with.

This technology allows the Cricut Builder to split with 10 times the strength of any such Cricut Explore Series machine.

Just because of that, the Builder would cut thick materials such as leather & wood.

17. Can you print with the Cricut?

Printing is not possible with the Cricut machine. All newer Cuttlebug machines, on the other hand, have the capacity to paint & create symbols, figures, & other things.

The solution to this question should be obvious when you're using a Cricut.

18. Is Ink necessary for the Cricut?

Because the Cricut cannot write, you may use it without ink.

But let's assume you're willing to utilize the painting option. For the drawing, you'll need their markers. They provide a large number of options from which to choose.

19. Is the Cricut a Chipboard Machine?

No, that isn't true. Lamination would not be available on Cricut machines. But wouldn't it be great if that were the case?

20. Is the Cricut willing to emboss?

The Cricut Cuttlebug seems to be the only Cricut machine that can emboss completely (discontinued).

You can get around it by creating stencils for a few of the machines & embossing anything very much. While

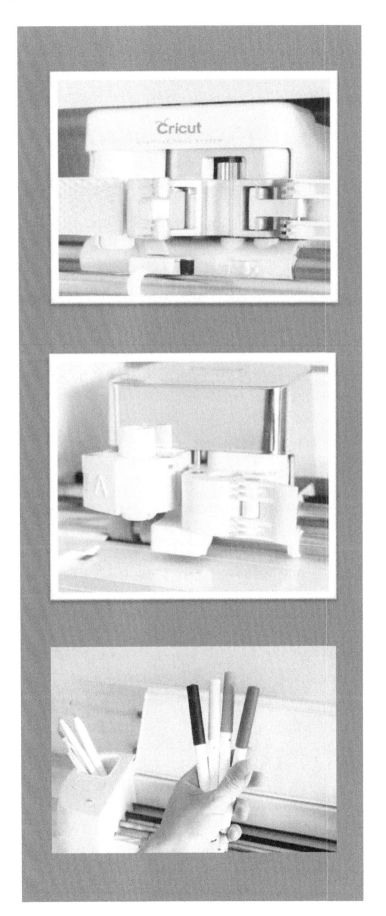

researching this problem, you discovered a plethora of fantastic Videos online that demonstrate how to accomplish it.

If you've a Cricut Creator, though, you need "deboss" using the debossing tip (the inverse of embossing).

21. Is the Cricut a Sewing Machine?

No, that isn't true. The Cricut might not be able to sew. It's simple to say that you can accomplish as a drain whenever you hear about all the amazing things you can accomplish.

22. Can you cut fabric with the Cricut?

In reality, the Cricut would cut fabric.

If you work in the garment industry and have to cut large amounts of fabric in a variety of sizes, the Cricut will be your best slicing companion.

A Cricut Maker would be used to cut fabric without the need for any bonded materials. You may acquire a Cricut when sewing is your job, and it's the main reason you desire one. Investing in Joy is strongly encouraged.

Any of those Cricut Explore Series machines would be used to cut fabric.

23. What is a backing material, and how would it apply to cloth cutting?

Fabrics may be cut using the Cricut Explore & Cricut Maker devices. But there is one important caveat: backing material may be used to cut fabric with the Explore Family machines.

Backing, also known as Heat & Bond in the realm of Cricut & die-cutting machines, is a kind of substance which helps you attach textiles to the cutting pad. In other words, if you don't use this material before cutting your textiles with the Cricut Explore Machines, the fabrics will be damaged & spread out.

24. Is the Cricut capable of cutting wood?

Both No & Yes are correct. This is the favourite Cricut cutting tool out of them. The Cricut Creator is the only way to cut wood. Two types of wood that may be removed are basswood & balsa.

You must also be aware that the Cricut Creator's standard cutter doesn't cut wood. These tasks need the use of a Razor Knife; this is a kind of blade designed specifically to cut thick materials.

25. What kind of projects should I make with a Cricut Maker?

The Cricut computer must be utilized for a wide range of projects. This is just a sample of the jobs you must do.

- The decor of the house: There are window & wall decals available. Personalize items like buckets and even culinary ingredients if that's something you prefer to do.
- Stickers: Stickers can also be utilized for many things, including organizing, journaling, & much more.
- Greeting Cards: Using this machine, you may create high-end cards. For instance, those seen at supermarkets.
- Items of clothing: For a beautiful & fitted appearance, T-shirt styles may also be trimmed & ironed over.
- 3D Projects: 3D crafts include things like gift boxes & paper toys.
- A Cricut Machine may be used to cut wood & make 3D, long-lasting sculptures.
- The fabric is cut, & design elements for the garments & other things are produced because the sky is the limit of your imagination.

26. What are Cricut cartridges, and do I even need them?

Throughout the Cricut world, the word cartridge does indeed have a different meaning than it is within the printing world.

Cricut Cartridges are a collection of photos, drawings, or typefaces that you may purchase and keep for as long as you like. They're usually themed on Disney or even a Pop Corn Group, or anything else comes to mind.

There are two types of cartridges available. The actual ones can go into the machine, but the digital

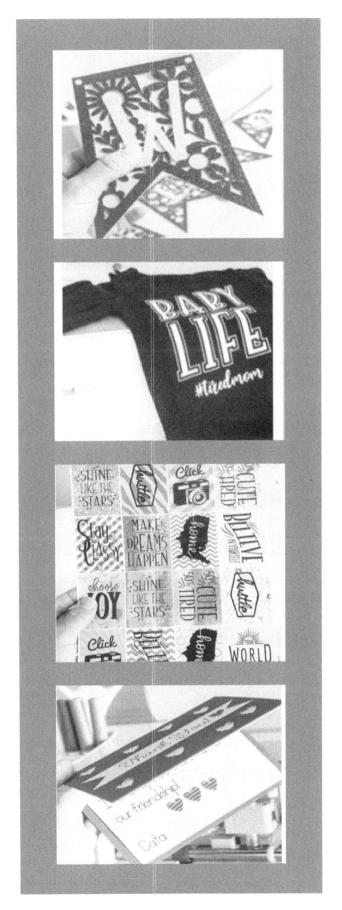

ones can't. Digital versions are available for purchase on the Cricut site or in Cricut Design Space. The cartridges would work on the application until they're activated, & you won't need the physical copies after that.

Cartridges are not functional in their original condition.

27. Cricut Infusible Ink, and how does it work?

Infusible Ink is a kind of technology which allows you to create patterns & then transfer those to a substrate. This technique becomes really unique when the Infusible Ink transference is combined with the raw material you choose.

The pictures are beautiful & consistent now that you're utilizing Cricut Infusible pigment. They're incredibly smooth, won't slide off, & may be permanently embedded in the underlying material.

28. What are Cricut Mats, and which one would I require?

A Cricut Mat is a cutting surface that may be used to cut many varieties of materials. They come in two sizes: 12" x 24" & 12" x 12".

Cricut Mats typically are sticky, & the amount of stickiness you apply depends on what you're cutting. And, as they're often referred to, handles.

Right present, there are 4 distinct mat styles available for a Cricut Explore & Maker:
- Light Grip (Blue)
- Solid Grip (Purple)
- Textile Grip (Pink)
- Normal Grip (Green)

A Cricut Joy comes with three different mats:
- Light Grip (Blue)
- Standard Grip (Green)
- Card Mat (Blue) For making cut-out cards.

Reminder: Cricut Joy Mats are available in sizes ranging from 4.5x6.5 to 4.5x12.

The basic grip is the perfect MAT for you if you're just getting started. The better the grip, the harder the material you use.

If you're cutting normal, thin paper, for instance, a Light Grip mat will suffice; but, if you're cutting heavy materials, including thick cardboard, a Strong Grip mat will suffice.

Almost every device comes with a basic grip mat. Read the term carefully before making a purchase.

29. What is a Cricut Blade, and how do I choose the right one?

The cutter is in charge of slicing the items. What are your thoughts?

But there is something you'd be aware of before you begin, especially if you want to cut heavy material. There are presently seven-blade types & three additional carving tools available online for bigger devices (Maker & Explore).

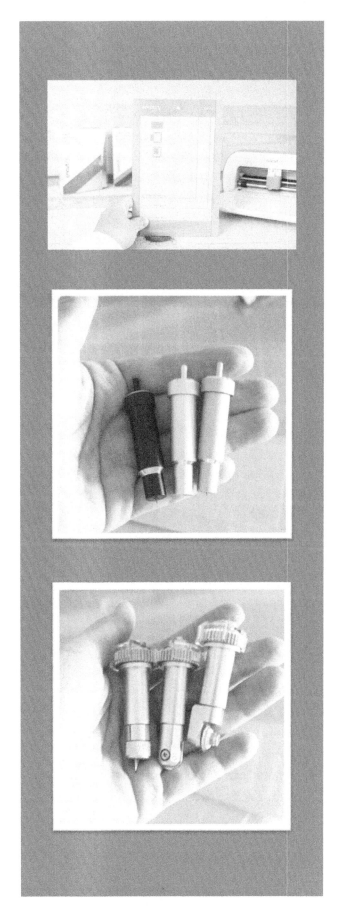

- **Fine Point Blade:** Paper, cloth, & cardboard are examples of light to intermediate textiles. There's also a gold variant.
- **Deep Point Blade:** The best materials are chipboard, stiff plastic sheets, cardboard, & heavy materials are the best materials.
- **Bonded Fabric Blade:** A Bonded Cloth Blade may be used to split a wide variety of textiles. The fabric must have a reinforcing layer connected to it.
- **Rotary Blade (Just for the Cricut Maker):** Cuts virtually any kind of fabric, & the material may be placed directly on the Mat. It comes as part of the Maker's bundle.
- **Knife Blade (Just for Cricut Maker):** This incredible tiny blade can trim through materials as tough as basswood.
- **Fast Swap Perforation blade:** You may create items using a tear finish with this blade. This

technology has given you access to a whole new world of possibilities. It can only be used with Cricut Maker.

- **Fast Swap Wavy blade:** The Fast Swap Wavy blade produces wavy results on final cuts rather than cutting clean lines such as rotary & fine point cutter. It can only be used with the Cricut Maker.
- **Fast Swap Debossing Tip:** You may push the material in & create beautiful, intricate patterns with this technique. Because of the level of detail, you'll be adding to your projects, and debossing will elevate them to a whole new level. It can only be used with the Cricut Maker.
- **Fast Swap Engraving Trick:** For many craftsmen, the Engraving Trick has become a long time coming. With this kit, you'll be able to engrave a wide variety of materials. It can only be used with Cricut Maker.
- **Tips for Quickly Swapping Scoring Wheels:** A Scoring Wheel is a technique for folding textiles in an attractive, edgy, and crunchy manner. It can only be used with Cricut Maker.
- **Foil Transfer Kit:** You may create beautiful foil effects on your drawings with the "Foil Transfer Kit." It's compatible with Cricut Maker & a few Explore series machines. Cricut offers fine, bold, & medium tips for better suit your project throughout this bundle, which includes three resources in one.

Read this comprehensive guide to learn much more about Cricut Blades & their variations.

Even though a Cricut Joy includes a "Fine Point Blade," it's only usable with such a device.

30. What blades does each Cricut machine come with?

When you buy a gadget alone (not part of a package), it usually comes with a blade. Let's take a look at these blades that every unit produces.

- Fine point blade for Cricut Explore Air 2
- Cricut Maker: fine point cutter, rotary blade
- Pointed razor for Cricut Joy.

31. What is the life expectancy of the Cricut blade?

Depending on the products & how often you use them, Cricut blades would last a longer time.

It still does not have a time frame attached to it. Let's say you observe the goods aren't being sliced as crisply and readily as they formerly were. Then you must choose a different one.

32. Do I Require Any Other Cricut Accessories?

This is a tricky topic since it depends completely on the items you want to split & deal with.

Cricut machines can do a broad variety of jobs, but they have to be utilized in combination with other tools to be completely successful. If you wish to use one from the Explore Series Machines to cut fabric, for instance, you'll have to have:

- Fabric Bonded Blade
- Standard Grip Mat
- Backing Material

If you just use Maker for cutting fabric, you may use the tool mentioned above or a spinning blade alongside the Silk Grip Mat.

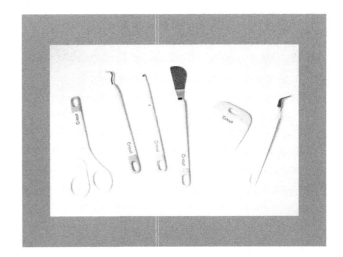

Most conventional & light fabrics may be cut using the Fine Point Blade (a razor that goes between every device) & the Basic Grip Mat.

It may become a lot easier as you understand more about a particular device & the item you're dealing with.

You know it isn't easy at first, but you'll become a pro once you get the hang of it. The software on this machine is helpful in that this will show you exactly what material you'll require when cutting a specific material.

The Main Tool Set includes
- Tweezers come in handy when working with delicate things.
- Weeder: Assists in the segregation of negative slices & their removal.
- Covered with a pair of scissors having a blade
- Spatula: It's what you'll utilize to clean a Mat Scraper while also helping with pattern transitions from a layer to the next.

The Essential Tool Set includes the following items:
- Stylus for scoring, plus everything stated above: It's a fantastic method to include folding edges into games, 3D projects, & other projects.
- A trimmer & a replacement blade are required for cutting items bigger than 12".
- Use the scoring blade to attach folding lines to your product (for a trimmer).

Whether or not you are fortunate enough to obtain a set, it will undoubtedly be featured in the Basic Toolbox.

33. Do I get the whole package or only the device?

There appear to be a number of packs to select from whether you visit the Amazon, Cricut App store, & other online shops. They are inexpensive & come with a starting kit to assist you in getting started straight away.

When purchasing packages, be certain they include everything you'll require for getting started.

If you're beginning with paper & vinyl cutting, for instance. Your perfect package could include a vinyl sheet, a particular machine, a basic grip pad, & a particular toolset could be included in your perfect package.

34. Is there anything else I need in addition to the Cricut & Items

There are a few more things you'll require that aren't typically mentioned:

You would like to understand how & where to cut certain products. It is recommended that you practice cutting on papers for a long period before moving on to expensive materials such as fabric or wood.

Persistence is a valuable asset. The learning curve is very steep. It won't be easy at first, but this will become easier.

Watching Video tutorials will teach you all you require to understand about this device.

35. What is a Cricut Easy Press, exactly?

The Cricut Easy Press is an excellent tool for ironing Iron-On vinyl onto quilts, sweaters, T-shirts, & other items. It's available in three different varieties, so you can pick the one which best suits your needs: Following are the measurements:

- 9"x9": Such size is perfect for scaling down prototypes to single sizes. T-shirts are a common choice.
- 6"x7": Ironing on small things, such as onesies & other baby goods, is a breeze.
- 10"x12": Ironing big surfaces like comforters & covers is a breeze with this iron.
- Easy press Mini: It's perfect for pressing HTV on tiny things like bags, hats, & small items.

36. Is it simple to use the Cricut?

In general, there is indeed a learning curve.

You confess that once your Cricut arrived, you were a bit perplexed. It may seem not very comforting initially, but it'll seem natural after you get the hang of it. Those dull days would be a distant memory for sure. So, the most crucial thing is to keep moving. It would be best to follow as many Channels on YouTube & Social media posts as possible. Search for videos with instructions.

Don't be disheartened. You live in a digital age when information is available just at the click of one button.

38. Do I need to be tech-savvy to be able to use the Cricut?

You don't need to be a tech whiz to accomplish this. However, you must have to be familiar with the basics & fundamentals of the machine.

For instance, you would now be expected to have a basic understanding of computers. You arrange the object you would like to cut by opening the tab & login into Cricut Design Space.

You may utilize the app to operate your machine if you've got a Smartphone. You must also understand how to install the program.

Is there any way you would not be able to get this done? That isn't the case at all. It's possible if you have the time & dedication.

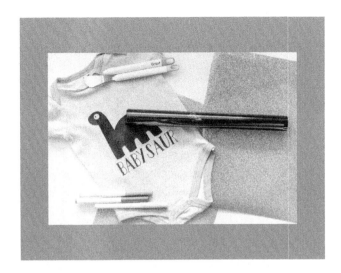

39. With whom will the Cricut be used?

In order for a machine to work, you must also be connected to a Cricut Design Space.

Its Cricut Design Space mainly supports Windows & Mac operating systems. To look at it another way, in order to use the Cricut Machines, you'll need a desktop computer.

If you wish to use the machine without it being connected to the Internet, you'll have to download a Cricut Design Space application. Because it connects to your smartphone through Bluetooth, that software is very useful. This software is only available for iOS devices (iPhone & iPad). If you're an Android user, don't lose up hope; Cricut has just released a beta version, & although it lacks many of the capabilities of the iPhone, that's a solid start.

40. Can I attach my Cricut to a mobile phone or device through Bluetooth?

It is mostly dependent on the kind of computer being used.

Bluetooth is integrated into the Maker, Explore Air 2, & Joy, allowing them to connect to any computer or smartphone.

41. Would I be able to use the Cricut if I don't have access to the Internet?

You don't have to be available on the internet all the time to concentrate on these designs.

However, in order to install Cricut Design Space & get the computer on & running, you should be connected to the internet.

You should first import Cricut pictures & fonts (while online) if you want to use those offline.

If you have any iOS device (iPad, Android phone), you still can cut & create designs offline; however, you won't store fonts or files for later use.

Cricut is also available for Android customers in an offline mode.

42. Is there any alternate software that can use Cricut?

Not in the least.

While it's not compatible with current computers, there was possibly a method to do it using third-party software.

You design what you want to use & cut it out on Illustrator, except instead of cutting it out on Illustrator, you cut it out on the printer. On another hand, let's pretend it's all text & basic forms. It's more than enough to use the Cricut Design.

43. What does the Cricut work?

So far, you've learned all you need to understand about your Cricut. Mats, materials, needles, and equipment suitability are just a few things to think about.

But how precisely will your Cricut work? In order for your Cricut Devices to carve, you would utilize your Cricut Design Space. You may use this to set out & design the cut pattern.

44. What is Cricut Design Space, and how does it work?

Your Cricut Design software assists you in planning, designing, & cutting your creations. You can't use your machine until you have the Design Space. That's why knowing when to utilize it is crucial.

Your Cricut Maker is wonderful, and however, if you don't know how to use the Design area, it's similar to having a camera & never using that. Purchase a Smartphone & tablet without a video call or voice as an alternative.

45. Is Cricut Design Space available for free?

Yes, absolutely.

If you've computer access, you must submit those fresh drawings for splitting. You may also make simple changes for free using the fonts & shapes on the computer.

Cricut Access, on another hand, does not come without a cost.

46. What is Cricut Access, and how does it work?

Cricut Access seems to be a large library that enables you to explore & create pre-planned designs. This is especially useful if you're just starting.

You may pick from a range of unique fonts, 3D projects, icons, & much more if you've Cricut Access. They offer designs for each occasion and whatever kind of information you want to utilize. It's a masterpiece.

47. What is Cricut Free Cut Friday, and how does it work?

Starting on the weekend of each week, Cricut would provide a few complementary cut templates. You are only allowed to use specific files throughout the week.

That's also great since it motivates users to keep using the gadget in order to find new features. You might look for those within Cricut Design Space.

You may also get an email with a tutorial to test them out if you're a member of their updates.

48. Can you tell me where I can get free Cricut cut files?

Cut files may be found unrestricted in a number of places.

- Daydream into Reality Library: The library is growing at a fast pace. You'll find not just Cut pictures, however, also a wide range of other great pintables suitable for any occasion.
- Cricut Design Space: Within your Cricut Design Space, cut all free images of the week.
- Jennifer Maker: It also offers a wonderful library that you may use.
- ME & SVG: Stunning & lovely library.
- Pixabay: Pixabay is indeed a completely free photo-sharing service. They offer a huge collection of SVG files that you may use for complimentary or for business purposes.

1.5 Cricut Joy: Step-By-Step Unboxing & Setup

So, you got yourself a little sidekick & want to begin with your Cricut Joy. Fortunately, unpacking the new Cricut Joy & getting it ready for your 1st project is a breeze!

From beginning to end, the whole procedure should just take a few minutes!
Are you ready to begin?

Step 1: Open Box

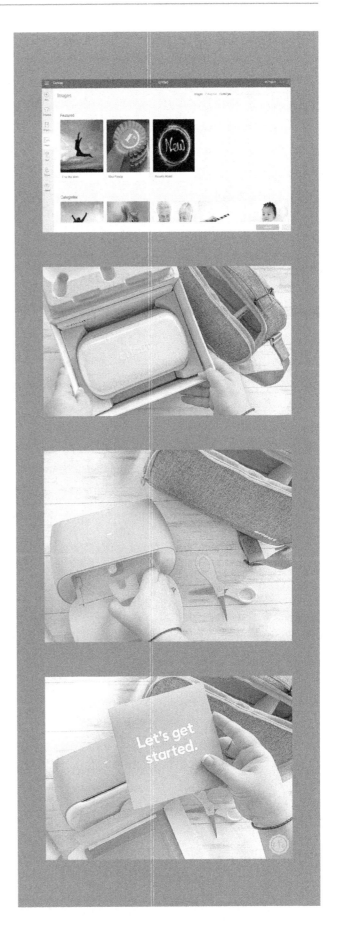

This one ought to be self-explanatory! Begin by opening the package & removing all of the contents. It shouldn't take too long. If you're like me, the thrill of buying a newer toy means you've already opened that package and inspected everything inside!

There should be four items within the box:

- Power Cord
- Cricut Joy
- Black Pen
- Instruction Booklet (Sample Paper, Sample Vinyl, Setup Booklet, Standard Mat)

Unboxing your Joy is indeed a breeze. It's only a question of ripping the cellophane, pulling the styrofoam protection from its blade, and taking off its clear sticker, which protects the region beneath the blade after you've had it out.

After you've gotten everything out from the box & removed the packaging, it is time to get to work on the exciting part: connecting this thing to your Cricut Design Space!

Step 2: Setup Joy With your Cricut Design Space

Okay, everyone... It's now time for the heavy guns to take the stage. Cricut Design Space is a software program that allows you to create your designs. You've registered many Cricut items with Design Space during this time, & the process has been quite simple... However, you'll be utilizing Cricut Design Space's desktop version instead of the online version for this time.

Which frightened you for a certain reason.

It's fortunately not difficult.

Open your Cricut Design Space & double-check that

it is modern (it will require you to update every five secs so just tap yes once it opens & asks you for an update). When you're at the Setup wizard, you'll see that your Cricut Joy choice is accessible.

Click on 3 little lines within the top left-hand corner after you've updated & chosen "New-Machine-Set-up" from the drop-down menu. Then choose Cricut Joy from the drop-down menu.

Design Space would guide you through all the procedures (which are quite simple), but the most important thing to remember is that your tiny Joy only can connect to any laptop, phone, or tablet via Bluetooth. As a result, if you can't get access through Bluetooth, this will be an issue.

Fortunately, most phones now have Bluetooth (although your PC does not), so you'd be OK.

Just remember that you'll need to connect the computer by its settings rather than Cricut Design Space. Fortunately, these are actions you'll need to take: Plug in the power cable & the Bluetooth from your computer to your Joy & get yourself ready for cutting!

Step 3: Start 1st Project

Now that it is time to get to work on your project! This tool may cut various materials (vinyl, paper, window cling, iron-on, etc.) & the basic fine pointed blade is small & adorable (exactly similar to the machine!).

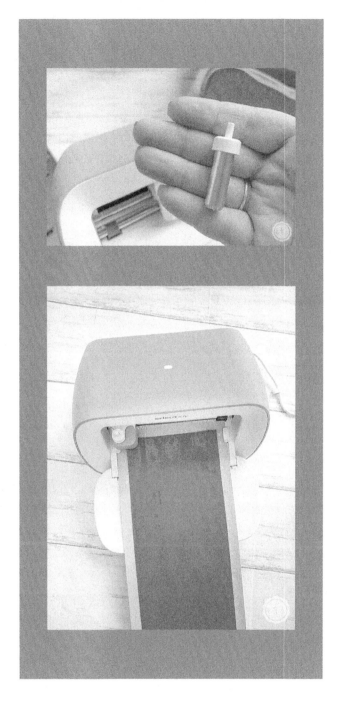

Any enthusiast who wants to save time doing his projects should invest in this Cricut machine. It enables you to cut a range of materials with precision, resulting in dependably great results. The most powerful Cricut system comes with a slew of benefits and features.

You'll take a look at a few of the finest Cricut machines throughout this chapter. You'll take a close look at nine Cricut machines as well as two useful toolboxes.

Before buying a product, this is critical to learn a great deal about it. Below is a detailed description of every model shown on the map.

1. Cricut Maker Machine

If you're looking for a device that's super-versatile, robust, and loaded with features, go for the Maker. Your Cricut Store is still open for business. This gadget allows you to make anything which comes to your mind. It's possible to make balsa wood crafts, vinyl decals, stitching jobs, paper crafts, leather crafts, & other crafts.

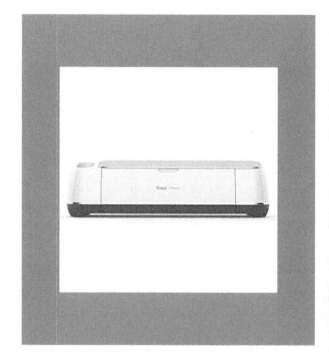

There's nothing these machines can't accomplish with a scoring tool, knives, & pens. It comes with a newer rotary blade which can cut through any kind of material.

You'll obtain clean and uniform slices each time. This knife blade would pass through mat-board and balsa wood, among other materials. If you would like to save effort, this equipment is really for you.

It's perfect for the wood carving & stencilling. You may wonder, "Is it the greatest cutting device for you?" The answer is yes since you're a competent craftsperson.

Advantages

- Custom layouts & designs may be imported.
- For any smartphone or tablet, a simple charging station is available.
- It will help you save time & make your chores more manageable.

- Powerful blades, a scoring tool, & pens are all required.
- It may be used with a wide range of materials.

Disadvantages

- There isn't much room for cutting.
- A knife blade is not included and must be bought separately.

2. Cricut Explore Air 2 Machine

You can create personalized vinyl patches, greeting cards, custom-made clothes, & home décor, among many other things if you give such cutting machine one try. With the quality carbide blade, you can count on precise & accurate cuts each time. This gadget is very simple to use.

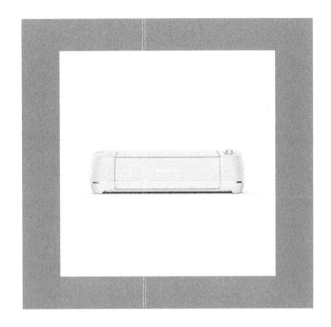

To create anywhere, just drag & drop your pictures into the program or pick from a vast collection of customized projects & themes. This machine comes with a two-tool holder for cutting & writing or maybe cutting & scoring.

You may create & design using your computer, tablet, or PC. This type is excellent if you require a machine which is extremely precise and reliable.

It works with a variety of materials, including paper, cardboard, fake leather, & more. You can buy it at any Cricut Store before everything sells out.

Frequently, don't neglect to purchase the necessary equipment to assist you in getting the most out of this machine & producing consistently excellent results.

Advantages

- With such a smart dial, you can slice along with the appropriate depth & pressure using wireless slicing plus built-in Bluetooth.
- Versatile, precise, & extensively utilized cutting device.

Disadvantages

- This has a larger volume than any of its predecessors (Cricut-Explore-Air)

3. Cricut Explore Air Machine

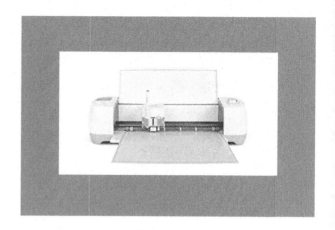

If you want to purchase a product which is well-reviewed by thousands of people & has a good reputation, go for your Cricut Explore Air.

It possesses a dual carriage which allows you to cut & write or also cut & score constantly. It is also possible to post your pictures for free.

That machine can handle more than 60 material varieties, including leather plus vellum. The smart dial for simpler material settings, one iPad app, & a complimentary Cricut Design subscription is also included. Your Cricut Explore Air would be compatible with each Cricut cartridge, ensuring smart & accurate cutting every time. It includes built-in storage space as well.

Advantages

- Cutting which is both sharp & precise.
- It has built-in storage compartments and is compatible with Cricut cartridges.
- The utilization of the smart dial simplifies material settings.
- The software is free on the internet.

Disadvantages

- This makes a loud noise while cutting.
- The blade is difficult to adjust.

4. Cricut Explore One

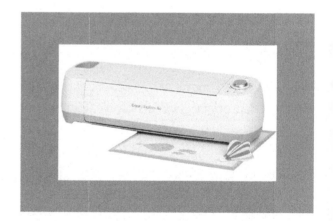

Do you want to buy an automatic cutting machine for assisting you in completing different DIY crafts? A Cricut

Explore One has an excellent option if that's really the case.

It allows to add & chop pictures arbitrarily. You can develop and customize any time with the freeware cloud-based applications for PC, Mac, & iPhone.

If you want to cut remotely, you'll need to get a portable Bluetooth adaptor for any cutting machine. The fact that this is sold separately is considered a disadvantage.

If you're looking for a cutting machine which can handle a range of materials, including iron-on, leather, vinyl, parchment, & more, be no more than explore one.

Advantages

- It's adaptable and may be used with a number of materials.
- For artists who are passionate about their job, this is the finest cutting machine.
- Your pictures may be clipped & inserted.

Disadvantages

- The dual carriage is not in use.
- There isn't any Bluetooth capability.

5. Cricut Easy Press 2 Machine

This Cricut Easy Press-2 is excellent for t-shirts, hoodies, blankets, banners, & similar items because of its 12"x11" size.

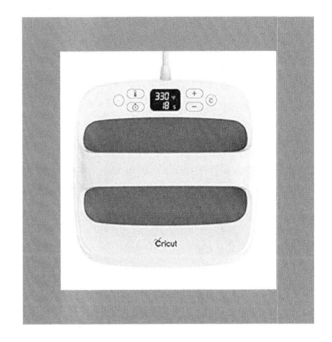

In just seconds, the enhanced heat plate shape with a ceramic-glazed surface provides an up-to-date iron-on effect. This gadget can accurately measure temperatures up to 400 degrees Fahrenheit. It's easy to understand & use. It's exclusively suggested for North American usage.

If you enjoy what you've learned about such a machine, grab yours before stock sells out at any Cricut Store.

Advantages

- This scale might be beneficial to larger crafts.
- A heat plate's structure has been enhanced by using a ceramic-glazed foundation.
- Precise temp control.

Disadvantages

- It's expensive, but it's worth buying.

6. Cricut Bright Pad

If you're looking for your crafting partner, go for a Cricut Bright Pad. When creating, it's excellent for lighting activities and minimizing eye strain.

A Bright pad of Cricut is simple to use & very effective. Quilting, tracing, & weeding are just a few of the things you may do with it. Because of the ultralow profile, you can track your movements while sitting on your favourite chair. The Cricut Store has become operational.

If weeding vinyl or iron-on, your design would be attractively lit for quicker & simpler outcomes. Paper assembling quilt blocks were never simpler, thanks to such a pad. It adds to the enjoyment by providing an evenly lighted, customizable board.

Clothing, templates, needlework, & crafts may all benefit from this instrument. It's only designed to work with US power sockets.

Advantages

- There are 5 distinct brightness settings to choose from.
- Quilting, tracing, & crafts are all possible with this fabric.
- There is a big, scratch-resistant surface available.

Disadvantages

- Glitter HTV has indeed hard to remove and is a bit expensive.
- Such a machine does not have any batteries.

7. Cricut Cuttlebug Machine

If you're looking for something like a mechanical die trimming & embossing machine, go no more than a Cuttlebug. It's the perfect model for craftsmen who are passionate about what they do.

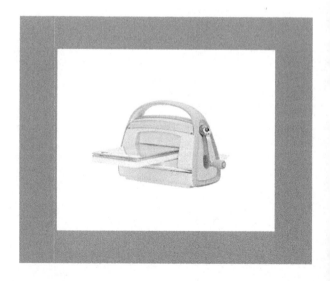

An embossing archive A2 and 2 metal dies are included in this package. If you buy this cutting device, you'll also receive a 6x8B plate, a 6x8A tray, & a mat for rubber embossing.

Such a machine's fold-&-store profile is one of its best

features. A bonus is a collapsible handle. Cutting & embossing materials like foils, tissue paper, acetate ribbon, & thin leather were never easier.

Cuttlebug is compatible with some cutting dies & other popular embossing folders. Let's take a closer look at the benefits & drawbacks of this little mechanical gadget.

Advantages

- Super-adaptable
- There are many free accessories.
- Works with a wide range of materials.
- For a tiny footprint, choose a profile that folds & stores.
- Handle that folds.

Disadvantages

- It is incapable of doing complex cuts.

8. Cricut Joy Machine

A Cricut Joy might be the smallest and most adorable cutting machine on the market. Don't be misled by its little size by thinking it's ineffective.

In Contrast, this compact setup is jam-packed, having incredible features. It will amaze you with what this can accomplish for your business. It's both light & affordable.

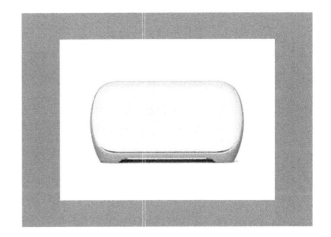

The machine is appropriate for both beginner and advanced craftsmen. This will, in contrast, benefits professionals. This Cricut has it all: simple customized card creation, precise cuts, & mat-less cutting.

If you're looking for a simple cutting device, go no more than your Joy. Software may be downloaded to any phone, tablet, or another device to operate it.

It has a lot of great features, like wireless cutting. It's time to place a Joy order with Cricut Store. The only disadvantage is the lack of features.

You'll need accessories, including card mats, cutting pads, & smart fabrics if you would like to get the most out of creative ideas. It's also not built to support heavyweight.

Your Cricut Joy has the ability to cut every form to perfection. This works well with materials such as vinyl, iron-on, cardboard, peel-&-stick label paper, & even regular construction paper.

Don't be fooled by the fact that the Joy is indeed the smallest into the Cricut series of machines. This little powerhouse makes creating distinctive designs simpler and quicker (which is why experts believe it's the greatest Cricut machine).

Aside from being a fantastic cutting machine, your Cricut Joy also serves as a personal scribe, allowing you to make gorgeous labels, engrave a personalized card, and even write the ideal monogram. You may choose your preferred colour, line weight, & font.

Advantages

- Compatibility with Bluetooth
- There are around 50 distinct materials.
- It would be ideal for newcomers & craftsmen.
- To work, smart materials are used.
- It's capable of cutting, writing, and drawing.

Disadvantages

- During the upgrade, there were issues with the program.
- It only has two functions (drawing & writing)
- There aren't any necessary accessories.

9. Cricut Easy Press Mini Machine

Is a tiny cutting machine required? This Easy-Press-Mini Cricut is a machine for you.

It may cut around 8.5"×12" of paper & other materials. You may cut tiny shapes & letters for such a model beginning at 1/4" and continuing around 11-1/2".

Such a model is ideal for individuals who need a highly detailed machine due to its extensive and precise cutting capabilities. But you'll need a PC or laptop with a stable internet connection.

This Easy-Press-Mini is a small, lightweight, & silent press. It's perfect for DIY makers who are passionate about what they do.

Advantages

- It's a discreet operation.
- Works with a wide range of materials.
- With such a tool, creating tiny shapes & fonts is indeed a snap.
- Precision and detail-oriented cutting capabilities.
- Lightweight & portable.

Disadvantages

- You'll require a connection to the internet for making cuts.
- You'll have to buy additional photos or cartridges.

03 CRICUT COST & COMPARISON CHART 2021

The fundamental characteristics for each Cricut model, including its warranty, are shown here. Hopefully, this chart can help you decide what unit is the best fit for you.

1. Cricut Machine Comparison Chart 2021

BEST CRICUT MACHINES	WEIGHT	DIMENSIONS	WARRANTY
Cricut Maker	15.02 pounds	22.6 x 7.1 x 6.2	1-year limited warranty
Cricut Explore Air 2	14 pounds	24 x 6.5 x 6.5	1-year limited warranty
Cricut Explore Air	16.89 pounds	25.4 x 10 x 6.2	1-year limited warranty
Cricut Explore One	13.75 pounds	24 x 6.5 x 6.5	Not specified
Cricut Easy Press 2	15.05 pounds	16.9 x 15.2 x 7.6	1-year limited warranty
Cricut Bright Pad	2.73 pounds	16.3 x 12 x 2	1-year limited warranty
Cricut Cuttlebug Machine	11.55 pounds	13 x 11 x 6.5	Not specified
Cricut Joy Machine	4 pounds	5 x 8	1-year limited warranty
Cricut Easy Press Mini	1.52 pounds	3.6 x 6.3 x 7.8	Not specified
Cricut Basic Tool Set	3.52 ounces	10.3 x 6.5 x 0.9	Not specified
Cricut Rotary Cutter	4.8 ounces	10.2 x 3.9 x 0.8	Not specified

2. How Much does a Cricut Cost?

Each Cricut comes with its price tag. Let's take a closer look at the costs of these gadgets, plus the accessories & equipment that you'll almost certainly need.

1. Cricut Maker

This amazing gadget is available for far less than $350 around the market. You'll wind up with a total of around $360 if you include $8 for the Cricut Access.

2. Cricut Explore Air 2

A Cricut Explore Air-2 is almost $ 70; however, if you would like Cricut Access, you'll spend around $280. Cricut Access will set you back about $8 each month.

3. Cricut Explore Air

On Amazon, a Cricut Explore Air costs around 380$. In contrast, a Cricut Access will set you back almost $390.

4. Cricut Explore One

This is among the most cost-effective models. It may be yours for around $200. If you want to add Cricut Access into your pricing, expect to spend about $8 per month.

5. Cricut Easy Press 2

This product is available for around $120 on Amazon. As you'll see, it's a low-cost option that performs well. It's small, light, & simple to operate.

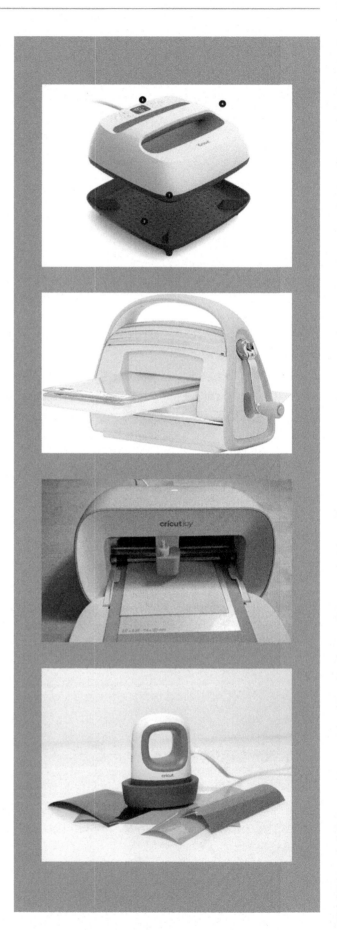

6. Cricut Cuttlebug Machine

The Cuttlebug version is available for around $100 in the market. Customers want it even though this is a manual cutting device for its flexibility.

7. Cricut Joy Machine

On this official Cricut website, your Cricut Joy has been offered for around $180. If you want to, you may use a variety of materials that are all under $15 per piece.

Generally, most insert cards are cheap, with each one costing almost $10.

8. Cricut Easy Press Mini

This small cutting machine costs around $100 on Amazon. If you're looking for a tiny, portable gadget, go to this model.

3. Cricut Basic Tool Set

Five essential tools for snipping, weeding, burnishing, & lifting different materials are included within Cricut Basic toolset. It's perfect for paper, iron-on, & vinyl projects.

There will be a scraper, a spatula, a weeder, a good set of scissors, & tweezers supplied. They're well-built, tidy, and dependable.

Cricut crafts equipment are present in a variety of colours to match the craft area & are intended to improve the DIY experience. They are simple & enjoyable to use.

You will also have the appropriate tool for any task if you purchase this package. When you're about to trim items down to size, snag an edge, & smooth things off, this package keeps you loaded.

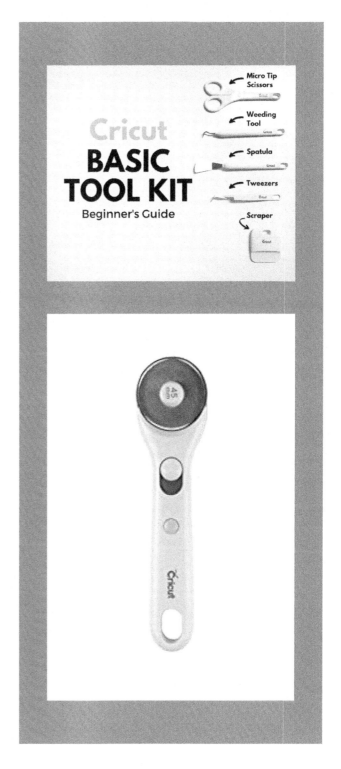

4. Cricut Rotary Cutter

Fabric cutting seems to have become simpler, quicker, & more enjoyable thanks to a rotary cutter of Cricut. It features a sturdy grip & a handy quick-release turn.

Its handle has full control, while the spin firmly holds its blade. It's a great-quality cutter that cuts in a controlled, precise manner.

For additional safety, it features a blade cap that pulls out easily.

Because it's made of quality steel (carbon alloy) & can be utilized by left & right-handed individuals, this 45 mm rotary blade has been one of the expert's favourites & recommended.

It's a tiny cutting machine that is 1/2 the length of a Cricut Explore & Cricut Maker, making it perfect for those dedicated to creating space. With just a single blade & a pen holder, it's less complicated than the different Cricut machines. However, don't be misled by its small size; it's packed with innovative new functions.

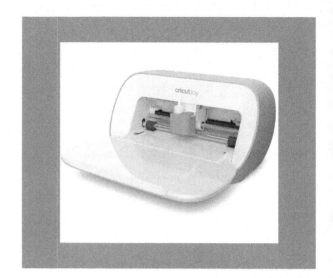

Cricut Joy is meant to be utilized in combination with a Cricut unit. Use it to do quick projects without pulling out a Cricut Maker or Cricut Explore and use it simultaneously with your other machines during super-crafting!

Cricut Joy would be a fantastic way to test whether Cricut is suitable for you. Some of you are hesitant to use a Cricut machine. Is it something you'll be able to figure out? Will any knives, mats, equipment, or supplies be understandable to them? Would you ever take advantage of it? Your Cricut Joy is a beautiful machine for 1st time Cricut customers who would like to make quick items without wasting a lot of time.

It's tiny & light enough just to take on weekends creating with friends, concentrate on organizing chores, or even simply about the house to make design projects simpler, whether you've owned a Cricut for years or are just taking your Cricut Joy out from the bag.

1. What can Cricut Joy do?

Cricut Joy made it simpler than ever to personalize your life. With this ingenious cutting and writing machine, you can personalize stickers, iron-on transitions, record decals, party banners, & more. Start with one of the selected projects & begin from scratch. Cricut Joy is in charge of the rest. Cricut Joy is portable and powerful enough even to cut duplicated shapes up to twenty feet, enabling you to make something unique for yourself & someone else at any time.

It's great for last-minute tasks like finding out your child's or teacher's anniversary is today (15 mins before the bus comes!). You can make a birthday gift in much less than 5 mins! Cricut Joy is excellent for producing beautiful cards since this not only cuts but also composes.

If you're in a hurry to label the pantry, this is the place to go. It just takes a few minutes using writable vinyl & a Cricut Joy's pen! Your Cricut Joy is a fantastic space-saving printer that can fit virtually any place in your house if you don't have much space.

On a Cricut Joy, there're two sensors under the rollers which draw material in. The machine may then straighten & quantify the materials which have been placed as a result of this. Your Joy machine would test the material prior to actually cutting it to ensure you've enough for your desired design.

Your Cricut Joy has ideal for all levels of crafters, from beginners to experts. Its small size creates opportunities for short, daily tasks as well as a vacation! I could see a lady's crafts retreat—could you? It'd also be fantastic to present to your children's schools and instructors!

The max material width is the major difference among your Cricut Joy & any Cricut series machine. The max material width for the other Cricut machine family is 12", while Joy's is 5.5". The number of available tools for the machines, the extra materials which may be cut using the machines, compatibility with both Bluetooth and USB cutting capabilities are also notable distinctions.

Whatever Cricut you use, you can anticipate a lot of assistance to optimize your pleasure due to the incredible resources accessible on Cricut's website or blog. Furthermore, the Cricut family is very helpful & friendly!

2. Cricut Joy Blade

A fine point cutting blade is included with the Cricut Joy. This technique can only be utilized with a Cricut Joy & not with every other machine. Your Cricut Joy's Fine Point Blade cuts through a range of materials with simplicity & precisely.

3. Cricut Joy Tools

Cricut Joy carries its own set of speciality pens & markers for creating one-of-a-kind creations. This collection includes Infusible Ink-Pens, conventional pens, & Gel Pens of various colours.

4. Cricut Joy Mats

Both light & regular grip mats are compatible with your Cricut Joy. As you may have observed, there's no Pur-

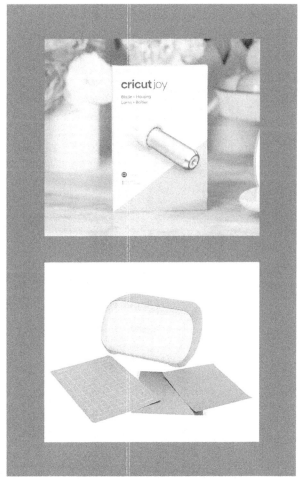

ple-Strong-Grip-mat. Because your Cricut Joy utilizes less force as compared to any other machines & isn't intended to cut through heavy or thick materials, that's the case. There's also a brand-new mat named Card Mat. It features an affixed transparent covering which enables cutting foldable cards simple.

5. What are Smart Materials?

Do you wish you could cut without the need for a mat? Find items labelled "Smart Materials." Because such materials have stronger backing, Cricut Joy can draw or cut on those materials without a mat.

6. Cricut Joy Materials

Iron-on, Infusible Ink, vinyl, Pens, Writable Labels, Adhesive-Backed Paper & transfer tape all are Cricut Joy suitable & proportioned precisely.

Newer Smart Materials are available for your Cricut Joy, allowing you to load and go with no need for a mat! Vinyl, iron-on, & other smart materials are available! Your Cricut Joy may also cut almost 20-feet at once, which is ideal for framing a favourite phrase, creating the galaxy of dazzling stars, or producing team jerseys.

From your birthday to the farewell, engaged to married because your Cricut Joy operates well on paper, enabling you to create a personalized card at a moment's notice. Choose the appropriate design, place any pre-scored card over a mat, & Cricut Joy would take care of the rest!

7. How Is Cricut Joy Dissimilar to Cricut Maker & Cricut Explore?

The Cricut Joy does have restrictions compared to other Cricut; however, it offers some capabilities that the others do not. Let's have a glance at those all:

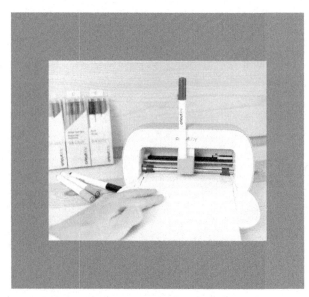

Cricut Joy would be a straightforward machine. It has no controls since it turns over once you plug that in. A Cricut Explore & Cricut Creator has a cutting diameter of 11.5", while a Cricut Explore & Cricut Creator has a cutting diameter of 4.5". This just has one blade, and it's a fine-point blade. No specific scoring tools & blades are required. A pen can also be utilized; however, shifting between both the pen & the blade is required.

Cricut Joy, in contrast, offers a number of features that have never been seen before. Your Cricut Joy Card-Mat is experts' personal favourite, and as you'll see in a future update, this will make creating cards a breeze.

Smart Iron-On & sticky Smart Vinyl may be cut without even a mat. These "good" materials feature any thicker backing materials that function as mats, enabling you to trim them without one.

Smart Vinyl comes in a range of lengths, among a 20-feet roll-in in specific colours. Solitary cuts may be almost 4-feet deep; you may cut the entire 20-feet of Vinyl in a single shot, even if you're creating smaller forms (like grocery labels & wall decorations). Because this is a smaller machine, the mat-less cutting feature allows one to cut any larger number of pictures in a single pass. In addition, there is no need to buy new mats.

8. What Can You Make with Cricut Joy?

Simple tasks are the secret to success when this comes to your Cricut Joy! Take a single colour, single cut, & single application as an example. It's perfect for contemporary Cricut users with simple concepts. You can have a little fun in minutes if you do the following:

- Labels for a sewing room, pantry, workplace, & other parts of the home.
- Mugs, phone cases, tumblers, & other items may have vinyl decals applied to them.
- Wall decals & borders.
- Using iron-on vinyl stickers, simple shirts & child bodysuits may be personalized.
- Cardstock is used to make cards, posters, & other group items.

You can customize, arrange, & modify just about whatever you want with this Cricut machine—I assure you it's the greatest! Pillowcases & bags, water bottles & tumblers, your birthday cards, team jerseys, pet's dish, & even house décor are all available! For inspiration, check out the DESIGN SPACE program of Cricut & app. They also have a blog with a lot of excellent ideas!

The most important element of project design is building space. Design Space is the fundamental software that creates all cutting templates & layouts. You must first visit their Cricut website before downloading your Design Space program. That service is accessible on your PC as well as other Android & iOS devices. After you've downloaded the file, you'll need to sign up for a Cricut account & create a customized profile. You're all prepared for your 1st creation now.

For some, learning about such a new program can be a daunting task. A Design Space, in contrast, is a program that caters to the general public. The user interface is clear & easy to use. Therefore, it is generally better to grasp the applications before starting any project. All projects at your Cricut Joy would need the program; thus, a prior understanding of the application is required before starting a project. In this chapter, Design Space is explained step by step using examples for making it simpler to understand.

1. The Design Space Home Page

Your Design Space is the 1st page you see when you start the app. The webpage is divided into four sections. The header is at the top, followed by the banner with all of the Cricut promos & offers. My designs & highlighted stuff are the other 2 sections.

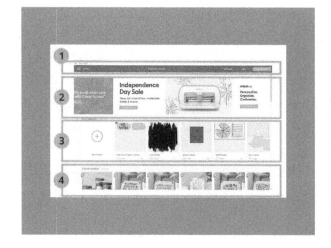

The homepage has 4 sections.

The Homepage of Design Space is described in full here. All 4 components will be thoroughly discussed.

- The Header
- The Banner
- My Project Section
- Featured Projects

2. The Header

A menu icon is located on the left side. The site & the canvas are the two choices. This symbol allows you to go from the homepage to the canvas & back. This menu has additional functions in addition to toggling among the homepage & canvas.

- New Machines Setup
- Print & Cut the Calibration
- Manage the Custom Materials
- Update film-ware
- Account detail
- Link Cartridge
- Cricut's Access
- Legal
- Settings
- New Feature
- Country's Selection
- Help

You'll have to build up your current machine via Design Space since it's the same software that's utilized for all previous Cricut machines. Any necessary calibration is changed during the cut, followed by print calibration. Users have control over their account settings. The Cricut Access symbol represents your subscription. The settings icon represents the canvas setting option. You may choose your nation, & there's also a Help button with a number of commonly asked questions & answers.

3. The Banner

This area is for the Cricut promos and advertising. Here you'll find information regarding new accessories, current promotions, discounts, & offers.

4. My Projects

When you initially start, this area will be empty. This is where you'll save your projects once you've created them and saved them. All of your projects would be featured in chronological order in this section, from the most current to the oldest. It'll also make it simple for people to scan all of the projects & replicate them if necessary.

5. Featured Projects

This part will describe to you all of the Cricut projects that are ready for making. You must choose a file & click Make This in these files, & the rest would be directed to you. Design Space would walk you through all of the materials, blades, designs, & the sequence in which your products must be cut.

6. The Canvas Layout

From the main page, go to your canvas. You may access the canvas from three different places. All three sites are indicated in the image:

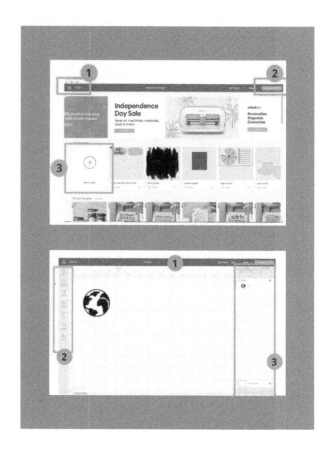

The Canvas is split into four main sections when you first open it. You'll go over each of these four components in depth throughout this chapter. This chapter will take you through every section one by one, & hopefully, you'll be done by the conclusion of this chapter. You'll be prepared for the 1st project after you've mastered all of these components. The following sections make
up your canvas screen:

- The Header & the Edit Panel
- An Insert Menu for Project
- A Menu for the Layers
- A Creative Field/Main Canvas

7. Header and Edit Panel

The upper area of the Design Space Canvas screen is split into 2 sections.

Header

A toggle menu is located on the far right of its header. The project's name will display in the middle. Untitled Project displays in the middle of the header if your project has not been saved. A system selection & a 'Make It' buttons are located on the right side.

Toggle Menu

When you click this button, a new choices menu will appear. This menu is similar as the one on your homepage.

Project Name

Your project name will be shown in the middle of your header. Untitled projects are displayed in this area unless you give them a title. Only once you've placed one picture or text within the canvas area you can give it a name.

Type of Machine

Because all the Cricut Machines have shared a Design Space, it's critical to choose Cricut Joy from the selection. Some features are unique to a Cricut Joy, so you won't see them in your design area if you don't have the Cricut Joy chosen.

Make It

Save & upload your files after you've finished designing. After that, choose to Make It. Then, you must choose the appropriate blades & materials for cutting. If you're dealing with many materials, design space would offer you all necessary instructions on what to put on your mats & which material should be cut first.

An Edit Panel is located under your header. Its purpose is to organize & modify components. Using that panel, you may decide what kind of fonts are best for your project.

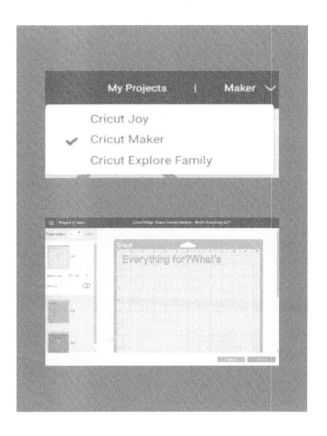

It's a taskbar with a large number of choices. You may feel overwhelmed at first, but if you get the hang of this, the features & icons are simple to use.

An Edit Panel

One such Edit panel allows you to manage the canvas's scaling, text addition, shape, project alignment, font addition & deletion, redo, and undo. The entire chapter has a detailed explanation of each component.

1. Redo & Undo Icon

When you work, you often make mistakes. Those icons are ideal for correcting errors. When you make a mistake, hit Undo. If you accidentally delete anything, click the Redo icon to restore it.

2. Fill, Line-type Icon

This decision would tell the device what kind of equipment & blades you'd be utilizing. Based on the model you possess, in this instance, the Cricut Joy, you have a variety of choices.

Line-type

You'll choose the kind of blade you'll use for a project here. You've got the greatest number of choices with the Cricut Joy. Cut, Score, Perforate, Draw, Wave, Foil, Deboss, or Engrave are all options.

Here's a detailed breakdown of all of these options:

Cut Option

The Cricut joy's default mode is a Cut option. When you choose this option, anything you draw on your canvas would be chopped when you click a 'Make It' button. So, if you'd like to utilize a different function, make sure you update the option.

Draw Option

You may utilize that option when you wish to sketch out any designs. If you choose that option, you must insert the Cricut joys & Pens into the machine's market sockets. Keep in mind that the Cricut Joy will not colour your creations.

Scoring Option

For this feature, the Cricut joys include a unique scoring tip.

Boxes & greeting cards may be made using this option. Users may utilize this function to score those lines where folding occurs if your project needs to fold. This aids in the completion of your task.

Deboss Option

The term "deboss" refers to the act of pressing the material into place. The deboss recommendation does this precisely.

On paper & different lightweight materials, that feature may be utilized. This is for embellishing your projects, such as cards & boxes.

Engrave Option

It may be used to engrave a variety of materials. On AL sheets & vinyl sheets, this option may be utilized for engraving monograms & designs.

Wave Option

This option is a part of the speciality tips of the Cricut Maker. If you want to make your project with wavy edges, you can use this option. It is ideal for cards, cake toppers, the name takes and invites.

Foil Option

It's a purely cosmetic choice. It can be utilized to adorn greeting cards, create gorgeous monograms, & provide a silver or gold tint to various materials. This feature is performed using special silver & gold foil sheets suitable with Cricut Joy.

Perforating Option

If you're working on a project that requires you to create tear-out sheets, this will come in handy. This feature allows you to create ticket sheets & coupons.

Fill

Printing is done using this option. Once the cutting line type is chosen, this option becomes accessible. If you don't want to fill the space, you'll have to trim. If you select a fill option, your product must be cut & printed.

You printed this project on the home printer & cut it out with your Cricut Joy.

3. Select All Option

This is a straightforward & practical solution. If you choose this option, anything on your canvas would be chosen, allowing you to pick up & move your entire project.

4. Editing Option

When you choose that Edit Icon, a drop-down menu appears with various choices. Copy, cut, paste, & replicate your work. All of these options may be used to chop items & move them around on your canvas. You may cut the same item or form numerous times during the project.

5. Align Option

That option is utilized to identify the centre of any project on your canvas. You may arrange any project on your canvas in a variety of ways.

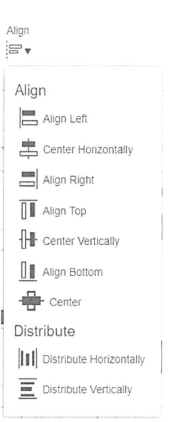

Align Left:

If you choose that option, all of your project's components would be guided from canvas's left side. This means that your project's orientation would be left.

Align Correct:

If you want to choose that option, your project would be oriented correctly throughout.

Center Horizontal:

Photographs are the most common usage for this feature. Once you select that option, all of the components would be horizontally aligned.

Center Vertically & Horizontal:

This option arranges all project elements vertically into a column format.

Align Top:

The components would be placed mostly on the topmost portion of your canvas in this arrangement.

Align Bottom:
Once you select that option, all of your components would be aligned to a canvas's bottom.

Center Align:
If you choose this option, the whole project would be precisely centred on canvas.

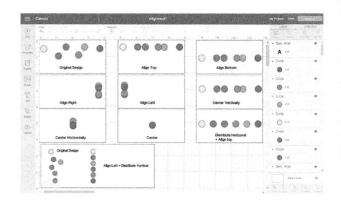

Distribute:
This feature is used to set the spacing among all of your canvas's components. If you've got many things and can't evenly place them, you may use that option to space them all properly. You have the option of spacing the items horizontally or maybe vertically.

6. Arranging Option
If you've many components on the canvas, this method will come in handy. Text, images, & forms are examples. This option assists you in determining the proper order of the components from the top towards the bottom. This allows you to choose what component is at the bottom & which is at the top. What component should go on the rear & which should go on its front? Your components may be organized as per your design. There are four choices available to you. You choose each component & arrange it according to the four choices.

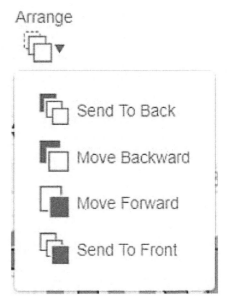

Send to the Back:
When this option is chosen, the highlighted element will be moved to the rear of all other components.

Jump Backward:
This option causes the chosen component to slide back a layer.

Going Ahead:
This option causes the chosen component to transfer a layer ahead.

Send towards Front:
Your component would be put in the first position if you choose this option.

7. Flip Option

This option produces a mirror of the component you've chosen. There are two choices for flipping the image: vertically or horizontally.

8. Size Option

This is for sizing your project's components. You may manually change the size of every component you require to trim by clicking on it and then clicking size & selecting self. A little lock symbol locks the dimension of your components. Once you click on the lock, you're indicating that you'd like to alter the dimensions.

9. Rotate Option

This feature is utilized to rotate an item at a specific angle. It may also be utilized to rotate an item on your canvas by 180 degrees or completely 360 degrees.

10. Position Option

This feature may be utilized to position objects on your canvas in a specific location. The option is similar to an alignment option; however, it is utilized for more sophisticated purposes. This may be utilized to place individual items on your canvas.

11. Font Option

To insert text to the canvas, simply choose this feature. Some typefaces are free for use, while some need payment or a subscription to your Cricut Access.

12. Style Option

You may make your fort italic, bold, or both using this option. It is all up to you.

13. Letter space, line space & font space

This feature is utilized to change the text in your document. The font size, the spacing between characters, & the spacing between distinct words may all be changed.

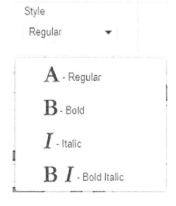

14. Alignment Option

This feature is just for text. You may wish to align if you've got the paragraph or a few phrases of text to cut. Center, Left, or right orientation are all options.

15. Curve Option

This is also a unique way to write the content. There is a slider in the centre of to the left, a rainbow-style word arrangement will appear. The text would be o manner if you go towards the right. The text will be organized in a circle if you go

16. Advance Option

This choice applies to the text over your canvas as well. It's a drop-down menu with a variety of choices.

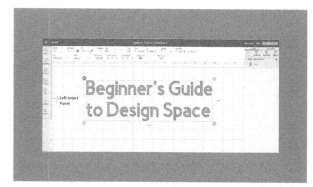

Advanced

Ungroup-to-Letters:

You may use this feature to personalize each of any text letters. This feature allows you to split each letter into its layer.

Ungroup-to-Lines:

This ungroup-to-letters choice is identical to this one. The main distinction is that it applies to every phrase or line in any text. You may use this tool to make changes to every sentence in a paragraph.

Ungroup-to-Layers:

This feature is only available for multi-layer typefaces. These fonts are either included in your Cricut Access membership or may be bought separately.

8. Left Panel

You may start a new project, examine your past endeavours, & discover photos and drawings for the new project on the left side. Let's take a look at each of the choices on the panel one by one.

New Button:

To begin a new project, click that button & you'll be presented with the blank canvas.

Template Button:

To begin a new project, your Design Space offers you with variety of basic templates. It would be used as either a project overview or a mock-up. You may choose from a variety of templates, including banners, aprons, T-shirts, tags, labels, & shorts.

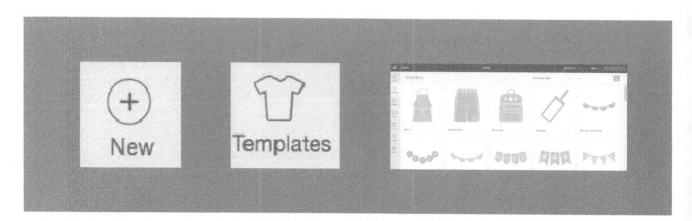

Projects Button:

This feature contains all of your previous projects. If you need to recreate a project, just pick the file & click Create. There's no fuss at all. Every of Cricut's pre-made projects is accessible to create here. Once you sign up for Cricut Access, you'll have access to a broad range of ready-to-make projects.

Images Button:

You may clip a wide range of pictures & image files from this page. With Design Space, there already are pictures. However, you'll need to subscribe the Cricut Access to have access to a lot more pictures. This is where you'll see the pictures & images you've uploaded.

Text Button:

This is a straightforward button. When you click on it, a window on your canvas opens where you may type your content. Your top taskbar may then be used to manage and create the style, size, font, & other aspects of the text.

Shapes Button:

This feature is used to add basic shapes to any design. All of the fundamental forms are provided. These basic shapes may be used to create more complex patterns. For your project, you may change the sizes & utilize more than a single form.

Score Button:

This is a really helpful feature. This is especially helpful if you're creating cards or boxes that need to fold after they've been cut. It is often used upon lightweight materials such as paper. When you use this feature on your design, your scoring blade will score along with the lines that need to fold in the design.

Upload button:

If you'd like to use a picture in your design, click upload and choose an image from the device. Your Design Space program will show you how you can upload & use the pictures correctly.

9. Right Panel – Layers

It's a fascinating section of any project. So, what are its layers, exactly? Layers in the entire Cricut universe represent each component or substance utilized in any project on your canvas. Due to its design, a basic project might have 1 or 2 layers, while a more complicated project might well have 5 or 6 layers.

Consider your birthday card as an example. As a result, each card will contain some shapes, some text, & a card itself. All of these individual components are now a layer.

Although most components and layers may be changed or updated, certain files, such as JPEG & PNG pictures, are not editable. The Layers Function's purpose is explained in depth.

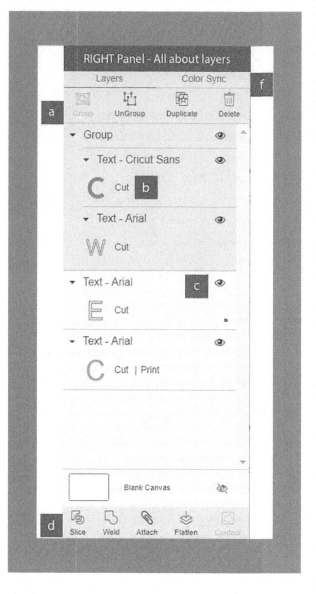

a. Grouping, Ungrouping, Duplicating and Removing

These settings may be found within the layers panel at the top.

To Group:

If you'd like to have certain project components share a layer & if you just want those particular components to stay together, you may use this feature to pick all the elements & group them all. It may only be shapes, & it may be both forms and words. Every single layer may include more than 1 component of the project.

To Ungroup:

This involves removing a specific component from the group, as its name implies. If you wish to display a shape/text as a distinct layer, select that component & ungroup this from any other components. It's also sometimes done to alter/resize a specific group, which may subsequently be regrouped within a single layer.

To Duplicate:

This option duplicates a previously created layer. This feature may be used to duplicate any layer/design within the same project.

To Delete:

This is a pretty simple choice. The delete feature is utilized if you believe a project component is no longer needed or needs to be removed.

b. Line-type & Fill

This feature allows you to choose the line type for every layer. The procedure to be utilized to cut your project is referred to as line-type. Your project must be foiled & it must be sliced, perforated, scored, & cut into waves. This feature allows you to choose a function for every layer.

c. Visibility of Layer

Every layer on your canvas has a small eye on the side. The layer would vanish once you click the eye. At that location, a little cross would emerge. When you would like to view each layer individually, this feature is useful.

d. Blank Canvas

This feature alters the canvas's colour. White is the colour of the canvas. You may like to view your ideas with a new backdrop from time to time. As a result, you may alter the canvas colour to observe the impact. This option is also applicable to templates. If any design is based on patterns, you may experiment with different colours to see how they impact your design.

e. To Slice, to flatten, to attach, to weld, & contour

All of these features are very helpful & their titles are self-explanatory.

To Slice:

Pick it, and then click slice to remove a portion of text/shape from the design. A section of the design would be isolated from the rest of the canvas, & you may put it anywhere you like on your canvas.

To Weld:

Welding is the polar opposite of cutting. This function may be used to combine two sections of a design. When you pick both pieces & click weld, the components you chose are combined. This may lead to the creation of a completely new design.

To Attach:

This feature is similar to a grouping feature; however, it is more powerful. When you pick two shapes & click attach, the components would be attached, and their colours would change. The colour of this layer on its back would be utilized in the attached result. During the cutting process, such components would also stay intact.

To Flatten:

This feature is only available if you want to print with no fill. You must first print and then cut your pattern. So, when you wish to print several layers simultaneously, pick them all & then select flatten for printing them all at once.

To contour:

If you wish to leave portions of your design out, choose this feature. Assume you don't want certain aspects of your project. You choose out certain areas & shape them. The sole exception is that this feature is only accessible for forms & designs that have curved or omitted parts.

f. Color Sync

A distinct colour represents each substance on any canvas design. It's OK if you require all of these colours in any design. However, if you've several colours of blue/yellow, you may wish to combine them into one shade. So, you click & drag the colour you would like to remove to the colour you would like to replace it with.

10. The Main Canvas Area

This is the location where all magic happens. On your canvas, all of the functions discussed throughout this chapter are used. The canvas is where the real designing & creating happens. We'll go through the canvas layout in more detail later.

Canvas Rulers & Grid

The x & y axes split the entire canvas into the grid. The grid's default measurement option is in inches. It's also possible to convert it to centimetres. The grid provides a visual representation of the project's size & scope. The visual/digital depiction of your Cricut Mats is this grid.

Selection

Every layer is represented in the painting by one blue box that encircles it. Within the right panel for the layers, you may pick that box & modify any layer/design. A small cross appears in the top left corner of each box. You may use that button to remove the layer once you want to. The curved arrow may be seen in the right corner. With the assistance of this, you may tilt or maybe rotate the design. A tiny lock may be seen within the bottom-left corner. It is intended to maintain the proportions of the design & picture. This, if left unlocked, may distort the picture. As a result, it is preferable not to enable this option. The ability to change the design's size is located within the bottom-right corner.

11. Cricut Access

Many individuals get confused about the Design Space & Cricut Access when they first start using the Cricut Maker. Design Space has been the downloaded software that every present Cricut Machines uses to design & cut items. Cricut Access, on the other hand, is Cricut's subscription plan. It's a premium service that allows you to utilize pre-made Cricut projects, over 400 different kinds of text, & 100,000 different pictures. Furthermore, you will get a 10 percent discount on each Cricut product when signing up for Cricut Access. You may save an extra 10 percent on discount goods as well. As the Cricut Access member, your orders are prioritized above those of non-members. All of your purchases will be sent for free if you subscribe to Cricut Access. It's worth mentioning that a Design Space offers some free typefaces, graphics, and ready-to-use projects. You receive a Cricut Access free trial when you initially join with the Design Space. However, after your membership has ended, you will be unable to save the image or typeface from Cricut Access. Cricut Access is available in monthly & annual packages, which may be renewed over a monthly/annual basis. You have complete control over when and how you terminate your membership.

1. Making Cards with Cricut Joy

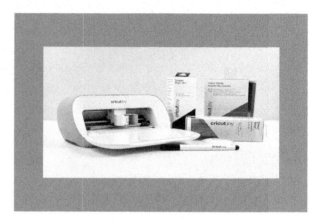

Supplies

- Joy Tools
- Joy Pen
- Joy Mat
- Cricut Joy

Instructions

- It's very simple, & the Joyful with a variety of free card crafts. Here are a few card samples.

- The 1st stage is choosing a "Perfect for a Cricut Joy" card under a "Perfect for a Cricut Joy" area. Click on the Make It tab to get started.

- It will offer you a sneak look at a card that will be placed on a Mat. Select "Go" from the drop-down menu.

- After that, you'll need to insert a card into the card mat. The reverse of a card should be slid among the Mat & a plastic guide. Slide your card up unless the top & sides are reached. As you've seen, the card fits the guidelines well. Place that card over the Mat by folding it top-down.

- Over your tablet or smartphone, choose insert card also as content.

- As directed by CDS, remove the blade assembly from the clamp & replace it with the pen.

- Once Design Space prompts you to load a Mat. Place it into the front of your rollers, & the mechanism would start rolling this in. (There aren't any buttons to push!)

- The computer would verify that it's inserted correctly before displaying a cut option on a CDS pad. Have a look at what happens if you push it!

- When the pen has done writing, your Cricut Joy would come to a halt, & CDS will prompt you to enter the blade. Remove its pen & use a clamp to hold it within blade housing.

- This should divide the rest till it is discovered. Cricut Design Space might stop & a computer with an unloading option would display. Once you push this, this would unload!

- Carefully lift the front of the card from your Mat. Remove the cutout parts from the paper if they don't stay on your Mat. Then put a card back in its place.

- The small holes within corners may be used to insert every one of the background cardstocks. The adhesive is not required.

It's finished! It's very simple and nice!

2. Shadow Box of Wine Cork

Supplies

- • Transfer Tape
- • Cricut Joy
- • Shadow Box
- • Cricut Tools
- • Vinyl
- • Wine Cork

Instructions

- Full design vinyl is required because the glass of a shadow box measures 8.5"x 8.5". You'll need to cut it into 2 parts since you're working with Cricut Joy, which can't cut anything longer than 5.25".

- Now change the message to "To your wine buddy" & choose Arab Brushstroke STD as the font. This was positioned for the central document, resulting in the height of about 6.3", & letters were connected (click at Attach within lower right-hand corner).

- Arab Brushstroke was utilized for the Est. 2002 textbox.

- Composed into Mark & Amy within a new-text window using Aphrodite Pro-font through Cricut Access.

- You initially decrease the Letter Space only at the end to bring your names' letters closer together. Then click Ungroup within the upper right-to-let the letters move independently of each other unless they were the same as they intended to be.

- Every letter was moved to its appropriate position by clicking & dragging it. The user didn't like the ampersand in this typeface, so he took it off.

- He drew one box around all of his letters & hit Attach when he was satisfied with his titles' words.

- Go to the Images & go through the ampersands until he locates one that suits his requirements. So put that in there.

- Then he enlarged it to realign the titles, choose the names & the ampersand, & hit Attach.

- To go among the sentence & the titles, he went back on Images & searched for flourish. Upon locating one, he implanted & measured that to make sure it was the same size as the other. Then select all & centre Horizontally underneath the Align tab.

- A flourish, titles, & Est.2002 were over the top part of a cork box customized decal, so choose it & click Connect. They may cut out together in their current state.

- Just save the project & ensure Joy is selected within the drop-down option at the end if you've more than a single machine.

- After clicking Make It, choose Without the Mat from the pop-up option to begin utilizing Smart Vinyl.

- According to Cricut Design Space, you'll require 15" of the Smart Vinyl for cutting this all out. Choose the Smart Vinyl-Permanent for the content environment.

- Then just follow the on-screen directions! Allow Cricut Joy to drag a vinyl roll in by placing it below the wheels.

- All the directions for the Cricut Joy may be found within Cricut Design Space. Whether you're utilizing a tablet, iPad, or laptop, follow the instructions and hit the load as well as unload buttons on your computer.

- Vinyl Cutting Using Intelligence Unless you click the Go button on your screen, your Cricut Joy may handle the rest. Long sections will shatter, & the vinyl might show up upon the reverse. Select an Unload symbol till the process is complete. Then, since the roll is long & smooth the next time you utilize it, utilize a trimmer to remove the ending. After that, pick out any remaining vinyl.

- While you like to start with the corks & work your way around the shadow box, you may do this in any sequence. The tabs were then raised & the supporting was removed with the help of the spatula.

- Numerous wine corks have been inserted once the inside of a bottle had been cleaned.

- There's no right or wrong answer when this comes to the amount of cork to utilize. At first, it introduced a bunch, but then realized it didn't intend them so high, so this removed some. It's not a huge problem; opening and closing the shadowbox is a breeze.

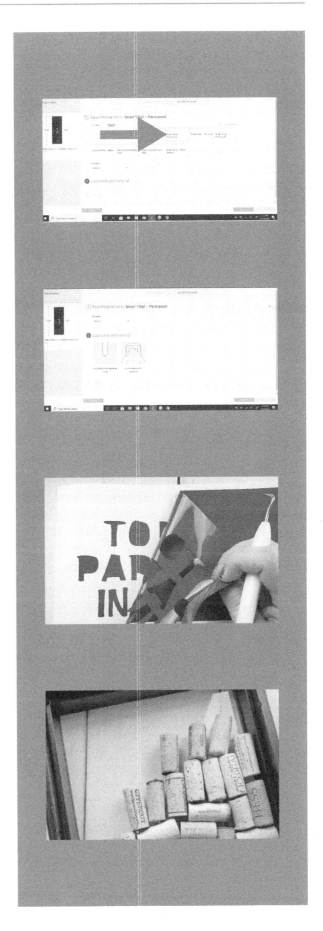

- Reset the display & close all of the tabs. Clean the glass on the front.

- Apply transfer tape to a weeded-off vinyl. Begin by ripping off the tiny side of the transfer tape wrapping and centring it with the edge of the vinyl backing. Pull the tape's liner away from the vinyl while you pull & push it down the 1st few millimetres.

- Scrape everything down till it's secure. Scrape the building's front & rear. After that, split the cup into half & place it on a shadow-box glass for lining it. Because the top of your vinyl backing is smooth, he lined up the top on the top & the bottom just at the bottom.

- Circle the center of each with the ruler & place this in the center of its frame. To hold it in place, the top vinyl piece may be attached to glass using blue painter's tape. Fold this over onto a tape, cut its lining, & place it gently upon this glass to ensure that everything is in order.

- Scrape down all transfer tape & remove it. Repeat the procedure for the customized names & dates over its bottom half.

- That's all! You may now give your wine-loving friend a personalized wine cork holding shadow case!

- Although this did dislodge some wine corks, this is completely a matter of personal preference! Even before the shadowbox has filled, you still need to add additional corks.

3. Hacks of T-Shirt Making

Supplies

- Smart Iron-On (White)
- Weeding Tool
- Black Shirt
- Easy Press 2
- Cricut Joy
- Easy Press Mat

Instructions

As a solo colour style, it'll be too small to fit over the front of your t-shirt on a Cricut Joy. But, using various colours cuts into numerous parts, enabling you to enlarge the design while keeping these individual pieces small enough to cut over the Joy!

- The handset has been utilized to cut the design that had been prepared on your screen. Also, you appreciate how a Cricut Design Space makes switching among devices a breeze!
- It may be tough to keep a multi-colour design similar to this sequence while pressing. Heat-Resistant Tape from Cricut was a secret weapon in making this shirt exactly right!
- Using the measuring tape, double-check that all the objects were correctly centred over the tee. Then, using the tape, mark all corners of your boards by crossing sections where these corners were.
- To iron an item, just line that up with corner markings made by the tape. This was the breeze because of a Smart Iron-On materials' stronger support.
- Simply cut that tape before you've pressed enough of your iron-on, & your t-shirt is good enough to wear! Such as the backer over a Smart Iron-On, won't give any stain & adhesive behind.

4. Little Tees with Cricut Joy

Making a tee has never been easier. Fill your vinyl with your design & cut it out using a Smart Iron-on of Cricut. It's easy and handy, & the kids will have a blast creating the tiny masterpieces.

Supplies

- Cricut Easy Press
- Weeding Tool
- Cricut Joy
- Unicorn Design
- Iron-on Vinyl

Instructions

- Open a unicorn layout into Cricut Design Room. Holographic Smart-Vinyl should be used to fill this unit. It was unnecessary to use a mat. Begin by cutting according to the device's instructions.

- Weed the template after removing it from your Cricut Joy machine.

- To press a design on the T-shirt, use Cricut Easy Press-2.
- You'll get a customized tee in mins after removing its iron-on backing.

These are all the cards that will save you far more time. Cricut joy card is great for making lovely cards. It's simple enough that even youngsters can do it.

5. Home Decor with Cricut Joy

Supplies

- Arts Canvas
- Weeding tool
- Smart Vinyl
- 3-4 Acrylic paints of different colours
- Cricut Joy
- Ziplock bag

Instructions

- Open your Ziplock bag all along two-seam sides. Position your canvas on one of the bag's sides.
- Using a similar shade of your acrylic paint, apply 6-8 paint blobs across the canvas. A rep for the last 3 or 4 paint colours.
- Fold the plastic bag cover over the entire canvas.
- Press down over the paint unless it has melded together.
- Take the bag's top off the canvas. Authorization to drive entirely.

- Click here to send cut files to the Cricut Joy.
- After this, weed the cut design & apply a transfer tape.
- Place your weeded pattern on the painted canvas.

You may now display it in the room or gift it to your friend.

6. Paper Bookmarks

Supplies

- Scissors
- Trimmer
- Cricut Joy Pens
- White card stock
- Cricut Joy Mats

Instructions

- In the Design Space application, look for the Bookmark design.
- Grab some white cardstock & a paper trimmer now.
- Cardstock would be cut down to fit on the Mat.
- Hit that "Make It" icon on a system design application & follow the instructions for the Cricut pen placement.
- You'll swap out a marker with a cutting blade after the design is finished.
- Follow the instructions to cut the Bookmark shapes.
- After cutting is completed, remove a Mat from your machine.
- Remove your Mat from a completed bookmark.
- You may now relax and enjoy it.

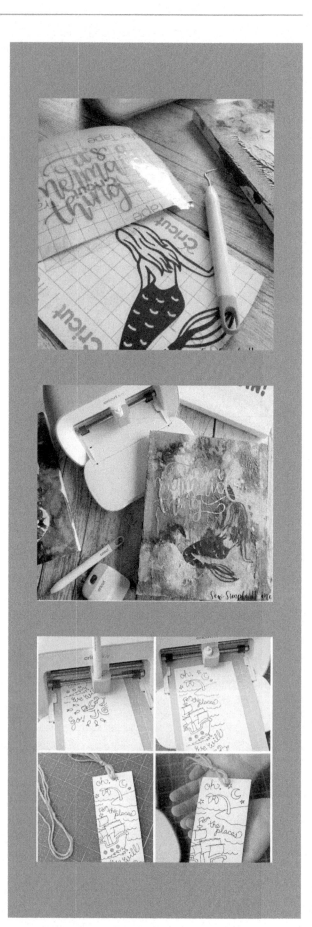

7. Smiling Flowerpot

It's a project that adults should make with their children to present to someone special on Teacher Day, Mother's Day, or simply as a nice surprise left in someone's doorway. It just takes a little amount of perpetual vinyl & the flower pot along with a flat surface to achieve success!

Supplies

- Transfer Tape
- Scraper
- Weeder
- Design Space Software
- Small Planter
- Cricut Machine

Instructions

- Within the design space program, look for the "Planter Face."
- The next step is to click on "Make It" & cut vinyl by following the instructions.
- Weeder would be used to eliminate the vinyl's unwanted bits after the cutting process has been completed on the machine.
- The next step is to put your happy vinyl images on a flowerpot using transfer tape & a scraper.
- That is! Your present is ready.

8. Acrylic Wall Planner

Supplies

- Cricut Weeding tool
- Whiteboard marker
- Cricut Transfer Tape
- Acrylic sheet
- Scissors
- Vinyl in black & tulip
- Rule
- Cricut Scraper

Instructions

- Begin by choosing and customizing your design within the Design Space program. The app's

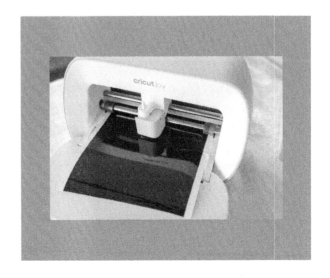

typefaces include (Bodoni & Drescher Grotesk) for producing words and specific forms on your canvas, such as arches & lines, enabling vinyl to be placed underneath the clear acrylic for easier printing & dry erasing. The front part of a mirror was chosen. Your Cricut prints this expression as a representation, but it corrects itself unless put to the bottom. Start the program after inserting your vinyl in a Cricut Joy.

- You'll see that a pattern has also been taken out when you withdraw the material from your printer. Using the weeding software, weed your templates to remove all negative space. Then this was preserved in one arm with vinyl to use.

- Cut the text off your larger designs.

- Cover the design with the transfer tape & scrape it to verify that it has properly adhered and is free of air bubbles. Peel the white backing from the transfer tape. It's important to take your time and gently removing any white backing since this may be difficult, especially when working with little letters.

- After putting the acrylic right-side-up, you mapped out the shape of a board using the whiteboard marker & ruler. After that, flip your board over & apply the vinyl towards the backside. Press your pattern & tape over the acrylic sheet together with the forms. Using lines on a transfer tape, ensure your vinyl is lined. To create a smooth bond, scrape your acrylic with a scraper. With care, remove your transfer tape from a template and leave it on a planner.

- Pink arches & black lines were also added.

- To put vinyl lines over the acrylic board, its board has been outlined for such a purpose.

- Finally, drill all holes & secure the board with gold standoffs.

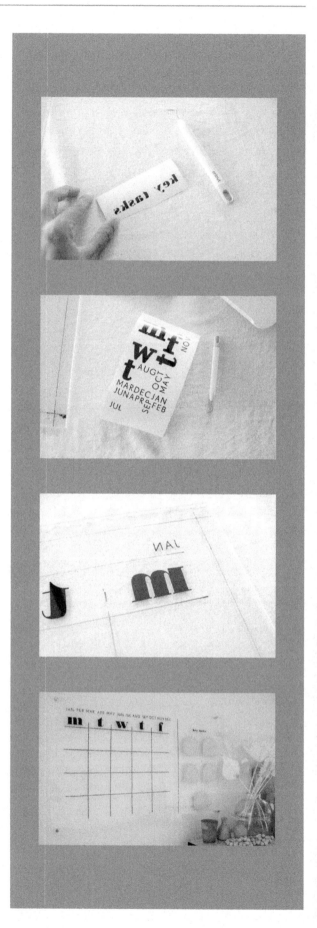

9. Make Cricut Card with the Card Mat

- The transparent lining of the Cricut Joy Cards Mat must be pulled away.
- By sliding the prepared card beneath the connected liner, you may align this with the instructions. Firmly push the card on the mat to secure it.
- Using Design Space, go to Images, Cartridges, & "Quick Cut Card."
- Select "Make It."
- Put the pen within the tool holder, choose the material, and load your card mat using the app.
- As far as you hit Go into Design Space, Joy would begin sketching.

Click with the pen on the sharp point blade. Once it has done sketching, continue cutting. Unload your mat after the cutting is done. Flip your mat over & gently pull it away from your card. Fill every one of the 4 corner slots with the lining.

In just a few minutes, you can make a number of different cards using the same instructions.

10. Make Cricut Label with the Cricut Joy Smart Label

- Click the pictures on the right-hand side.
- Insert the mark image into the search box & then enter Labels into the search bar.
- On the left-hand side, click text & type the words you wish to display upon the mark. Make sure you choose a typeface that is appropriate for blogging.
- Centre a text above a label using that align button just at the top of your page.
- Select both the type & the label using the button within the bottom right corner of the display, next "Attach" both.

- Choose "Make It" in the top right corner. Pick "No Mat" below Kind if you're using Smart Label.
- By clicking "Continue," you may go to a Joy machine.
- After putting the pen in the tool holder, pick the material & load a Smart Label.
- As quickly as you select Go into Design Space, Joy will begin sketching.

Once the pen has completed sketching, move it to the fine point blade & click "Go" for cutting. Unload your mat once the cutting is done. Carefully remove the sticker off the backside and place it on the appropriate surface.

Made in the USA
Las Vegas, NV
26 October 2021